MAKING DISABILITY
Exploring the Social Transformation
of Human Variation

ABOUT THE AUTHOR

Paul Higgins is a Professor of Sociology at the University of South Carolina, Columbia. He writes primarily about disability, an interest that has developed out of his parents who are/were deaf and his wife who teaches deaf children. Among his books are *Outsiders in a Hearing World*, *Understanding Deviance* (with Richard Butler), *The Rehabilitation Detectives*, *Understanding Deafness Socially* (coedited with Jeffrey Nash), *Personal Sociology* (coedited with John M. Johnson), and *The Challenge of Educating Together Deaf and Hearing Youth*.

MAKING DISABILITY

Exploring the Social Transformation of Human Variation

By

PAUL C. HIGGINS, PH.D.

Department of Sociology
University of South Carolina
Columbia, South Carolina

CHARLES C THOMAS • PUBLISHER
Springfield • Illinois • U.S.A.

Published and Distributed Throughout the World by

CHARLES C THOMAS • PUBLISHER
2600 South First Street
Springfield, Illinois 62794-9265

© *1992 by* CHARLES C THOMAS • PUBLISHER

ISBN 0-398-05769-9

Library of Congress Catalog Card Number: 91-34208

With THOMAS BOOKS *careful attention is given to all details of manufacturing
and design. It is the Publisher's desire to present books that are satisfactory as to their
physical qualities and artistic possibilities and appropriate for their particular use.*
THOMAS BOOKS *will be true to those laws of quality that assure a good name
and good will.*

Printed in the United States of America
SC-R-3

Library of Congress Cataloging-in-Publication Data

Higgins, Paul C.
    Making disability : exploring the social transformation of human
variation / by Paul C. Higgins.
        p.   cm.
    Includes bibliographical references and index.
    ISBN 0-398-05769-9
    1. Physically handicapped—United States.   2. Physically
handicapped—Rehabilitation—United States.   3. Social work with
the physically handicapped—United States.   I. Title.
HV3023.A3H54   1992
362.4'0453'0973—dc20   91-34208
                                                                                    CIP

To my family—who increasingly enrich my life.

ACKNOWLEDGMENTS

No book, even single-authored, is the product of one person's work. The Department of Sociology, University of South Carolina, generously provided secretarial and other assistance. Without the ideas of many authors upon whose works I have drawn, I could not have written this book. For more than a decade, my colleague Bob Stewart, has encouraged me in my teaching and research. His concern with how we can live and act together successfully has enabled me to think—to research, write, and teach—more usefully about social life. My thanks to all.

CONTENTS

		Page
Introduction	Making Disability	3
Chapter 1	Framing Disability	22
Chapter 2	Manufacturing Disability	65
Chapter 3	Depicting Disability	80
Chapter 4	Interacting and Identifying Disability	99
Chapter 5	Experiencing Disability	123
Chapter 6	Servicing Disability	151
Chapter 7	Policy(ing) Disability	188
Chapter 8	Managing Disability	227
Conclusion	Remaking Disability	250
References		257
Index		277

MAKING DISABILITY
Exploring the Social Transformation of Human Variation

Introduction

MAKING DISABILITY

Imagine a society in which its members make distinctions among one another that are similar to what we call "strength." (Speaking a language different than ours, members of that society use a word whose meaning is also slightly different than "strength." But I will use "strength.") Those known to be stronger can walk, lift, pull, push, twist, and manipulate objects more easily than those known not to be as strong. Most members are comparably strong, but their strengths are recognized as differing. Some are unusually strong, while others have little strength. Strength is useful.

Most members have the strength to live adequately in their society. They can open and close doors; walk up and down steps; pick up, carry, and put down objects; lift; twist; push; pull; and do so much more that enables them to live satisfactorily. Their strength enables them to go to school, to work, to play, to move about their communities, and to participate in the other activities of their society. Some members experience a little difficulty with such activities and tasks, but with extra effort, they can manage. However, members of the society do notice that some of their fellow citizens do not have enough strength to do what members typically do. They cannot pick up, carry, and place ordinary objects, though some can do so with very light objects. They typically cannot open and close doors. Some cannot walk up and down steps or walk very far at all. These members have great, but varying, difficulty participating in their society.

Generations ago members called those recognized as having inadequate strength "feebles." Members of the society knew feebles were greatly different from them. Some members pitied them, but many believed the feebles were a threat to the safety and prosperity of the society. Through bearing children, the feebles might multiply and weaken the strength of the country. At a minimum they were an unproductive drain on society. Some claimed that they were not fully human. Scientists developed and debated various theories as to what caused feebleness. Some believed that immoral behaviors of feebles' parents were to blame. For several decades society segregated many feebles in special villages where the feebles lived out their lives. Feebles were often sterilized to prevent perpetuating their burden on society. If some of the feebles became stronger (miraculously it seemed), then the other members occasionally let them leave those special villages. Some of these former feebles joined traveling shows where they amazed the audiences with their rejuvenated strength. (But audiences soon wondered whether the former feebles who performed for them had actually been feeble or were frauds.) However, most former feebles were typically ashamed of their prior feebleness. They tried to keep secret their past.

Today the society's members take pride in their self-proclaimed more enlightened ideas about feebles. In fact, most members no longer call them feebles, which seems pejorative. Instead, members call them "weaklings," though some weaklings and some who are not weaklings debate the most appropriate terms to use. Weaklings are no longer feared—at least not much by most people. However, nonweaklings have ambivalent feelings about weaklings. Many nonweaklings greatly pity weaklings. The nonweaklings cannot imagine what it must be like to be a weakling. Not knowing what to do or say, some are apprehensive around weaklings. Others believe that weaklings would be better off with their own kind. However, most believe that weaklings deserve a greater chance to get ahead. When asked what that greater chance might be, many nonweaklings reply that weaklings should have the same rights and opportunities to participate as others do—if the weaklings can manage. If the weaklings cannot manage, then nonweaklings believe that special care should be provided to make the lives of weaklings comfortable.

Not surprisingly, many parents whose children are weaklings experience a great deal of anguish, doubt and uncertainty about what to do. They often receive conflicting advice from professionals and inconsistent services from their community that they claim are inadequate. While investigators have had difficulty checking allegations that parents and their doctors have let severely weak newborns with birth defects die rather than repair the defects, rumors persist. Some doctors have even published reports suggesting how medical personnel should decide which newborn weaklings with birth defects should be aggressively treated and which ones should be allowed to die. The allegations, investigations, and doctors' suggestions received nationwide attention for a short while.

Most weaklings are not born weaklings. Due to accidents, disease, unsafe work practices, the effects of poverty, aging, and such, youth and adults become weaklings. Some who become weaklings see their lives dramatically change. Where they were once valued friends, schoolmates, employees, and neighbors, they become something else—a burden, an unhappy reminder of what was and could have been, "one of them." They become outsiders to the world of the nonweaklings, some even to their families. Those who regain some of their independence (but not their strength) are held up to other weaklings as models of what they might strive to become. But many do not—their weaknesses cannot be "overcome" (or so it seems to the nonweaklings). With little fanfare, others satisfactorily make their lives out of the mundane sorrows and joys that nonweaklings assume to be denied them.

Presently the society is debating, changing, and reconsidering the wisdom of changing its policies regarding weaklings. For example, weakling children were formerly taught at home, if at all, and primarily to learn to entertain themselves since it was known that they could not work. Nowadays, through re-designing their educational facilities and practices, communities are opening neighborhood schools to weaklings. However, educators often place weaklings in separate classes from nonweakling students—for the weaklings' benefit, of course. Some concerned observers wonder if the present educational practices do more harm than good; others demand further reform.

Weaklings, advocates, and government officials continue debating the housing, transportation, and other concerns of weaklings. Without a clear, consistent policy, communities vary greatly in how they meet the needs of their weaklings. (A few observers argue that the society's housing policy, transportation system, and other arrangements that provide for the public welfare do not meet well the needs of many citizens, whether weaklings or not.)

Others are concerned that benefits paid to weaklings who do not work may perpetuate their dependency—either because the benefits are too generous or because they provide disincentives for weaklings to try to work. Some even claim that nonweaklings are posing as weaklings in order fraudulently to obtain benefits. Soaring benefits have led officials to proclaim that a crisis has occurred and to "get tough" with those claiming and receiving benefits. The crackdown has led to countercharges that the officials are more concerned with "pinching pennies" than providing for people. Those making the countercharges remind the citizens of their society's past, inhumane treatment of weaklings. Recent, major legislation seems to expand the opportunity for weaklings to participate in their society, but at what cost counter some critics.

Many weaklings, however, have recently belied their designation. Through public protests, legal suits, and quiet organizing, many weaklings have confronted the nonweaklings. The weaklings have demanded that the nonweaklings recognize that many of the difficulties experienced by the weaklings are not due to their lack of strength but to the attitudes and actions of the nonweaklings. Those who are weak criticize how doors are made, the unnecessary use of steps, the lids on jars, the weight of ordinary objects, and on and on. They claim that how nonweaklings have (often unthinkingly) built society needlessly oppresses them. Strength need not be as crucial to living adequately as nonweaklings assume. The weaklings also criticize the discrimination of the nonweaklings who after making doors unnecessarily difficult to open hold them closed when weaklings try to enter for a job, for an education, or for some other opportunity. They denounce the paternalism of the nonweaklings, who good-heartedly give the weaklings charity when the weaklings are demanding rights. The weaklings do not want to become nonweaklings, but they want to live with dignity as citizens who are weak—and who are much more. They wonder why their society cannot enlarge itself to include all of its members. However, the weaklings have not spoken with unity, which weakens their collective voice.

The protests have some nonweaklings commenting about the ingratitude of the weaklings and other nonweaklings dismissing the weaklings as agitated. Other observers agree with much of the protests—the lack of strength of the weaklings is not the crucial restraint shackling the weaklings. However, some wonder if the protests of citizens who are weak ignore those among them who are so weak that meaningful interaction with them is all but impossible to imagine or to sustain. For those severely weak citizens, their inadequate bodies, not discrimination, are surely their problem—and sympathy the only solace, claim these concerned observers. Weaklings and nonweaklings wonder what will happen next.

We could imagine more about the above society. Yet, we all realize that we do not need to rely more on our imagination in order to know what more we might include. All we need to do is look around. However, not any kind of looking will enable us to see well, to see beyond the obvious. In order to see well about disability, we may need to use our imagination after all.

Important changes in the worlds of disabled—and nondisabled—people and in our understanding of disability have taken place in the past several decades. Those changes continue. This work grows out of those changes and, if successful, may become a small part of them, particularly a small part of our understanding of disability—and of ourselves. In brief, my understanding is:

> We make disability. Disability is not a natural quality of people or of their individual traits. Through responses to people with variations that we have made meaningful within a world that we have often unthinkingly built, we produce disability. Those of us made disabled and those of us not can make disability in an infinite number of ways, ways yet to be tried or even imagined. However, not any way will work well. We are responsible for whatever disability is, even though we are not responsible for nor can we control everything in our lives. Our challenge is to explore how we make disability and how we might make it more successfully. In doing so, we will have understood better how we make all of us.

The rest of this book takes up that challenge, primarily the first part—how we make disability. The remainder of the introduction sketches more fully my briefly stated (and still inadequate) understanding of disability.

Making Disability

We create disability. Those of us known as disabled and those of us who are not make disability. Through our beliefs and our behaviors, through our policies and our practices, we make disability (Albrecht, 1981: 275; Ferguson, 1987). Through interpersonal, organizational, and societal activities, we make disability (Bogdan and Biklen, 1977). In all arenas of social life we make and remake disability: in the family, among friends, in impersonal encounters, in school, on the job (and long before a job is gotten on), in the media, in human service agencies, within self-help groups, through governmental policy, within cultural beliefs (nurtured by and displayed through all of the above and more), through technology, through sweeping societal changes, and even through the writings of observers of disability (Fine and Asch, 1988). And we make disability even when our intentions have nothing to do with disability. Through all of the above and more, we create disability.

To claim that we make disability is not to deny the importance of our bodies. Our bodies provide us our most fundamental capacities—to symbolize, to sense, to exert force. We vary in those capacities, in how we have developed those capacities into abilities, and in how we exercise those abilities. We all know that.

However, to state above the obvious is to state too much too easily. Our bodies and our capacities to symbolize, to sense, and to exert force cannot be known independent of us. Through our observations, which can be very sophisticated but need not be, we come to make claims about our bodies and our capacities. The history of medicine and of other disciplines concerned with human functioning can be read in part as the history of the claims that we have made about "the" body and its functioning (Cartwright, 1977; Rosenberg, 1989). Claims change. What is taken as obvious may later be discarded as obviously wrongheaded. Medieval physiologists *knew* that the balance of the four humors—blood, phlegm, black bile, and yellow bile—determined people's health and temperament (Conrad and Schneider, 1980). Nowadays we "know" better. However, our claims are understood by most of us to be what our bodies and capacities "really" are. Others, emphasize the tentative nature of our claims, but still claim that our knowledge is increasingly approximating how we "really" are. Both understandings mislead us.

We can never know what our bodies and capacities "really" are. At best, we can observe and make claims about our observations—not about the body as it is independent of our observations (Rosenberg, 1989; see Stewart, forthcoming, for a broad foundation for this discussion). But some claims may momentarily enable us to meet more successfully the challenges we confront. Claims about viruses help us more than claims about humors. But we do not always agree on which claims are most useful, and we may later realize (claim?) that we too quickly accepted some claims and dismissed others (Skrabanek and McCormick, 1990).

Thus, we must be careful. While recognizing the importance of our bodies, I do not assume that we merely *uncover* the nature of the human body and its capacities or the qualities of our particular bodies and their capacities. Instead, through exploring and making claims about people's bodies, capacities, and functioning and acting on those claims, we make our bodies what we "know" them to be. An important—and often useful—claim is that we vary in our capacity to symbolize, sense, and exert force.

That variation is itself our doing. While we speak of "recognizing" variation as if the variation exists independent of us, merely to be known and recorded if we choose to do so, that is misleading. We produce the variation that we recognize. How we classify people as we respond to the challenges we confront—challenges in educating ourselves, developing governmental policy, attending to our health, everyday living, and so on—creates the variation that we believe we simply notice.

In creating that variation, we often take for granted the experiences of the dominant group (white, advantaged, able-bodied men) as the "natural" way of life rather than seeing those experiences as one partial set among many, a point I take up later in this introduction. The dominant group's experiences in the guise of the "natural" way of life become the standard by which other experiences are evaluated and are said to differ. Thus, "difference is not discovered but humanly invented"—and invented in ways that favor some people over others (Minow, 1990: 55).

We "mark off" some of that variation as significantly different. We do so by how we understand that variation, experience it, and manage it. When we do so, *we are creating disability.* Disability *is* what we have made of physical, mental, and emotional variation. We make disability, not merely respond to it. (1)

As I have implied above, we also make "the" body and its capacities and the variations that we embody. The making of disability does occur at this "organic" level, but my exploration does not—at least not much. (Look to others in the history and social sciences of medicine; Cartwright, 1977; Lehrer, 1979; Rosenberg, 1986; Rosenberg and Golden, 1989.)

Disability then is a social accomplishment (Sarason and Doris, 1979). As Joseph Schneider (1988: 65) notes, "Epilepsy, illness, disease, and disability are not 'givens' in nature . . . but rather *socially constructed* categories that emerge from the interpretive activities of people acting together in social situations." Disability is not a trait of individuals, though we have often understood it to be an individual trait, this understanding itself being an important production. We have typically assumed that the significance of disability, such as the often lessened lives of those with disabilities, was completely due to "flawed" bodies. Today we "know" differently. Yet we have just begun to develop the imagination that *enables* us to see that whatever disability may be, it becomes that through our efforts.

Consider briefly learning disability, which I take up in more detail in Chapter 1. Before the late 1800s when observers began to write about "word blindness," and, more significantly, before the mid-1960s when educators and others began to popularize learning disability, it did not exist. Learning disability did not exist as a means for making sense of difficulties people experienced in learning (Coles, 1987). Even the human variation (i.e., the learning difficulties) to which it refers has not existed for most of human history (see Chapter 1)! However, today almost 2 million students are served as learning disabled, more than are served through any other disability category (U.S. Department of Education, 1990: 12).

Or take hearing impairments. Most people with impaired hearing become hearing impaired as adults. But as they do, what they and others make of it may change dramatically over time. As they begin to experience what later they and others come to call a hearing impairment, they make something else of it. They experience bad telephone lines and mumbling talkers. Their world has changed, but not yet them. Others around them may take them to be inattentive. Later, without necessarily a change in sensory capacities, they become hearing impaired people. They, family members, doctors, colleagues, and acquaintances and perhaps still others have made them hearing impaired people. The telephone lines are no longer bad and talkers no longer mumble, though the now hearing impaired people still have trouble understanding what is being said. But their trouble is now a different trouble—one of hearing impairments. Their identities and interactions with others are no longer the same. Their understandings and expectations may be changing. They are becoming perhaps "words apart" as they make a new world in which they are hearing impaired (Jones, Kyle and Woods, 1987).

As the two brief examples suggest, we make disability in complex ways. Through individual, interpersonal, organizational, and societal activities we create human variation and give it—and ourselves—profound significance.

The making of disability is not static, but ongoing. Even when disability is the same this moment as it was in a previous moment, we made that so. But we can also make it different, perhaps better, though it may be difficult to do so. Dramatic change does not occur in a moment.

However, we typically take our present world for granted. We assume that matters have always been as they are or they have naturally become what they are. What exists is either right or cannot, should not, be changed much. If the social world changes, it will change in due time, as it should. At best, we can tinker with our world in minor ways—and even then we should be careful, for we are likely to do more harm than good (Stewart and Reynolds, 1985; Sowell, 1987). We have difficulty realizing that we create the social worlds in which we live, the social worlds created by people vary tremendously, and the social worlds that we could create could vary even more. We imprison ourselves within the worlds we create without realizing that we are the jailers. Yet we are also the ones who can unlock our present cell door and make another, less confining place for ourselves. So it is for disability.

I imagine that as many of us read the description of the "imaginary" society that begins the book, we nodded in recognition that that is how society "treats" disabled people. But it isn't—at least not universally so. People have made disability in many fashions, if only for a short time or on a small scale (Scheer and Groce, 1988). And I imagine we have not come close to how we could make disability—with dignity. For example, in

traditional societies, a single personal characteristic, such as the ability to hunt successfully or grow abundant crops, does not seem to define one's total identity (Gluckman, 1962). An individual who is disabled may well be viewed as a fellow villager or clan member, age-mate, skilled artisan, and so forth, rather than solely as someone unable to see, hear, or walk. For example, Thomas (1958) describes the case of Short Kwi, a reportedly outstanding Bushman hunter who, in his 40s, lost a leg from a snake bite. His wife and kin rallied around him while he recovered, and although he never again became the outstanding hunter he had been prior to his accident, he learned to participate in the hunt with the help of a walking stick and his male kin. His subsequent status in the community apparently continued to be high, reflecting his achievements through his entire lifetime (Scheer and Groce, 1988: 30).

We do not need to romanticize the Bushmen to appreciate that how they made Short Kwi disabled was far more liberating for him and them than how we often today make people disabled.

How we make disability may be more or less useful to us. Our actions may create possibilities or close opportunities. They may be the best that we can do *and* still be not "good enough." Our making may be more useful today than yesterday, but not necessarily. Making one another learning disabled or hearing impaired (and how we do so) may lead to more satisfying lives through services provided, understandings developed, interactions modified, worlds recreated, but it may not. Our makings may liberate or limit ourselves.

Our Concern

The making of disability speaks to us all. It does so for several reasons. Most obvious, many of us are disabled, will become disabled, or know well someone who is disabled. All of us interact with fellow citizens who are disabled. Creating disability speaks to us on this most personal level (Zola, 1989).

Creating disability also speaks to us as *citizens* of our country. Our society's disability making affects our lives even though we may not be disabled or may have little, if any, involvement with people who are disabled. For example, making buildings more accessible to people who move in wheelchairs also helps those with strollers or who are temporarily on crutches. Redesigning procedures to assist mentally retarded workers may enable workers who are not mentally retarded to perform better, too (Zola, 1989: 420). But if our makings limit those with disabilities, then we handicap all of us, because all of us pay the great costs of lessening the lives of those with disabilities—financial, social, and most important, moral (Bowe, 1978; Chirikos, 1989).

More generally, to understand the making of disability enables us to understand ourselves, whether disabled or nondisabled. First, to be disabled only has significance in its relation to being nondisabled. For example, how can a student be a slow achiever without some standard of acceptable (i.e., "nondisabled") achievement (Withers and Lee, 1988)? Similarly, being *nondisabled* makes no sense without some contrast to those made disabled. To claim that one sees satisfactorily makes sense only in contrast to those known as seeing poorly. Disability and nondisability cannot exist without the other (Higgins, 1980: 174–178).

Further, we cannot understand the making of disability apart from our larger social world that we have made. Disability exists within and grows out of that world. For example, we cannot understand "special education" without realizing how typical education sets the context within which education for children with disabilities is made "special." If "regular" education had been created to speak to the diversity of our youth, rather than as a means to educate advantaged children and too often control or ignore disadvantaged children, then all of it would be special and no

"special education" would be developed (Lazerson, 1983; Barton, 1988).
Or, more specifically, in order to understand the development of learning disability, we should explore the development of middle-class subur-
bia whose citizens expected success but often experienced disappointments
and difficulties. The educational difficulties of some of their children
became part of their unfulfilled expectations and resulting strains. As I
explain in Chapter 1, learning disability became a response to these
difficulties (Coles, 1987).

Take disability payments as another example. We cannot understand
our policy of income transfers to those with disabilities (such as worker's
compensation or SSDI benefits) without recognizing how such policies
respond to and help produce our political economy. Our society is based
on a work ideology—everyone should work (or take care of children) and
through work people obtain what is desirable. However, our society does
not provide employment for all. Disability and disability payments can
be understood in part as a flexible, societal safety valve. Through
expanding definitions of disability, the government can absorb some
unemployed workers while also preserving the "legitimacy of the work
ideology" (Stone, 1984: 168). Yet, too expansive definitions and too
generous payments may undermine the work ideology and create fiscal
concerns (Stone, 1984; Berkowitz, 1987; Mezey, 1988).

Some governmental policy even recognizes that disability is a consequence of the "normal functioning" of a society (Kronick, Vosburgh, and
Vosburgh, 1981: 195). The disabled person is "part of the cost of progress,
or even of the normal operation of society as a necessary incident"
(Kronick, Vosburgh, and Vosburgh, 1981: 198). Part of that "normal" (but
unnecessarily oppressive) functioning is how we have literally built our
world. Our

> society is not constructed to accommodate the wide variety of physical differences
> that exist. Buildings, work sites, and homes are built for "normal" people,
> but normal is usually narrowly defined. Because of this, many people, both
> those traditionally considered disabled and others are shut out from jobs, decent
> living arrangements, and from seeking fun and pleasure (McMurray, 1987: 144).

We make disability within the worlds we make for all of us—and as we
make those worlds we disable some of us.

And we make disability in the same way that we make all of us. The
processes through which we make disability—many of which I explore in
this book—are the same ones we use to create all of us and our worlds
(Meyerson, 1988: 174). For example, "blind men are made, and by the

same processes of socialization that have made us all" (Scott, 1969: 14). We do not need a different understanding for disability and for non-disability. But we do need an enlarged understanding for all. Too much of our present understanding based on those without disabilities is unthinkingly assumed to be a basic understanding of us all (Gliedman and Roth, 1980: Part 2). It is not (Minow, 1990: Afterword). Our under-standing does not capture the variety in us and in our worlds.

In understanding the making of disability we create the opportunity to understand ourselves, whether disabled or not. We do so because we all are made of the same "stuff" (Higgins, 1987). Our experiences and concerns, our hopes and our fears, transcend the distinction we make between disability and ability and bind us in a common humanity. However, we have typically not believed that, which itself is part of the making of disability.

Yet, even when we celebrate differences between disabled and non-disabled people, understanding disability can help us to understand those of us who are not disabled. Understanding the celebrated differ-ences of disabled people may enable nondisabled people to view criti-cally what they take for granted as natural, without need of consideration. What was taken as obvious may now become understood as a partial view among many competing partial views.

> Opening up to another point of view could allow us to see how we are *all* different from one another and also how we are all the same. It depends upon how we look at it—and we all reflect the partiality of our own perspective (Minow, 1990: 376).

For example, as I explore in Chapter 5, Experiencing Disability, people with severe disabilities can be comfortable with their bodies, taking pride in them, which should make us question the great emphasis that in myriad ways we place on physical beauty. Or, a classic joke told in the Deaf community and discussed in Chapter 8 points to the "obsession" hearing people often have with noises, noises that range far beyond the one mentioned in the joke (an obsession not only with the volume of sound but also the appropriateness of it). Because most hearing people take their concern with noise to be "natural," not shaped by them and perhaps "obsessively" so, many may not "get" the joke or only superfi-cially so.

Finally, making disability occurs within the tremendous variation that is humanity. Disability is experienced and becomes significant within the lives we live as women and men, old and young, people of color and of varying "means," citizens of different societies and of varying sexual orientations, and on and on. (These differences are also our creations and ones, which, when used unthinkingly, may hinder us from making useful differences among people with the "same" characteristics or creating common bonds among those taken to be different.) While we typically have reduced people with disabilities to "the disabled," those with disabilities (and those without) are vastly more than their physical, mental and emotional conditions. Their lives and the lives of all others make up the mosaic of humanity. For these and still more reasons, the making of disability speaks to us all.

Our Challenge

The task we have is challenging: to understand how we make disability and to be involved in that making in ways that enhance us all. If we take seriously the making of disability, then we realize that we must take responsibility for what we have made. If we too easily point to bodily conditions as the explanation for the significance of disability (for example, as justification for our segregation of disabled children in separate educational programs), then we blame those whom we have victimized and we lessen the likelihood that we will more humanely remake disability (Ryan, 1971).

Many of us may find it difficult to keep before us the idea that we make disability. We realize now more than ever that our bodies do not determine our lives. We "know" that how we respond to those with different capacities often limits them more than their bodies do. But without even realizing so, we lapse back into an individualistic, pathological framework that has dominated much thinking about disability (see Chapter 1). We unthinkingly abandon the powerful, liberating (but also unsettling) idea that we make disability and fall back to the familiar refrain:

> After all, the bodies of "the disabled" are flawed, and those flaws do indeed limit them. No matter how well we eliminate our hindering behaviors and beliefs, disabled people are essentially different. No matter how small those differences, they matter.

Thus, two keen observers argue that "we cannot separate the essence of disability from the social construction of disability," but then immediately add that "we must continue to struggle to ensure a life free of the kinds of oppressions we have described so that disability can refer to the physical or mental limitation alone" (Asch and Fine, 1988: 300). I agree that we must struggle to eliminate the oppressions experienced by those with disabilities—and those without. But my argument is that physical and mental limitations do not exist "alone." They do not exist apart from how we put together our worlds and live our lives. Through our activities we have greatly expanded how people with varying physical, mental and emotional characteristics live, though we have not done so for all. Where is that "alone," that boundary between the limitations imposed upon people solely because of their bodies (as we presently "understand" our bodies) and the limitations we create, both knowingly and, more important, unknowingly? (2)

Or, in an assessment of federal laws and programs affecting those with disabilities, the National Council on the Handicapped (now the National Council on Disability) (1986: 1) noted that "people with disabilities have been saying for years that their major obstacles are not inherent in their disabilities, but arise from barriers that have been imposed externally and unnecessarily." This statement recognizes that (in significant ways) we make disabilities. But a paragraph earlier, the council noted that "a disability may be considered to be the lack of some mental, physical, or emotional 'tool' which most other people can call upon in addressing life's tasks."

This is an appealing, sympathetic metaphor. *It may be a useful one, too.* Yet is also a very individualistic conception of disability in which a "real" "defect" resides within the disabled person. Knowing the great strides we have made recently in assisting children with Down syndrome to develop their selves, can we easily say what "tools" children with Down syndrome lacked? Did they lack tools or did we make of them people with fewer tools than we presently make of them?

If we were to continue the metaphor, why not say that people with disabilities and those without have different tools, though it may never be clear how and in what way they are different. The tools, themselves, may change over time and across social circumstances. People made disabled might build the same objects as those not disabled in similar and in different ways as built by nondisabled people. For example, one "mobility impaired" individual might walk from place to place, perhaps with much greater effort than others, while a second, similarly "mobility impaired" individual might use a wheelchair, ramps, and elevators to get around. Or, one deaf person might converse with a hearing person through the use of paper and pencil while another deaf person might speechread and speak quite well. Conversations have been conducted in both cases but in different ways. Disabled people might build different objects, some of which people without disabilities may find difficult to build because how they use their tools doesn't suggest to them other objects they could build. As I noted earlier, severely disabled individuals may be quite comfortable with their "imperfect" bodies, whereas nondisabled individuals may become obsessed with the "perfect" body. Or, we—disabled and nondisabled—may build objects together, and on and on. This slightly different metaphor begins to suggest very different possibilities. Yet, some other metaphor may be more useful, still.

Again, I am not denying the importance of our bodies and our "natural" capacities. But I am urging us to not assume that we know where immutable limitations of people exist and where social practices begin. We can continually "amaze" ourselves with how we all can live our lives, but only if we are willing to be amazed. If we assume physical, mental and emotional conditions limit us, then we will ensure that they do by not challenging them. If we assume that these conditions naturally compel us to act in certain ways (e.g., to segregate disabled people from nondisabled people), then the conditions will do so with our complicity.

However, if we realize ever more fully that we make disability, then what we make, we can remake—or at least strive to do so. Not any making will be successful, but we can make disability in many more ways than we typically do. We may also realize that we are comfortable with how we have made disability and may try to resist others' remaking.

Consider Breta, a "deaf-blind, alingual, nonambulatory, retarded" twelve year old who transferred "massive amounts of saliva to objects before touching them more thoroughly" (Goode, 1984: 238, 239). Breta had "no oral or gestural language," "almost no self-help skills," and "required virtually twenty-four-hour custodial care" when met by a social scientist (Goode, 1984: 239). No doubt, many people would find Breta to be almost inhuman. Breta's sympathetic teacher, who worked with her "fairly effectively," called her "slug-like." However, her mother thought her beautiful and claimed that her daughter communicated with her "completely" (Goode, 1984: 239). The social scientist initially could not imagine what Breta's mother meant. Later, however, he, too, came to see Breta as being able to communicate in important ways. In Chapter 4, I explain how he revised his understanding of Breta.

I do not believe that we can successfully make Breta whatever we wish. If we conclude that Breta's organic condition limits what she can become, what we—and she—can make her, fine. It certainly may be useful to "claim" that her organic condition will not enable us to help her do many activities, such as drive a car—or much more modest activities. But, we have made that claim, and we should be cautious in how far reaching we will make such claims. Will we claim that Breta is inhuman, and in doing so, make her so? Or, will we, as her mother has done, claim that Breta can communicate and strive to enable her to do so? The latter making is much more liberating than the former—and may be successfully made!

However, recognizing our responsibility for disability can be frightening. No matter what we do, matters can always be better. People with disabilities—and without disabilities—can always be more self-determining, experience greater opportunities, enjoy more fully life, and on and on. We could respond to falling short by berating ourselves and then fleeing from the challenge altogether. After all, if we cannot ever succeed (absolutely), then why try? But we can also recognize that satisfaction comes in our working at the everpresent challenges—and at times working more successfully than before.

Plan of the Book

In the following chapters I explore how we make disability. I do not explore all that we do. I focus on some important, interrelated social means through which we make disability, issues that arise in that making, and what we have made. I do not know as well as I would like how we make disability, what we have made, and what we could make. Yet, this book will succeed if readers begin to question what they take for granted, if they begin to take up our collective responsibility for making disability and nondisability, for living as disabled and nondisabled people.

The materials I have used to write this book, to develop and illustrate ideas about the making of disability, primarily come from and concern Western society, particularly America. Yet 90 percent of disabled people live in the developing world (Groce, 1990: 2). Thus, much that I explore may turn out to be useful within a very limited time and place. However, to the extent that I am examining basic ways that we make disability, the processes of disability, then my discussion may be more widely useful. Specific, substantive examples may not travel as well. Those living and working within or familiar with other worlds will need to decide how useful my discussion is for them.

As I noted earlier, the making of disability occurs within the tremendous variation that is humanity. When making disability we are necessarily making people with other widely varying characteristics and relationships. We do not just make ourselves disabled or nondisabled, but we also make one another female and male, old and young, of color and differing sexual orientations, and so much more. To a great extent I will not address that variation. However, it is beginning to be done by others (e.g., Fine and Asch, 1988). By not addressing that wider complexity, I encounter the ironic risk of disembodying people with disabilities and unintentionally encouraging readers to see disability as the key, even only, feature of disabled people. In doing so, I may support the very making of disability that I do not find useful. However, I believe I can write usefully about disability even while remaining silent about the interwoven complexity that is us, a complexity in which disabilities—and abilities—are some among many threads.

My focus is the making of disability. In pursuing it, I do not explore greatly any particular disability. Instead, I use material that involves first one then another specific disability or material that itself explores a basic issue regardless of disability. This work is not the place to learn in detail about any particular disability.

In making disability, we develop general, taken for granted orientations by which we understand our selves and our worlds, including disability. We *frame* disability. We conceptualize disability as a particular kind of phenomenon, categorize human variation to create specific disabilities and then count what we have created. We take our conceptions as "true," as "that's the way it is," rather than understanding them to be our handiwork. Our conceptions have primarily been individualistic, often deterministic. Disability is some kind of internal flaw. More recently, we are beginning to conceptualize disability as a social phenomenon, particularly as a clash of majority and minority groups. This book is itself one framing of disability. Chapter 1 explores how we frame disability.

Not only do we make disability in the complex manner that I have briefly introduced, but we also make it in a much more specific, recognizable way. We "literally" produce in one another the mental, emotional, and physical characteristics that we then mark off as disability. We impair one another's hearing, seeing, thinking, and feeling. We hinder people's physiological capacities. We "cut off" their extremities and we paralyze them. In so many ways we produce those characteristics that we know as disability, often in the name of progress, honor, freedom, or some other seemingly worthy cause. We *manufacture* disability—the topic of Chapter 2.

Through language, the media and other publicly visible means, we present images of disability and disabled people. Our images reflect our other makings of disability and help maintain those makings. We present disability as primarily an internal condition that estranges disabled people from others. Chapter 3, examines how we *depict disability.*

Through interactions disabled and nondisabled people construct the identities of disabled people (and nondisabled people) and based on those identities further develop their interactions. While most of us take as obvious that people have one identity—unless they have split personalities—another view may be more useful. If we make identities for one another through interaction, through how we act toward one another, then as our interactions with others vary, so may our identities—and sometimes greatly so. We are each of those people and all of those people but not to everyone we encounter. In Chapter 4 I explore disabled and nondisabled people's *interacting and identifying.*

Disabilities do not determine our experiences of them. Those with disabilities, their intimate others, and those less personally involved make their experiences of disabilities. They may do so in ways that confuse and conflict. Nondisabled people may experience disabled people as homogeneous. However, disabled people and their intimate others may make more varying and less static experiences of disability than nondisabled people can imagine. Disabled people's experiences of disability may even challenge what nondisabled people seemingly hold dear. Chapter 5 takes up *experiencing disability.*

In schools, rehabilitation agencies, and other service organizations, we (too) often work on disabled people in order to "fix" them. In doing so, we further disable them. Even if we "repair" particular disabled people, we make disability a master identity that separates those known as disabled from those known as nondisabled. In Chapter 6, I discuss *servicing disability.*

With good intentions and often with no intentions at all, we have controlled people with disabilities. Our disability policy has kept them in "their place"—after having made a place within which to keep them. Much of our disability policy has not been made with disability in mind. Our unrecognized and often unintended disability policy has been a response to and a furtherance of our becoming a capitalistic, industrialized society—a society with new capacities and great challenges.

Consequently, our present, intended disability policies can often be understood as inconsistent, uncoordinated attempts to grapple with the consequences of our unintended and unrecognized policy of the past. Legislation of the past two decades has revolutionized our making of disability by implementing a rights rationale. However, our policies still greatly individualize disability through segregated, exceptional responses that make people with disabilities dependent. Alternative policies that emphasize the interconnectedness of our lives, that create commonality/communality among us, that develop universal programs and arrangements that include all of our citizens are needed (Zola, 1989). Chapter 7 explores our *policy(ing) disability*.

Many disabled people (and supporters) have increasingly become dissatisfied with their experiences. From individual to collective action, from strategies that enable them to live better with the oppressive making of disability to those that challenge that making, disabled people are *managing disability*, which I take up in Chapter 8.

If we make disability, then we can remake it. But the challenge is great. We make disability within the building of our larger society. To remake disability successfully necessarily entails fundamental changes in how we educate all of our students, transport our citizens, work, house one another, distribute our resources, think about ourselves—in how we live and act together and apart. To remake disability will remake us all. In the Conclusion I point to the challenge of *remaking disability*.

A Note on Naming

I end the introduction with a note about what we call one another. I do not plan to use consistently "disabled people" or "people with disabilities" or "physically challenged" or other more recently developed terms. At times I will use a phrase that may grate on some of our sensibilities, "people made disabled." However acceptably or awkwardly I refer to disabled people, the idea of "people made disabled"—by us—should be kept in mind. That is what I explore in this book.

In explaining why he prefers the term "disabled people," Michael Oliver (1990: xiii), a disabled social scientist, argues:

> It is sometimes argued, often by able bodied professionals and some disabled people, that 'people with disabilities' is the preferred term, for it asserts the value of the person first and the disability then becomes merely an appendage. This liberal and humanist view flies in the face of reality as it is experienced by disabled people themselves who argue that far from being an appendage,

disability is an essential part of the self. In this view it is nonsensical to talk about the person and the disability separately and consequently disabled people are demanding acceptance as they are, as disabled people.

Oliver makes well his point from the stance of some disabled people. However, disabled people are not the only ones who make disability. We—disabled and nondisabled—make ourselves, our disabilities, and our abilities. And we do so at times in very different ways. Our language is one of those differing ways (see Chapter 3). Let my inconsistency reflect the different terms we use. It also reflects my and many other people's difficulty in deciding what to call one another, a seemingly simple, but actually profound, matter in making ourselves.

Endnotes

1. Observers rightly call our attention to the complexity of disability. They do so by differentiating it from impairment, handicap, and other concepts, though they may do so with conflicting terminology (Wood, 1980; Albrecht and Levy, 1984). I will say more about that in Chapter 1. Such distinctions attempt to differentiate between the "real" bodily states of people, a "firm" organic foundation, and the murkier personal and social consequences of those states. In making such distinctions, participants are attempting to develop a firm, objective, nonmanipulatable basis upon which to classify people as disabled or not for all kinds of programs (Stone, 1984). In making the distinctions, specialists are also dividing the "work" to be done on/with disabled people—medical specialists concentrating on the organic limitations, therapists of various kinds on the personal and social limitations. However, the distinctions too easily mislead us to believe that our bodies and organic capacities can be "really" known, that our observations merely record rather than produce what we know our bodies to be.

2. See, too, the attempt by Albrecht and Levy (1981) to draw a distinction between socially constructed disabilities and objective impairments. A firm belief in our making disability is radical—and it is difficult to keep in sight.

Chapter 1

FRAMING DISABILITY

Consider drunken behavior. Some people repeatedly drink a "great deal" and behave in ways to which others take offense. At times we have called this habitual "problem" drinking sinful, immoral behavior. At other times it was willful violation of community regulations, a crime. Most recently we understand such behavior as a chronic illness, alcoholism (Conrad and Schneider, 1980). Widely different responses may follow from those different understandings. We cast the sinners out or try to save them. We throw "the drunk" in jail. But we treat the person with alcoholism, even treating the alcoholic person as disabled. Those responses embody our varying understandings, reflecting them and reproducing them. But which is "problem" drinking? It is all of them—depending on how we frame the behavior and act toward it.

Or, imagine a seven-year-old boy who is black. He lives in poverty with his mother and several siblings in a public housing "project." He achieves academically below grade level. In school he often gets up and wanders throughout the room, talking with classmates or examining items in the room. Instead of promptly starting his assignments, he may play with his pencil, chat with another classmate, or stare out a window. He occasionally yells and curses at other children and the teacher. Sometimes he fights with other children if they have "bothered" him. And, of course, he does so much more that is ordinary, appealing. How might we understand this child and his behavior? We could see him as emotionally disturbed due to the pathological single-parent household and neighborhood in which he lives and assign him to a special education program for children with such disabilities. His emotional disturbance unfortunately makes it impossible for him to fit into the regular class. We can serve him best in a program geared to his needs. However, we might see him as an ordinary child coping with a challenging, often difficult, life and succeeding fairly well. He and his family may need a different set of services than children who come from a privileged middle-class family, but the little boy is not fundamentally disturbed.

22

Perhaps it is the society that disturbs the boy, his family, and many others like them (Kugelmass, 1987).

Our world does not wait for us to come to apprehend it (Bruner, 1986). Instead, we make the world as we comprehend it. We give our world its various, shifting meanings. Through framing our world, through conceptualizing and categorizing it, we make our world as we make sense of our world. So it is for disability.

Through conceptualizing and categorizing humans, we begin to make disability. We begin to invent and transform human variation into the disability that we "know" it to be. We come to understand human variation as one kind of phenomenon and not another. Through framing we produce disability, not merely understand what it "really" is.

However, that is not typically how we understand our frames. Instead, we overlook our framing and take our frames to be "real." Human variation becomes this or that disability, with these or those characteristics. That is what it is. We do not realize that through our framing (and much more) we have made what we know disability to be. Perhaps that making is useful; perhaps not.

When we develop alternative frameworks to the dominant ones, we may realize that disability might be something other than what we "knew" it to be. However, proponents typically dismiss their competitors as uninformed, misguided, or worse. Should we change our framing of disability, then we will claim that our understanding has improved. *Now*, we know what disability "really" is. We fail to realize that through "knowing" disability in a new way (through framing it differently), we have reconstituted it. It becomes something it was not previously. "Problem" drinking changes from sinful behavior to alcoholism, a disease and a disability, with very different and enormous consequences for all.

Framing disability is practical. We put our understandings into practice by how we act toward disability, through our practices we create our understandings of disability, and our practices provided further testimony to our understandings. Each gives rise to and justifies the other.

When we frame disability we not only know what it is, but we also know what we should do about it (if only generally) and who should be in charge. Think of the two examples that opened the chapter. If we know that repeated problem drinking is sin, then we may pray for the offender, expect the offender to repent or excommunicate the offender from the church. Religious officials must take charge. If it is a willful violation of our laws, then the police and other officials of the criminal justice system must step in. But if we know it is a disease, then we provide medical or other kinds of clinical treatment under the direction of medical officials. If we know the boy to be emotionally disturbed, then we assign the boy to special experts. But if we know that the boy is "normal," but economic, educational, and other policies disturb him, then we work on those policies so that they serve better the boy and his family. Our framing tells us what to do.

Framing is ultimately a political means for managing ourselves—for those of us with and without disabilities. We may have varying, often competing interests. Framing may give rise to and support some people's interests, but not others. It bestows authority upon some participants, but not others. It sanctions some kinds of responses, but ignores others.

Again, think of the previous example of the seven-year-old boy. If we see him as disturbed, then we provide him special, expert assistance, but we may not change our regular educational arrangements in order to best serve him. Nor may we concern ourselves too much with his and his family's difficult circumstances. Yes, we may provide some counseling, a little bit of disparaged welfare, and other modest assistance, but nothing that fundamentally challenges the present arrangements encountered by the boy and his family. Our understanding protects our present arrangements—in the classroom and in the society. However, if we believe that he is a fairly typical boy behaving reasonably well within difficult circumstances, then we realize that we need to alter the circumstances in which he is living. The circumstances are the problem, not the little boy (though the boy may be acting in ways that we find unacceptable and to which we decide to attend). But some of us have created part of those troubling circumstances (as educators, politicians, business people, citizens perhaps). Who we are and what we do are bound up in those circumstances that now may become challenged. To challenge the troublesome circumstances would trouble us. Thus, we do not consider doing so or resist when others do so.

When framing disability, we conceptualize, categorize, and count it. Through *conceptualizing* disability, we formulate it as one kind of condition or another. We have primarily understood it as a trait inside of individuals, though more recently we have claimed that it expresses a social relation. Conceptualizations are broad understandings of human variation. Through *categorizing*, we develop and give shape to some of our physical, mental, and emotional variation. We transform the variation into specific kinds of disability with various characteristics. For example, we turn some difficulties in reading into learning disability due to minimal neurological dysfunctions (Coles, 1987). When *counting* disability, we do not record disability statistics, we produce them. We create how much disability exists, how many people are disabled, and the characteristics of those disabled. Counting turns people and their relations to one another into discrete, hard numbers. Through conceptualizing, categorizing, and counting human variation, we begin to make and give shape and magnitude to disability.

Our concern is not whether our framing is right or not. Our concern is how useful is our framing. What have been and what may be the consequences of one framing as compared to another? Can we frame disability more usefully than we presently do?

Conceptualizing Disability

Most conceptualizing *individualizes* disability. We understand disability as a trait within individuals that limits them. Our focus is primarily the particular "flaw" that disables them. Recently, participants have emphasized that disability is a *social phenomenon.* It is not merely, not even primarily, an individual condition. Instead, disability develops out of the interaction among people with varying physical, emotional, and mental characteristics and their circumstances (Oliver, 1988). We presently individualize and "socialize" disability. While advocates and disabled people increasingly promote a social conception of disability, our individualizing conception still dominates. It does so often unrecognized and even within expressed attempts to make disability a social phenomenon.

Individualizing Disability

We typically have individualized disability. Through various conceptions we have understood disability as a defect within individuals that limits them. The interactions among people with varying physical, mental, and emotional characteristics and our larger social arrangements that set some people apart as disabled are overlooked. Instead, "flawed" people naturally cannot live easily within a taken-for-granted world.

A *medical-clinical* perspective presently dominates our individualistic conceptions, but an *economic/work-limitation* perspective is important, especially for government programs. However, throughout most of human history a *traditional* (or supernatural) perspective has dominated our thinking about disability (and the world in general). This traditional point of view remains important in many countries considered to be less "rational-scientific" than the West. However, many people in the West still rely on this perspective even as they use other individualizing conceptions of disability. The *consequences* of these individualizing perspectives are significant.

Traditional Conceptions

We traditionally have understood disability as the result of evil spirits, the devil, witchcraft, or the gods' (even God's) displeasure. Supernatural entities were behind disability. Those with disabilities (and/or their families) were possessed, cursed, sinful, wicked—or perhaps even blessed in a mysterious way. For example, according to various passages in the Old Testament, those who displeased the Lord might be "smitten" with a consumption, a fever, inflammation, extreme burning, madness, blindness, a sore botch that would not heal, or in the knees or legs (Obermann, 1965: 53). Since prehistoric times people have cut holes in the skull to permit evil spirits to escape (Bowe, 1978: 3). We have particularly perceived epilepsy as the result of possession:

> In the Middle Ages epilepsy was called "the falling sickness" or "the falling evil." All diseases were considered punishment for sin, but epilepsy was particularly singled out because of its association with possession. The victims were believed to be under the power of a supernatural being whose will dictated their conduct (Temkin, 1971: 86), and they were seen as tormented by evil spirits (Schneider and Conrad, 1983: 24–25).

We have especially connected disabled infants to evil spirits or the devil. "The belief in the linkage between evil spirits and/or parental misconduct and the birth of a disabled newborn appears widespread," existing among "primitive" tribes as well as in preindustrial and industrial Europe and America (Scheer and Groce, 1988: 28). For example, the "Dogon . . . believe women who have copulated with a bush spirit will bear disabled infants," while the "Nuer . . . believe a disabled infant represents a hippopotamus that has mistakenly been born to human parents. They return the child to its proper home by throwing it into the river" (Scheer and Groce, 1988: 28). Others, like Luther, believed particular children that we would call disabled to be changelings, nonhuman creatures in which the devil sat where the soul should have been (Wolfensberger, 1975, 7–8). Today, we may still wonder what people with disabilities did wrong or the disabled infants' parents did wrong that brought this "affliction" upon them. Parents may wonder as well what they did to deserve such "misfortune." A traditional conception not only individualizes disability, but often casts a moral shadow over persons with disabilities.

But a traditional perspective may also conceive of disabled people as God's chosen. Those now known as mentally ill have been understood in past times as possessing divine gifts (Chambliss, 1974). We still apply today a touch of divinity to disabled people. Consider one woman who contracted infantile paralysis in 1951 when she was 7 years old. Both of her legs became partially paralyzed. Her Polish community turned her into a marginal member through, in part, "revering" her:

> I was called a saint. "God loves her so much to have given her this cross to bear." I heard that so many times. I felt an enormous amount of pressure to be perfect because I was "one of God's favorites" (Phillips, 1988: 206).

Through making the woman spiritually special, her community separated her from them. Sin or sanctity individualizes disabled people and separates them from others.

Medical-Clinical Conception

A medical-clinical view of disability has become dominant within industrialized societies, though it has existed for thousands of years. We have increasingly viewed "troubles" of all kinds as medical matters (Conrad and Schneider, 1980). Within a medical model, those with disabilities have some kind of physical, mental or emotional defect that not surprisingly limits their performance. We cannot expect flawed people to function as well as others.

For example, a medical-clinical model dominates our understanding of mental retardation. In 1900 one student of mental retardation wrote:

> Idiocy is mental deficiency, or extreme stupidity, depending upon malnutrition or disease of the nervous centers, occurring either before birth or before the evolution of mental faculties in childhood. The word imbecility is generally used to denote a less decided degree of mental incapacity (MacMillan, 1977: 33).

In 1932 the Committee on Nomenclature of the American Association on Mental Deficiency (the name of the association is telling) recommended seven classifications of mental deficiency, each due to a different set of diseases, such as prenatal influences, infection, trauma, convulsive disorders, and so on (Scheerenberger, 1983: 184).

Along with a change in name to the American Association on Mental Retardation, has come a change in definition, but not nearly as much in conception as some may have imagined. Mental retardation is now a "significantly subaverage general intellectual functioning concurrently with deficits in adaptive behavior and manifested during the developmental period" (Ysseldyke and Algozzine, 1990: 161). While the "causes" of mental retardation may have broadened to include environmental deprivation as well as physiological abnormalities emphasized in past conceptions, mental retardation is still a deficit possessed by people—a deficit in intellectual functioning and now in behavior appropriate for one's age and cultural group. This conception begins to acknowledge that people live and act with others, that what is expected of us varies by who those others are, but ultimately it emphasizes that some people do not have the wherewithal to think and act appropriately.

As I noted in the Introduction, the National Council on the Handicapped, sympathetically expressed that lack of wherewithal, which to the council *is* disability. The Council (1986: 1) has called disability the "lack of some mental, physical, or emotional 'tool' which most other people can call upon in addressing life's tasks."

Within a medical model participants distinguish among several concepts: pathology, diagnosis, impairment, functional limitations, disability, and handicap (Albrecht and Levy, 1984: 51–55). Active pathologies are "abnormal organic" states and the "concurrent" struggle of the organism "to regain health." Diagnosis is the "art of determining the type and nature of the disease. Impairments are anatomical losses or physiological disruptions resulting from the pathologies . . . Impairments produce disability if they cause functional limitations in the performance of expected activities such as eating, bathing, and paying bills" (Albrecht and Levy, 1984: 53). While handicap and disability are often used interchangeably, a handicap is a "functional limitation that disadvantages a person in a competitive situation such as interviewing for a job or producing work" (Albrecht and Levy, 1984: 51). For example, due to cancer, an active pathology, a person may be missing part of a lung, thus impaired, but not be disabled. Or, an individual may be missing a fourth toe, an impairment, without any present active pathology, disability, or handicap (Albrecht and Levy, 1984: 53–54). Handicap points us toward seeing disability as a social phenomenon, though a medical model understands handicap as the "natural" disadvantage suffered by disabled people in competitive situations due to their individual limitations.

Unfortunately, those making the above distinctions do not always do so in the same way or with the same terminology. Confusion results (Locker, 1983: 1–2; LaPlante, 1990). For example, first make the distinction between actions and activities, between the "finer" tasks that make up "gross units of performance" and those larger units of performance:

> Talking, thinking, remembering, walking, seeing are examples of *actions.* Playing, working, reading a newspaper are examples of *activities.* Moreover a specific activity can be accomplished by different sets of actions. Individuals can sometimes modify how an activity is performed by changing the actions that are required . . . A person with paraplegia may not be limited in the activity of driving if he or she has a car fitted with hand and arm controls (LaPlante, 1990: 15).

Now, one prominent student of disability "refers to problems in performing actions due to impairments as *functional limitations* and problems in performing activities as *disability.* The W.H.O. (World Health Organization) refers to problems in performing actions due to impairments as *disability* and problems in performing highly valued activities as *handicap*" (LaPlante, 1990: 15). Differing definitions lead to differing understandings and counts of disability. Regardless of the confusion, the focus remains much the same—flawed people do not function "normally."

A clinical view individualizes disability as does a medical perspective. However, the defect need not be due to an organic abnormality. Whether a bodily flaw, maladjustment, lack of motivation, abnormal learning style, or some other individual defect, the disability resides within the individual (DeJong, 1983).

Medical and clinical views may point to different procedures and professionals for dealing with disability due to the different kinds of abnormal states upon which they focus. Physicians may treat those with bodily flaws, whereas clinicians may counsel, rehabilitate, and educate those who behave abnormally. Consequently we might see these two perspectives as competitors while missing their essential similarity: An internal, abnormal state is the essence of disability.

Economic/Work-Limitation Conception

Economists have typically viewed disability as a "health-related inability or limitation upon the amount or kind of work that can be performed" (Hahn, 1983: 37). Disability becomes an abnormal state that inherently limits people's capacity to work. A medical-clinical perspective becomes wedded to the economy. Government surveys, policies, and programs concerning disability often employ this frame (Stone, 1981). For example, physicians help determine whether or not people have impairments that qualify them for governmental assistance (Stone, 1984).

Those who work successfully cannot be disabled within this conception (Gliedman and Roth, 1980: 276). The two are mutually exclusive. While this may seem absurd:

> Given a medical definition of the "disabled worker" as "economically sick," the exclusion of the successful but handicapped worker makes perfect sense: if he is successful, he is, by definition, "cured" of his economic "illness" and is no more interest to the economist and his policy-making audience (Gliedman and Roth, 1980: 277).

An economic/work-limitation view narrows the complexity of disability to whether (working-age) adults who are physically, mentally and/or emotionally "flawed" work or not.

Through traditional, medical-clinical and economic/work-limitation conceptions, we individualize disability. While not necessarily precisely, we tell ourselves what is disability, what is significant about it, what should be done about it, and who should handle it. Through these conceptions we create important consequences.

Consequences of Individualizing Disability

In individualizing disability, we produce several important, interrelated consequences. We burden disabled people with their disabilities, separate them from those not disabled, lessen them, and, perhaps most important, conserve present arrangements (Hahn, 1985; Minow, 1990: especially Chap. 2).

Through individualizing disability we put the burden of disability that we have created on those with differing physical, mental, and emotional conditions. Whether or not we cast a moral shadow on those who are disabled, we "know" that disability is largely disabled people's (and their families') burden to bear. Whether deserved due to some moral transgression or not, disabled people are flawed. Their defects naturally limit them. Therefore, their responsibility is to do their best to accept their conditions, to work to improve them, and to overcome them if fortunate, but not to burden others with their conditions, even if that requires ending their lives (Longmore, 1985).

When the community individualizes disability, it may still intervene. Out of fear, it may segregate disabled people, perhaps in institutions or colonies or through death. If concern replaces fear, the community may work with, but typically work on, disabled people. The community counsels, prescribes, operates on, gives to, and through other ways addresses the flawed individuals. The community does so often through experts who specialize in the particular abnormal conditions. Religious officials but more so today doctors, counselors, educators, and professionals of all kinds treat disabled individuals. No matter the intervention, they are all directed toward disabled individuals and their defects (see Chapter 6).

When we individualize disability, we "blame the victims." We hold disabled people responsible for the challenges they encounter but conveniently overlook the responsibility of those of us who are not disabled (Ryan, 1971).

If disabled people "suffer" from or are "afflicted" by some internal defect—sin, possession by evil spirits, pathology, disease, or inherent work limitation, then they are different from those not disabled. One is flawed; the other is not. We then "appropriately" deal with disabled and nondisabled people quite differently. The difference demands it. We create different laws, serve through different agencies, educate in separate schools, house in separate "facilities," transport through different means, employ in different (sheltered) settings, and so on. Individualizing disability separates disabled and nondisabled people (see Chapters 6 and 7). The separation in turn supports the individualization. We point to all of those separate arrangements as evidence that disabled people are indeed different individuals than those not disabled.

To individualize disability is to lessen those we make disabled. We focus on their "flaws," tending to overlook the complexity of their selves. They become narrower people. Their internal flaws make them less capable, even less human (Goode, 1984; see Chapter 4).

To individualize disability is to preserve our present practices and policies that produce disability. If disability is an internal flaw to be born by those "afflicted," then we do not question much the world we make for ourselves. Our actions that produce disability go unchallenged because they are not even noticed (Gliedman and Roth, 1980). Our present arrangements (from how we educate children to constructing our buildings to arranging work to making assumptions about humanity and much, much more) are not recognized as *our* accomplishments, but are understood as how the world has naturally come to be. If we turn many reading and other learning difficulties experienced by children into a learning disability due to minimal neurological dysfunctions, then schools do not need to alter fundamentally how they educate students; minor adjustments are satisfactory (Coles, 1987: especially Chapter 10). Whatever is, whatever is natural, must be appropriate (Stewart and Reynolds, 1985; Minow, 1990: Chapter 2). Individualizing disability protects the advantages of those without disabilities (Blythman, 1988), but in doing so ultimately handicaps us all (Bowe, 1978). It does so because, as I noted in the Introduction, our lives as disabled and nondisabled people are intertwined.

Deafness as a deficit: an example

Think of people who are deaf. We have commonsensically understood their disability to be the result of an individual, internal impairment. They cannot hear when the world naturally demands it. We have taken that deficit and made it into a pervasive defect (Padden, 1980: 90). They lack an important, even an essential, element of being human:

> Scholars and ordinary people, in fact society in general, traditionally considered the deaf to be on a subhuman level, incapable of education or culture, bereft of human intelligence (Furth, 1966:7)

"Deaf and dumb" continues to depict this individualizing frame. Perhaps

> denoting only the inability of deaf people to speak (which is incorrect), but certainly connoting their inability to think, this view of deaf people has greatly influenced their lives. Out of this assumption have come in the past restrictions on deaf people's right to marry, to vote, and to make wills. Due to this assumption, deaf people were placed in the same category as fools and minors in early Hebrew law. If cattle entrusted to them broke away, then the owners were liable for damages because they had shown so little sense. Some states such as Alabama and Georgia passed laws to prevent carnivals from bringing deaf people with them and then abandoning them in local towns (Higgins, 1980: 23–27). Based on a related assumption, deaf people have encountered difficulty in obtaining driver's licenses and insurance at reasonable rates. After all, goes the assumption, one must be able to hear well in order to drive well. Not necessarily so (Schein, 1968)! Due to this assumption that deafness is a deficit there continues a long tradition of psychologically investigating the possible (or is it probable?) pathological development of deaf people (Neisser, 1983: 65). Because of this assumption, "deaf education, by definition if not by design, has had a long history of low standards" (Neisser, 1983: 144). And due to this assumption, it has only been recently recognized (and certainly not universally so) that sign language is a language, *not* a shorthand, a broken-form of English or some other inferior means of communication (Higgins, 1987: ix–x).

When hearing people have not "benignly neglected" deaf people, they have worked on them, typically to turn them into hearing people. Until recently, "fixing" deaf people was only dreamed about. Now, through surgery and other means that dream seemingly becomes more possible. (Or will that dream once again become the nightmare of misguided hopes and damaged lives that it often has been?) More typically, the hope has been that through arduous efforts of deaf people and hearing specialists, deaf people might learn to speak and lipread. If deaf people could not become hearing, at least they could become like hearing people. But they typically did not. However, their "failures" testified further to the significance of their defect. When deaf people did not quite succeed at becoming hearing and in the hearing world—when they did not learn well through an oral approach that banned signing, were passed over for promotions, left out of conversations among hearing colleagues and family members, misunderstood in public places, and experienced many other indignities for not being hearing—that was a shame, but they needed to accept it (Higgins, 1980). After all, to hear (and speak) was naturally necessary to succeed.

The world made according to hearing people was taken for granted. The presumed necessity of hearing to perform various jobs, the lack of interpreters and captioning, the emphasis on spoken English to the neglect of language development, the denigration of signing, and so on were not challenged. But then why should they have been? They were not the issue. The problem lay within deaf people.

When others, such as the pioneering deaf educator of deaf youth, Laurent Clerc, who did not individualize deafness claimed that deafness was part of the diversity of humanity, they were countered or attacked by those who "knew better." Those who individualized deafness as a defect attacked whatever they perceived as giving legitimacy to alternative ways of living and being.

For example, Alexander Graham Bell, whose wife was deaf and mother was hard of hearing, was the most forceful proponent in the late 1800s and early 1900s of individualizing deafness. He viewed deafness as a "physical handicap; if it could not be cured, it could be alleviated by covering its stigmata; hearing people of goodwill would aid the deaf in a denial of their particular language (sign language) and culture, in 'passing' as hearing people in a hearing world" (Lane, 1984: 340).

In an influential paper, "Upon the Formation of a Deaf Variety of the Human Race," presented to the National Academy of Sciences and widely distributed (Lane, 1984: 357), Bell expressed his concerns. He criticized any arrangement that he believed encouraged deaf people to live apart from (though among) hearing people. He criticized the practice of educating deaf children in residential schools separate from hearing youth (an issue that continues to receive much concern today (The Commission on Education of the Deaf, 1988; Higgins, 1990)), the use of teachers who were themselves deaf, reunions of former residential pupils, print media published by and for deaf people, their "gesture language" and more because they constituted the:

> elements necessary to compel deaf-mutes to select as their partners in life persons who are familiar with the gesture language. This practically limits their selection to deaf-mutes and to hearing persons related to deaf-mutes. They do select such partners in marriages, and a certain portion of their children inherit their physical defect. We are on the way therefore towards the formation of a deaf variety of the human race. Time alone is necessary to accomplish the result (Bell, 1883: 44).

Individualizing deafness continues today. It is not a relic of the past. In writing about educating together deaf and hearing students in Great Britain, one author notes that a:

> deaf child who could talk would be more acceptable than one who could communicate only by means of sign language. One might suggest that the more normal the speech and language, the more acceptable the hearing impaired child would become (Lynas, 1986: 63).

A British professional involved in "special education" encountered a shock when he became involved in the education of deaf youth. In 1985 when he was gathering material for a television program on the politics of the education of deaf students:

> one teacher of the deaf referred to the adult deaf community as the "deaffies" and to one deaf man who had the temerity to challenge her as "some deaf Jamie". Another spoke of the use of sign language as akin to "barking at print for hearing children"; having the surface trappings of a real skill but without involvement or comprehension. The same teacher of a postgraduate course in deaf education began a lecture to postgraduate students by telling them how the eating of baked potatoes by a group of deaf people in the lounge at a conference she had attended confirmed the relative inability of deaf people to acquire social skills. Another suggested that signing challenged God's physiological acumen: "If he had meant us to sign, the functions of language would not have been organized in the left hemisphere of the brain". Another educator ... moved from a discussion of the medieval doubt of the presence of a soul in the deaf to a sudden espousal of his own present views:

> If you look at a Minister signing the Lords Prayer it can look beautifully
> expressive—but what does that waggling of hands mean to the deaf? No-one
> knows what they are thinking about. We were not intended to learn the language
> of signs... Faith can only come through hearing... isn't it a fact that faith was
> transmitted orally (Booth, 1988: 109)?

Individualizing deafness or disability profoundly separates people who vary physically, mentally, and emotionally. It may even separate them into different kinds of people or make some not people at all.

"Socializing" Disability

Out of dissatisfaction with individualizing disability, some have begun to "socialize" disability. Some have begun to claim that disability is not merely, perhaps not primarily, maybe not at all, an individual attribute. Instead it is a social phenomenon. Disability is a product of the interplay between people who vary physically, mentally, and emotionally and their worlds (Hahn, 1985: 93).

Those who socialize disability do not ignore physical, mental and emotional characteristics of people. They know that (it may be very useful to claim that) people differ in their capacity to sense, think, and exert force, that some have quite little capacity to do so, and that the lack of capacity is due to physiological conditions. However, that is just a beginning for understanding disability, not the end as individualizing perspectives primarily make it. Even with that recognition, some who socialize disability encourage us to be skeptical about how much the "physiology limits the performance"—and even when it does, to realize that we set the tasks, the standards, and the means by which the tasks are accomplished, and we could do so otherwise. To whatever degree those who socialize disability retain the significance of individual flaws, they direct our attention to what we say and do concerning disability. The "destiny" of disabled people becomes due less to anatomy, more to attitudes, actions, and arrangements.

Socializing disability, as does individualizing disability, is embodied in our actions that make disability. Our actions reflect and give further testimony to our framing. For example, out of socializing disability come laws designed to provide more rights and opportunities for disabled people, which in turn support conceiving of disability as a social phenomenon (Barnartt and Seelman, 1988). Socializing disability is part of a different making of disability, a making that is becoming more widespread, that is diverse, that is in flux, that is being assessed and challenged, that needs to be better understood. Socializing disability is presently the future for disability.

In socializing disability, some have stressed the *social deviance of disability.* Stigmatization lessens the opportunities of disabled people. Others have argued that disabled people are a *minority group.* Disability becomes a sociopolitical phenomenon in which conflicting groups may be pursuing competing interests, with, too typically, oppressive consequences for disabled people.

Disability as Deviance

Rather than emphasize the presumed inherent bodily limitations of those with disabilities, some participants stress society's negative reaction to some of us who vary physically, mentally, and emotionally. These reactions, not their individual, often bodily attributes, make people unacceptable (Freidson, 1966). In advanced, industrialized societies, we typically expect those we encounter to

> walk normally, speak intelligently, not to have sight or hearing impaired, have the usual level of physical stamina, and be able to follow the train of a normal conversation with relative ease. Any alteration in these attributes leads . . . (many of us) to define these individuals in less than positive terms (Lindesmith, Strauss, and Denzin, 1975: 535).

While the above quote skirts the complex issue of how people decide what is "normal," "intelligent," and "usual" and still holds quite strongly to an individualistic perspective, it also points us toward the importance of people's reactions in disabling one another.

Many of us stigmatize people who (we "know" to) differ physically, mentally, and emotionally (Goffman, 1963). Not believing them to be equally human or like us, we do not accept them. Not knowing what to do or say, we are uncomfortable when interacting with them. Impersonal encounters between those with and without disabilities become strained and awkward (Higgins, 1980: Chapter 5; Jones et al., 1984; Ainlay, Becker, and Coleman, 1986; see Chapter 4). Through the "process of being seen and treated as different," those who vary in their physical, mental or emotional conditions are made deviant (Rains et al., 1975: 94).

Consider again mental retardation. Typically we have individualized it as a physiological deficiency. The deficiency naturally made some people incompetent. However, we could understand mental retardation as a devalued status into which some people have been put. If we do, then the term "mental retardate does not describe individual pathology but rather refers to the label applied to a person because he occupies the position of mental retardate in some" group (Mercer, 1973: 27–28). Thus, people with similar "mental pathology" from a medical-clinical perspective might occupy very different positions in different groups, some being reacted to ("known" to be) mentally retarded, others not.

> If a person does not occupy the status of mental retardate, is not playing the role of mental retardate in any social system (i.e., group), and is not regarded as mentally retarded by any of the significant others in his social world, then he is not mentally retarded, irrespective of the level of his IQ, the adequacy of his adaptive behavior, or the extent of his organic impairment (Mercer, 1973: 28–29).

Those who view disability as deviance claim that we are more likely to make deviant some people than others. Continuing with mental retardation, we have historically more readily labeled minority group children, such as Mexican American children and African American children, mentally retarded than white children. We then place the minority group children in special institutions or classes from which it may be very difficult to "escape" (Mercer, 1973). This recognition of the unequal, even inequitable, labeling of some people with varying conditions as deviant points toward a minority group perspective, the dominant way of socializing disability, to which I turn shortly.

To view disability as deviance is an important, yet small, step toward socializing disability. Our reactions to one another become important. Our reactions, not individual traits, make disabled people devalued. However, disability as deviance largely conceives of disabled people as passive pawns buffeted about by the reactions of the nondisabled. Those with disabilities are marginal people, who interpersonally cope with their lack of social acceptance. (That they and nondisabled people may create acceptance is largely ignored (Bogdan and Taylor, 1987 and 1989; Taylor and Bogdan, 1989)). By primarily emphasizing nondisabled people's "misguided" or negative attitudes toward disabled people or by emphasizing the awkward and unsatisfying interactions between those with and without disabilities, this point of view often fails to pursue larger societal arrangements and processes, such as policies and services, that oppressively make disabled people (Hanks and Poplin, 1981; Albrecht and Levy, 1984; Hahn, 1985; Oliver, 1988). To that extent, disability as deviance is quite conservative. By not focusing on the larger social arrangements and processes that subordinate those with disabilities, this conception protects those arrangements and processes. While disability as deviance goes beyond the internal flaws of individualistic views, it moves primarily only to attitudes and interpersonal interaction. A minority-group perspective emphasizes a broader, more critical stance.

Disabled People as a Minority Group

When we conceive of disabled people as a minority group, we consider the myriad ways that we oppress people who differ physically, mentally, and emotionally from the majority. Through a minority-group conception we recognize the prejudice and discrimination of individuals but go beyond that to the harmful policies and practices of our society. When understood as a minority, those with disabilities are recognized as being denied equal opportunities and treatment because of their membership in an identifiable group (Wright, 1960; Safilios-Rothschild, 1970). "Disabilities are regarded as no different than other bodily attributes such as skin color, gender, or aging which have been used as a means of differentiation and discrimination throughout history" (Hahn, 1985: 93–94). Disabled people

> comprise a minority group with many of the same problems as other disadvantaged ethnic or racial segments of the population. Disabled persons not only form a sizeable proportion of welfare recipients, but they also have one of the highest unemployment rates in the United States. Disabled citizens have confronted barriers in architecture, transportation, and public accommodations which have excluded them from common social, economic, and political activities even more effectively than the segregationist policies of racist governments. Most disabled children in America have been assigned to "special" or separate schools, and many have not received any education whatsoever. Disabled individuals have been subjected not only to stereotyping, but also to stigmatizing, which has made them the targets of aversion and ostracism. Studies of public attitudes have revealed extensive intolerance of disabled persons which is related to indicators of discrimination against other minority groups. Like the plight of other minorities, the problems of disabled persons can be viewed as raising the fundamental issue of the extent to which a society is willing to take compensatory action for the discrimination and inequality imposed upon portions of the population that have become the objects of widespread prejudice (Hahn, 1985: 94).

As I discuss in Chapter 7, federal and other governmental legislation and regulations have helped to define disabled people as a minority group. Disability legislation of the past twenty years that prohibits discrimination based on handicaps has often "borrowed language from laws concerning racial, religious, or gender discrimination" (Scotch,

1989: 390). Governmental practices have helped to reframe disability; reframing disability has bolstered revised practices.

The minority-group frame contrasts greatly with the individualistic conceptions of disability. Flawed bodies and functional limitations are not the problem; oppressive practices and policies, even oppressive perspectives, are the problem. This is so even when they are unintentionally oppressive or well-meaning. Instead of being grateful patients, clients, and recipients, disabled people become activists and wary consumers. Instead of submitting to professionals of all kinds who know best, disabled persons (and their allies, including professionals) band together to confront professional dominance, to demand their rights through legal means, and to determine how they will best be served. Economic calculation (How much will it cost and what will be the return?) cannot be a prime consideration (perhaps not one at all) in guaranteeing fundamental rights, as an economic/work-limitations approach assumes (Hahn, 1985: 97–98; Berkowitz, 1987: 188–191). Better adjustment, improved functional capacity, and a closer resemblance to those without disabilities are not the key goals. Self-determination and equal opportunity (however unclear that may be) are. Civil rights legislation, court action, and political mobilization become key strategies for creating equality. A minority-group perspective challenges the individualizing of disability (Gliedman and Roth, 1980; DeJong, 1983; Hahn, 1985).

Disabled people are beginning to understand themselves as a minority group. According to a recent survey, almost three-fourths of disabled Americans identify to some degree with other disabled people. Almost half say that those with disabilities are a minority group in the same way that black people and Hispanic people are minorities. And three-fourths believe that civil rights laws that cover minorities against discrimination should also cover those with disabilities. Even those who judge themselves to be slightly disabled, who do not consider themselves disabled (but were included in the survey on other grounds—see the section, "Counting Disability," that ends this chapter), or who are not limited in their activities have similar views (Louis Harris and Associates, 1986: 110–115). A scholarly framework is becoming the consciousness of disabled citizens and vice versa.

Questioning the minority-group conception

Viewing disability as a minority-group issue enables us to make disability more clearly a social phenomenon, not only an individual one.

However, some participants point to shortcomings in this perspective. In comparison to other minority groups, a disability minority lacks intergenerational continuity and experiences tremendous heterogeneity. Civil rights legislation used to prohibit discrimination against other minority groups is not completely applicable to disabled people. A minority-group perspective overlooks the limitations of people who vary physically, mentally, and emotionally, limitations that exist independent of prejudice and of discrimination, whether practiced by individuals or institutions. Because of these claimed shortcomings and its relatively recent challenge of more dominant understandings of disability, a minority-group perspective is not firmly accepted or applied. Finally, I believe that while a minority-group perspective is an important step toward understanding that we make disability, it does not go far enough. How far *can* we go in developing the understanding that we make disability?

Disabled people are not bound together as much as are other minority groups. Most disabled persons are not born with impairments (to take from the medical-clinical conception), but black citizens and women are born with their ascribed, "minority" characteristics. Disabled persons typically do not have disabled parents. Consequently, intergenerational continuity is absent for disabled people, but it exists for ethnic and racial minorities. While ethnic, racial, sexual, and other minorities are heterogeneous, the heterogeneity among disabled people is enormous. Their racial, ethnic, sexual, social class, disability, and other characteristics and experiences may vary greatly (United States Commission on Civil Rights, 1983: 145–146). For example, our "modern" policies and services have typically separated categorically disabled people. We have "served" people who are blind, mentally retarded, orthopedically impaired, deaf, and so on through different programs and policies. Continuity, similar statuses and experiences, and a common culture that could bind together disabled people do not exist in the same way that they do for other minorities (Gliedman and Roth, 1980: 4; Berkowitz, 1987: 193–194). Disabled people may be in search of collective cohesion. Perhaps this criticism points to the challenge faced by disabled people when they try to organize and mobilize themselves to counter their oppression (Scotch, 1988).

Civil rights legislation used to prohibit discrimination on the basis of race, sex, national origin, religion, and age is not completely applicable for prohibiting discrimination on the basis of handicap. Even though legislation concerning "handicapped" persons uses nearly identical language as other civil rights legislation and even though courts have "directly applied civil rights concepts, precedents, and analyses to cases involving discrimination against handicapped people," to redress the discrimination experienced by handicapped people and to ensure their full participation in society will take action different from that appropriate for other minority groups that are protected classes (U.S. Commission on Civil Rights, 1983: 148, Chapter 7).

For example, many people who are termed handicapped are not able to perform in ways that others who are not handicapped can perform. While the metaphor may be problematic as I noted earlier, they are lacking a "tool," to use the National Council on the Handicapped's (1986:1) phrase. Laws defining handicap often "require as a component that the condition affect performance or function" (U.S. Commission on Civil Rights, 1983: 143). Unlike members of other civil rights classes based on characteristics such as race or sex, to be legally defined as handicapped may require people to have "real, functional differences" (U.S. Commission on Civil Rights, 1983: 144). Those "real, functional differences" may be the basis for exclusion of handicapped persons that is not legally discriminatory. Yet, those "real, functional differences . . . may need to be taken into account and accommodated if . . . (handicapped people) are to participate fully in society" (U.S. Commission on Civil Rights, 1983: 144). Thus, to be neutral toward those who are handicapped in the same way that "antidiscrimination laws aim to eliminate consideration of race, sex, and national origin from decisions regarding rights, benefits, and services" may be to discriminate against handicapped persons (U.S. Commission on Civil Rights, 1983: 153). We cannot simply apply a civil-rights approach based on other minority groups to handicapped persons (Minow, 1990: especially Chapters 5 and 6).

Further, advocates who are sympathetic to a minority-group perspective wonder if it overlooks the "very real" limitations experienced by disabled people due to their varying physical, mental and emotional characteristics (Gliedman and Roth, 1980; Berkowitz, 1987: 224; Ferguson, 1987). Some argue that

> not all handicapped children fit the minority-group model. Perhaps 10 percent of all handicapped children possess a disability so limiting mentally or emotionally that they would not be able to lead normal lives even if prejudice against them melted away. Some moderately retarded children fall into this category, as do nearly all children with severe or profound mental retardation.

So do most victims of childhood psychosis and other severe emotional distur-
bances (Gliedman and Roth, 1980: 4).

Others note that the very notion of a minority group

assumes that humans are agents in the social interpretation of their world,
rather than reactors to our confrontations with an unchanging world of facts
that are "out there," in the "real world." The challenge of profound retardation,
however, is precisely how close it seems to come to the absence of agency . . .

(T)o be severely cognitively impaired is not a difference like skin color or
gender. It is not even a difference in the same way that getting around in a
wheelchair instead of walking is a difference. There is nothing inherent in
being a woman that is necessarily undesirable. There is nothing innately
unfortunate about being a Black, a Native American, or a homosexual. There
is something profoundly unfortunate about severe cognitive limitations.

It is easy to imagine a society where gender, skin color, age, nationality, and
sexual preference have no social inequities attached. It seems much harder to
imagine a world where it would not be preferrable to be capable of abstract
thought. Indeed, the very act of imagination required therein contradicts the
world we would have to conceive (Ferguson, 1987: 54).

Whether or not it is useful to conceive of people who are severely disabled as a minority group, a minority-group perspective has not yet served
them well. A minority-group perspective as well as both civil rights legislation and the disability-rights movement that are compatible with it have
made relatively little difference in the lives of the most severely disabled
individuals (Ferguson, 1987). Such people are considered beyond the
scope of the perspective and perhaps even the movement. Compassion
and pity remain their lot. As long as those with disabilities are viewed as
a minority group limited by prejudice and discrimination, but otherwise
capable of assuming their rightful and "normal" place in the world of
work, then, claim some participants, those with severe disabilities will
remain the odd ones out (Ferguson, 1987; Minow, 1990: Chapter 6).

While a minority group perspective has emerged as an alternative to
the individualistic perspectives, it is still tentative, not firmly accepted.
For example, we speak of mainstreaming instead of desegregation (Hahn,
1987: 195). When buildings are inaccessible, we do not make the connection to "white's-only" facilities of previous decades. Those with disabilities are oppressed with pity rather than horrifying hatred encountered
by other minority groups (Hahn, 1987: 197). And civil rights legislation,
which has been used by governments to address the discrimination
experienced by minority groups, is seen as not completely applicable to
disabled people (United States Commission on Civil Rights, 1983: Chap-

ter 7; Barnartt and Seelman, 1988; Davis, 1988). However, a minority-group perspective pushes us further toward understanding disability as a social, not merely individual, phenomenon.

Beyond the minority-group conception?

Yet, I do not believe a minority-group conception pushes us far enough. Both the perspective *and* some of the criticisms of it don't dare us to examine continually and fundamentally how we make our lives—as disabled and nondisabled people. Too much is taken for granted in a minority-group conception. Too much is still individualized. I cannot offer clear directions as to how to move beyond this useful view (though this book may be a modest step toward developing some), but I can mention some of my concerns.

In conceiving of disabled people as a minority group, we are likely to view disabilities as traits of people, "as no different than other bodily attributes such as skin color, gender, or aging which have been used as a means of differentiation and discrimination throughout history" (Hahn, 1985: 93–94). This view does not forcefully encourage us to consider that these traits only exist through what we make of one another. We make the traits and we differentiate people based upon what we have made—whether we do so usefully or not.

Consider skin color/race. While Americans make a crude distinction between white and black people (children with one "black" parent or even a single grandparent or great-grandparent who is "black" are black), Brazilians make between 300 and 400 distinctions—and anthropologists make yet other kinds of distinctions (Harris, 1989: 106–110). But this example is not powerful enough. Some of us might understand it to indicate merely that we differentiate people in different ways according to their natural characteristics. No, we make those characteristics—and we differentiate people according to them. We create the concept of race, the different races that we claim exist, and put people into those categories. None of that exists independent of us.

Or, consider mental retardation. We have created and continue to create the concept of intelligence, have developed and continue to develop the notion of mental retardation, and have designated and continue to designate people as retarded. Mental retardation is

> never a thing or a characteristic of an individual but rather a social invention stemming from time-bound societal values and ideology that make diagnosis

and management seem both necessary and socially desirable. The shifting
definitions and management of mental retardation are not understandable in
terms of the "essence" of the "condition" but rather in terms of changing social
values and conditions (Sarason and Doris, 1979: 417).

A minority-group perspective too easily sees disabled people as
possessing traits—and then emphasizes how we unfairly discriminate
against people based upon them. Crucial questions go unasked. What
traits have we made? How have we made them? What are the consequences of our making them this way or that? Can we make them more
usefully? Should we make them at all? I briefly take up some of this in
the next section when I explore our categorization of disability. We do
treat people differently according to their attributes, but let's not overlook our making of those attributes (with the differential treatment being
one part of that making).

Second, the United States Commission on Civil Rights cautions that
the "real, functional differences" of "handicapped" people "may need to
be taken into account and accommodated" if they are to "participate fully
in society." Therefore, to be neutral toward those who are "handicapped"
in the same way that "antidiscrimination laws aim to eliminate consideration of race, sex, and national origin from decisions regarding rights,
benefits, and services" may discriminate against "handicapped" persons
(U.S. Commission on Civil Rights, 1983: 144, 153). That caution reflects a
bedrock, nondisabled ("able-ist") construction of the world, which many
of us have difficulty recognizing. The caution states that we must address
the characteristics of "handicapped" people (i.e., their "real, functional
differences") while implying that we do not do so for those not handicapped. The caution implies that the world is simply as it is—natural,
neutral—and within it those not disabled perform more easily. This is
absurd!

We have deliberately, often painstakingly, constructed our world in
ways that "accommodate" those not known as "handicapped." Often
without reflection we have done so, too. For example, when we build
stairs, we fit their height to many (but not all) people's capacity to climb
them. Of course, until recently we have built stairs when ramps could
have worked just as well. We run our "regular" schools so that the
majority of children can at least survive within them, if not thrive. We
design our factories, offices, and other work sites to nondisabled people's
"specifications." We develop our transportation system with only some
people in mind. Examples are never ending. We "accommodate" non-

disabled people in all realms of living. The "problem" is that we have narrowly constructed our world in ways that "accommodate" a fraction of our citizens, continue to do so, but do not fully realize that we do so. Taking responsibility for our handiwork will eventually be more useful.

The Commission's caution relatedly assumes that meaning is inherent in objects and actions. Not considering variation in physical, mental and emotional attributes in decisions regarding rights, benefits and services would be "neutral" for "handicapped" and "nonhandicapped" people according to the Commission, though doing so might also discriminate against "handicapped" people. Thus, a different tack must be taken with "handicapped" people—one of "reasonable accommodation" (U.S. Commission on Civil Rights, 1983: 153–156).

But actions are not inherently neutral. We make them (i.e., act toward them as) neutral in comparison to some standard. That standard may be taken for granted, rarely questioned carefully (see Minow, 1990: Chapter 2). Our standard is that bedrock nondisabled construction of the world. Are we being "neutral" when we advertise a job opening and will interview all interested parties after they have traveled up three flights of stairs? At first glance it may seem that we are. All who come will have a chance. But upon further reflection, our employment practice is obviously not neutral.

If it is not obvious, then let me momentarily turn our world upside-down. Imagine that a company advertised for openings to be filled. The company's office was unusually built with very low ceilings. People of typical height had to squat to get around. Even though they could do the tasks, they could not traverse well the office. The company did not exclude people of typical height from applying, but after evaluating their ability to work in the office, the company rarely hired them. Instead, the company hired short people. Is that "neutral" or not? Many of us would say that the example is absurd. It doesn't make sense. How could one then claim that the procedures were "neutral"? And that is my point. If you are short, the procedures are "neutral." If you are not, the whole world (or at least the company) seems "stacked" against you. Presently our world is "stacked" against many people—disabled or not. Our layout of places of employment and of jobs within them are designed with nondisabled people in mind (and even then often badly). When we redesign jobs we believe we are modifying neutral practices to accommodate the capacities of disabled people. No. We are modifying jobs designed for some (nondisabled) people so that others can also work. (And we are learning that in designing jobs and other features of our world so that disabled people are included, many nondisabled people are better served, too (Zola, 1989)). Neutrality (and everything else) do not exist independent of how we construct our world and lives. Neither, of course, does disability.

One last example, perhaps a difficult one: Many of us might assume that to be a newscaster, one must hear and speak. It's an essential feature of the job (Davis, 1988). We might admit that deaf people can be newscasters on special programs viewed by a deaf audience, but not for hearing people. Why? Deaf people could sign the news with a voiceover for hearing listeners. Now, many of us might claim that would not work well, the audience would be disoriented. Perhaps; perhaps not. But let's not deceive ourselves into thinking that hearing and speaking are essential for that (or many other tasks). They are not. We make hearing and speaking seem to be essential or necessary by how we arrange our world. In some cases, we may be able to arrange it otherwise only at great cost—and then claim that it cannot be done. No, it can be done, but we have decided not to do so—and perhaps *our* decision is sensible. In other cases, we may not be able presently to arrange matters otherwise but could with more work and wisdom. We continue to mislead ourselves that our arrangements are natural and that they require us to act in certain ways. In doing so, we limit what we can do and who we can become.

While the Commission appropriately raises its concerns, it has done so within a taken-for-granted, nondisabled view of the world. That view becomes the standard by which others are judged, though the judgments are claimed to be neutral. Thus, *deviations from it* are "accommodated." The Commission does not recognize how much it takes for granted, how imprisoned it is.

The important concern that a minority-group perspective does not apply well to the most severely disabled people indicates how difficult it is to escape that taken-for-granted, "natural" view of the world. Yes, those known as severely disabled may never live like those not severely disabled. Put better, they may never live as full and varied lives as we all might wish for ourselves. But how they live will be our mutual responsibility. To emphasize that their severe disabilities limit their lives too easily overlooks how we act toward and interact with people who are severely disabled. That emphasis may too easily be interpreted to mean that only

the severe, seemingly immutable "defects" limit their lives. That emphasis may hinder us from realizing that good intentions can oppress just as
can prejudice and discrimination. That emphasis discourages us from
exploring what we could do in making severe disability less limiting.
After all, severe disabilities "naturally" limit people—or so we think.

But consider Down syndrome. In 1924 one authority "concluded that
persons with Down syndrome represented a regression to a nonhuman
species (i.e., to an orangutan)" (Rynders, 1987: 3). Down syndrome was
known as a severe disability. Approximately 50 years later a well-known
theologian comforted a parent who had emotionally struggled to the
decision to institutionalize his child with Down syndrome by asserting
that putting away a baby with Down syndrome was "sad," even "dreadful,"
but carried no guilt because it was not an offense against a "person"
(Rynders, 1987: 3). A few years later the *Encyclopedia Britannica* listed
Down syndrome under the heading "Monster" (Rynders, 1987: 3). Yet,
today we know that people with Down syndrome can and do learn to
read, compute, and live in the community (Rynders, 1987). Claiming
that a minority group model does not apply well to severely disabled
people may unintentionally discourage us from challenging ourselves to
see what we can make of one another, to see how encompassing a world
we can create.

As do individualizing conceptions, a minority-group perspective makes
disabled people different from nondisabled people. Disabled people are
a *distinct* class of people discriminated against because of bodily attributes.
Like other minorities whose rights have been violated, they deserve
special consideration and require particular remedies. Legislation is
written to ameliorate *their* oppressive conditions. Even as the minority-
group perspective and practices based upon it aim to bring together
disabled and nondisabled people, the perspective and practices unintentionally tell us that disabled people are different kinds of people.

For example, the Education for All Handicapped Children Act of
1975, P.L. 94-142 (now named the Individuals with Disabilities Education Act) was landmark legislation. It was intended to provide a free,
appropriate education to disabled children who often had been denied
any education. However, mechanisms such as an Individual Education
Plan, IEP conferences, and due process hearings where parents could
contest educational decisions are available only for disabled students.
They are "special" procedures. Consequently, the mechanisms set disabled and nondisabled children apart. The legislation attempts to bring

together disabled and nondisabled people, but it also reinforces the pervasive belief that disabled and nondisabled people are different kinds of people (Biklen, 1989). A minority-group perspective may not strongly encourage us to develop flexible, universal policies that encompass the diversity of all of our citizens (Zola, 1989).

A minority-group perspective has enabled us to go far. It has encouraged us to explore our practices that limit disabled people. It has underlay the civil rights legislation for disabled people of the past several decades. It has tremendously broaden our understanding of our collective responsibility for living as disabled and nondisabled people.

However, I believe we must eventually move beyond a minority-group model. It ultimately lets us off the hook. It does not insist that we are completely responsible for how we live as disabled and nondisabled people. In taking the world we have created that suits nondisabled people as natural, neutral, it requires only reasonable accommodations or else justifies more on charitable grounds. In claiming that severely disabled people do not fit the model, it does not force us to struggle with the fact that we are still responsible for how we live as disabled and nondisabled people even when our efforts seem so meager. In letting us off the hook (though keeping us on it longer than an individualistic frame), it does not fully challenge us to devise ways for transcending the apparent opposition between disabled and nondisabled people, between minority and majority group (Zola, 1989). It does not fully challenge us to develop ways that disabled and nondisabled people can live together—and apart, recognizing the common humanity that binds us together and celebrating the distinctiveness that separates and enriches us. By letting us off the hook, it does not encourage us to imagine how varied we might make our world. I tackle again these concerns in Chapter 7, especially when I explore the emerging rights rationale that underlies our disability policy.

Making disability social begins to give us responsibility for disability. We may not be able to succeed in that responsibility, but it is ours. What we do matters. We no longer can use individual traits as the excuse for what we do. The traits do not make us do what we do, even though we may not yet (or never) be able to do what we wish.

Categorizing Disability

Conceptualizing disability sets the broad orientation within which we make disability. As we frame disability, we also categorize it. We mark off some physical, mental, and emotional variation as distinct phenomena, create an etiology for and attribute other characteristics to the phenomena and the people marked by it, and develop strategies to manage the disabilities. As Joseph Schneider (1988: 65) notes, disabilities "are not 'givens' in nature . . . but rather *socially constructed* categories that emerge from the interpretive activities of people acting together in social situations."

Here I very briefly discuss the categorization of disability. I note the *differentiation* of human variation into distinct categories and subcategories of disabilities and the *expansion* of categories to cover new phenomena and more people. This categorization has primarily taken place within individualized conceptions of disability, either traditional or, more significantly, medical-clinical views. As participants have categorized disabilities, they have attributed *clusters of characteristics* to the disabilities and to the disabled people. These clusters are overwhelmingly negative. I end the section with a discussion of the development of learning disability, the largest, and a rapidly increasing, category of disability for school-age children.

A significant trend in the categorization of disability is the differentiation of human variation into distinct categories and subcategories. Early people made few distinctions among one another (Rosen and Gregory, 1975: 17). They did not separate physical from mental functioning. All of life was explained by supernatural spirits. Eventually, people separated physical from mental difficulties, attributing the later more so than the former to supernatural spirits. Primarily, but not only, with the development of medical expertise and specialization, doctors and others made distinctions within physical and mental realms and developed subcategories of disabilities (Conrad and Schneider, 1980: 52).

For example, by the end of the 1800s, students of "mental defectiveness" had clearly separated mental retardation from mental illness (Scheerenberger, 1983: 87). Moreover, whereas early observers conceived of mental retardation as a single phenomenon, those in the 1800s distinguished between idiocy and imbecility, the former being "extreme stupidity" and the later a "less decided degree of mental incapacity" (Scheerenberger, 1983: 59). In the first comprehensive textbook on mental retardation published in 1887, the author created ten categories of mental retardation based primarily on physical characteristics and causes (Scheerenberger, 1983: 59). Nowadays educators often distinguish among mild, moderate, severe and profound mental retardation (Ysseldyke and Algozzine, 1990: 162).

Perhaps more than any discipline, psychiatry has been greatly concerned with classification (Conrad and Schneider, 1980: 53). Beginning with the ancient concern with "madness," psychiatrists have now developed more than 200 categories and subcategories of mental disorders (American Psychiatric Association, 1980). Specific categories have given way to new, differentiated categories. For example, neurosis no longer exists as a distinct category. Instead, affective, anxiety, somatoform, and dissociative disorders have "divided and conquered it" (Cockerham, 1981: 5–6).

As we have categorized disabilities, we have also expanded our classifications to cover more phenomena and people. A fundamental expansion has been the shift from understanding unwanted human behavior as sin (or punishment for sin) to increasingly understanding it as a medical phenomena (Conrad and Schneider, 1980). For example, in understanding drinking and drug difficulties as an illness instead of as a sin or as a willful violation of our laws, we have turned them into disabilities as well.

We have also widened our categorization. We have enlarged the scope of our categories to include "milder" forms of unwanted behavior and less extreme variation (from what is taken to be typical human functioning) and created new categories that classify variation as disability.

For example, early people probably only categorized as mentally retarded people whom today are classified as "severely" retarded. With the development of IQ tests, an IQ of 70 became a popular cutoff for separating retarded from nonretarded people. However, in 1959 the American Association on Mental Deficiency developed a definition of retardation that used an IQ of 85 (or 84) as a cutoff, which would include one-sixth of the American population. The definition represented the association's concern that people who were performing marginally be eligible for services and their belief that greater intellectual abilities were needed in a complex society. However, by the early 1970's, parents, advocates, court officials and other participants were concerned about the treatment of mentally retarded children and adults and about the labeling of minority children as mentally retarded. In response to that concern, the AAMD revised its definition such that an IQ of 68 or 70 (depending on the test) became the cutoff. With the raised cutoff, fewer children are now classified as mentally retarded (MacMillan, 1977: 36–38; Walker, 1987). However, the past decade's decrease in students classified as mentally retarded has been counterbalanced by the increasing classification of children as learning disabled (Coles, 1987). A more "respectable" category has begun to replace a less desirable one, a point I take up shortly.

The expansion of categories has occurred in other realms of disability. The emphasis of Freud and his disciples on neuroses, the psychogenic development of mental symptoms (as opposed to organic development), and the importance of the family and early childhood experiences expanded greatly the realm of mental disorders. "Madness, hysteria, obsessions, compulsions, phobias, anxiety, homosexuality, drunkenness, sexual deviation, chronic misbehavior in children, and delinquency, among others" became psychological disorders (Conrad and Schneider, 1980: 54).

We have especially widened our net in dealing with children. Nowadays, students may receive special services not only if they are deaf but also if they are hearing impaired. With the development and popularization of hyperkinesis in the 1960s and 1970s, what before were behavioral and learning difficulties have become the most common childhood psychiatric problem. Moreover, observers are slowly expanding hyperkinesis to adolescents and adults (Conrad and Schneider, 1980: 155–161). And professionals are increasingly finding the interconnected difficulty, learning disability, in children as young as one year old. Perhaps they are doing so because some argue that learning disabilities can lead to frustration in school and hostility toward society, which in turn may lead to even more disastrous, violent outcomes such as the *presumed* link between a *tentative* diagnosis of Lee Harvey Oswald's dyslexia and his assassination of President Kennedy (Coles, 1987: 20).

While occasionally we contract our categories (witness the AAMD's 1973 definition of mental retardation) or even delete them (homosexuality is no longer officially a mental disorder), we continue to modify them and typically expand their domain. Our categorization (and its implementation) are making more and more people disabled.

When categorizing disability, we also attribute characteristics to the disability and the disabled people. We "discover" the nature of the disabled people whose disability we have categorized. These natures, like the categories themselves, may change. However, our professional characterizations typically depict disabled people very negatively (Schneider and Conrad, 1983: Lane, 1988; Ysseldyke and Algozzine, 1990: 172). For example, the following are terms found in the professional literature to describe youth who are mentally retarded: apathetic, concrete, disruptive, easily manipulated, erratic, frustrated, impulsive, inattentive, perseverative, rigid, slow, stubborn, unmotivated, unstable, and withdrawn (Ysseldyke and Algozzine, 1990: 172).

Or, consider deafness. Professionals have created a "psychology of the deaf." Deaf people are said to be: asocial, disobedient, dependent, immature, irresponsible, submissive, unsocialized, egocentric, have poor insight, naive, unaware, aggressive, hedonistic, rigid, stubborn, depressive, explosive, irritable, and/or paranoid among other negative and sometimes inconsistent traits (Lane, 1988: 9). Not too surprisingly, mentally retarded and deaf people often disagree with the professional characterization of them (Bogdan and Taylor, 1976, 1982; Lane, 1988).

Our professional characterizations of deaf people, mentally retarded individuals, and others with disabilities underlie the nondisabled's paternalism toward disabled people. The nondisabled's burden is to take care of their less civilized, less competent charges for whom they have a mixture of pity and contempt. Such paternalism has been paralled by the paternalism of the colonizers toward those they have colonized (Lane, 1988). The professional characterization of disability also finds an everyday counterpart in the mass media's portrayal and other public depictions of disability, an issue I take up in Chapter 3.

Disabilities do not exist independent of our creating human variation and categorizing it. The domination of medicine as a major means of managing "unwanted" behavior and its increasing specialization partly underlies the development, differentiation, and expansion of disability categories (Conrad and Schneider, 1982). However, categorization of disabilities grows out of other concerns as well. As I mentioned in the Introduction and take up in Chapter 7, disability has provided a flexible tool for bolstering our often threatened work ideology that proclaims that everyone should work (or take care of children) and work is the prime means for obtaining what is desirable. Our categorizations and paternalistic characterizations of disability provide economic benefits to nondisabled people. The categorizations and characterizations provide employment and status to professionals who expertly and patiently serve people now known as disabled. The categorizations (as well as the larger framing of disability and its fuller making) may provide a cheap supply of labor (inside or outside of institutions) and a market for "disability products and services" that primarily enriches nondisabled providers (Lane, 1988). Our categorizing may also provide more "respectable," and still conservative, means for managing our disappointments, particularly the disappointments of mainstream members of society. Consider learning disability.

Categorizing Learning Disability: An Example

In the mid-1960s learning disability became an important category for understanding (perhaps misunderstanding) difficulties youth, especially middle class youth, experience in learning, particularly in reading (Coles, 1987). While it has gone by many names, learning disability has

> always been formally defined as a specific subset of low academic achievers whose serious academic failures could not be accounted for by their sensory functioning, intellectual ability (as measured by IQ tests), or emotions, which were generally normal. Nor can unfavorable circumstances or experiences explain the disabilities. These children by and large come from the middle class (Coles, 1987: 10–11).

Instead, the essence of learning disability is minimal neurological dysfunctions that "biologically disable" youth (Coles, 1987: xi).

Before the late 1800s when observers began to write about "word blindness," learning disability (whatever its name) did not exist, though the human variation to which it ambiguously refers did—sort of! People who today might be known as learning disabled may have formerly been known as "slow," "retarded," or "odd." But mostly they would not have been known as unusual at all. The learning difficulties experienced today by learning disabled youth have not been experienced by most youth throughout history. For example, most youth have not been asked to learn to read. Thus, they could not experience any reading difficulties, the most common learning disability. As we have expected youth to learn to read and have tried to teach them to do so, many youth have experienced difficulty. However, until the mid-1960s we typically did not understand those difficulties as the consequences of a learning disability. Instead, we offered other explanations, from low intelligence to little motivation to inadequate family functioning.

Even if we accept that minimal neurological dysfunctions are the essence of learning disability (and we should be skeptical of doing so, though a very small portion of learning disabled youth may experience some dysfunctions) and that these dysfunctions have existed throughout history, we should realize that minimal neurological dysfunctions have been insignificant for most of human history. Most people with minimal neurological dysfunctions throughout history would not have been known as different. They would not have experienced any significant consequences because of their dysfunctions; and when they did, as in misunderstanding an oral direction, they would certainly not have been called learning disabled.

However, with important changes since World War II, we have produced learning disabilities where they did not previously exist. Since World War II middle-class adults moved to the suburbs where they expected success but often experienced difficulties and disappointments. The adults expected to succeed within the postwar expansion of the economy. Many did, but others did not. Long-term mortgages, utilities, taxes, repair bills, and other costs produced economic strains. Periodic job transfers, the increase in divorces beginning in the mid-1960s, the widespread use of Valium® and Librium®, job-related stress, and youth disenchantment led to and indicated the significant strains that middle class suburban families experienced (Coles, 1987).

The educational difficulties of some of the children of suburban, middle-class parents became part of the parents' unfulfilled expectations and resulting strains. Middle-class children's "learning disabilities were not an anomaly—some kind of 'fluke,' as LD specialists have often concluded; rather, they were part of the larger failure of U.S. middle-class life to achieve post-World War II promises and expectations" (Coles, 1987: 194). Schools have always failed to educate well many children, but middle-class parents expected their children to succeed. Some middle-class parents of children who were doing poorly in school began "demanding that schools do more for *their* children" (Coles, 1987: 195). The activism of these parents was part of the wider social activism of the 1950s and 1960s. As parents arranged meetings with physicians and psychologists in the 1950s and 1960s, they encountered the LD explanation offered by the professionals—and took it to heart (Coles, 1987).

The creation of learning disability became the major response of parents, educators, researchers, and government officials to the otherwise unaccountable educational difficulties experienced by middle-class youth. The essence of learning disabilities, minimal neurological dysfunctions, was appealing to parents and educators. In locating the difficulty within the youth, the field of learning disability did not blame parents and educators, provided the possibility for improvement, and led to educational adjustments (i.e., techniques for working with the new category of disabled children), *not* institutional change (Coles, 1987: Chapter 10). Learning disability provided hope without the turmoil of "blame" or fundamental change.

With the passage of Public Law 94-142, the number of children identified as learning disabled has increased dramatically. From 1976–77 to 1982–83 an additional 1 million students were identified as learning disabled. At the same time, the number of children diagnosed as mentally retarded declined (Coles, 1987). However, participants disagree greatly on how to define learning disability, and educational programs for students classified as low-achieving and as learning disabled do not differ significantly (Walker, 1987: 103). Nevertheless, learning disability has become a "respectable" category for managing children who experience academic difficulties, especially white, middle-class children but also minority-group children (Coles, 1987; Walker, 1987).

The creation of learning disability should not by itself trouble us. We must categorize in order to understand and manage the world. However, what should concern us is whether or not our making of learning disability (or any category) has been helpful to us. Gerald Coles (1987) argues that making minimal neurological dysfunctions the essence of learning disability has not been helpful. Instead, he suggests an alternative for understanding learning disability, an "interactivity" approach. This emphasizes the active interaction between and among children, parents, educators, and others concerning learning within larger "social, economic, political and cultural" arrangements (Coles, 1987: 140).

The concern about learning disability is one we should have for all disability. Does our categorizing help or harm those we categorize?

Counting Disability

Forty-three million Americans are disabled and 500 million worldwide (Zola and Kirchner, 1990; Bowe, 1986: 202). *Perhaps*. Maybe as "few" as 14 million Americans are disabled, but then perhaps as many as 75 million are disabled (Bowe, 1978: 17; Pfeiffer, 1989). Maybe 30 percent of the American population is disabled, but then perhaps "just" 8.5 percent of adults are disabled (Pfeiffer, 1989; Bowe, 1985: 4). While 43 million (disabled Americans) has become a widely mentioned figure (being mentioned in the preamble of the Americans with Disabilities Act of

1990), counts of disabled people and disability vary greatly (Zola and Kirchner, 1990).

Counting disability is complex, even controversial. The consequences are significant. From nationwide surveys to agency tallies, we count disability.

Through counting disability, we help to make it. Counts are not objective reflections of some "real" number of disabled people. Instead, just as disability does not exist independent of our interpersonal, organizational, and societal efforts to manage human variation, neither do counts exist independent of our efforts to tally what we have made. When we count disability, we give further shape and size to the phenomenon that we make. Through the interplay of government agencies, disability groups, and other participants, who may have varying interests, we count disability (Zola and Kirchner, 1990).

Counting is consequential. Counts can be used to justify the importance of disability, the provision of more resources and the necessity of new legislation. They provide information for planning, implementing, and evaluating our programs directed toward disability. Counting is used to demonstrate accountability, to show often skeptical publics and regulators that an agency or group is effectively, efficiently, and appropriately meeting its mandate. But counts can also be used to downplay disability, to justify the relative inattention it might presently be receiving (Zola, 1979: 454; Zola and Kirchner, 1990). For example, in many less developed countries

> in view of the deceptively low estimates of chronic illness and disability used, and therefore of rather limited need for rehabilitation, no justification could be found for the provision of rehabilitation services under the institutional model of rehabilitation tied to an expensive specialized hospital with very expensive equipment and specialized personnel. Many passionate appeals to the UN and other international organizations in the 1960s and early 1970s, like the one made by the author in 1971 on behalf of disabled children, had no results (Safilios-Rothschild, 1981: 112–113).

In an important sense, to count disability is to bring it into existence. To government, to be recorded is to exist. Counts record disability whether the records be of disabled students, rehabilitation clients, or "disability" recipients.

Thus, what we count and how we count matters. The technical issues of how we count does not concern me here, though they are important (Gleidman and Roth, 1980: 280–282; Safilios-Rothschild, 1981:112; Higgins and Butler, 1982: 32–33; Berk, 1985; Bowe, 1985; Zola and Kirchner, 1990). Instead, what we count concerns me. How we define disability shapes what we "find." Our present counting fundamentally and dangerously misleads us.

In America two approaches have dominated until recently: a health-conditions approach and a work-disability approach (National Council on the Handicapped, 1986: 3). The medically oriented health-conditions approach focuses on "all conditions or limitations which impair the health or interfere with the normal functional abilities of an individual" (National Council on the Handicapped, 1986: 3). This approach typically produces very large estimates of disability prevalence— 160 million impairments and chronic conditions, according to one survey. While it includes conditions that many of us do not call disability, it also neglects others that are nowadays taken to be disabling, such as learning disabilities (National Council on the Handicapped, 1986: 3).

The other major approach is work disability, an economics approach. Those who have a health-related condition that prevents them from working or limits their ability to work would be work disabled (Hahn, 1983: 37; National Council on the Handicapped, 1986: 3). This approach, which is used in almost all surveys (Hahn, 1983: 37), has been criticized for many reasons. For example, it

> underestimate(s) the numbers of people at lower age ranges—the 16 to 24 age group, for example—some of whom are not ready to join the work force and for whom the self-identification as either work disabled or not is often not meaningful. (It) also skew(s) the population counted. Persons who are out-of-work or who are not seeking work have psychological motives for reporting themselves as having a work disability, whether or not they truly have a disability. Independent disabled persons with a strong work history and who are currently employed, on the other hand, will often refuse to categorize themselves as having a work disability, even if they have a significant disabling condition such as blindness, paralysis, or absence of a limb. For these reasons, work disability studies tend to underestimate the total numbers of people with disabilities, and to overestimate the unemployment and nonparticipation in the labor force rates of people with disabilities (National Council on the Handicapped, 1986: 4).

Others criticize the work-disability approach for overlooking approximately "three-quarters of all . . . (adults who were) classified as handicapped during childhood—the mildly mentally retarded, the learning-disabled, and the emotionally disturbed" (Gleidman and Roth, 1980: 285).

Reread the above criticisms. While useful, they reflect unstated assumptions as does a work-disability approach. The National Council on the Handicapped seems wedded to an objective, absolutist approach, implemented by officially sanctioned experts. People may not "truly" have a disability but claim that they do; others who "truly" are disabled may not claim so. Apparently self-perceptions are given less credence than the "objective" perceptions of experts.

Or, the authors who criticize the work-disability approach for overlooking many adults who were classified as disabled as children are sensitive to the social construction of disability. However, their criticism (partly) implies that once disabled always disabled and, of greater importance I believe, that disability is a trait inside individuals that they take with them from one setting to another, in this case, from one age arena to another. By itself, this criticism fails to recognize that schools are the prime setting for identifying and treating people as disabled. (The explosion of learning disabilities mentioned earlier is a good example.) Nowhere do we scrutinize people more closely and differentiate them more finely than in school (though some may argue that we do both very badly). Nowhere do we construct such a narrow notion of normal against which many may come up short. (A notion that includes excessive emphasis on some intellectual skills and rigid boundaries for behavior.) We should not be surprised that many whom we deem to be disabled as children are not known as disabled as adults. Their physical, mental and emotional attributes may not have changed (though they may have improved once away from what is too often a disabling world), but what others and themselves make of them has (Mercer, 1973). Thus, with irony, mild mental retardation has been called the "six-hour" disability (the time the "retarded" child spends in school) (Edgerton, 1979: 72 noted in Mehan et al., 1986: 161).

Another, perhaps more useful, criticism of the work-disability approach is the confusion its users create. Those who use it often take it as a definition of disability without the qualifier "work" (Hahn, 1983: 37). By doing so, they assume (and lead others to believe) that to be disabled necessarily means that one has work difficulties and that if one does not, then one cannot be disabled. The successful but seemingly disabled worker is defined out of existence (Gliedman and Roth, 1980: 276–277).

Relatedly, the work-disability approach reduces people to their (economically) productive selves. It clearly tells us that disability is only important so far as people cannot work well. The potential complexity of disability is ignored. However, rather than seeing this merely as a shortcoming of a work-disability approach, we might more usefully see this as the outcome of important societal (governmental) practices toward disability. Disability becomes important only as it may hinder the economy. I take up this issue in Chapter 7.

Most importantly, both the health-conditions approach and the work-disability approach to counting disability reflect the individualistic framework out of which they have developed. Each takes disability to be a flawed attribute of people, and one, from the work-disability view, that necessarily obstructs people's ability to work. Disability exists within people. Each takes disability to exist independent of how we produce and manage human variation, how we make disability. How we make disability out of human variation is obscured. Thus, these approaches fundamentally produce conservative figures; conservative in that present arrangements, practices, and policies are not questioned as to their role in disabling people.

If we believe that we make disability, then to ask how many people are "really" disabled is nonsensical (Mercer, 1973: 255). However, by asking and providing answers, by counting, we seemingly comfort ourselves. By trying to get a fix on how many people are disabled, we

> delude ourselves into thinking there is some finite number of disabled people. In this way we try to distance ourselves from the reality of disease, disability, and death. But our safety is illusory. Any person reading the words on this page is at best momentarily able-bodied. That person will, at some point, suffer from one or more chronic diseases and may be disabled, temporarily or permanently, for a significant portion of his or her life (Zola, 1983: 56–57).

What might counting be like if we begin to move beyond our individualistic conceptions of disability? If disability expresses a relation among people and their worlds, if it is a product of complex actions of many participants, if we make one another disabled at some moments but not at others, if the making varies by the maker, and so on, then how would we count disability? I don't know. Given that numbers are crucial in making policy, we will need to continue to count, but how?

Perhaps a tentative step would be the recent national survey of disabled Americans conducted by Lou Harris and Associates (1986) for ICD–International Center for the Disabled. In that self-report survey, a person was defined as disabled if he or she

> had a disability or health problem that prevented them from participating fully in work, school, or other activities(;) . . . said that he or she had a physical disability, a seeing, hearing, or speech impairment, an emotional or mental

disability, or a learning disability(;) . . . or considered himself or herself disabled, or said that other people would consider him or her disabled (Lou Harris and Associates, 1986: iii).

The survey includes health-conditions and work-disability approaches but moves beyond them by recognizing that how we and others "see" ourselves can be an important feature of disability. But the variability that I noted above, such as being made disabled in some circumstances but not in others, has yet to be addressed. Nevertheless, our counting is beginning to recognize the complexity of disability.

Demography of Disability

Our present disability counting provides us a demographic picture of disabled Americans. Given the complexity of counting disability and the many concerns noted above, I cautiously, not comfortably, present the demographic picture of disability that follows.

Disabled people are *older* than nondisabled people, *poorer* than nondisabled people, are significantly *less educated* than nondisabled people, are *less likely to be in the labor force* (i.e., to be working or looking for work) than nondisabled persons, and slightly *less likely to be married but more likely to be divorced or separated* than nondisabled people (Bowe, 1985; U.S. Commission on Civil Rights, 1983: 10–15). Black Americans (and perhaps Hispanic Americans) are more likely to be disabled than white Americans (Bowe, 1985; U.S. Commission on Civil Rights, 1983: 14–15).

The older people become, the more likely they are to be disabled. Approximately 10 percent of those under 21, between 9 and 17 percent of those working age, and nearly half of those over 65 are disabled (Asch and Fine, 1988: 1). (These and other figures noted below may change as data from the 1990 census become available.) As we live longer, we presently can look to being disabled (Zola, 1989). And as the populations of other countries age, those countries will increasingly confront disability issues (Safilios-Rothschild, 1970: 39–40).

Disabled people are poorer than nondisabled people. One-fourth of American disabled people (in 1980) earned income less than the federal poverty line, but only one-tenth of nondisabled Americans earned so little. Conversely, (in 1980) less than 5 percent of disabled Americans had incomes of $25,000 or more, but more than 10 percent of nondisabled Americans did so (Bowe, 1985). Those who live in poverty are more likely to become disabled due to their harsh living and working conditions, and those who grow up or become disabled are more likely to become poor.

Disabled people are less educated than nondisabled citizens. One in five disabled persons has attended college but one in three nondisabled Americans has gone to college. However, almost 17 percent of disabled Americans have less than eight years of schooling, four times as great as nondisabled Americans (and the older age of the disabled population cannot completely explain these differences). While disabled children have been excluded from school, the educational gap cannot be primarily understood as a result of our educational policies. Most disabled people become disabled later in life. Instead, persons who are less well educated live more difficult, poorer lives (e.g., they work at more physically strenuous jobs), which give rise to their becoming disabled (Bowe, 1985: 14).

Disabled people are also less likely to be working. Only one in three are in the labor force. Approximately 40 percent of disabled men and slightly less than 25 percent of disabled women are in the labor force compared to almost 90 percent of nondisabled men and more than 60 percent of nondisabled women. These great differences cannot be completely accounted for by the older age of disabled people or their lesser education (Bowe, 1985: 20-23). Less income, less education, and less employment are bound together for many disabled people.

However, when disabled people work full time, their incomes are comparable to that of their nondisabled colleagues (as are their jobs) (Bowe, 1985: 29). Work is a prime determiner of status for disabled and nondisabled people (which should not surprise us given the work ideology upon which our society is based) (Louis Harris and Associates, 1986: Chapter 5).

Disabled people are slightly less likely than nondisabled people to be married (55 to 59 percent) and more likely to be widowed (9 to 2 percent), divorced (11 to 7 percent), and separated (5 to 3 percent). The older age of disabled people helps to account for their higher rate of widowhood. Observers commonly attribute the greater likelihood of being divorced or separated to the "strains attendant to disability" (Bowe, 1985: 20). However, we must be careful with this explanation. Are the strains inherent in personal attributes known as disabilities or do they arise out of the complex interpersonal, organizational, and societal ways in which we respond to those with varying physical, mental, and emotional attributes? Further, the differences are slight

Finally, black Americans (and perhaps Hispanic Americans) are more likely to be disabled than white Americans (U.S. Commission on Civil Rights, 1983: 14–15). Almost twice as many black Americans are disabled as white Americans (14 to 8 percent) (Bowe, 1985: 4). Black Americans live poorer, harsher lives than do white Americans. Their more difficult existence gives rise to their higher rate of disability (Bowe, 1985: 4). Likewise, the more difficult existence of those in less developed countries gives rise to their high rates of chronic health conditions (Safilios-Rothschild, 1981).

Our counts of disability are likely to increase in the future, as they have in past decades (see Safilios-Rothschild, 1970: 38–40). For example, medical, surgical and pharmaceutical improvements are controlling acute illnesses and infections, which enables those with chronic illnesses and disabilities to survive. However, we have not been notably successful in controlling chronic diseases. Life expectancies throughout much of the world are increasing. As populations age, a greater percentage of the citizens will likely be disabled (Zola, 1989). Disablement from automobile accidents (which I take up in the next chapter) continues to rise (Safilios-Rothschild, 1970: 39; U.S. Department of Transportation, 1986: x).

We are also likely to increase our disability counts as we expand our categories of disability (which I have previously mentioned), heighten our evaluation of our citizens and increase our efforts to record disability. The search for disabled students is a prime example of our greater scrutiny (Walker, 1987; Zola, 1989). We are also increasing our efforts to record disability, especially in developing countries (Safilios-Rothschild, 1981). Disability counts are growing. Perhaps a "universal" phenomenon requires universal policies (Zola, 1989), a point I take up in Chapter 7.

Counting provides us a complex picture of disabled people. In examining the demography of disability, most observers focus on differences between disabled and nondisabled people, especially differences which indicate the difficulties experienced by disabled people. That is appropriate. Many wish to see those difficulties lessened. However, we must be careful that in contrasting disabled people to nondisabled people we do not mistakenly believe that disabled people are homogeneous and that they are different from nondisabled people.

Disabled people vary greatly demographically. They are not homogeneous. For example, as an aggregate disabled people are older than nondisabled people, but disabled people are young, old, middle aged, and all other ages. They are poor and they are well off. They are illiterate and well educated. They are unemployed, but they are also heads of companies. They are white and they are people of color. They are married, single, divorced, and widowed. Disabled people vary in every way imaginable. While we often think otherwise, disabled people are extremely diverse in their characteristics and experiences (Asch and Fine, 1988: 3).

We must also be careful that we do not overlook the (demographic) similarities among disabled and nondisabled people. As an aggregate they do differ in significant ways, which is important to know and act upon. However, just as disabled people are diverse, so are nondisabled people. Thus, many disabled and nondisabled people share similar but varying experiences. Some disabled and nondisabled people are poor in contrast to some who are not. Some disabled and nondisabled people are unemployed, but other disabled and nondisabled people work. Some disabled and nondisabled people are divorced, but others are married (happily or not). And so on. Put another way, the differences between disabled and nondisabled people as aggregate differences are much smaller than the differences within the disabled and nondisabled populations. Disabled people are diverse, and they share that diversity with nondisabled people (even though as an aggregate they differ from nondisabled people in ways that rightly concern us).

Conclusion

Through framing disability, through conceptualizing, categorizing, and counting disability, we create it. We establish what it is and how much of it exists. We have typically individualized disability. We have conceptualized it as sin, a medical flaw, a health-related work limitation or some other kind of defect. We have categorized human diversity and difficulties into discrete biological entities (e.g., learning disability). We have counted in order to fix the number of disabled people.

Individualizing disability conserves present practices and policies. Our attitudes and actions go unchallenged. However, those practices and policies presently (but shortsightedly) benefit some people but harm others. For example, our paternalistic characterizations provide economic benefits to the suppliers of disability products and services and to employers who have a cheap source of labor. As will become clearer throughout the book, how we presently make disability benefits some to the harm of others. However, by individualizing disability, we overlook our handiwork.

Yet, some challenge how we have framed disability. They question an individualistic view. Instead, they urge us to understand disability as a social phenomenon. Whether disability is understood as deviance or, more usefully, as the basis for a minority group, they draw our attention to the attitudes, actions, and arrangements that turn some into disabled people. They encourage us to take responsibility for what we make.

And we are making more disability than ever before. Through increasingly framing our lives in terms of disability—by categorizing more phenomena as disability, by scrutinizing and evaluating ourselves more closely, and by attending more to recording disability—we are producing more disability. That need not be troubling. But what may be troubling is how we make ourselves disabled. As I explore next, we literally *manufacture* those characteristics that we turn into disability.

Chapter 2

MANUFACTURING DISABILITY

I magine we were aliens, unfamiliar with the manner and customs of humans. If we were to observe carefully (for example, in America), we would probably be amazed, perhaps appalled, to notice how often humans wrecked physical, mental, and emotional havoc on one another.

We would often notice humans harming one another. We would witness people crashing into one another with their motor vehicles, frequently killing and maiming each other. However, we would also learn of how poorly manufacturers constructed the automobiles and how much more they could do to ensure motorists' safety. We might wonder why poor, pregnant women took little care of themselves and their not-yet-born babies, but we would also wonder why others did so little to assist them. We might be astonished as employers maimed workers and contaminated the environment of fellow citizens in the pursuit of profits. We might be amazed that people consumed great quantities of alcohol and cigarettes to the detriment of their well-being. And we would surely be perplexed about the aggressive advertising and sale of cigarettes, alcoholic beverages, and other merchandise whose (too great) consumption was widely known to debilitate its users. We might be dismayed that people put so much pressure on one another to "measure up" in so many ways that many became mentally and emotionally distressed. We would be horrified at the tremendous death and destruction that humans inflicted on one another in armed conflict for reasons that would often be difficult to discern. We would have difficulty believing the carelessness with which people lived and the tremendous costs they suffered for it. Everywhere we looked we would see humans physically, mentally and/or emotionally harming each other or permitting that harm to develop. (Of course, we would also notice efforts by humans to prevent that harm.) We might conclude that an important goal of humans is to produce disability. After all, they seem to be so successful at doing so.

We manufacture disability! We significantly produce the physical, mental, and emotional characteristics that we turn into disabilities,

65

Throughout this book I examine how we make disability. Through interpersonal, organizational, and societal means, we turn human variation (that we have developed) into disability. We make disability what it is. Our creative efforts may be more or less useful, though many of us realize that they must be improved. However, here I mean to be much more literal. Much of the human variation that we make into disability is not due to "natural" processes, such as the "natural" aging of humans (and all life). It is not due to the "accidents" of birth. It is not due to unforeseen, unknown, or unknowable happenstance. Instead, we literally produce in ourselves and in others the physical, mental, and emotional attributes that we commonly call disability.

I call our production of disability "manufacturing" for several reasons. "Manufacturing" captures the spirit of industrialized countries, especially America, whose disability production I primarily explore. Some claim manufacturing is what has made America great, even though we have moved to a "postindustrial" era, according to some observers (Harris, 1981). Manufacturing *is* America, but so is the production of disability.

While I focus on America, developing countries produce disability, too. Perhaps 90 percent of the world's disabled people live in developing countries (Safilios-Rothschild, 1981; Groce, 1990). However, industrialized countries often "assist" developing ones in producing disability. Through depletion of the world's resources; exportation of dangerous products such as cigarettes; exploitative economic policies; and support for, tolerance of, or involvement in armed conflicts and wars among other means; industrialized countries help to disable citizens of developing countries (Byrne and Martinez, 1989; Werner, 1990).

The industrialization of America and other countries (typically through the development of capitalism) has been a source of progress: higher standards of living, greater freedoms, better health, raised expectations about the quality of life and about safety, and so on (Stark, 1989; Viscusi, 1989; Wildavsky, 1989). "Manufacturing" has made America great (or so goes the slogan). However, we produce significant amounts of disability as we manufacture goods or as the consequence of that manufacturing. Cost-benefit calculations for determining the appropriateness of health and safety regulations reflect this production (McCaffrey, 1982). Ironically, our "manufactured" progress may also be debilitating. Even as we improve our lives, we manufacture disability.

Yet we also have a darker image of manufacturing (and a recognition of less desirable consequences of capitalism). We have the picture of the worker as a cog, of profits at any cost. This darker picture emphasizes that manufacturing is hazardous to our welfare. Producing disability harms our welfare, too. Manufacturing also connotes intent and action. Through purposeful action manufacturers produce different kinds of goods, even if they are not aware of all of the consequences of their manufacturing. Unfortunately, the goods may be disability. For all these reasons I call the literal production of disability "manufacturing disability."

Nowadays, many of us are aware that we manufacture disability. However, we may not realize how much we produce, and we are not likely to dwell on that production. Perhaps we do not dwell much on that production because, ironically, we seemingly benefit from it—at least those of us who are not early and evidently made disabled. Critics of government's regulations of industrial practices often remind "us that society in general benefits from the production processes which can cause death and disease" (Wilson, 1985: 170). Governments recognize that as well. New Zealand's Accident Compensation Act of 1972 recognized that accidents (which may disable) originate in the

> normal operation of the society: the production, distribution, and consumption of goods and services. Accidents were . . . (an) undesired by-product of these activities. The plight of the victim was a social cost of a basic social good, of the very processes that defined the society itself (Kronick, Vosburgh and Vosburgh, 1981: 191).

Through the development of our society and particularly the production of material benefits, we have manufactured disability. The following is a brief examination of how we do so.

We manufacture disability throughout all realms within which we live. We manufacture disability within big—and small—businesses. We create it on the assembly line, in front of the video terminal, and in the executive suite. We produce it on the highway and at home. We create it in far away countries during armed aggression and in our neighborhoods during equally dangerous assaults. We make it while working and when we play. We grow and produce the substances with which we disable ourselves, and we glamorize them in order to turn a profit. We produce disability primarily among our poorest, least powerful people, but we make some for those well off, too. Others disable us, and we also do it to ourselves. In a tragically ironic and shortsighted way, making disability is big business—figuratively and literally.

I focus on five major means by which or realms within which we manufacture disability: *injuries, war, work, poverty,* and *self-disabling* practices.

These five are not mutually exclusive. However, through these means or in these realms we disable millions of us each year. We have found the manufacturers of disability—and we are they.

A note: The statistics I present concerning our production of disability should be taken as suggestive, not definitive. Recording the manufacturing of disability is as difficult as counting disability. Neither "captures" some "real" phenomenon independent of our activities. For that reason, my use of the following numbers can be understood as an attempt to make a case for the importance of our manufacturing disability (Best, 1989). No neutral reporter am I—nor could I be.

Injurying

Injuries are the "most serious public health problem facing developed countries . . . Few (will) escape the tragedy of fatal or permanently disabling injury to a relative or friend" (Baker, O'Neill and Karpf, 1984: 1). Each year one American in three experiences a nonfatal injury, approximately 150,000 die, and the cost (which we always seem to want to know) is as much as $100 billion (Baker, O'Neill and Karpf, 1984: 7; National Research Council, 1985: 1).

Injuries also permanently impair. Due to impairments resulting from injuries, more than 6 million Americans are unable to carry on the major activity of their group (such as play, school, or work), are limited in the amount or kind of major activity they can perform, or are otherwise limited (U.S. Department of Health and Human Services, 1986). More than 80,000 Americans each year become permanently impaired due to injuries of the brain or spinal cord, including "2,000 who remain in persistent vegetative states" (National Research Council, 1985: 1; U.S. Department of Health and Human Services, 1988: 78). More than 2 million injuries on the job resulted in lost work days (U.S. Department of Labor, 1988). Annually approximately 150,000 are permanently impaired due to motor vehicle injuries, 70,000 due to workplace injuries, 80,000 due to injuries in or around the home, and 60,000 in public places (Budnick, 1987: 169). Through injuries, we annually disable hundreds of thousands of Americans and obviously millions worldwide. (And this is so even though the rates of many kinds of accidents have declined in America in this century as our demands for greater safety have increased and as technological developments have made safety less costly (Viscusi, 1989).)

Many of us think of (unintentional) injuries as due to unavoidable accidents, as the result of regrettable but chance occurrences (Robertson, 1983: 2). Not so! Through our manipulation of the world, we produce most injuries. Further, we know how to prevent many injuries, reduce the severity of most of them, and do so inexpensively in relation to our benefit (Robertson, 1983: 1–2; Baker, O'Neill and Karpf, 1984: 1, 269). Injuries are avoidable, but we have avoided preventing and reducing them.

Due to neglect, politics, mistaken notions of costs and benefits, concern with profits, and still other reasons, we produce and permit injuries to occur (Robertson, 1983; Baker, O'Neill and Karpf, 1984). We know how to reduce injuries with technically feasible and cost-effective means (Robertson, 1983: 191). For example,

> Protection against serious injury in crashes at impact speeds below 50 mph not only is theoretically possible but was incorporated several years ago in prototype cars that were also lightweight and fuel efficient and that would have been reasonable in cost if mass produced. These lifesaving features, however, have not been incorporated into cars produced for the public. In addition, most roads today are not designed to provide state-of-the-art protection against foreseeable events. Nor have available knowledge and technology been adequately applied in the designs of trucks, aircraft, boats, tractors, cranes, forklifts, and other products associated with high injury rates (Baker, O'Neill and Karpf, 1984: 270).

By not implementing what we know and not improving what we could, we injure people unnecessarily—killing, hurting, and disabling them.

However, when we do attend to injuries, we individualize the issue much as we individualize disability. We focus on the behavior and motivations of those directly involved (which is appropriate because we are responsible for what we do), but we give too little attention to how we design and use our environment and how we organize our activities.

For example, many disabling injuries in vehicle crashes are sustained due to the "careless" actions of the participants: the failure to use restraint devices and drinking (U.S. Department of Transportation, 1988, 1989). Occupants in passenger cars who do not use lap and/or shoulder safety belts are "about 50 percent more likely to be injured in a crash, and three times as likely to require hospitalization" as those who use restraints— but about 40 percent of occupants of passenger cars involved in crashes did not use safety belts in 1986 (U.S. Department of Transportation, 1988: ix). Likewise, approximately 40 percent of all fatal crashes in 1987

involved a drunk driver or pedestrian (U.S. Department of Transportation, 1988). Consequently, through education, surveillance, threats, and
punishment, we focus on "careless/reckless" drivers (and now those who
provide them the alcohol by which they become reckless).

However, in giving most of our attention to the behavior of crash
participants, we have put "little emphasis . . . on the relationships between
high-risk groups and effective means of protecting people" (Baker, O'Neill
and Karpf, 1984: 270). Teenagers, intoxicated drivers, and others at high
risk of being involved in crashes are also likely not to use seat belts.
Those least likely to change their behaviors are the ones most likely to be
injured. For injuries

> as for diseases, the most effective way to protect high-risk groups as well as the
> rest of the population is with measures—such as pasteurization and household
> fuses—that do not require individual motivation and frequent effort (Baker,
> O'Neill, and Karpf, 1984: 270).

Accordingly, air bags, which the automobile industry has historically
resisted, do not require individual motivation or much effort to be
effective—and the American public in the past has preferred them to
automatic seat belts (Robertson, 1983: 76, 169, 177–178, 194–195, 198).
Only since the mid-1980s has automatic protection for passengers been
gradually phased in with all passenger automobiles manufactured after
September 1, 1989 required to provide such protection (which could, but
need not, include air bags).

We individualize other injuries, too. Consider falling by children and
older persons. We admonish them to be careful as they move about, but
we could more effectively prevent injuries by placing beds closer to the
floor, especially for elderly people, or redesigning furniture, which may
cause as many as half the childhood injuries from falls (Smith and Falk,
1987: 153).

Or, approximately 10,000 workers died in 1986 from work-related
accidents and 10 million traumatic injuries were sustained (Reiman,
1990: 61; U.S. Department of Health and Human Services, 1986: 109).
However

> to say that some of these workers died (or were injured) from accidents due to
> their own carelessness is about as helpful as saying that some of those who died
> at the hands of murderers asked for it. It overlooks the fact that where workers
> are careless, it is not because they love to live dangerously. They have produc-
> tion quotas to meet, quotas that they themselves do not set. If quotas were set
> with an eye to keeping work at a safe pace rather than to keeping the production-

to-wages ratio as high as possible, it might be more reasonable to expect workers to take the time to be careful (Reiman, 1990: 61–62).

Through how we develop our world and organize our actions with one another, we injure and disable ourselves. We often do so shortsightedly with an eye toward profits (Ehrlich and Ehrlich, 1989).

Warring

Wars disable. We sometimes forget that. I do not mean to ignore the many lives that are sacrificed or taken in war. I do not mean to downplay the heroism shown by many participants. I do not mean to question the motives of those who put us at war (though certainly we should be skeptical about the proclaimed "necessity" of and pronounced justifications for war). While we may believe that wars (certain wars?) are justified, if also regrettable, we must also recognize that *we* war with one another. No one or no force makes us do so. War is our making. The alternatives to the death and destruction of war may appear to us as less tolerable, even intolerable, but alternatives do exist. Many urge that we develop and explore alternatives, that we strive more diligently for less violent resolutions to our conflicts. Nevertheless, in warring with one another, we disable ourselves—and we do so in great numbers.

In the more than 125 wars since 1945, 1,200,000 people have been injured in an average year (and 525,000 have died). Yes, people have fought more than 125 wars since World War II (Sivard, 1989)! Most of us do not realize how much warring the world is doing. Most of it occurs in developing countries, far from the light of publicity. For example, perhaps 500,000 people in Angola have been disabled in the 1980s due to their ongoing war (and 500,000 have died) (Werner, 1990).

However, through supporting one faction or another and through supplying the arms, developed countries such as the United States, the Soviet Union, and European countries participate significantly in the warring even when they don't do the shooting. In Vietnam, Afghanistan, and most recently in the Middle East among other countries and regions, the developed countries do the shooting, too (Sivard, 1989).

Warring directly disables military personnel and civilians. However, it indirectly disables, too. By diverting resources from social and health programs to the military, warring debilitates countries' most needy citizens. In developing their own military, developed countries also have less nonmilitary assistance to provide to developing countries. Thus, while military budgets were increasing in developing countries on the average of 35 percent from 1980 to 1987, social budgets per capita either declined or remained at low levels in most of those countries. In 1987, developing countries spent on the average thirty-nine dollars per capita on health and education; some as little as two dollars (Sivard, 1989: 21).

When "Johnny gets his gun" to go off to war, he (and many others) may get much, much more than they expected. Ironically, but not surprisingly, much of America's early (and intentional) disability policy was in response to the returning wounded veterans (Obermann, 1965). We disable ourselves through wars and then seek to make amends with our disability policy.

Working

The workplace provides us opportunities to earn a living. It also disables (and kills) us. It is "not facetious to think of the ghetto and the factory as the major settings in America in which disability is manufactured" (Krause, 1976: 206). (I take up the ghetto, i.e., poverty, next). The amount of disability we produce when working is astounding.

Here are some figures. I do not take them to be precise. They sensitize us to how much disability we produce in the workplace. While some of the figures do not refer to long-term impairment, many of the figures likely underestimate how much disability working creates. They likely underestimate the production of disability due to our inability to connect workplace experiences to later disabilities and to some participants' willful failure to report accidents and illnesses (Reiman, 1990: 58).

American workers sustain 10 million traumatic injuries at work each year; most requiring medical treatment only. However, approximately 325,000 workers of the almost six million workers injured each year on the job become permanently disabled (whether totally or partially) as defined by worker compensation laws. Another 400,000 workers become ill from exposure to hazardous substances. These annual figures accumulate, contributing to the present prevalence of disabled people. By the late 1970s nearly two million Americans attributed their difficulty in or inability to work to job-related injuries or occupational diseases (U.S. Department of Health and Human Services, 1986: 109; Worrall and Butler, 1986: 97–98).

Jobs injure, make ill, impair, and harm workers in many ways. For example, tens of thousands, perhaps hundreds of thousands, of workers have acquired or will acquire occupational lung diseases. These disabling diseases are due to the inhalation of materials in the workplace. Byssinosis or brown lung disease, caused by the inhalation of cotton dust, coal worker's pneumoconiosis or black lung disease, caused by the inhalation of carbonaceous dust, silicosis, due to the inhalation of silica, and asbestosis, due to the inhalation of asbestos fibers, are four major occupational lung diseases experienced by workers (Farer and Schieffelbein, 1987; U.S. Department of Health and Human Services, 1986: 115; 1988: 67–68).

Work harms our hearing. Approximately 10 million American workers are exposed to noises of 85 decibels or more. Exposure to high levels of noise has produced hearing impairments in many of these workers and will eventually produce it in others. Slightly less than 20 percent of these workers presently experience a mild hearing loss (hearing threshold greater than 15 dB), 10 percent experience a "material" loss (threshold greater than 25 dB), and 5 percent experience a moderate to severe hearing impairment (threshold greater than 40 dB). Approximately 3.5 million workers are presently hearing impaired due to their jobs (U.S. Department of Health and Human Services, 1986: 116; 1988: 69).

When working, we are exposed to dangerous chemicals that impair our health and threaten our lives. Between 3 million and 9 million workers are exposed to carcinogens, and almost 8 million workers are exposed to neurotoxic chemicals (U.S. Department of Health and Human Services, 1988: 68, 69).

Working also stresses us, sometimes so greatly that we die or become disabled. For example, a substantial amount of heart disease (which kills 750,000 people each year) is likely due to the hazards of the workplace, particularly stress (Reiman, 1984: 54, 170). Thus, female clerical workers have rates of coronary heart disease that are almost twice the rate of housewives (U.S. Department of Health and Human Services, 1988: 68). Between 8 and 10 percent of American workers, approximately 10 to 12 million workers, experience disabling emotional or physiologic ill health (U.S. Department of Health and Human Services, 1988: 69; U.S. Bureau of the Census, 1990: 380).

Some of these workers have been harassed into becoming emotionally disabled (Brodsky, 1976). When we repeatedly and persistently attempt to "torment, wear down, frustrate, or get a reaction" from another person, we are harassing them (Brodsky, 1976: 2). Scapegoating, name-calling, physical abuse, sexual harassment, and the "selective exercise of work pressure" (i.e., the hurry-up tactic) are several major forms of workplace harassment (Brodsky, 1976: 24). For example,

> from the moment Albert entered the police department, he loved it . . . most significantly, he loved and admired his chief . . . Unfortunately, five years later, when this chief retired, life changed abruptly for Albert. The new chief was a "white glove man," who constantly checked up on everybody and everything . . . The new chief knew about Albert's relationship with his predecessor and thought Albert was very manipulative. He decided to stop Albert's manipulations and became especially hard on him, criticizing him, humiliating him in front of others, and threatening him with loss of his job. The new chief accused Albert of living with a woman to whom he was not married, and even demanded to see his marriage license . . . Albert continued to be known throughout the department as the chief's "number 1 target . . . "
>
> Albert's life was hell. He began to dread going to work in the morning. He was unable to sleep. Because of anxiety and tension, he felt he could no longer relate to anyone. His marriage broke up and his wife and stepson left him. His parents died. He went to a physician who prescribed Valium but questioned whether Albert could safely continue his duties while taking drugs. As he took more medication, Albert felt he could not think and at times functioned in a daze. Finally, his physician sent him to a psychiatrist, and the psychiatrist urged him to stop working.
>
> Albert left the police department and for a short period of time continued his second job as a maintenance man for an industrial organization. Within four months, he had to stop working there, too, because his anxiety had become so intense. Slowly, he had phased himself out of the work world, unable to express his rage and sadness effectively.
>
> After he stopped working altogether, Albert seemed unable to organize himself. He said that he spent most of his time "going crazy" (Brodsky, 1976: 12).

Working disables (and kills) us in these and many other ways. The "refusal of management to pay for safety measures and of government to enforce safety standards" makes jobs hazardous to workers (and to citizens affected by contamination, pollution, and other industrial practices) (Reiman, 1990: 58; McCaffrey, 1982; Wilson, 1985). Organizations cut corners to make a profit and disable workers (and others) in the process. However, even when business takes an upswing, disabilities may, too. Employers may hire inexperienced workers unfamiliar with the workplace hazards and push the existing workers harder in order to meet production demands (Robinson and Shor, 1989). Our lack of effective opposition makes us accomplices to disabling work.

Poverty

Like the workplace, poverty produces a great deal of disability.

Poor diet, severe life stress, and poor or nonexistent health care are the well-known concomitants of a poverty-level existence. Combining with these physical and mental disability-producing conditions for the poor are the conditions for the blue-collar, working class in American industry (Krause, 1976: 207).

Poor people face great physical and social demands but have fewer resources than others to meet those demands (Kaplan et al., 1987). Disability (and "premature" death) may often be the result.

Worldwide this happens (Sivard, 1989). Approximately "90% of all disabled people today live in the Developing World, 80% of these individuals live in rural areas, and a high percentage of these live in poverty" (Groce, 1990: 2). Sixty percent of all disability in the Developing World is caused by malnutrition (Groce, 1990). Even those who live in the cities in developing countries are at great risk of becoming disabled. The majority are poor and live at the "edge of the development transition during which the negative effects of development are more tangible than the benefits" (Safilios-Rothschild, 1981: 114). For example, they experience unchecked pollution from industries and businesses before enjoying employment, or they become maimed or killed in traffic accidents (due to the congestion of pedestrians, bicycles, and vehicles) before enjoying efficient public transportation (Safilios-Rothschild, 1981: 114–115). Poverty disables worldwide.

It does so in affluent countries, such as the United States. As I noted in Chapter 1, disabled Americans are more likely to be poor than those who are not disabled. For example, in 1980 25 percent of disabled Americans, 16–64, had incomes below the official poverty line. Only one in ten nondisabled Americans was poor. Only 30 percent of nondisabled Americans enjoyed at least $8,000 in incomes from all sources in 1980, but half of all Americans did so (Bowe, 1985: 23). Those who live in poverty are more likely to become disabled, and those who grow up or become disabled are more likely to become poor due to educational, employment and other barriers.

Poverty disables Americans in many ways. Americans who are less well-off are more likely to experience heart disease, arthritis, diabetes, hypertension, angina, epilepsy, rheumatic fever, anemia, various cancers, injuries, and other health problems (Kaplan et al., 1987). While children from all backgrounds may experience elevated blood lead levels (from paint, gasoline, food, water, and other sources), those who have few resources are most likely to do so. Lead poisoning can lead to delayed cognitive development, reduced IQ scores and impaired hearing (and to coma, convulsions and death at more severe levels of exposure) (U.S. Department of Health and Human Services, 1988: 1, 5). Similarly, children born to low-income mothers are more likely to have low birth weight than those born to more advantaged mothers. Low-birth-weight infants are more likely to die and more likely to experience cerebral palsy, autism, mental retardation, developmental delays, vision and hearing impairments, and other disabilities (Hughes et al., 1988: 33; U.S. Department of Health and Human Services, 1988: 137). Poorer people are more likely to be injured (at least fatally so, about which more research has been done) (Baker, O'Neill and Karpf, 1984: 26). In these and other ways, poverty disables.

"Self"-disablement

Not only do the policies and practices of others disable us, but we do it to ourselves (and our children) as well. But we do it with the assistance of others. Through smoking, excessive drinking and drug use, poor diet, little exercise, and in other ways, we disable ourselves. However, these disabling practices of individuals are supported by the policies and practices of government and business. Through regulation, taxation, subsidies, manufacturing, promotion, and other means, government and business make these self-disabling practices possible, even desirable. For example, through direct and indirect assistance, our government annually subsidizes the tobacco industry by almost $100 million (Reiman, 1990: 72). The industry does a multibillion-dollar business. We subsidize an industry that massively advertises a product that we know kills and disables us. With a "little help from our friends," we disable ourselves.

Approximately 50 million American adults regularly smoke cigarettes. Each day they smoke about one billion cigarettes (U.S. Department of Health and Human Services, 1988: 16). Smoking not only kills— approximately 390,000 in 1985—but it also disables (U.S. Department of Health and Human Services, 1989: 12). The Surgeon General has concluded that smoking is a cause of coronary heart disease, atherosclerotic peripheral vascular disease, lung and laryngeal cancer in women; oral cancer, esophageal cancer, chronic obstructive pulmonary disease, intrauterine growth retardation, and low-birth-weight babies. It is a probable cause of peptic ulcer disease, a contributing factor for cancer of the bladder, pancreas and kidney, and associated with cancer of the stomach (U.S. Department of Health and Human Services, 1989: 20).

For example, 10 million Americans experience chronic obstructive pulmonary disease (COPD). More than 1.5 million Americans are diagnosed each year. Emphysema, chronic bronchitis, and other respiratory problems constitute COPD. While only 10 to 15 percent of smokers develop severe COPD, most who develop COPD are smokers.

> Typically, COPD begins when a young person starts smoking cigarettes. Several years may elapse without recognized symptoms, although measurable abnormalities of pulmonary function may be present. Later, a chronic, productive cough develops. After about the age of 40, shortness of breath begins to occur. Advanced, incapacitating disease typically appears after age 55 but may occur earlier ... (It) disables them (people with COPD) with unremitting shortness of breath, destroys their ability to earn a living, results in their frequent use of the health care system, and disrupts the lives of their family members for one or two decades before death eventually occurs (Farer and Schieffelbein, 1987: 116).

Smoking may not be the taste that refreshes. However, it is often the practice that destroys and disables.

So are excessive drinking and drug use. Approximately 9 million Americans are alcoholics (Herring, 1987: 201), and 2.5 million Americans have a serious drug problem (Goldstein et al., 1987). The government recognizes alcoholism and drug addiction as disabilities in their own right, though others have objected because of the "connotations of moral deviance if not (at least in the case of drug addicts) moral depravity" (Scotch, 1984: 110).

Drinking and drug use also produce other disabilities, for the users and for their children. The use of alcohol and other drugs increases the risk of injuries, which themselves can be very disabling (Budnick, 1987: 166). Excessive use of alcohol can cause cancers of the mouth, tongue, pharynx, and esophagus. It can lead to liver diseases, stomach problems, and chronic pancreatitis. It can also damage the heart muscle. Heavy use by pregnant women may lead to Fetal Alcohol Syndrome in their newborns, who may experience growth deficiency and impairment of intellectual and motor abilities. From 1,800 to 2,400 babies had been predicted to be born with FAS (in 1983) and another 36,000 babies to be affected with less severe adverse alcohol-related effects (U.S. Department of Health and

Human Services, 1988: 142). As many as one-fourth of the children born on Native American reservations have Fetal Alcohol Effect (Newsweek, 1989). Pulmonary difficulties, arthritic conditions, neurologic disorders, psychosis and other impairments may result from regular use of other drugs such as heroin or cocaine. Newborns of drug addicted and dependent mothers may become addicted and dependent themselves (U.S. Department of Health and Human Services, 1988: Chapter 2). Excessive drug use is debilitating.

Poor eating and exercising disable us, too. Millions of us, perhaps the great majority of Americans, eat and/or exercise inadequately. For example, most Americans have undesirably high blood cholesterol levels (U.S. Department of Health and Human Services, 1986: 216). An elevated cholesterol level raises the risk of developing coronary heart disease. Hypertension, diabetes, some cancers, and low-birth-weight babies are other possible consequences of inadequate diets (U.S. Department of Health and Human Services, 1988: Chapter 3). We may not be what we eat, but what we eat (or fail to eat) can surely disable us.

So, too, can inadequate exercise. Most of us do not exercise very much. Sixty percent of us do not exercise regularly, and less than 10 percent of us exercise "vigorously" (i.e., at least 3 times a week for 20 minutes or more each time at an intensity that requires at least 60 percent of our cardiorespiratory capacity—approximately the amount of exercise needed for developing and maintaining cardiorespiratory fitness for healthy adults) (U.S. Department of Health and Human Services, 1988: Chapter 4; 1986: 229). Adequate physical activity reduces the risk of coronary heart disease, hypertension, osteoporosis, and possibly diabetes and depression (U.S. Department of Health and Human Services, 1988: Chapter 4). Eating and exercising can be joyful. Done poorly, they can be debilitating.

From smoking to not exercising, from drinking too much to eating poorly, from listening to loud music ("30 to 60 percent of college freshmen—the Walkman® generation—have hearing deficits" (Will, 1986: 112)) to driving carelessly, and on and on, we disabled our selves. Yet we do so with the assistance of others—of our broader policies and practices— government support of the tobacco industry; aggressive advertising of alcohol, tobacco, and "junk" food; favorable media depiction of drug use; and so on. Even when individuals manufacture their own disabilities, their handiwork is not an individual accomplishment.

In many other ways we disable ourselves, too. Through polluting our environment; exposing ourselves to toxins; assaulting one another in our homes and on the streets; inadequately and inappropriately, even dangerously, providing health care; and still other practices; we impair ourselves.

Conclusion

We manufacture disability in many ways. Injuries, war, work, poverty, and self-disabling practices are some of our means for harming ourselves physically, mentally, and emotionally. Even as developed countries "manufacture" progress—higher standards of living, more freedoms and rights, better health, and greater concern with safety and quality of life among other improvements—they also manufacture disability. Disability manufacturing is not an aberration of developed countries. Instead, it has been an integral product of developed countries. Unfortunately, poor people have been most likely to experience our disability manufacturing.

It could be otherwise. We have the capacity to prevent many, if not most, of the disabilities we manufacture. We have increased our concern about safety and have developed technological means to provide safety (at less expense) (Viscusi, 1989). Prenatal and infant care, safer work environments and safer vehicles, and education are some of the means through which we are presently reducing our manufacturing of disability but could reduce much more (National Council on the Handicapped, 1986, 1988). (More farreaching changes such as a more equitable distribution of resources and the reduction of armed conflict worldwide would save millions of lives and reduce disability immeasurably.) "Effective preventive measures would reduce the costs of disability and health care for Americans, reduce ... spending for disability in the near future, and decrease the incidence of disability for future generations (National Council on the Handicapped, 1986: 30). However, in the still dominant pursuit of profits and power, we increase the cost of "doing business."

Once we have manufactured disability, we create and disseminate images about disability and disabled people. Through the media and other means, we *depict disability*, to which I turn.

Chapter 3

DEPICTING DISABILITY

Have you heard the following: How many morons does it take to screw in an overhead light bulb? Three—one to hold the light bulb and two to turn the one holding the light bulb. Or consider Frankenstein's monster, Dr. Jekyll and Mr. Hyde, the character Benny in the popular television series *LA Law*, Corky in *Life Goes On*, the award winning *Children of a Lesser God*, Zero in the comic strip *Beetle Bailey*, the exhibition of "freaks" in (primarily) yesterday's sideshows, telethons, and other charity campaigns for chronic diseases and conditions, terms such as "afflicted with" and "the handicapped," and newspaper headlines such as "Ex-mental patient held in starlet's stabbing carried 'Death Petition'" (*The Columbia Record*, 1982). We depict disability through these and many other means.

Through words and pictures we "tell" one another what disability is, who people with disability are. Much of this telling is suggestive, not detailed. We create images of disability (Gartner and Joe, 1987).

Our depictions produce disability and are the product of our making disability. Our depictions, beliefs, and actions concerning disability are bound together. Our depictions embody our basic beliefs about disability and disabled people and are a source out of which we develop anew our beliefs. They both reflect and provide the rationale for our actions toward people with disabilities. A change in our depictions indicates a change in our beliefs and actions. Changing our depictions can alter our understandings and responses. "Stick and stones may break my bones but words can never hurt me" is not so. Our words about and pictures of disability are powerful (Biklen, 1987; Kent, 1987; Bogdan, 1988; see also Wolfensberger, 1975).

I primarily explore two major, "popular" depictions of disability: the names by which we refer to those with disabilities and the media portrayals of disability. We all participate widely in *naming* and *portraying* disability. But we depict disability through other means, too. We depict disabled people when we *display* them in sideshows, on tours of facilities that serve disabled people, and in fundraising drives of all kinds. Scholarly pronouncements can be thought of as depictions, too—and often have been as oppressive as other forms (see Chapter 1). This book can be considered a depiction. By exploring briefly these other displays, I point to varying means by which we depict disability.

I do not exhaust the depicting of disability. For example, when people with disabilities present themselves and others with disabilities, either in formal occasions, as when representing an organization of disabled people, or more mundanely in the encounters of everyday life, they, too, are depicting disability. They are signifying what disability is and who disabled people are. I take up the everyday encounters in Chapters 4 and 8.

Depicting disability is one of the interrelated processes that "makes up" the making of disability. In depicting disability, we create images that reflect how we frame disability. Because we have primarily individualized disability, our depictions do likewise. The images we create present disability as a defect of individuals that separates them from those not disabled. As we begin to make disability a social phenomenon and thereby challenge our individualizing perspective, so, too, are we changing our depictions.

Naming Disability

Naming is important in constructing disability. Through naming (and other means of symbolizing) we objectify our world. We create objects that we can consider. To name something enables us to (more easily) discuss it, think about it, relate it to other objects, to explore it, to act toward it, to make it "real." Names put together and set apart. To call many objects by the same name is to make them meaningfully similar. To call objects by different names is to make them meaningfully different. Of course, the naming is not all that makes the objects similar or different, but the naming is part of a package of responses that do so. Names focus our attention on some qualities but not others. Names are not neutral. They create connotations of varying worth and take on connotations of worth from our other responses to the objects so named. Names identify. Who names what and how matters. All of this is so for disability.

Nondisabled people have dominated naming disability. They have typically named themselves and disabled people. They have taken themselves to be the standard against which disabled people are named and known—and disabled people are known not to be "normal." Thus, nondisabled people have named disabled people through "negation" (Roth, 1983: 56). Disabled people are not whatever "normal" people are. Disabled people are *dis*abled, *in*valid, *ab*normal, *un*sound, and so on. (As I noted in the Introduction, I do not know what terms to use in naming people with and without disabilities. My inconsistency reflects my and our uncertainty.)

Nondisabled people also "know" that disabled people are homogeneous. Because they are the same, they can be referred to as an aggregate and by referring to them as an aggregate, we identify them as the same. Thus, disabled people are "the disabled," "the deaf," "the retarded," "the handicapped," and so on (Longmore, 1985: 419; Zola, forthcoming). Such naming also tells us that the essence of disabled people is their disability, since that is how we refer to them. They are first and foremost— and maybe completely—*not* able.

In naming people with disabilities through negation, referring to them in the aggregate, and devaluing them (in so many ways), it is not surprising that the names we call people with disabilities conjure up that lack of worth. If you are told that someone is a "cripple," you are likely to be oriented much differently than if you are told that someone has various characteristics, one of which is "difficulty in walking." While studies of people's attitudes toward individuals with disabilities have many problems, ironically, one of their problems provides telling support for the power of names. Studies of people's attitudes toward those with disabilities often ask them to evaluate in some way their attitudes toward names and only names, such as toward "blindness" or "the mentally retarded." These studies show that people do make such evaluations (with little hesitation, even though they are told nothing else), and when they do so, they evaluate less favorably those termed (in some way) disabled (Altman, 1981; see also Foster, Ysseldyke, and Reese, 1975). Switching to other terms that have less negative connotations may be momentarily successful in improving people's responses to those with disabilities, but it is not sufficient by itself (e.g., Hollinger and Jones, 1970). Naming has put down people with disabilities. (1)

It has also medicalized them. We refer to those with disabilities in medical terms: "patient," "afflicted by," "sick with," "suffering from," and such (Longmore, 1985: 420; Zola, forthcoming). By individualizing disability primarily through a medical-clinical frame, we "know" disability is a flaw of the body or the person. Our names tell us so. Naming disability develops and displays our individualistic, pathological view of disability (Shapiro, 1981). Our language tells us what we know and helps to make it so.

By calling people with disabilities "vegetables," "creatures," and "things," we very clearly dehumanize them (Longmore, 1985: 420–421). Such terms reflect and provide the rationale for our dehumanizing people with disabilities. After all, *we* do make sense when we call people "creatures" whom we have stripped of dignity by warehousing them in institutions or denying them life-saving medical services among other practices. We name them what we have made them. Naming and knowing them as "creatures" then further justifies our making them so.

As present names become recognized as pejorative, professionals, parents, and others may develop new terms. Those with disabilities have recently become "exceptional," "with special needs," "developmentally disabled," or "learning disabled" (Longmore, 1985: 421). Among other organizations, the National Easter Society has developed a set of guidelines for how to refer to disabled people and disabilities, *Portraying Persons with Disabilities in Print* (Henderson and Bryan, 1984: 91–93; Zola, forthcoming). But this isn't new. When " 'idiots,' 'morons,' and 'feeble-minded' became objectionable, the phrases 'severe, moderate and mild mental retardation' and (later) 'developmental disabilities' were coined. Institutions for people so labeled have experienced corresponding name changes" (Bogdan and Biklen, 1985: 48). Accepted professional terms seem to become the future schoolyard epithets. As they do, new terms may be coined.

Unfortunately, the new naming remains problematic. To the extent that our practices do not change, then the negative connotations of the old terms soon "catch up" with the new names (Bogdan and Biklen, 1985: 48). Without other changes, name changing can be a futile attempt to destigmatize the oppressed group (Raspberry, 1989). It still sets those with disabilities apart from those without disabilities. It hinders our ability to see the complexity of those with disabilities as people, not categories (Bogdan and Biklen, 1985: 47–51).

For example, in an investigation of the integration of disabled and nondisabled students, observers noticed that in one school that integrates severely autistic and nondisabled children, the term "handicapped" was not used. Thus, a preschool child did not know what it meant, and only after being told what it meant did she identify two of her classmates as handicapped. ("Actually" three were.) The child knew that some of her classmates had difficulties in walking or talking, but she did not see these difficulties as "all-defining." Instead, she knew and could describe to the observers her disabled classmates as individuals (Bogdan and Biklen, 1985: 49–50). Changes in naming and in practices produced the supportive response of the child to her "handicapped" classmates.

To the extent that professionals control the naming, it still suggests that disabled people are dependent on professionals for their welfare (Longmore, 1985: 421). They remain the professionals' responsibility and charges. The new terms also seem euphemistically to skirt issues of minority-majority conflict. Thus, students with disabilities are "mainstreamed" into local schools, not "integrated" into them (which, of course, implies that they had been "segregated" from them) (Longmore, 1985: 421; Hahn, 1987: 195). And persons with disabilities may object to the new (and old) names.

In objecting to the names applied to them, individuals with disabilities respond in various ways. Of course, some object to the stigmatized, master status that the name "gives" them. They are both more than and not "the disabled," "the crippled," and so on. (Others embrace such terms as starkly descriptive (Mairs, 1986: 9–20).) For some, the objection includes being "lumped" with others who they believe are not the same as (perhaps not as worthy as) themselves. Those with disabilities may stratify one another just as those without do so. Thus, less severely hearing impaired people may resent being called "deaf." Instead, they may prefer "hard of hearing" or the now fashionable, "hearing impaired." Even more politically, disabled activists (as well as Congress and others) were concerned how the term "handicapped" was defined in Section 504 of the Rehabilitation Act of 1973, which many see as the preeminent civil rights act for disabled citizens. "Virtually no one outside of OCR (Office for Civil Rights, within the then Department of Health, Education, and Welfare) supported defining alcoholism and drug addiction as disabilities, because of their connotations of moral deviance if not (at least in the case of drug addicts) moral depravity" (Scotch, 1984: 69, 102, 110–111). They were included. Similar concerns were raised with the recently passed Americans With Disabilities Act of 1990.

As part of their larger efforts to gain control over their lives, people with disabilities (and advocates) are also seeking control over naming themselves—and naming those without disabilities. Remember, non-disabled people have historically monopolized the naming of those with disabilities and have taken themselves as the standard against which they name those with disabilities. By coining terms such as "handicapism," "physicalism," and "normalism," disabled people (and their advocates) identify the practices of nondisabled people that oppress them (Longmore, 1985: 421; Zola, forthcoming). Likewise, by calling those without disabilities "TABs" (temporarily abled bodied), "ABs" (able bodied), "normies," "regulars," "walkers," or "the nondisabled," those with disabilities control the "name game." In doing so, they remind nondisabled people of their own precarious status, try to reduce the gap between disabled and nondisabled people, perhaps deprecate those without disabilities, even define them through negation (i.e., those without disabilities become the *non*disabled.), and express a "hard edge of pride in differentness due to disability" (Longmore, 1985: 423; Zola, forthcoming).

Those with disabilities also express pride in themselves through how they name themselves. They reject the stigmatization of the terms applied to them by those without disabilities. Thus, they create alternatives such as " 'able-disabled,' 'handicapable,' 'disABLEd,' (and) 'differently abled.' A number of wheelchair athletes have expressed a preference for 'challenged' or 'physically challenged' " (Longmore, 1985:422). Deaf activists (and their advocates, often researchers) may refer to those who are social-culturally deaf as "Deaf," whereas "deaf" is used to refer to an audiological status and those who possess such status (Baker and Battison, 1980).

These attempts at (re)naming have followed various strategies (Zola, forthcoming, drawing upon Phillips, 1986). One strategy has been to accept the oppressive practices of society. "Cripple" and "handicapped" reflect that acquiescence. Another strategy euphemistically personalizes disability. Terms such as "physically challenged" and "physically inconvenienced" may inadvertently foster a "blaming the victim" approach by overlooking the oppressive practices of society, confuse people about who is being discussed, and aid in the denial of being disabled (Zola, forthcoming). Others emphasize a more activist stance. Whether using such terms as "handicapper," which is intended to stress what people with disabilities can do, or through the private, "inside" talk of people with disabilities (e.g., referrences to "crips" or "gimps") that at times may be made public, disabled people proclaim their disabilities to be an essential feature of themselves with which others must deal.

Instead of changing the names of disability, perhaps the *grammar* might be changed. Irving Zola (forthcoming) argues that the use of disability nouns and adjectives such as "the blind" or "deformed" makes the disability the entire person, a point noted earlier. Instead, the more awkward phrase "with a disability" implies both a connection to the person and a separation from the person. The disability is part of the person but not all of the person. Such phrases make the users and receivers pause to consider what is being meant. (But recall Michael Oliver's explanation of why he prefers "disabled person" to "person with a disability," mentioned at the end of the Introduction.) Further, active construction such as "uses a wheelchair" indicates that the person with the disability is in control, whereas the passive construction of "is bound to a wheelchair" indicates that the disability controls the person. Similarly, "to be" disabled indicates much greater pervasiveness than "to have" a disability. By indicating an essential difference between those with and without disabilities, "to be" separates disabled and nondisabled people. However, Zola cautions that the affirmation of "I am disabled" may be necessary when those with disabilities politically mobilize themselves.

Those with disabilities do not agree on how to name themselves. The disagreement can even become divisive as participants criticize one another for inappropriate language (Zola, forthcoming). Nevertheless, attempts to create alternatives to references developed by "the non-disabled" clearly convey the desire of disabled people to control their lives, including identifying names. Black Americans (or should it be African Americans) and other minority groups have likewise created alternatives to the names applied to them by the dominant white majority. Renaming is an important means for dealing with oppression.

Naming identifies people. It points to what the users take as the important characteristics of those named. It tells who are similar and who are different, drawing boundaries around and between people. In doing so, names orient us (however generally) toward people. Too often, "disability names" have oriented us toward people "known" to be fundamentally different from those without disabilities. Our naming has helped to devalue people made disabled.

Portraying Disability

From Captain Hook to the Hunchback of Notre Dame to Frankenstein's monster to Captain Ahab to Ironsides to Zero in *Beetle Bailey* and more recently to Sarah in *Children of a Lesser God,* Benny in *LA Law,* Corky in *Life Goes On,* and Christy Brown in *My Left Foot,* the mass media have created some of our most vivid images of disability. With their vast audiences, movies, television, radio, literature, journalism, and theater are important in depicting disability and disabled people.

The media's portrayal of disabled people both reflects and produces our beliefs about and actions toward disabled people (Biklen, 1987; Kent, 1987: 48). While the media's images have changed over time, vary somewhat by the medium, and have not been equally explored for all media (Kriegel, 1982; Zola, 1985), several *disabling images* dominate. The media have primarily portrayed those with disabilities as monsters, evil or demonic, objects of charity, "vegetables," or maladjusted (Bogdan and Biklen, 1977; Bogdan et al., 1982; Kriegel, 1982; Quart and Auster, 1982; Longmore, 1985; Zola, 1985, 1987; Biklen, 1986, 1987). The *media's message* individualizes disability and sets people with disabilities apart as primarily defectively different. While the media's portrayal of disability is *changing*, much remains oppressively the same.

Disabling Images

Horror films present monstrous disabled people. Quasimodo, the Hunchback of Notre Dame; the phantom in the *Phantom of the Opera;* Frankenstein's monster; crazed killers in "fright" films; and others frighten and fascinate us (Bogdan et al., 1982; Longmore, 1985). The monsters' disabilities "typically involve disfigurement of the face and head and gross deformity of the body . . . These visible traits express disfigurement of personality and deformity of the soul . . . (and the) disability may be presented as the cause of evildoing, punishment for it, or both" (Longmore, 1985: 33). "Normal," respectable people may become deformed monsters and change back again, as does Mr. Hyde or the Incredible Hulk (Bogdan et al., 1982). In becoming monstrous, they give up their humanity (if only for the duration). Even when presented sympathetically as a victim of an accident or others' bigotry, monstrous disabled people are a menace to citizens. Their unpredictability, violent rages, or quests for revenge against those who torment them make them unfit to live among the rest of us (Longmore, 1985).

Complementing the media's depiction of monstrous disabled people is their portrayal of disabled people as demonic, evil, or criminal. Evil disabled people often seek revenge for their disablement (Kriegel, 1982, 1987; Bogdan et al., 1982; Longmore, 1985). In raging against the whale that has torn his leg from his body, the demonic Captain Ahab abandons "normal life . . . (and the) ties that bind men to one another . . . (He) inspires fear . . . because others cannot really understand his quest for vengeance" (Kriegel, 1982: 18). Gangster movies and adventure programs may involve disabled criminals or characters who seek revenge for their suffering. *Dick Tracy* (the movie and comic strip) includes a rogue's gallery of disabled criminals. Classic children's tales tell us that disabled people are evil. The deformed, cannibalistic witch in *Hansel and Gretel,* Captain Hook, the "limb-missing, patched-eye pirates of *Treasure Island,*" the queen in *Snow White,* who becomes a "wart-nosed, hunched-over witch" to poison Snow White, and other disabled characters are wicked (Bogdan et al., 1982: 34). Television presents similar images of evil disabled people: the one-armed murderer in an extremely popular series, *The Fugitive;* a "greedy and vengeful oilman who walked with a limp" in *The Yellow Rose* in the mid-1980s; mentally ill characters who are violent (one-fourth of all programs that portray the mentally ill use that image); and the like (Longmore, 1985: 32; Bogdan et al., 1982). If not monstrous, then disabled people are still dangerous.

Disabled people are also dependent. Whether objects of charity, a burdensome responsibility, or perhaps even "vegetables" with little reason for living, disabled people cannot do for themselves (Kriegel, 1982, 1987, Longmore, 1985; Biklen, 1987). Tiny Tim, like other objects of charity, "soothes middle-class society." In giving alms to pitiful disabled people, nondisabled donors can self-righteously believe that they have done all that they should do. Virtue and an untroubled life are their rewards—even if only indirectly through consuming media depictions of pitiful disabled people (Kriegel, 1987: 36). Less appealing are the burdensome disabled, who become an "impediment to others' freedom" or who are handed over to service organizations to be "disposed" of (Biklen, 1987: 522). And still less appealing are the "vegetables."

Plays, movies, and television programs of the past two decades, such as *Whose Life Is It, Anyway?* and *The Elephant Man,* depict severely disabled people's lives as so difficult, even so worthless (even if the difficulty is due to other's bigotry), that ending those lives may be the best solution. Severe disabilities make people inhuman the media tell us. They become "vegetables" (Longmore, 1985).

Journalism has similarly treated severely disabled people. Stories about Elizabeth Bouvia, a woman with severe cerebral palsy who "requires assistance in order to live . . . (and who) sought to have a hospital give her pain-killing drugs to aid her suicide through starvation" and "Baby Doe" emphasized the hopeless, inhuman existence for these disabled people (Biklen, 1986: 45). The story of "Baby Doe" pitted the parents and doctors of Baby Doe, an infant born with spina bifida, against disability advocates . . . Baby Doe was deemed to be "doomed" by the impairments that she had been born with. Her life would be, according to the medical profession, a "difficult" and "valueless" one. Her parents would "suffer unduly" by having this child live. Much of the media attention focused on the pathos and tragedy (Ruffner, 1987: 6).

Journalism can present as sensational and stereotypical stories of disabled people as do the entertainment media.

In the past several decades, television and movies have emphasized maladjusted disabled people (Longmore, 1985: 34). The media tell us that disabled people are bitter because they have never accepted their impairments and themselves. Consequently, they unjustifiably treat harshly nondisabled people. However, some nondisabled people realize that they must "get tough" with the disabled people in order for the latter to become better adjusted. The maladjusted disabled person became a dominant image after World War II, perhaps in "response to the large numbers" of returning disabled veterans (Longmore, 1985: 34).

The media have portrayed disabled people in other, less dominant ways: as victims, as survivors who "endure and in (their) endurance discover survival as a cause in itself" (Kriegel, 1987: 38), as possessed of special compensations or gifts such as "goodness of heart" (Longmore, 1985: 34), as heroic in overcoming their adversity (e.g., in nonfictional television that focuses on the exploits of "real" people) (Longmore, 1985: 34), or through "realism" in which the disability is merely part of the disabled person's self (Kriegel, 1987: 37). Some of these portrayals complement the dominant depictions, as do those that emphasize the heroic overcoming of adversity in which adjustment is still the focus. Others, such as the "realist" portrayals, contrast with the dominant images. Whether complementary or contrasting, these are less prominent depictions.

Media's Message

While the media have portrayed disabled people through several dominant and lesser images (and while the images have shifted over time and vary across the media), the message has not been particularly mixed. The media have quite consistently individualized disability. They have told and shown us that disability is an individual attribute that makes disabled people defectively different from nondisabled people.

Whether presented as monsters, villains, "vegetables," objects of charity,

maladjusted, "super crips," or in other ways, the media individualizes
our understanding of disability. Television, which particularly centers
on personalities, not social processes, emphasizes the individualistic
nature of disability (Zola, 1985). Whether dealing well or not with their
disability, disabled people's "difficulties" are themselves, particularly
their impaired selves. A technological fix or better adjustment may
resolve the problems. The former speaks to our faith in gadgets and the
latter to our widespread belief that with the proper attitude people can
do anything. If not, then death may be appropriate—for the demonic,
evil, or "vegetable" disabled persons. Societal arrangements, actions, and
attitudes that oppress disabled people are given little, if any, attention
(Longmore, 1985; Zola, 1985).

Complementing this individualizing of disability is the media's depiction of disabled people as different, especially defectively different.
Disabled people's "defects" become their defining characteristic, their
essence. Our media depictions (and our terms) tell us so. While some
researchers have commented on how widely the media have portrayed
disabled people (Longmore, 1985) and while many of us can easily
remember a host of riveting depictions, disabled people appear in television (at least) far less than they "appear" as citizens (Zola, 1985). But
when they do appear (in television or elsewhere), their involvement in
the story revolves around their individual disabilities. Moreover, hospitals,
special schools, and other "disability places" are often the settings for the
disabled characters (Zola, 1985). Because disabled people appear relatively infrequently in the media, in special settings when they do appear,
primarily in terms of their disability and in sensational and highly
stereotypical ways, the message is clear: Disabled people are different.
They are not "us"—us being the unstated, nondisabled population.

If disability is a matter of individual misfortune, shortcomings, perhaps serious moral flaws, and/or adjustment, and if disabled people are
different than those without disabilities, then whatever befalls them, no
matter how undeserved and tragic, can be more easily accepted. After
all, what could nondisabled people do if they play no part or only a
peripheral part in the "disability drama." When the media do focus on
the role of nondisabled people in the struggles of disabled people, they
primarily point an accusatory finger at some clearly offensive characters,
not at typical nondisabled citizens. When "average" citizens are the
culprits, their ignorance and insensitivity, only secondarily their prejudice,
create the difficulties for disabled people. Disabled people must be

patient with nondisabled individuals and educate them. More important, policies and practices of all kinds that oppress disabled people get short shrift in media portrayals (Longmore, 1985). For example, relatively little was written in the stories about Baby Doe or Elizabeth Bouvia of the woefully inadequate services provided to people with severe disabilities. The "prevailing framework for covering disabilities, a combination of charity, pity, tragedy, and 'overcoming disability,'" typically ignores our larger arrangements and actions that handicap people with disabilities (Biklen, 1986: 49).

The media's portrayal is a reflection of and a component in the making of disability. Typically, the media have individualized disability, portraying as defectively different people it helps to make disabled. But the media can also be a force for and a reflection of positive change. Witness the expose of Willowbrook, a New York facility for mentally retarded people, which eventually led to more mentally retarded citizens living in the community (Rothman and Rothman, 1984). Or, consider the media attention given to "Baby Does." While much of it inadequately addressed the policies that oppress disabled people, that attention underlay the efforts leading to legislation to prevent future "Baby Does" (even though the legislation seems to be ineffective (Moss, 1987)). While more exploration is needed, media portrayals can be used to enable people to develop a more "positive" stance toward disabled individuals. However, the media alone are unlikely to be dramatically effective (Horne, 1988). Improvements in the media indicate important social change and can further that change.

Changing Media

And the media are changing. Disabled citizens are becoming more involved in various ways and more positive, complex portrayals are appearing. Newspapers more regularly run stories about disabilities and not merely in the health section. Disabled actors, actresses, producers, newspeople, and others in the media are working in greater numbers and with greater visibility. Scholarly and popular "disability publications," such as *Disability Studies Quarterly* and *The Disability Rag*, are becoming more available. (*The Rag* appeared in 1980 and complements the great range of specialized media by and for disabled people that have existed much longer than it.) These "disability media" inform disabled people about issues that otherwise get little attention in the "mainstream" media and provide some opportunity to challenge the "mainstream" media's depiction of disability. Movies and plays such as *Mask* and *Children of a Lesser God*, and some television such as *LA Law* and *Life Goes On*, are depicting disabled people less stereotypically, more complexly (Longmore, 1985). Disabled people are appearing in commercials, signing lovingly to one another or "popping wheelies" in their wheelchairs (Longmore, 1985; Ruffner, 1987). The emerging conceptualization of disability as a social phenomenon, particularly the minority-group perspective, is the impetus for these changing portrayals of disability, which in turn encourages the emerging social view.

Disabled people and their advocates have worked to improve the media's making of disability. Disability activist groups have pushed the entertainment industry to improve the depiction of disabled characters and to increase their casting of disabled actors and actresses. Chris Burke, who has Down syndrome, plays Corky on the highly acclaimed television program *Life Goes On*. A nine-month letter writing/information demonstration campaign by disabled volunteers at an independent living center in Kansas City significantly improved the local newspapers' use of "acceptable" terminology concerning disability (Longmore, 1985; Ruffner, 1987). Disability activism has been effective.

But not surprisingly, to many much more remains to be done. Journalists and other commentators continue to use disability terms to criticize those of whom they disapprove. A nationally syndicated columnist suggested that an unmindful former Secretary of Housing and Urban Development, known as "Silent Sam," might be appropriately called "Blind Sam" for permitting a multimillion-dollar, perhaps billion-dollar, scandal to occur (Raspberry, 1989). Television characters continue to make jokes at the expense of disabled people. In one program a girl wrote for a class assignment that she had visited her grandparents who had become "retarded" and moved to a community in Arizona for "retarded" people. The "joke" was that the granddaughter meant "retired." Or, Academy Award winner, Marlee Matlin, followed up her winning performance in *Children of a Lesser God* with a television portrayal of a deaf woman who was also angry and bitter. If hearing actresses can be typecast, then so, too, can deaf actresses, though typecasting the latter probably harms not only the actress but also distorts our understanding of deaf people. Disability typically remains the focus when characters with disabilities are included in the entertainment media, but the larger disability-rights struggles go unscreened (*The Disability Rag*, May/June 1990: 32–34). Nondisabled actors continue to play disabled characters in movies, such as the lead characters in the highly acclaimed *Born on the Fourth of July* and *My Left Foot*. This is a controversial practice. These and other shortcomings indicate the need for further change in the media's depiction of disabled people—and for efforts by disabled people and advocates to create that change—in the media and elsewhere. (See *The Disability Rag* for continuing examination of the media's portrayal of disability.)

Displaying Disability

While I have focused on naming disability and the mass media's portraying disability, we depict disabilities in other ways, too: scholarly writings, jokes, telethons, fundraising campaigns of all kinds, during tours of facilities that serve disabled people, in (primarily) yesterday's "freak shows," and so on. These other depictions largely complement, not contradict, the two popular ones that I have explored. Some even predate the two that I have discussed. While some may be offended at my making a connection among the following, "freak shows," telethons, fundraising campaigns of all kinds, and presentations of disabled "clients" during tours of service facilities present some very similar images of disabled people. These depictions are (or have the potential for becoming) *displays* of disabled people for "amusement and profit" (Bogdan, 1988).

Whether through (primarily) yesterday's "freak shows," fundraising campaigns, or presentations of disabled clients during tours of service facilities, displays complement our naming and portraying disability. They show us that disabled people are different kinds of individuals than nondisabled people. They are unique, odd, pitiful, or amazing (in what they have accomplished—and could accomplish with additional support). By playing to our curiosity or sympathy, these displays separate those with disabilities from those without. We do not display fellow citizens, only those who are different than "us."

Consider "freak shows." From approximately 1840 to 1940 freak shows crisscrossed the United States. Many who performed in them would now be termed disabled: legless and/or armless or with extra limbs, with microencephaly (a "condition associated with mental retardation and characterized by a very small, pointed head and small overall stature"), with skin disorders, Siamese twins, and so on (Bogdan, 1988: 111–112, 7). Promoters often presented them as "freaks of nature"—nature's "jokes or mistakes" (Bogdan, 1988: 6). Because money could be made, some people "feigned disability in order to qualify for freak roles" (Bogdan, 1988: 268). Audiences marveled at these human "oddities." Today, many of us are aghast at what we take to have been those cruel exhibitions, but we may still sneak a peak at the tamer sideshows of today's fairs and carnivals. Outrage at and attempts to ban "dwarf tossing" (in which citizens pay a fee, often at a bar or club, to compete at tossing a dwarf onto a padded surface) express our present shock at today's "freak shows." (2)

But telethons and other charity campaigns are not so different. Fundraisers still exhibit disabled people for "profit." Audiences marvel at the accomplishments of the disabled people who are presented to tug at our heartstrings—and our purse strings. Perhaps we marvel even more at the telethon hosts who go on and on for hours. Can they (physically) make it? Can the goal be reached? Stay tuned! As one observer of a well-known telethon noted:

> Mix pathos and bathos, fold in cloying clubbiness of old-time showbiz, add a few stars and a bunch of hacks and retreads, season with fatigue and you have the kind of event that could only happen in Las Vegas (Barol, 1987: 66).

If it could only happen in Las Vegas, then does that telethon and others like it (though less "spectacular") emphasize the common humanity that binds people with and without disabilities or (unintentionally) imply that presumably profound differences separate disabled and nondisabled people? What images of disability do they create?

I do not mean to disparge the motives of the participants nor the worthiness of the causes, but telethons and fundraising campaigns of all kinds typically depict disabled people in troubling ways.

> The American public gives billions of dollars each year to charity, much of which is solicited in the name of helping the handicapped. This system of collecting funds demeans its recipients by supporting the prejudice that the handicapped are inferior people. Moreover, professionals who require charitable contributions to support their programs tend to distort the image of the handicapped in order to play on the public's pity. Thus, the crippled child becomes a poor soul whose disability evokes pity and guilt and the spirit of giving, but also lessens the possibility that disabled people can be regarded as people with personalities, with individual aspirations, and with an interest in being perceived as ordinary people (Bogdan and Biklen, 1977: 18). (Notice some of the terms in the above quote that jar. Naming does change.)

Such fundraising individualizes disability. The proposed solution becomes a technological or medical fix that charitable contributions may make possible. Societal policies and arrangements and individual's prejudices and practices are not addressed. If anything, fundraisers lessen our responsibility for disability, hindering our recognition that in important ways we create disability. Instead, our "duty" is done through donating (Scott, 1969: Chapter 6).

Tours of facilities serving citizens with disabilities may also become displays of disabled people. The professionals may present disabled clients to the tour group. Such tours can take on the flavor of visiting a zoo with the disabled citizens as the caged animals or a vaudeville show with each disabled citizen asked to present his or her specialty act. Professionals may even take their "charges" to the public, legislators, or other potential benefactors (Lenihan, 1976–77: 23). Once again, the danger of such displays is that they may easily separate disabled people from those who are nondisabled. The common humanity is downplayed; the wonder of it all emphasized.

Scholarly work concerning disability may also be understood as displays of disability (see "categorizing disability" in Chapter 1). Scholarly work that individualizes disability or more recently makes it social creates images of disability. Beyond presenting (possibly) technical information, scholarly work creates a sense of what disability is and who disabled people are.

Scholarly work does not, cannot, just present the "facts." "Disability facts" do not exist apart from the efforts to make and convey some sense about disability. Scholarly efforts do not discover facts waiting to be found but create what is then taken to be uncovered.

But scholarly efforts draw power from their presumed objectivity. Those efforts do not display disability but explain what disability "is," so we believe. After all, no "profit" is to be gained in displaying disability— unless we consider the financial and other kinds of support to continue the scientific work, the acclaim, the opportunities to advance, and the like (Barton, 1988).

However, "research is not a value-neutral activity. It is a social experience in which subjects of research can suffer and perceive particular forms of study as oppressive" (Barton, 1988: 91). Scholarly work is not separate from the social era and circumstances within which it is conducted. It is often intimately tied to and does the bidding of the most powerful institutions in society. For example, the dominant emphasis in educational research and particularly "special educational" research to identify the individual defects and needs of youth (e.g., psychometric testing) enables educators to segregate youth into greatly varying educational opportunities, which helps perpetuate a stratified society (Barton, 1988).

Or, consider mental retardation. We have created various images of mentally retarded people: as sick, as subhuman, as menace, as objects of pity, as burdens of charity, as holy innocents, as developing individuals, and still others (Wolfensberger, 1975: Chapter 1). During the late 1800s and early 1900s concern with mentally retarded and other "defective" people and how best to deal with them swept the country (Rothman 1971: Chapters 10 and 11; Wolfensberger, 1975: 33–56; Lane, 1984: 353–361). During this era, scientists launched some of the most devastating attacks upon mentally retarded individuals.

Henry Goddard, a well-known American psychologist, explored the connection between mental retardation and social deviance. He became famous with the publication of his (now-discredited, but for many decades widely-referred to) book about the Kallikaks (Smith, 1985). Goddard reconstructed the lineage of Deborah Kallikak, a resident at the Training School for Feeble-Minded Boys and Girls in Vineland, New Jersey, where Goddard was director of the research laboratory. He claimed that during the Revolutionary War Martin Kallikak, a young soldier from a respectable family, had an illegitimate son with a barmaid thought to be feebleminded. Later Kallikak married a "good" woman from a respectable family. The descendants from the liaison with the feebleminded barmaid, including Deborah, were deviant: feebleminded, illegitimate, sexually immoral, alcoholics, and such. The descendants from the marriage to the "good" woman were conventional, upstanding citizens: doctors, lawyers, and educators (Goddard, 1912). Based on that and subsequent research, Goddard concluded that:

> For many generations we have recognized and pitied the idiot. Of late we have recognized a higher type of defective, the moron, and have discovered that he is a burden; that he is a menace of society and civilization; that he is responsible to a large degree for many, if not all, of our social problems (Goddard, 1915: 307 in Wolfensberger, 1975: 34).

If "feeblemindedness" was hereditary, as Goddard and others believed, and if the "feebleminded" were a menace, then the solution to this problem was either euthanasia or the prevention of the reproduction of mentally retarded people. Both have been tried (Wolfensberger, 1975, 1980, 1984; Meucci, 1988).

Scholars have developed important displays of disability. They have primarily individualized disability, presenting disabled people as abnormal. More recently, scholars have helped to develop frames that make disability social. But whether they individualize disability, make it social, or develop more specific images of disability, we should not believe that they are reporting their findings about disability, about a phenomenon that exists independent of what they and we make of human variation.

"Freak shows," fundraisers, tours of service facilities, and other displays such as scholarly works complement our naming and portraying disability. These displays primarily show us that disabled people are defectively different. That difference is their essence and their bane. They must live with it or try to overcome it—perhaps with citizens' charitable donations and professionals' know-how.

Conclusion

Through naming, portraying, displaying, and in other ways we depict disability. We create images of people we make disabled. These images reflect how we make disability and become the unspoken justification for our further actions. Our depictions have primarily individualized disability. Disability is an individual defect that sets people with disabilities apart from nondisabled people. It is the essence of disabled people. But changes are occurring. As we begin making disability a social phenomenon, more complex depictions are appearing; disabled people are becoming involved as actors, actresses, producers, newspeople and in other ways in the depiction of disability; disabled people are actively naming themselves and those without disabilities; and people with disabilities and others are pushing for still more change. Words and pictures are powerful means for making disability.

Through our depictions of disability we develop basic feelings about disability. These feelings permeate the *interactions and identifications* between disabled and nondisabled people, the issue that I take up next.

Endnotes

1. Names do matter. Residents of Hodgkins, Illinois were apparently encouraged by some Chicago radio announcers and editorial writers and the United Parcel Service, which was locating a package sorting center there, to change its name (*The Disability Rag,* May/June 1991: 8). However, according to a town employee, the town voted to retain its name.

2. The inconsistency of condemning or banning "dwarf tossing" for short people's "own good," which denies a few short people the opportunity to earn a significant amount of money; the acceptance of short people as clowns in the circus; the worship of big people running up and down courts, tackling and blocking one another or boxing each other for tremendous sums of money; the widespread stigmatization of short people; the still acceptable display by women (and men) of their bodies for profit; and still other "related" practices seems to have gone largely unrecognized by all of us, perhaps particularly by those outraged by "dwarf tossing."

Chapter 4

INTERACTING AND IDENTIFYING DISABILITY

Consider Christina, a "deaf-blind Rubella" child who resided in a state hospital when "befriended" by a social scientist. Clinically, she was profoundly retarded and without any language (i.e., alingual). However, she could "ambulate, grasp, and eat normally" (Goode, 1984: 242). Within the state hospital, Chris had three distinct (but also similar) identities.

> One "version" of Chris was produced by custodial personnel on the ward, who talked about her in terms of her abilities (or lack thereof) to perform those tasks which they required of her during eating, bathing, dressing, pottying, playing, etc. Another identity was afforded Chris by clinical staff at the hospital who were charged with examination, diagnosis and remediation of her condition and health in general. These staff employed a mechanistic-medical model (in which Chris...was construed in a deeply pejorative way) coupled with a people work identity (in which Chris was described as difficult to examine, diagnose or cure). Finally, Chris's teachers described her somewhat differently, although in equally negative terms—as unable to be taught, lazy, stubborn, without an attention span, etc. (Goode, 1984: 242–243).

To the social scientist who worked with her for three years, Christina was yet a different child, one with great competence. She and the others who resided at the hospital were

> excellent hospital residents. They were "institutionalized" which meant (for better or worse) that they understood something of the hospital's routines and rules... One very common scenario involved "pushing". The children would typically wait to be taken from one activity to the next. They might be lying on the floor lost in some autostimulatory behavior when a staff member would come up and fairly abruptly pick up a child and push her to her "next" in the wards' routine. If it was 11:30 AM and lunch was approaching, a child would be picked up and pushed toward the bathroom (they were always taken to the bathroom before lunch). The typical reaction, and the child had a wide range of possible things she could do after being pushed, was to understand "the push" (as I came to call it) as the communication it was intended to be. The child would wander to the bathroom, find a toilet, do her business, stick her

hands in the running faucet after she was done, and walk to the (locked) door to the dining area.

To me these actions were clear indications of active intelligence at work . . . Even stereotype, rocking and repetitive actions without any apparent instrumental value, may be interpreted as institutionally adaptive behavior . . . During a thirty-six hour observation period . . . I realized just how much time she (Chris) was left to her own devices to occupy her time. The *vast* majority of the day this was her situation and she did not have external distractions of our culture such as television. She loved the radio (Chris had good sound reception but did not process the sound in a normal way) and whenever one was available she did her best to get close enough to it to listen. She loved to rock to the music and built some fantastic constructions from available furniture to climb up to a small radio kept, for obvious reasons, on a high shelf away from the hands of the children. But in most places there was no radio and she was left alone to provide herself with amusement. She rocked, played with her sight and sound reception, masturbated and so on, *not* because of her organic deficits but because she was bored and these were things which she could do by herself and from which she received pleasure, reduction of anxiety or other gratification . . . She literally waited for everything and I developed a healthy respect for her abilities to entertain herself in solitary pursuits (Goode, 1986: 94–95).

While she was certainly not diagnosed as having multiple personalities, Chris had four identities (some similar, one very different), each as "real" as the other, but with importantly different consequences for Chris. How can that be?

Interaction between disabled and nondisabled people is pregnant with possibilities and potential problems. Most important, whether disabled or not, who we are is distinctly a matter of with whom we interact. *Interactional identities* are made when disabled and nondisabled people encounter one another. When they do, nondisabled people often create *spoiled identities* for the people with disabilities. How disabled and nondisabled people manage the spoiled identities further affects their interaction. Yet, when interacting with nondisabled people, disabled people are not only, perhaps not even primarily, concerned about managing their (potentially) spoiled identities. *Navigating the encounters* successfully in order to accomplish the purpose at hand is also important.

The interplay between disabled people's identities and their interaction with nondisabled people is important for producing disability. That interpersonal interplay arises out of the larger social arrangements and practices that we create. As I illustrate in the chapter's conclusion, the interplay is a social phenomenon, not merely an interpersonal matter.

Interactional Identities

Many of us understand identities to be a (more or less) coherent bundle of traits or perhaps a core essence that each of us possesses. Just as we have a complexion, eye and hair color, height, weight, body shape and the like, so do we have a self, a "who we are," an identity that is us if not physically within us. When interacting with people, we learn who they are and they learn who we are. As we commonsensically say, "we come to know" who each other *is*, which assumes that who we are is "inside" us, waiting for others (and even ourselves) to discover in more or less full detail. That is not the only way to understand who we are, and it may not be the most useful way either.

Instead, whether disabled or not, who we are does not reside somewhere within us. Instead, our identities are distinctly a matter of with whom we interact and how we do so. Our interactions with people, the understandings we develop about them, and our responses to them *are* them—for us. And vice versa. No matter how we try, we cannot know people independent of our experiences of them, independent of what we think and say about them and behave toward them. Those actions *are* the people as far as we know (though we are likely to believe that who we know the people to be is who they are to anyone, anytime, anyplace, who they are, period). And, of course, each of us thinks and talks about and acts toward ourselves, too. We also create identities for ourselves. In interaction our identities are made and exist (Stewart, forthcoming: Chapter 5).

If people's identities seem to be relatively consistent, then their interactions with others are similar. When interactions with others vary greatly, so, too, do their identities—and vice versa.

To think of identities as created in interaction is perhaps particularly crucial for those with disabilities, especially those with the most severe disabilities. If who people are is merely some kind of internal trait, then it becomes much easier to conclude that disabled people, particularly those with severe disabilities, have diminished selves. To put it plainly, "they are not much." However, if we realize that we create identities in interaction with one another, then we may be able to produce greater, more competent, more complex identities. More complex, competent identities become possible in part because that realization also enlarges the responsibility for who people are. Whoever interacts with a person is socially responsible for who that person is (if not legally so). Our actions when encountering others can enhance who those others are—to us, to them, and to others.

Recall the four identities "possessed" by Chris. While the custodial, clinical, and educational staff each knew Chris "to be" (not merely "as") grossly incompetent and a problem, who she was varied from one set of interactions and interactional partners to another. The social scientist, who interacted with Chris in dramatically different ways than did the staff, knew her to be someone the staff could not even recognize. The social scientist's Chris did not exist for the staff. And once the social scientist made his own Chris, the staff's Chrises did not exist for him as a lived experience but only as other people's making.

However, the scientist's Chris is no more "real" (and no less real), no more who Chris actually is, than are the staff's Chrises. Nevertheless, we all recognize that the scientist's Chris is a much more complex, competent, interesting person than is the staff's. If we were Chris, we would rather be the scientist's Chris than the staff's. If we were interacting with the social scientist's Chris, we would probably have a more satisfying experience than if we were interacting with the staff's Chris—but to interact with the scientist's Chris would require us to "know" and act toward Chris as the scientist did. Further, interactions with the social scientist are likely to be much more enabling for Chris than those with the staff. Chris is more likely to interact competently with the social scientist than with the staff. Interactional identities make us realize the responsibility we all have for who all of us are.

Don't think, however, that Chris (or any of us) are passive pawns merely moved about by our interactional partners. While most of us can act and sense in more varied ways than can Chris (notice the Chris I just made), she, like all of us, is making her world as she acts in it. (Or should I say that if we are willing to understand Chris as making her world, then to us she is doing so.) Again, recall the social scientist's appreciation of the ability of Chris and others who resided with her to understand the hospital's routines and rules.

While we create identities for one another in interaction with each other, we cannot successfully create any identity. I do not believe that we can successfully make Christina whatever we wish. We are not likely to make her competent enough to do most of what you and I do. However, we can make Christina in many more ways than did the staff in the hospital. The social scientist created one alternative. Many others were yet untried. The challenge is not to "see" which is the "real" Christina, but to see in what ways we can make Christina—and she herself—that will enhance her life and ours.

How we identify disabled people can have enormous consequences. It can be a matter of life and death (see Chapter 6). For example, Phillip Becker, a teenager when national attention was focused on him, had Down syndrome. His parents, who institutionalized him on the advice of doctors, refused to permit his congenital heart defect to be repaired. The Heaths, a couple that befriended him through a volunteer program, eventually initiated legal proceedings to be declared Phillip's guardian and to obtain court authorization for the surgery. In deciding to grant guardianship to the Heaths and permit them to authorize medical treatment, the judge compared the

> conceptions each couple held of Phillip and his quality of life. According to the court, the Beckers regarded Phillip as an unskilled devalued person, incapable of loving others; this was the conception they had acquired when Phillip was born, based on the assessment offered by doctors at that time. The Heaths, in contrast, pictured Phillip as an educable and valuable person, capable of love. The court treated these comparative assessments as central evidence concerning both who should make the medical treatment decision and whether the heart surgery should go forward. The Heath's conception was more persuasive, reasoned the judge, and offered the least detrimental alternative for Phillip: a life worth living (Minnow, 1990: 344–345).

Through our interactions we create identities for one another, for those of us disabled and nondisabled. In creating identities, we enable or hinder one another in our interactions. Out of those resulting interactions, we further create one another, which, in turn, obstructs or promotes the ongoing interaction. *And on it goes.* Identities and interactions are interwoven. Each is profoundly significant for the other.

Consider the following account of "Robert, or, as he preferred to be called, Bobby . . . a fifty-year-old man with Down's Syndrome who lived at a board and care facility" (Goode, 1984: 234). It is made by the same social scientist who knows Chris.

> I first got to know Bobby through his clinical records . . . which summarized his career in human service contexts . . . (They were) testament to the clinical identity which Bobby had been given by clinicians. Nowhere was Bobby discussed in terms of his having any sort of competence and human value; instead an exclusively fault finding perspective was employed . . . This method afforded Bobby an essentially *devalued, incompetent* and *hopeless* identity . . . (Excerpts from the records indicate) "speech or language therapy is not recommended as prognosis is poor . . . client can communicate basic needs but

can not express complex ideas and understands very little . . . difficult to com-municate with . . . " (or) a quick test of intelligence yielded a mental age of approximately 2–8 years. Clinician concludes that Bobby is "severely mentally retarded with severe brain damage" . . . (and) "time and effort in this area (occupational therapy) is not suggested as prognosis for improvement is poor . . . maintain client in a protected environment as he can never function independently" . . .

By the time I had got to know Bobby as a friend, I was not shocked when his peers (in the board and care facility) reported that Bobby talked as well as you or I but "you [the researchers] just didn't understand him." As far as the general population of the facility was concerned, Bobby had "no communica-tion problems" and "talked fine" . . .

With his friends at the board and care facility Bob was more relaxed, more assured, more knowledgeable about the affairs going on around him, more willing to volunteer remarks and literally pronounced utterances more clearly and forcefully. Within the "strange" world of the clinic . . . he was tense, lacked confidence, was frustrated at not being understood, did not participate and, when he spoke, enunciated poorly and failed to project his voice . . .

In some areas, communication assessment for example, the very logic of the procedures contributed to "Bobby's" incompetencies. In one interview he was asked to communicate with a stranger without aid from one of his more verbal intimates. The task, as he and I knew, was problematic if not an impossibility under the circumstances. While I can recall how little I understood of Bobby's speech when I first met him, I can also remember, after getting to know him better, sitting in during a clinical interview and getting incredibly frustrated at the inability of the interviewer to understand what were to me clear and sensible utterances from Bobby. To identify with Bobby's position one need only imagine that every time he would open his mouth, persons would take the utterances as gibberish (Goode, 1984: 234–237).

Clinicians made Bobby a different person than did his friends in the board and care facility. Each group also interacted differently with Bobby. Out of those diverse identities and interactions, Bobby acted differently toward the clinicians and toward his friends. His actions supported the identities each group had made for him. Bobby became what the clini-cians and his friends knew him to be.

We need not, and often do not, behave in ways that fulfill the beliefs that other people hold about us, that fit the identities they know we possess. However, to the extent that other people act toward us in ways consistent with their beliefs of us, it becomes more difficult for us to act other than they know us to be. And even when we do so (according to the understandings of still others), the people may be very unlikely to understand that we have done so. A potential self-fulfilling prophecy is set in motion (Merton, 1957). Often that prophecy involves spoiled identities for people with disabilities.

Spoiled Identities

When people with and without disabilities encounter each other, the interaction may often be awkward, uneasy, inhibited, strained. But, of course, it need not be—and isn't always. But when it is, the stigmatization of disabled people may be the strain. Disabled people have been "reduced in . . . (the) minds (of the other participants) from a whole and usual person to a tainted, discounted one . . . (They) are not quite human" (Goffman, 1963: 3, 5).

In short-term, impersonal, public encounters with nondisabled people, those with disabilities may be uncertain how they will be treated. Will they be treated as ordinary persons with a variety of attributes, or will their disabilities become stigmatized master statuses, which over-shadow their other attributes? Will their stigmatization based on their disabilities spread to other realms of their existence so that a particular variation (others would say limitation) in functioning now becomes a more generalized incompetence? Will they become simply another instance of a category of disabled people to whom nondisabled people will indiscriminately apply past experiences with other disabled people or conceptions of that category? If others act civilly toward them, is it genuine or is it merely a matter of manners? In short, will they be accepted or (subtly) rejected? For others with disabilities, past experiences underlie their all too certain predictions about present and future encounters (Goffman, 1963).

Nondisabled people may be equally uncertain of what will transpire, but for differing reasons. With relatively little experience interacting with disabled people, they may be unsure of what to do. For example, should they offer assistance or not? Should they acknowledge the disability or not (Sagatun, 1985)? Assuming that those with disabilities are greatly different from them (part of our larger social construction) compounds their uncertainty. Yet, even if they "know" how to act, they may be unconfident that they know so (Fichten, 1988). Wishing to act in a way acceptable to those with disabilities, they may unknowingly act offensively, patronizing disabled people with unwanted sympathy (Makas, 1988). And if those without disabilities have less regard for disabled people, they may wish to have little to do with those who are inferior, even repugnant to them.

Hence, encounters between disabled and nondisabled people are pregnant with potential problems. Consequently, those with and without disabilities manage these fateful encounters in various ways. To do so, they manage their identities and help produce identities for their interactional partners. Many of the strategies (particularly those that students of disability have focused on) separate disabled and nondisabled people—from their experienced selves, from one another, from the possibility of developing deeper, more meaningful relations and identities. Other strategies eventually bind disabled and nondisabled people.

Disabled People's Managing Stigma

Disabled people may cope with their potential stigmatization in various ways (See Goffman, 1963; Elliott et al., 1982; Jones et al., 1984). *Passing, covering, and disavowal* are three major approaches.

Those whose disabilities are not readily apparent may present themselves as nondisabled. By concealing their disabilities, they create for others a nondisabled identity. They avoid their anticipated stigmatization. Wearing long pants to conceal an artificial leg; having a hearing aid in the frame of eyeglasses; using timing, rhythm, and judicious selection and rearrangement of words to conceal stuttering; or keeping quiet about epilepsy on an employment application may enable some with disabilities to be taken by others as nondisabled (Petrunik and Shearing, 1983; Schneider and Conrad, 1983; Kaiser, Freeman, and Wingate, 1985). Some may use "disidentifiers" that attest to their being "normal," such as a job for those previously served within a mental health facility. Others may present the signs of their disabilities as indications of other, less stigmatizing disabilities. If so, then the disabled people are not passing as nondisabled, but as disabled in a way different than they know themselves to be. A hearing impaired person may encourage others to see him or her as absentminded or as a daydreamer. In order to pass as nondisabled, those with disabilities may confide in a small set of nondisabled people— family and friends—who then participate in the deception. Minimizing contact with nondisabled people may enable disabled people to keep their disabilities secret. And nondisabled people may act as if the disabled person has no disability in order to produce a counterfeit secrecy (Ponse, 1977). Thus, parents may act as if the seizures by their child with epilepsy were nothing to notice—just "fainting fits" (Schneider and Conrad, 1980: 36). In this case, the counterfeit secrecy keeps the person with the disability "in the dark."

Those who pass may encounter various pitfalls (Goffman, 1963: 83–86). The deceptions may grow larger and more complex in order to keep the disability secret. Thus, a person who was previously in a mental health facility may have to invent an ever-grander story to conceal stretches of time when he or she was unemployed. Passers may inadvertently be identified as having other shortcomings, some potentially more damaging than the actual disability. A person with mild cerebral palsy may be mistaken for being drunk or a visually impaired person for being clumsy. Those who pass leave themselves open to hear what others think of people with their disabilities, which may be more honesty (or is it insensitivity?) than they can presently endure. They may also become uncertain about who knows what about them. Is it only those they told or do others now know—and what do they know? Those who pass may often be "on," having to be alert to the social interaction so that their disabilities do not abruptly appear. Instead of being able to take social interaction for granted, to participate casually, they may need always to plan ahead. Those who attempt to conceal their stuttering may look ahead to what they will say next, trying to figure how best to express themselves without revealing their selves (Petrunik and Shearing, 1983). Of course, disabled people who pass can be found out which may involve three "strikes" against them—their stigmatized disabilities are now known, so is their deception, and, last, their "lack of regard" for the understanding and sensitivity of the nondisabled people is exposed, too. Minimizing contact also minimizes the opportunities to live a fuller, richer life. As one person who stuttered noted:

> I never went to the dances at school because I was afraid of stuttering and looking silly. Because I didn't go, I didn't learn to dance or mix socially. I always felt bad when people would ask me if I was going to a dance or party. I would make up some excuse or say that I didn't want to go. I felt that people thought I was some sort of creep because I didn't go. Each time I wouldn't go because of my fears, I felt even weirder (Petrunik and Shearing, 1983: 128).

Finally, those who pass may feel ambivalent about themselves. They live double lives but may not be comfortable with either one. They may be torn between who they know themselves to be and who they are known to be to others. Instead of embracing their selves, they deny their selves to others. Who are they?

Ironically, even when passing is personally successful, it may be a social failure. When those with disabilities successfully pass as nondisabled, they do not provide the opportunity for nondisabled people to reassess their beliefs about disabled people. Through interaction nondisabled people may develop more positive views of disabled people, but passing prevents such possibilities (Link and Cullen, 1986).

Other disabled people may choose not to pass or they may not be able to pass, their disabilities being quite evident. Instead, they may try to cover their disabilities, lessening the impact of their disabilities in the interaction with nondisabled people and for their identities (Goffman, 1963: 102–104). Many who do not attempt to pass do routinely cover. Strategies that enable those with disabilities to pass can be used to cover. For example, disabled college students who cannot pass may dress similarly to nondisabled peers. At least their clothing does not make them stand out. Others, however, may dress distinctively to lessen the focus on their disabilities. Clothing may also cover catheters, braces, and other para-phernalia that accompany the disabilities (Kaiser, Freeman, and Wingate, 1985). Additional strategies are possible, too. Visually impaired people may refrain in front of others from putting their noses to newspapers in order to read, or they may "look at" those with whom they talk. Individuals who move in wheelchairs may check if they can maneuver easily throughout a restaurant, office or other enclosed space so as not to bring unwanted attention to themselves, or they may position themselves behind tables or near chairs when conversing with others. Deaf speakers may depend on hearing companions to signal them when they speak too softly or too loudly. When covering, disabled people attempt to downplay their disability.

Many people with disabilities, unwilling to accept a spoiled identity, disavow their stigmatization. They attempt to break through others' stereotypes and stigmatization. By revealing their disabilities where they are not easily evident, they also learn sooner rather than later how others think of them. If others are going to be put off by their disabilities, then perhaps it is better to learn that early in a relationship (Schneider and Conrad, 1980).

In disavowing their spoiled identities, disabled people may build upon the civil, superficial acceptance they often receive from non-disabled people. They do so in order to develop a more satisfying relation. Through continuing interaction, disabled people may call attention to their disabilities so that they do not remain known-about-but-unacknowledged obstacles. They may do so humorously or by referring to their disabilities from an "insider's" perspective (e.g., referring to themselves as "cripples"). By doing so, they attempt to acknowledge and lessen the uneasiness of the nondisabled individuals. They reveal the complexity of their selves. If the disabled and nondisabled people break through the laters' stereotypes, they may be able to establish a fuller, more regular relationship. They may do so in one of (at least) two ways. The nondisabled persons may "overnormalize" the disabled people, not attending to the constraints encountered by disabled people in a world not built for them (e.g., overlooking that a restaurant may not be accessible). More satisfyingly, the nondisabled individuals may join the disabled people in a skepticism of the world of nondisabled people. Together they may recognize that some nondisabled people speak of opportunity for disabled individuals but provide only meager handouts for which disabled people are expected to be grateful, that nondisabled people may worship appearance to their own detriment, that other nondisabled people are rewarded for seemingly selflessly "helping the handicapped" when they are paternalistically controlling the lives of disabled people, and so on. The disabled and nondisabled individuals who have broken through share a jaundiced view of the oppressive making of disability. They recognize, even embrace, the legitimacy of living and being disabled, whatever the disabled people make that to be. Through disavowal, disabled people attempt to develop mutually respectful relations with nondisabled people (Davis, 1961).

Nondisabled People's Managing Stigma

Nondisabled people, likewise, manage their encounters with disabled people (see Elliott et al., 1982). Some minimize their contact with disabled people, either avoiding them or, if that is not possible, ignoring them. Thus, when visiting local schools, school district administrators may avoid the classrooms in which special education students are located. Or, a waiter may ask the companion of a disabled person what the disabled person would like to eat. Those who use such strategies may justify their practices by generalizing the taint of the disability to a wider incompetence and undesirability. They may fear that the stigma of the disabled person will become their stigma as well, a discrediting by association. Or they may take unrelated, minor "shortcomings" (such as misunderstanding what was said, being nervous, or being "emotional") or "quirks" of the disabled person (that we all possess but often pay little attention to) and emphasize them as further proof of the disabled person's being radically different from them (Elliott et al., 1982). What we give little thought to when interacting with nondisabled people we may give great weight to when interacting with disabled people.

> If people are mindless much of the time in their day-to-day interactions, they may have a very abstracted notion of normal. That is, so much repeated experience with normals may result in mindlessness with respect to individual idiosyncracies . . . That is, tics, gestures, and other physical characteristics are typically not noticed in a mindless interaction with a normal person. However, thoroughly typical characteristics should be noticed in a mindful interaction — for example, when interacting with someone who is disabled. Thus these accurate perceptions should be evaluated as atypical, since they typically go unnoticed (Langer and Chanowitz, 1988: 77–78).

Others may ignore the disability, which may be difficult if the disability is prominent in the interaction and may be dangerous if the constraints of the disability are not taken into account in arranging activities. Ignoring the disability may enable a superficial acceptance to develop, but until it is acknowledged and given meaning it always lurks in the interactional background.

Lowering their expectations of the disabled person, some nondisabled people accommodate the presumed limitations of the disabled person. Nondisabled people do for disabled people and praise greatly modest accomplishments. While such patronizing does not enable disabled people to be equal partners in the interaction, at least it includes them in the interaction. For example, a principal stopped in the hall during a change of class a thirteen-year-old boy, who is educated in a mainstream class for "trainable mentally retarded" students:

> Billy does not have a hearing impairment, but Mr. P(eters) talks to him as if he does. In a very loud voice he says, "How was the trip to the vocational program?" Mr. Peters has a big smile on his face and appears to be self-conscious in Billy's presence. Many people are looking at Mr. Peters and Billy because it is unusual for the principal to stop someone in the middle of the busy hall to talk.
>
> Billy is red in the face and grinning ear to ear. Mr. Peters continues, "You go down town." He is still speaking loudly. He puts his hand on Billy's shoulder and gives a patting motion. He pronounces his words as if he were talking to a non-English speaker. He talks in broken English. Billy, who now has his head down and is blushing, responds, "Yha."
>
> Mr. Peters remarks further, "Going down to shop hey. Hey, I saw the bird feeder you are making and it is absolutely fantastic. You're going to have to go into business." Turning to the teacher's aide, Mr. P. continues, "Did you see

Billy's bird house? Fantastic. If it were big enough, it would be nice enough to live in yourself" (Bogdan and Biklen, 1985: 34).

Some may see the disabled person with whom they are interacting as the exception to the general category of disabled people—and still others may work to develop an accepting relation, "even" with those disabled people who are most severely impaired.

Developing accepting relations

While much has been written about the stigmatization and rejection of disabled people by those without disabilities, sustained, accepting relations develop, too (see Bogdan and Taylor, 1987, 1989 and Taylor and Bogdan, 1989 for the bases of the following discussion). Perhaps a focus on impersonal, public encounters (often through one-time experiments) has led many observers to emphasize rejection without attending to the development of more varied, often accepting relations.

At least four bases exist for the development of accepting relations: family, religious commitment, humanitarian concern, and feelings of friendship. Whether that family orientation is based on birth, marriage, adoption or foster placement, it "appears to be the most pervasive and most enduring (sentiment of acceptance) in our current society" (Bogdan and Taylor, 1987: 37). While certainly conflict exists within families with a disabled member, "being a family" with a brother, sister, mother, father, or whomever who is disabled provides a basis upon which a valued relationship may develop. A religious commitment or appeal to spiritual values may underlie some people's acceptance of disabled people. For still others, humanitarian concerns from helping those in need to righting wrongs are a basis for accepting relations. Those who are professional human service workers may go beyond their official provider-client relationship and develop deeper attachments. Finally, friendships, involving a reciprocal liking of one another, may grow out of relationships that began on other grounds. For example, the director of an agency that serves disabled people, commented:

> Joan and I are genuine friends . . . I like her. We have similar interests in music, watching people. We are both physically slow, not athletes, and we don't like physically aggressive activities. We enjoy each other. I, we will keep in touch with each other when I leave my job here (Taylor and Bogdan, 1989:32).

While these four orientations underlie the development of accepting relations, the orientations may change as the relationships develop (for example, from primarily a humanitarian stance to one of friendship), and a mix of sentiments may become the basis for the accepting relations.

Accepting relations do not develop immediately. While accepting relations develop in various ways, they seem to develop in stages in which the disability and presumed differences may be initially central to the relationship, but eventually similarities become prominent and differences become positive rather than negative. (Recall the previous discussion of disavowal.) The disabled and nondisabled partners break through the presumed differences and uncertainty to a deeper, accepting relationship. First encounters are colored by the differences, but if an accepting relation is to develop, continued contact occurs, perhaps due to obligations (of family or work) or due to an initial attraction. The nondisabled person becomes more comfortable with the disabled person, beginning to see beyond the stereotypes to the individual with a disability. Comfort increases and the nondisabled person may come to believe that he/she understands what disability means to the disabled person, something that others without this relationship could not understand. They come to share a bemused, perhaps skeptical or contemptuous stance toward those who stigmatize disabled people, hold to mistaken notions about disabilities, or are awkward in the presence of disabled people. They question the concerns of nondisabled people, such as their great emphasis on superficial appearances. And the nondisabled person emphasizes positive features of the disabled person, perhaps regarding favorably differences that others would see negatively (Bogdan and Taylor, 1987; Davis, 1961).

For example, the relationship that Jim, a mentally retarded individual, and Mike, a former volunteer at a social service agency where Jim was a client, developed illustrates how disabled and nondisabled people may create caring relationships. They see each other at least once a week and talk regularly on the phone.

> At first (Mike) wasn't sure how to behave. He knew Jim was mentally retarded, and this "fact" dominated his thoughts. He did not want to say anything that might offend him, but he had some concerns about him. He thought that he might not have the ability to control his moods and that he was in danger because of latent violence. He was also concerned that Jim would become dependent on him. In addition, Jim's behavior and speech patterns were different enough that he had trouble understanding him. He also thought that Jim would feel awkward around his wife and friends, and they would feel awkward around him.
>
> Mike was cautious at first, but after a few encounters he began feeling more

comfortable with the idea of Jim as a friend. He felt less self-conscious about his label and began enjoying him. He especially appreciated Jim's candor. As he put it, Jim seemed to have an uncanny ability to "cut through the bullshit" of life . . . Mike also appreciated the fact that Jim talked about his feelings and, on occasion, cried. He saw Jim as having many of the attributes he respected in men, but were too often missing.

Jim shared stories of the abuse he had experienced and the shame he had felt when he was ridiculed for being dumb. The two began talking about Jim's life and the label mental retardation, and they even began joking about it. As the relationship evolved, Mike increasingly questioned what the label of mental retardation could tell him about Jim. Jim had talents and sensitivities that the term "mental retardation" did not capture.

As Mike got to know Jim better, he introduced him to his wife and invited him to dinner at the house. While Mike's family is not as close to Jim as he is, they do consider him a friend. Mike feels that he has a special relationship with Jim that his other friends might not fully appreciate. While he did not withdraw from his other friendships, his relationship with Jim remained separate from his other friendship groups (Bogdan and Taylor, 1987: 38).

Written from the viewpoint of Mike, the nondisabled partner, the above passage suggests that when disabled and nondisabled people develop a caring relation that the nondisabled partner must do much of the work, changing his or her understandings and guiding the development of the relationship. But that is probably not so. (Again, recall the discussion of disavowal.) Instead, disabled people may shoulder much of the interactional responsibility — making initial encounters with nondisabled people go smoothly, putting up with the uncertainty and even the unintentional slights of the nondisabled partner, eventually enabling nondisabled people to see beyond their stereotypes to the individuals before them (Davis, 1961; Fisher and Galler, 1988). After all, disabled people continually encounter these interactional challenges; nondisabled people do not. If caring relationships have developed, then typically disabled and nondisabled people have mutually worked to create them.

However, in relationships with severely (cognitively) disabled people, nondisabled (or less disabled) people may have more of the responsibility for establishing an accepting relation (though more careful scholarship is needed). Just as nondisabled people spoil those who are disabled, particularly those known as severely disabled, so too can they "make" them richly human.

Consider Jean, a twenty-year-old woman who cannot walk or talk (her name and those of her surrogate parents that follow are pseudonyms):

Her clinical records describe her as having cerebral palsy and being profoundly retarded. Her thin, short—four feet long, forty pounds—body, atrophied
legs, and disproportionately large head make her a very unusual sight. Her
behavior is equally strange. She drools, rolls her head, and makes seemingly
incomprehensible high pitched sounds...Some scholars and professionals
would argue that Jean and others like her lack the characteristics of a human
being...(but) to Mike and Penny Brown...Jean's surrogate parents for the
past six years, she is their loving and lovable daughter, fully part of the family
and fully human (Bogdan and Taylor, 1989: 138).

How is that possible?

Instead of using a fault-finding perspective (Goode, 1984: 232) that
sets disabled people (and all people) against a rigidly narrow notion of
being nondisabled/"normal," Mike and Penny Brown and others who
make severely disabled people fully human use an alternative human-
enhancing perspective composed of four dimensions: "(1) attributing
thinking to the other, (2) seeing individuality in the other, (3) viewing
the other as reciprocating, and (4) defining social place for the other"
(Bogdan and Taylor, 1989: 138).

Nondisabled people who know their severely disabled partner to be
human attribute thinking to their partner. Even though the severely
disabled partners may move extremely little and make minimal sounds,
their nondisabled partners know that they can reason and express their
reasoning. For example, a completely paralyzed young boy only makes
"slight in and out movements with his tongue and slow back and forth
rolling of his blind eyes," movements considered involuntary by professionals (Bogdan and Taylor, 1989: 139). However, the paralyzed young
boy's foster parents see their son change the speed of his tongue movement when certain people enter his room and occassionally "look" toward
the person who is talking. To the parents, this is an indication that their
foster son can hear and recognize others even though professionals have
said that he cannot understand or communicate.

Nondisabled people who have formed caring relations with severely
disabled individuals see their disabled partners as unique individuals.
They understand their severely disabled partners to have likes and dis-
likes, to have different personality traits, and to have feelings and motives
(which crying, laughing and other outward signs "attest" to). Recall from
the Introduction Breta, a "deaf-blind, alingual, nonambulatory, retarded"
twelve year old, who transferred "massive amounts of saliva to objects
before touching them more thoroughly" and was referred to by one of

her teachers as "slug-like" (Goode, 1984: 238, 239). Her mother thought Breta was beautiful and claimed that her daughter communicated with her "completely." Everyday incidents led the social scientist (who knew Chris and Bobby) to realize that Breta's mother made sense, a more useful sense than the sympathetic teacher who referred to Breta as "slug-like." As the social scientist remarked about one such incident:

> Once, when I was having trouble giving Breta her milk during one of my initial attempts at mealtime, Betty turned to me and remarked, "Oh, you're using the wrong cup, that's why she's making a fuss." And, as was usual, after supplying me with the correct cup, the problems with Breta ceased (Goode, 1984: 241).

The nondisabled partners create a life history for the disabled person, often a before and after story—before the relationship was formed, especially if the disabled person was institutionalized, and then after the relationship developed. The life history tells how the disabled person survived the dehumanizing institutionalization and now is improving, even thriving. And nondisabled individuals manage the disabled person's appearance in order to lessen differences and accentuate characteristics consistent with who the nondisabled people know their partners to be (e.g., frilly dresses for a feminine little girl). Stigmatized categories the disabled people are not.

Whether through the expansion of their lives due to their relationship with the severely disabled individual, companionship, making them a better person, seeing progress in the competence of the disabled person, or still yet other ways, the nondisabled people understand their relationships with their disabled partners to be reciprocal. They receive as well as give.

Finally, nondisabled people make the severely disabled partners integral members of their social group, such as their families. The foster child becomes "our daughter," and "our daughter" participates in family activities. A firm social place is created for the severely disabled individual. Thus, just as we can make disabled people not people at all, so, too, can we make the most severely disabled as human as any person. Whichever we do has enormous consequences for all of us. But neither outcome is determined by the "impairments" and other individual attributes of the disabled people.

Identities and interaction are interrelated. In interaction with one another, people with and without disabilities create identities. In turn, the identities "inform" the ongoing interaction. Nondisabled people often spoil disabled people's identities. Yet, disabled people may resist that damage. However, like nondisabled people, disabled people are also concerned with successfully accomplishing their transactions whether or not their identities become spoiled. They attempt to order food in a restaurant, attend classes, go to a movie, obtain information from a clerk, and the like. Identities are made in these transactions, but making identities, particularly countering spoiled identities, is not all that concerns disabled people.

Navigating Encounters

When people with disabilities encounter those without disabilities, stigma is not disabled people's only concern. Successfully accomplishing the transaction is important, as it is for anyone. Disabled people purchase items, order meals, carry on conversations, move with other people, and conduct other transactions. To navigate successfully those encounters, disabled people may show little regard for being stigmatized, but still a great deal of concern with their identities. Think of visually impaired people who use guide dogs or canes in order literally to navigate their environment. They identify themselves as disabled (and potentially stigmatized) in order to get about successfully. To make an identity acceptable to others and to accomplish the transaction may at times be incompatible. When they are, the former need not take priority over the latter (Petrunik and Shearing, 1983: 136).

Encounters between those with and without disabilities are potentially problematic *not* only, or even primarily, because of the disabled people's disabilities. Instead, the (potential for) disruption arises out of the taken for granted practices and beliefs that underlie interaction and which typically work well. However, when people unthinkingly use them in interaction with disabled people, disruptions may occur. A "breach in the taken-for-granted interactional order has occurred" (Higgins, 1980: 146). Nondisabled people assume the disruptions to be the consequence of the disabilities, at times even part of the essence of the disabilities. Instead, by applying inappropriate assumptions or using inadequate strategies, we produce the disruptions. Disabled people (as well as nondisabled people) may try to restore the interactional order which has broken down or prevent its disruption. To do so, disabled people do need to manipulate their identities, but they do so not necessarily with stigma in mind. Consider those with communicative disabilities.

Communicative Disabilities/Conversational Disruptions

Conversation is built upon the assumption of an "easy exchange of speaker-hearer role" (Goffman, 1974: 498). However, this and other conversational assumptions (Higgins, 1980: 148) may be very inappropriate when applied to those with communicative disabilities. Consequently, people with hearing impairments, those who stutter, and others with communicative disabilities often experience disruptions or the potential for disruptions (Higgins, 1980; Petrunik and Shearing, 1983; Sweidel, 1989). Nevertheless, people with communicative disabilities may take into account these assumptions in order to prevent or repair disruptions.

For example, we typically take conversational pauses by others as an indication that we may resume our talking. This assumption may not apply well to people who stutter. Those who stutter may manage this potential disruption by "making two claims: first, that they are competent persons who understand the conventions of talk; and second, that they have not relinquished their speaking turn—even though they are lapsing into unusually long silences—and should be permitted to continue speaking uninterrupted" (Petrunik and Shearing, 1983: 131).

Through confronting a block "head on" or through voluntary disclosure, those who stutter attempt to make those two conversational claims and thereby preserve interactional order. By trying to "force out the word or sound" through a "deep breath followed by muscle tension and visible strain," stutterers attempt to "break through" the interruption (Petrunik and Shearing, 1983: 131). By visibly struggling with this "mysterious intrusive force," stutterers tell conversational partners that they are still talking and that they are trying their best to limit interruptions (Petrunik and Shearing, 1983: 131).

However, observers who realize that their interactional partners are stuttering may not know how to proceed. Should they finish the stutterers' sentences, avoid looking at the stutterers, or fill the long pauses in some way? Consequently, through voluntary disclosure, stutterers may "instruct" their listeners. They tell their listeners what to expect so that they will not be taken aback when the stuttering starts. They may suggest how listeners can fill the pauses, as did one professor who told his students to catch up on their note-taking during his stuttering. Those who stutter may even intentionally stutter so that their listeners will not later expect better fluency than those who stutter can typically achieve. While stutterers are certainly concerned about their identities, and at times limit or modify greatly their interactions in order to avoid being stigmatized, stigmatization is not their only concern. Successfully accomplishing the everyday transactions of life is important, too (Petrunik and Shearing, 1983).

So, too, is it for those with hearing impairments. Deaf people routinely participate in problematic or potentially problematic encounters (Higgins, 1980: Chapter 6). They do so because hearing people take it for granted that everyone can hear and speak and that "nothing unusual is happening." All of us typically assume that nothing unusual is happening, even in what later become known as problematic situations (Emerson, 1970). Hence, hearing people assume that those with whom they interact are typical hearers and speakers. Of course, deaf people are not. Consequently, hearing people may mistake deaf people for uncooperative hearing people, even tragically so as in a fatal shooting where a deaf person could not obey a robber's demands. Hearing people may unthinkingly leave a deaf person out of the conversation as they turn to talk with someone else. Or making the assumption that speaking and hearing go together, which they do but not invariably so, hearing people may be amazed that the now recognized deaf person can speak so well. Or the hearing person may no longer be able to understand the deaf person (because after all deaf people cannot speak). Deaf people who speak to hearing people may be spoken to in return, even when they tell the hearing people that they are deaf. (If you speak well you must be able to hear well.) Or, they may be mistaken for being foreign because their speech sounds unusual to the hearing listener. Of course, the assumption that nothing unusual is happening may crumble in the face of conversational disruptions.

As do all people, deaf people attempt to transact successfully their encounters with others. They may be able to maintain hearing people's assumption that nothing unusual is happening by nodding, smiling, and in other ways pretending to understand what is spoken to them. Unimportant conversations may be handled this way, though such conversations could turn important without deaf people realizing so. By being alive to other features of the encounter, deaf people can successfully manage the interaction; for example, by handing the clerk enough money to cover the purchase or by positioning themselves to see the total on the cash register. Speechreading may enable deaf people to substitute one sense for another, but speechreading is frought with many potential difficulties—poor sight lines to speakers, sounds that look similar on the lips, well intentioned hearing people who move closer to deaf people or speak loudly and with distortion, etc. When hearing friends order for deaf friends in a restaurant, signal them that their voices are too loud or soft, or collude with them in other ways, they are assisting deaf people in maintaining the stance that nothing unusual is happening.

However, often it is not possible nor desirable to sustain the impression that nothing unusual is happening. Instead, deaf people actively manage the understanding that something unusual is happening. They may openly disclose that they are deaf and then attempt through gestures or writing to proceed. However, hearing people may be uncomfortable with such novel conversational procedures or still rely on the assumption that everyone is a competent hearer/speaker. Deaf people may use children, hearing friends, or other third parties to act as go-betweens, interpreting the conversation between the deaf people and the naive hearing people. However, go-betweens may become involved in complex or private matters that should not be their business, or hearing people may focus their attention on the go-between, not the deaf persons. Deaf people become left out of their own conversations. Or deaf people may manipulate the impression held by hearing people of what is happening. For example, those deaf people who are mistakenly identified as hearing when they use their speech may in brief encounters write their messages to hearing people. In order to transact the encounter successfully, these deaf people are displaying themselves as less competent than they are. Or, some whose speech becomes unintelligible after hearing people learn of their deafness may wear a hearing aid in order to maintain understandable speech. Their speech has not changed, but hearing people's understanding of them has. Now, they are hard of hearing people who can speak acceptably instead of deaf people who cannot. Of course, wearing a hearing aid to combat one potential disruption may lead to others as the hearing people shout or move closer to the deaf people (Higgins, 1980: Chapter 6). However, others hope that by displaying their hearing aid, hearing people may speak more slowly and less softly. This could assist those who depend on their residual hearing and speechreading to understand spoken conversations (Lynas, 1986: 233).

People with other communicative disabilities also face transactional disruptions. Those who use a communication aid to express themselves may find their interactional partners slowing their speech, using a lot of gestures, raising their voices, repeating themselves, and the like. Assuming that hearing and speaking go together, their interactional partners assume that those who use communication aids to express themselves have difficulty hearing. The interactional partners may also get no feedback, such as "I see" or "um-hmm," from the users of communicative aids that they would understand as indicating comprehension. The partners may have difficulty reading the body language of the user of communication aids or generalize the inability to talk well to the inability to think well, an assumption that has also created difficulties for deaf people (Sweidel, 1989: 168). Other difficulties may occur, too.

The interactional partners may try to manage these disruptions. By indicating that they recognize a disruption has occurred, utilizing a standard phrase such as "new word," explaining how the communication system works, and in other ways, the nonvocal individuals manage the conversational difficulties. Through repeating or writing the letters or words as the nonvocal person produces them, asking the nonvocal person to establish the tone of the conversation (e.g., humorous or serious), using context to fill-in the nonvocal person's message, and through other strategies, the vocal people, too, may try to minimize the disruptions (Sweidel, 1989: 173–174; Phillips, 1985: 51–53).

But note, these and other disruptions that nonvocal and vocal people, and more broadly those with communicative disabilities and those without, experience and manage are not produced merely by the communicative disabilities but by the actions of the interactional partners. These actions "help" create the communicative limitations that the nondisabled interactional partners assume inhere in the disabled people.

When interacting with nondisabled people, those with disabilities are concerned about their identities, but they are also concerned with successfully navigating the encounters. To do the latter does involve the making and displaying of identities, but it need not focus on managing spoiled identities. Managing spoiled identities and successfully accomplishing the transaction may be in conflict. Disabled people, like nondisabled people, may need to make fateful choices about how they will proceed.

Conclusion

Through interaction people with and without disabilities create one another's identities and manage the interaction based on the identities they have made. Nondisabled people often spoil disabled people's identities, making them tainted, even less than fully human. In managing that stigmatization, disabled and nondisabled people may create accepting relations. However, managing spoiled identities is not the only concern of disabled people. They, like nondisabled people, navigate their everyday encounters in order to accomplish successfully the transaction.

The interplay between identities and interaction seems to be an interpersonal phenomenon, being performed by the particular disabled and nondisabled participants. However, the interplay arises out of larger social arrangements and practices created by others. The interplay is very much a social phenomenon. Throughout the book I explore some of those larger social arrangements and practices. Here, I briefly conclude with some illustrations of the social basis for the interplay between identities and interaction.

Consider the fault-finding, stigmatizing orientation (Goode, 1984: 232) that so many nondisabled people bring to an encounter with disabled people. That orientation is a product of diverse practices and policies. It is a result of our framing that individualizes disability (Chapter 1). It arises out of how we depict those with disabilities through negation (i.e., "not able") and portray them as monstrous, evil, criminal, maladjusted or in other dehumanizing ways (Chapter 3). It flows from the servicing paradigm, in which defective people are to be fixed, which underlies much of our assistance to people with disabilities (Chapter 6). It is a product of our "disability policy" that has created a society that does not suit the great variation of its people (Chapter 7). And it develops out of still other practices and policies. That fault-finding orientation is not any individual's singular achievement.

Or, we know that continued, equal status contact in which those with and without disabilities cooperate in small groups to achieve common goals promotes best the development of accepting relations between those with and without disabilities, as it does between members of different ethnic or racial groups (Yuker, 1988; Higgins, 1990: 118). But consider how infrequently we create such contact. Instead, we routinely segregate disabled people from nondisabled people, often still in large institutions; place dozens of disabled people in a community residential facility without building those small cooperative groups with nondisabled citizens; permit those released from mental health facilities to wander aimlessly without any secure social place; grudgingly, tentatively, and only marginally mainstream disabled youth in public schools; develop special recreational activities for disabled children; and in still other ways create social arrangements that are opposite of those conducive for the development of caring relations.

Further, and much more serious, we have created communities, businesses, government organizations, schools, and other social worlds so large that it is difficult for many of us, disabled or not, to develop deep, personal relations among one another. (Compare our large schools of thousands of students with one of several hundred.) We are creating massive worlds in which we estrange ourselves from one another (Harris, 1981). Our "disability policy" and more fundamentally our creation of our society makes interaction perilous for disabled and nondisabled people.

Contrast our world to small scale, traditional societies. In such societies disabled and nondisabled people interact routinely. They are tied together by kinship, common residence, similar activities, and in still other ways. Nondisabled people know disabled people as individuals with diverse characteristics who occupy a secure social position in the community, not impersonally and through stereotypes. While disabled people do not live easy lives in simpler societies and can experience extreme rejection, even death, the social basis for their interaction with nondisabled people is conducive to being identified as complex, unique individuals (Scheer and Groce, 1988). We cannot "return" to simpler societies. However, we can think seriously about creating communities, neighborhoods, schools, businesses, and other organizations that enable all of us to interact cooperatively in smaller groups. We do not have to live in large, impersonal worlds (Harris, 1981). Thus, we should not overlook our larger social practices and policies when we explore the interplay between disabled people's identities and their interaction with nondisabled individuals.

Through interacting with one another and developing identities of each other, people with and without disabilities develop their *experiences* of disability. I take that up next.

Chapter 5

EXPERIENCING DISABILITY

We experience disabilities in diverse ways. However, the disabilities do not dictate our experiences. Instead, people with and without disabilities make their experiences as they live and act with others. Disabled people may experience disability very differently than do nondisabled people.

Consider Professor Sam Suppalla, who is deaf and whose parents and several older brothers are deaf. He and his family are not merely hearing impaired; they are also Deaf. (The uppercase "D" is being increasingly used by social scientists and community advocates to denote deaf people who communicate through American Sign Language and share a culture based on that language.) However, as a child enveloped in his family, he experienced neither his hearing impairment nor his Deafness as a "remarkable condition" until he became friends with a hearing girl next door:

(Sam) had never lacked for playmates; he was born into a Deaf family with several Deaf older brothers. As his interests turned to the world outside his family, he noticed a girl next door who seemed to be about his age. After a few tentative encounters, they became friends. She was a satisfactory playmate, but there was a problem of her "strangeness." He could not talk with her as he could with his older brothers and parents. She seemed to have extreme difficulty understanding even the simplest or crudest gestures. After a few futile attempts to converse, he gave up and instead pointed when he wanted something, or simply dragged her along with him if he wanted to go somewhere. He wondered what strange affliction his friend had, but since they had developed a way to interact with each other, he was content to accommodate to her peculiar needs.

One day, Sam remembers vividly, he finally understood that his friend was indeed odd. They were playing in her home, when suddenly her mother walked up to them and animatedly began to move her mouth. As if by magic, the girl picked up a dollhouse and moved it to another place. Sam was mystified and went home to ask his mother about exactly what kind of affliction the girl next door had. His mother explained that she was HEARING and because of this did not know how to SIGN; instead she and her mother

TALK, they move their mouths to communicate with each other. Sam then asked if this girl and her family were the only ones "like that." His mother explained that no, in fact, nearly everyone else was like the neighbors. It was his own family that was unusual. It was a memorable moment for Sam. He remembered thinking how curious the girl next door was, and if she was HEARING, how curious HEARING people were (Padden and Humphries, 1988: 15–16).

Sam's experience of deafness had just "begun." No doubt, "Deaf" was a part of his sign vocabulary and matter of factly used in reference to his family and other Deaf people. Of course, he and his family signed to one another. Yet, Sam likely took for granted the sign, "Deaf," and the signing. They were unremarkable features of his world, of *the* world—or so he thought. Even his hearing impairment would have had no significance *known* to him. He was simply who he was—not deaf or Deaf. Yet all this would be changing as he came to understand how hearing people experienced deafness and how they built a world based on those experiences with which he would contend. In that world he, not the girl next door, would be unusual, though Sam had not yet learned that when the above incident occurred.

People with and without disabilities experience disability. "Experiencing" disability suggests that our feelings, thoughts, and perceptions of disability "wash over us." We live through whatever is *there* that we encounter. The disability produces the experience that we have of it. No doubt, much experience has that quality. The disability is "happening" to us, whether we are the disabled person, a family member or other intimate, or some individual who has impersonally encountered a disabled citizen. However, such a view is misleading. In whatever ways we experience disability, we *make* our experiences.

The experiences of disability are not inherent in the impairments. We give meaning to ourselves and others, we create and counter our feelings—and we do so as we encounter and respond to others and the larger worlds that have been made. As individuals we experience disability, but we do not as isolated individuals make our experiences. Experiences are socially produced, not merely individually undergone.

We may make all kinds of disability experiences. Some experiences may be difficult to make and sustain. However, we might be surprised how people can experience disabilities in ways that (from an "able-bodied" perspective) seem unrealistic, even impossible, but are fully lived.

Recall my discussion in the previous chapter of Breta, a "deaf-blind, alingual, nonambulatory, retarded" twelve year old who was called "slug-like" by one of her sympathetic teachers in reference to her transferring "massive amounts of saliva to objects before touching them more thoroughly" (Goode, 1984: 238, 239). Her mother thought Breta was beautiful and claimed that her daughter communicated with her "completely." While the social scientist who came to know Breta was sympathetic to the family, he found it difficult to take seriously Breta's mother's claim of effective communication. He could not even imagine what might be meant by that. However, after six months observing in Breta's home, he came to experience and even document what that "complete" communication was. He experienced hundred of incidents similar to the one I recounted in Chapter 4: While having difficulty giving Breta her milk, Breta's mother told him that he was using the wrong cup, which was the reason for Breta's fussing. When he used the correct cup, he and Breta had no problem (Goode, 1984: 241). His experiences of Breta changed dramatically; he came to see her beauty, though it could not be seen with the eye.

While it is difficult, even impossible, to make and sustain some experiences of disability, we presently make and sustain experiences of disability that vary more than most of us imagine and could vary even more so. Instead of deciding if experiences are "real" or not, it may be more helpful to see if experiences are more enhancing or not. We "live" our experiences, but the experiences we create for one another may more or less enrich our lives.

We develop our experiences of disability out of the complex relations we have with one another. We are children, adults, parents, spouses, and siblings. We are women and men. We are white and people of color. We are homosexual and heterosexual. We are employees and employers. We are human service providers and clients of services. We live in industrialized societies and in impoverished countries. We are so much more. We participate in complex relations with others in which disability (whatever participants have made of it) is only one feature of who we are and of our relations. This is so whether we are disabled or not.

I overlook that great complexity of experiencing disability. Thankfully, others do not (Asch and Fine, 1988: 3). In doing so, I greatly simplify the experiences of disabled people and others of them. Unfortunately, I may give the impression that to make sense of experiencing disability all we need to do is focus on what people make of their experiences of disability, as if those "disability experiences" are separated from their other experiences. I also risk the danger of creating the impression that disability is the central feature of the experiences of disabled people, their families, and of others who encounter disabled people. At times it may be, but often it is not.

Instead, we weave the threads of disability with many other threads into the tapestries of our lives as disabled people and our lives as nondisabled people who live and act with disabled people. The weave of those threads of disabilities may vary greatly in our human tapestries. In pulling those threads out to understand them, I know I am distorting those threads and the tapestries they help to make. Yet, in doing so, I believe some useful sense can be made.

We experience disability as *disabled people*, as members of *families*, and as *impersonal others* such as schoolmates, neighbors, coworkers, and citizens. While disabled people, their families, and impersonal others at times may experience disability similarly, typically they produce important differences, too. I focus on particular topics in experiencing disability for each set of participants. However, one could also explore basic issues in experiencing disability that arise for all three sets of people, even if the three sets of participants (and the individuals within each set) manage those issues differently. For example, I explore how disabled people learn to be disabled. But all of us must learn (i.e., develop) whatever significance disability has for us.

Disabled People's Experiencing Disability

Disabled people experience disability more complexly than we imagine. The experiences of disabled people are diverse, and experiencing, itself, has many features. Disabled people *learn to be disabled.* Whoever disabled people become, their experiential selves are not determined by the disabilities. When experiencing disability, disabled people experience their physical, mental, and emotional states that are made into disabilities, and they experience their encounters with others. Their *realms of experience* vary from those particular states to encounters with others, including larger social arrangements such as service agencies. Thus, discussion in the preceding and following chapters concerning the interaction between disabled and nondisabled people and the provisions of service to disabled people are useful here. Out of living disabled, people with disabilities develop *experiential orientations*, general stances toward their disabilities and themselves, which often change over time. I explore these few threads of the experiential tapestry.

Learning To Be Disabled

Disabled people learn to be who they become. Whatever disability comes to mean for disabled people, they produce it in interaction with others. Disabilities do not determine disabled people's selves. People with disabilities—with characteristics that we routinely turn into disabilities—do not automatically, "naturally" experience themselves as disabled people, even as deaf people, blind people, arthritic people and so on. Recall the early experiences of Professor Sam Suppalla with which I began this chapter.

People who become disabled may do so through several interrelated processes: the potential application of *stereotypes* about disability by people with disabilities to themselves, the *encounters* people with disabilities have with those who are not disabled, the *interaction* people with disabilities have with others "similarly" disabled, and the dealings those with disabilities have with *organizations* designed to serve them. (See Scott, 1969 for a partial basis of this approach.) In all of these processes, people who may become disabled are actively making sense of who they are and what they are encountering.

The importance of these processes varies among disabled people. For example, many people with epilepsy do not know others with epilepsy (Schneider and Conrad, 1983). Yet, for many deaf people, interaction with others who are deaf, typically first within schools (and less frequently initially in families of deaf members) is a powerful avenue for becoming a deaf person (Higgins, 1980; Padden and Humphries, 1988).

First lesson

If people become disabled, the primary lesson to be learned, both first and fundamental, is that they vary in ways that others and themselves can and do mark as (some kind of) disability. Of course, the meanings they give to that variation continue to develop over a lifetime, sometimes shifting dramatically. The teachers of this primary lesson are the disabled people themselves and others, such as family members or professionals. Through direct instruction and through personally making sense of their experiences (such as comparisons to others and reflections on prior experiences), people who become disabled learn this lesson.

For example, children who are mentally retarded may sense that they are different, but not know how or why. Those with nondisabled brothers and sisters may particularly develop this sense. They compare how they and their nondisabled siblings are treated by others. Teachers and parents may tell the children, but they may disagree about whether the children should be told before an unpleasant experience with inconsiderate others or after such an experience. They may also not be sure who should tell (teachers or parents), when the child is competent enough to be told, or how to do so. In one school the teachers in the vocational classes informed students of their mental retardation by equating it "with an inability to do the thinking and work some other people can do. Many lessons were prefaced by comments such as 'Some of you will be able to learn to do this, and some of you will not' " (Evans, 1983: 136).

Adults who gradually lose their hearing do not immediately experience their sensations as a hearing loss. As they begin to ask for repetitions, turn up the television set or radio, complain that people are talking quietly on the telephone or that the connection is bad, and are told by others that they have a hearing problem, they may redefine their experiences as a possible hearing loss. Confusion may give way to uncertainty that is reluctantly replaced with a realization that one is likely hearing impaired. A visit to the doctor (and perhaps then to a specialist), typically years after that initial and still developing realization that one is hearing differently, and the subsequent diagnosis (itself perhaps taking several visits) provide official certification of what had been suspected perhaps for years (Jones, Kyle, and Wood, 1987: Chapters 4 and 6).

Even disabling conditions that occur suddenly and seemingly incontrovertibly do not announce themselves. People must make sense of them. Those who become paralyzed give meaning to what is happening to them. Perhaps out of prior knowledge of others with apparently similar conditions, comments by doctors and others that may change, experiences of their body, and more, people who become paralyzed may over time develop changing understandings of who they are. As one young man recalled the onset of his paralysis when he was 18:

> I was at a drive-in with my girlfriend . . . and I started getting sharp pains in my back, and they started getting worse. I felt as if I was going to pass out or something. So I had her go up to the snack bar and call my parents to come and pick me up, because I didn't know what was wrong. (Eventually) . . . I couldn't move anything, my arms or my legs.
>   . . . In the first hospital there was a guy who had broken his neck and he was all right after a bunch of therapy. I figured spinal cord injuries were all the

same, that I would be like him. And there was a guy in my room that I knew and went to high school with who had broken his neck and he was all right. After a month or two he got up and left with no problems at all. I figured I would be recovering over a long period of time. That is what the doctors had told me, too, that it would take a long time to get better . . .

Then I sort of realized that they had been saying *well* for a year or two, and after that they said you will get *better*. But I was not getting any better any more . . . so I started figuring that I wouldn't get any better. Then I transferred to the next hospital and saw a lot of other disabled people who weren't recovering even years after spinal cord injury. At that point I didn't want to face it, but I knew down deep that I wasn't going to get any better (Roth, 1981: 38–41).

Learning that primary lesson, that one can be and is marked as "disabled" (as mentally retarded, deaf, permanently paralyzed, or whatever), takes effort. Those who become disabled do not learn that lesson instantly. At times, they may not learn that lesson for many years, perhaps to their detriment.

Teachers of all kinds are important in whether or not disabled people learn that primary lesson. Parents can be particularly powerful interpreters of the world for their children. At times they may be able to teach their children what most others would take to be "wrong" or "nonsensical." They may not teach what others routinely expect they will teach. Parents may teach their children who others would recognize as being disabled that they are not disabled or at least not in the manner that others would recognize. Not teaching the primary lesson to be learned in becoming disabled when others routinely expect that lesson to be taught can be troubling. The "students" may later believe that their parental teachers lied to them. Or, what the children learn may not enable the children to make satisfactory sense of their experiences:

One middle-aged woman (with epilepsy) . . . said her parents had never told her she had epilepsy: "They just told me I suffered from fainting fits." She had filled this vacuum of silence by concluding that she must be "going mad" (Schneider and Conrad, 1980: 36).

Parents are powerful teachers, but they are never the only ones.

Learning that primary lesson is a fundamental beginning. However, those who become disabled develop throughout their lifetimes much richer, more detailed, and changing understandings of who they are becoming. They do so, in part, as they grapple with common beliefs about who they are; encounter others, disabled and nondisabled; and possibly deal with agencies that serve them. Class is always in session and the teachers are many!

Teaching disability lessons

Most people with disabilities acquire them. Therefore, growing up as nondisabled people, they experience the common beliefs, the stereotypes, about disabled people as do other nondisabled people. As I explored in Chapter 3, through naming, the media, charity campaigns, and other means, we have typically portrayed disabled people as incompetent, helpless, hopeless, malevolent, and/or pitiful people. Those who acquire a disability must grapple with these stereotypes and their applicability to themselves. The stereotypes may now be personally relevant (Link et al., 1989). Being unfamiliar with disability, they may apply a fundamental negative bias to themselves—just as impersonal others are likely to apply to them. If the disability is salient, stigmatized, and unfamiliar, then newly disabled people may primarily use that negative evaluation of disability in guiding their initial thinking about themselves (Wright, 1988).

> A part of the socialization experience in any society involves learning attitudes, beliefs, and values about stigmatized people such as the blind. These beliefs concern the effects that the condition is alleged to have on personality, and how a person who becomes blind is changed because of it. It is by reference to these beliefs that a putative social identity for the blind is constructed. When the blindness belongs to ourselves, these beliefs we have acquired about blindness become internal guidelines for our own behavior. In this sense, we have all in a general way learned the role of blind man; however, for most of us, it is a role we will never have to play (Scott, 1969: 16).

However, as people become disabled, their further, diverse experiences may provide them opportunities to challenge the stereotypes. As one young woman with a collagen-vascular disorder, in which she oscillates from able-bodied to being in pain and in a wheelchair, noted:

> Being disabled is not as traumatic to me now as it was when I first became disabled, because I had twenty-two years worth of all the biases and prejudices and fears that every able-bodied person has to get past (Roth, 1981: 164–165).

Some may be able to "get past" those stereotypes, as did the woman mentioned above. As she further explained:

> When I first went into the wheelchair I didn't know what to expect of myself, but once I went into the wheelchair I realized I was still me; I mean, going into

the chair didn't change my essence. It made me realize these are human beings with disabilities, not disabled people (Roth, 1981: 165).

Others, however, may wonder if their "essences" have changed.

Family, friends, acquaintances, and strangers directly and indirectly instruct disabled people. Interactions with others provide lessons from which disabled people continually give meaning to who they are. Some lessons may be demeaning, but others are not.

For example, some parents of children with epilepsy may subtly (and unintentionally) teach their children with epilepsy that they are not capable individuals. The parents worry about the safety of their children and/or the disclosure of their epilepsy. They repeatedly remind their children to take their medicine. They continually caution their children about what they cannot and should not do. These and similar responses may heighten the significance of epilepsy for the children and "become a kind of control that isolate(s), restrict(s), and further disable(s) the children" (Schneider, 1988: 71). One young woman with epilepsy noted of her mother:

> When I go out shopping by myself, my mom worries about me. When I'm home late, my mom worries about me. When I'm taking my bath, my mom pounds on the door—"Are you all right?" "Are you all right?"—you know, to make sure . . . and that bothers me (Schneider, 1988: 70).

The same young woman believed that by being "extra careful" she probably could live on her own, separate from her parents, but she had reservations:

> The only thing that bothers me now is I have convulsions mostly in my sleep, and I'm afraid of . . . what if I swallow my tongue? What if I can't get out of this? . . . I'll die. And I feel like when my parents try to wake me up and I wouldn't wake up, you know, that would be really scary. It scares my mom, but she checks up on me (Schneider, 1988: 70).

But disabling lessons do not need to be believed. Others with epilepsy turn similar lessons by their parents into a challenge. By testing the disabling message of their parents, they determine their competence and define who they are. By "overcoming the actual or supposed limitations of epilepsy," people with epilepsy disavow the stigma their parents attach to them (Schneider, 1988: 69). Yet, I wonder if those who succeed also set themselves apart from those with epilepsy who are not able to overcome the supposed limitations? Do they create a more positive view of themselves at the expense of others with epilepsy?

Still others with epilepsy are never taught the lesson that epilepsy limits who they are and what they can do. Instead, their parents treat epilepsy as "merely" a medical condition to be controlled with medicine. It is unimportant for their lives, should not be used as an excuse for unsatisfactory performance, and is not stigmatizing (Schneider, 1988: 69).

Encounters with nondisabled people are also instructive. Disabled people learn who others take them to be. But instructions do vary. If nondisabled people act hesitantly, awkardly, condescendingly, sympathetically, and the like toward disabled people, then disabled people learn that they are not who they once were or who thought they were—at least to these nondisabled people. Visually impaired people may find that others treat them according to the stereotypes that most hold about blindness. Sighted people may provide unsolicited help or handouts. They may not know whether to pull up the chair for the visually impaired person, order for them in a restaurant, or do many other things that typically they would take for granted. Interaction becomes awkward (Scott, 1969: Chapter 2). Adults who experience a hearing loss may find themselves left out of ordinary conversations with family members, friends, and colleagues. Their role as parent, spouse, or colleague may diminish as others consult them increasingly less frequently. Their world becomes smaller as they grow "words apart" from others (Jones, Kyle, and Wood, 1987). Such interaction is perhaps "destructively" instructive.

However, some disabled and nondisabled people move beyond that awkward, unsatisfying interaction. As I explored in the previous chapter, disabled and nondisabled people do disavow the stigmatization of disability and develop accepting relations. These encounters are also instructive, but now "constructively" so. They teach lessons through which disabled people can enhance their experiences of themselves.

People may also learn to be disabled through encounters with service agencies (Padden and Humphries, 1988: Chapter 1; Albrecht, forthcoming: Chapter 8). A significant, but perhaps overlooked, activity of service agencies is to tell people who they are and what they may become. When service agencies evaluate, place, categorize, transfer, educate, rehabilitate, and so much more, the agencies are informing people who they are and who they are becoming. When service agencies transform people into clients, the agencies are telling them that they are disabled people (at least disabled people who fit certain criteria). At times, the applicants may have had to work hard to convince the service agencies that indeed they were such people. Serving people together, whether in the same program, on the same ward, in the same unit, in the same group, or in other ways, tells them that they are similar in some way. Transfering people to another facility, program, or status tells people that they are no longer what they previously were but are now something else. Suggestively then, some research indicates that visually impaired people who have not been served by blindness agencies are much less likely to identify themselves as *blind* people than are similarly visually impaired people who have been aided by blindness agencies (Scott, 1969: 107).

As service professionals work with disabled people, expecting the disabled people to think and act in certain ways, to understand themselves as do the professionals, specific lessons about disability are taught. If disabled people do not learn these lessons, then they are not "good" clients (Scott, 1969: 76–80; Gubrium and Buckholdt, 1982: 31–33, Chapter 3) (See Chapter 6).

For example, agencies that serve visually impaired people have expected clients to realize that one or a few services will not adequately address their radically altered worlds. Blindness is "one of the most severe of all handicaps, the effects of which are long-lasting, pervasive, and extremely difficult to ameliorate," according to "blindness workers" (Scott, 1969: 77). Therefore, extensive and comprehensive services are needed for visually impaired people to address adequately their serious handicaps. If visually impaired people come to accept completely that they are blind, that their sighted self is dead, then through their hard work and that of the service professionals, visually impaired people may be able to become successfully functioning *blind* people (Scott, 1969: Chapter 5).

However, according to other professionals, many visually impaired people will not be able to become independent blind people, and therefore the agency and the people will need to make accommodations: sheltered workshops instead of independent employment, a fleet of cars to pick up the clients and deposit them at the agency, praise for trivial accomplishments, food served in the cafeteria that can be "easily" eaten by blind people, and the like. These accommodations may make it less possible for visually impaired people to live within as wide a world as they might choose. Visually impaired people may refuse to learn these lessons, but they are taught them and must contend with them (Scott, 1969: Chapter 5).

However, just as encounters between disabled and nondisabled people may teach constructive lessons, so too many service agencies. Mainstreaming in schools is one such attempt (Biklen et al., 1985). While much of our present mainstreaming is woefully inadequate (Biklen et al., 1985; Higgins, 1990), it can aspire to a vision of a just society (Higgins, 1990: 8–9). Mainstreaming can aim to teach youth and adults with varying characteristics that they can live together and separately, that they can create ties that bind one another while also cherishing differences (Higgins, 1990). It can aspire to legitimate disabled people's experiences as disabled people, not as defective versions of nondisabled people.

Encounters among disabled people also instruct one another in becoming disabled, whatever the particular content of the lessons learned. For many, those initial encounters occur in service agencies. Service agencies provide disabled people the opportunity to learn from one another, to develop common experiences, to create shared understandings, to develop ties that may strongly bind them together.

For example, people known as mentally retarded who work in the same rehabilitation center may develop shared experiences and ties among one another. While they need not define themselves as mentally retarded, they may develop a strong in-group identity. At one rehabilitation center several individuals known as mentally retarded or psychiatrically disabled spoke well of one another, criticized "young" and "colored" persons for trying to be "cool" or for being a potential threat to their own safety, and together engaged in leisure activities such as going to restaurants, eating at one another's homes, and shopping (Mest, 1988).

However, disabled people may also differentiate themselves from others being served, distinguishing themselves from whomever they take the others to be. For example, hard of hearing students and deaf students may distinguish themselves from one another, each thinking themselves to be better than the other. The hard of hearing youths may emphasize their oral and English skills; the deaf students, their signing (Evans and Falk, 1986: 119, 140, 165).

By providing disabled people the opportunity to learn from one another, service agencies may unintentionally create competing teachers and lessons. The disabled "clients" develop shared experiences at odds with the official view of disability.

For example, most deaf children and youth have first widely encountered other deaf people in school; until recently in separate, residential schools, now increasingly mainstream schools. Through the comfortable communication that often developed, the shared experiences (some of which concerned their unpleasant experiences with hearing people), and the years of interaction among one another, the deaf youth typically created strong ties among one another, ties that directed them toward the deaf community as adults and saw them through their old age (Becker, 1980; Higgins, 1980; Padden and Humphries, 1988).

However, this has not always been welcomed. As I mentioned in Chapter 1, Alexander Graham Bell and others understood deafness to be a defect that must be overcome according to the standards of the hearing world. They criticized any arrangement that they believed encouraged deaf people to develop their own communities and to live socially apart from hearing people. Residential schools and the use of a "gesture language" were two of Bell's greatest concerns. Many schools banned or greatly limited signing, but deaf students signed outside of the educators' view.

Today, the tension between the worlds created by deaf students and educational officials may be more subtle but not always. Deaf youth may object to the emphasis on manually representing English through signs to the neglect of American Sign Language, to not being able to communicate comfortably with teachers who do not sign well, or to being left out in the mainstream because students who hear and "regular" teachers cannot sign (Padden and Humphries, 1988; Higgins, 1990). For example, students at one residential school for deaf youth were suspended when they resisted the requirement to sign in English word order (Lane, 1988).

Or, at a mainstream high school program some deaf youth used for a couple of years the ASL sign glossed "stuck" in order to tell some of their "deaf education" teachers that "I've (the student) got power over you; I am able to put you in your place" (Wilcox, 1984: 160). The students seemed to use the sign as a way of reasserting themselves in the face of misunderstanding and cultural clashes. Eventually deciding that the sign was not nice, many teachers banned it from their classrooms and some even from their presence. When it spread to the middle school program for deaf youth, the teachers concluded it was a "dirty word" and forbid it (Wilcox, 1984). Service agencies enable disabled people to develop shared experiences, but the agencies cannot completely control those experiences.

Encounters among people with disabilities do not occur only within service agencies. Disabled people interact with one another in self-help groups, voluntary associations, "communities" of disabled people, advocacy associations, and other groups run by disabled people. Disabled people create such groups as responses to their dissatisfaction with a nondisabled world. But through participation in such groups, disabled people may develop ties among one another and new understandings of themselves and others. They may become people who embrace their disability and themselves, becoming both different and more complex than nondisabled people allow (See Chapter 8; Higgins, 1980; Goldin, 1984; Padden and Humphries, 1988; Deshen, 1991).

Individuals who become disabled people learn to be who they become. That which is used to mark them as disabled—hearing impairments, paralysis, epilepsy, mental retardation, and so on—does not make them disabled people. Those characteristics do not naturally make them people who understand themselves as deaf people, paralyzed people, people who "are" epileptic or mentally retarded.(1) That understanding and its complex substance are developed throughout people's lives. We continually become who we are.

Realms of Disability Experience

The experiences of people with disabilities involve various realms of living. Disabled people experience others, themselves, and their physical, mental and emotional variations out of which disability is produced. It is the latter that concerns me here. Disabled people make sense of their diminished hearing, their unusual bodily appearance, their visual impairment, and so forth.

Disabled people may focus on a mix of various features of their disabilities: pain and other bodily sensations; a disrupted, everyday order; uncertainty; and the relation of the disability to oneself among other features. For some such as those with rheumatoid arthritis or TMPDS (i.e., temporomandibular pain and dysfunction syndrome) the meaning of their disabilities may greatly or at times revolve around the pain they experience (Locker, 1983; Lennon et al., 1989). As one woman with TMPDS said of her worst, recent experience, "It's a dull and drawing pain (not throbbing) that feels like an old fashioned ice tong is pushing in on both sides of the head" (Lennon, et al., 1989: 118).

Some who are disabled experience the disruption of their everyday order. For those who become blind, their remaining sight may lead them to experience a "'haze' or 'fog' or continuous 'blur,' only occasionally broken by movement or color" (Ainlay, 1988: 84). The lack of vision disrupts their sense of spatial and temporal order. Objects disappear though they are within one's grasp, the world may become foreign terrain, and more time is needed to accomplish tasks (Ainlay, 1988).

For others, whose conditions have changed or may change, uncertainty becomes a central feature of their experiences. As one woman with rheumatoid arthritis noted:

> I often feel this when I'm talking to my consultant, it doesn't show a precise pattern does it. I mean sometimes people say 'Does the weather affect you?' Well it does but not always. The pouring rain and the bitter cold sometimes does. On a day like today when it's warm and humid it can be absolute agony yet another time when it's bitterly cold I'm going around merrily. I just don't know, it doesn't follow a precise pattern at all and this is what fools you, you wake up in the morning and you just have to wait and see how you are going to be that day (Locker, 1983: 22).

Disabled people also experience the relationship of the disability to themselves. Some may experience their disability as an alien force that is not part of themselves but does afflict them. Those who stutter often speak of their stuttering as "it." They experience stuttering as an

> alien inner force . . . which takes control of their speech mechanism. Stuttering is something which stutterers feel happens *to* them, not something they do: "somebody else is in charge of my mouth and I can't do anything about it" (Van Riper, 1971: 158 quoted in Petrunik and Shearing, 1983: 127).

Others may come to experience their disabilities as essential features of themselves. Their vision loss, paralysis, or absence of limbs *is* them (though not all of them). Diane DeVries, born with "quadrilateral limb deficiencies" noted:

> Most handicapped kids, when they hear they're going to get a new arm or a new leg, get really excited. It's going to be a neat thing to use . . . But I never could get excited about it because I knew it was going on my body. And that would add more sweat, and more asthma, because I'd have to work harder with it. So I always saw my body as something that was mine, and that was free, and I hated anything kind of binding anything (Frank, 1988: 59).

When experiencing disability, disabled people may focus on various features of their physical, mental and emotional conditions.

Managing the disability

Disabilities create consequences for everyday life. Activities may take longer to accomplish, energy may ebb, previous routines may need to be altered, everyday devices adapted, difficulties worked around, treatments worked into one's life, and so on. People with disabilities manage the "inconveniences" of being disabled.

For example, because visual impairments do disrupt the spatial and temporal order of previously sighted people's lives, blind people (with the help of family and others) may try to create and consistently maintain order within their worlds. Objects are placed and replaced in the same location. Furniture is not moved. In anticipation of further vision loss, visually impaired people may consciously try to familiarize themselves with their world, even practicing what it may be like to see less well:

> I go around the house (with the lights out) and I make sure I feel my way around in the dark to see how it would be. I will be all right if nobody moves the furniture or something like that. I do this alone—I pretend that I'm completely blind and go around (Ainlay, 1988: 85).

Elderly people who are beginning to lose their sight experience a disruption of their temporal order. Activities take much longer, goals may seem difficult to reach, the future may hold additional vision loss. Hence, there does not seem to be enough time to accomplish what one may wish. Consequently, elderly people with new vision losses may begin to focus on the present, enjoy one day as it comes, and devote less of themselves to contemplating the future:

> I just go from one day to the next. I just want to do the best I can with every day. I don't really have any special goals. I think maybe it's because I don't know just how bad my sight will get. And maybe I'm kind of thinking that I'll want a certain goal and I won't be able to do that. I don't want to try to do too much, you know?—something I can't handle. So I think it's better if I just take it day to day and live each day to the fullest. Not planning too far ahead, you know (Ainlay, 1988: 87)?

Those with disabilities may "redesign" their lifestyles in small and large ways in order to manage the consequences of their disabilities. Some with disabilities conserve their energy for essential activities, such as the return home of spouses with whom the disabled individuals wish to share a pleasant evening (Locker, 1983: 39). People with emphysema may plan their routes to their everyday destinations such as a grocery store in order to know where they can stop and "catch their breath." They turn mail boxes, telephone poles, benches, and other places into "puffing stations" (Fagerhaugh, 1975: 104). Others make sure that they have everything they need for the day when they come down from the second floor so that they need not go upstairs until they are ready to retire for the day

(Strauss and Glaser, 1975: Chapter 3). If possible, people may move to homes that are one story or that are surrounded by a flat terrain.

Because the world is constructed primarily to suit nondisabled people (and then suit well only a narrow segment of nondisabled people), disabled people may plan ahead more in order to live with their disability. Mobility impaired people may reserve accessible transportation days in advance or scout out access into and through buildings, stutterers may think ahead in the conversation in order to skirt words that typically give them trouble, others check ahead to be sure that appropriate food is available on airplane flights, and so on. Spontaneity may decrease. As disabled people manage their disabilities, they may primarily experience their disabilities as individual, personal troubles to bear.

Disability as an individual phenomenon

While recognition grows that disability is not merely an individual phenomenon (see Chapter 1), many disabled people continue to experience their disabilities as their individual problems. In a recent national survey of people with disabilities, many mentioned that they are not as active in community events, social activities, and getting around as they would like to be.

However, many of these disabled people explained their continuing difficulties in very individualistic ways. Something wrong with them limited their participation. Disabled people mentioned fear of getting hurt, sick, or victimized; dependency on others; and their self-consciousness as important reasons for their unsatisfactory participation. (Fewer also mentioned socially created obstacles to participation such as transportation difficulties and lack of access to buildings.) Many disabled people did not connect those feelings of trepidation or personal inadequacy to the actions and arrangements that they encounter. For example, they did not argue that their self-consciousness might arise out of nondisabled people's stigmatizing disabilities.

When those who said they still faced barriers were asked what could be done, many gave answers that indicated that they experienced disability as a "personal trial which they, and not society, are responsible for facing" (Louis Harris and Associates, 1986: 68). One-fifth replied that nothing could be done, more than one-tenth did not know what could be done or did not reply, and more than one-fourth mentioned improve their health, have a good attitude, get specific treatment, get medication and other individual medical/psychological approaches. Less than one-half percent mentioned improving government policy (though many also believed that changes in federal laws since the late 1960s have helped provide better opportunities) (Louis Harris and Associates, 1986: 68–69, 20–21).

People with disabilities also explained their employment difficulties in individual terms. Those who were not working at all or were not working full time most often mentioned (78%) as an important reason for their reduced work the limitation imposed upon them by their disability/ health problems. The second most mentioned reason (52%) was the medical treatment or therapy they needed. Less frequently mentioned reasons referred to social obstacles such as the attitudes of employers or inaccessible or expensive transportation (Louis Harris and Associates, 1986: 72). And among those who were working but believed without a disability they would have a better job and among those who were not working, most believed that their disabilities, not employers' attitudes, had been a bigger obstacle to getting better jobs (Louis Harris and Associates, Inc., 1986: 75).

While many disabled people (45%) did see themselves as a minority group in the "same sense" that black Americans or Hispanic Americans were a minority, many also experienced disability primarily as a personal trouble, not a public problem (Louis Harris and Associates, 1986: 114, 68).

Experiential Orientations

How those with disabilities experience their disability and themselves varies dramatically. Our stereotypes of disability tell us that disabled people are homogeneous, typically burdened by their disability, and static in their experiences: Disabled people feel badly about themselves and do so forever; if they could, they would become nondisabled.

Experiential orientations to disability are more complex than that, much more complex than even the following discussion indicates. For example, disabled people do not necessarily wish to become nondisabled, and those who may at one time, may not at another time, especially as they more fully experience themselves and make their lives (Weinberg, 1988: 142–147). One hearing impaired woman, a member of the deaf community, had an operation that improved her hearing. However, it became a "mixed blessing":

> But at times I wish I could go back to where my hearing was 83 db loss (a major impairment; it is now only a 20–30 db loss) in this ear because (laughter) when you have screaming children and you're in a noisy group and during that time (before the operation) when the noise stopped me I could always turn my

hearing aid off and that helps the rest of you. But now I can't turn my ear off. Once in a while I wish I could go back to (that time before the operation). Have my hearing improved more, no (Higgins, 1980: 92–93).

To simplify greatly, some disabled people may be "forever bitter and unhappy," others view their disabilities as "facts of life," and still others may actively "embrace" their disabilities (Weinberg, 1988). The disabilities do not determine these orientations. Instead, as people make their lives, producing accomplishments and experiencing obstacles, they develop and change these orientations.

Some disabled people experience their lives bitterly. They continually regret being disabled and believe that their lives would be much better if they were not disabled. Disability has made their lives tragic. As one man with cerebral palsy who had never been able to live on his own, marry, or obtain steady employment noted:

> I am angry—no, damned mad—most of the time every day. This should not have happened to me—there is no reason, no fairness to the way I am. I have to accept my condition, but nobody's going to make me like it. I hate it, and much of the time I hate everyone: those more fortunate than me, because they are, and those as badly or worse off, because they remind me of my own state. I am no cheerful Tiny Tim, with a sweet nature developed by affliction, I am bathed in anger almost always. Don't worry, I won't leap up out of my wheelchair and run amok. If I could, I wouldn't need to be angry (Kiser, 1974: 204 cited in Weinberg, 1988: 149–150).

Those newly disabled rather than those who have lived disabled for years may more likely be bitter (Fine and Asch, 1988: 10–11). Recall my earlier discussion of how recently disabled individuals may apply a fundamental negative bias to themselves.

Many others, perhaps most people with disabilities, come to see their disabilities as another feature of who they are. It may be inconvenient, but they do live with it. At times they may regret being disabled, but they do not dwell upon it. All people encounter obstacles, inconveniences, or limitations. So, too, do they. One young man who as a result of polio as a child is paralyzed from the waist down and has limited upper-body movement explained his not being able to do certain activities by asking an interviewer to imagine that

> everybody is going to go ice skating and you are not so hot on ice skates. So you don't go. Everyone goes out and ice skates and you are there all by yourself, and it kind of depresses you because you can't ice skate. But it is not an overwhelming thing. It is like, if you had money, you could go on a trip to

Florida or the Bahamas, but you don't, so you can't do it, but you will get over
it (Weinberg, 1988: 150).

Perhaps a smaller, but increasing, proportion of people with disabilities embrace their disabilities. With the development of a disability
rights movement, a growing number of people with disabilities are
embracing their disabilities as valued features of their selves. Whatever
their physical, mental, or emotional states, that is who they are. An
internationally acclaimed author with cerebral palsy, who takes twelve
hours to type each page, was asked by a journalist what he would do if he
could leave his wheelchair. The author shocked the journalist by reply-
ing that he would "get right back in" (Minow, 1990: 155). These disabled
people cannot imagine being otherwise.

Consider a young woman, Jill, who "was born with no legs and only
one arm, which ended at the elbow" (Weinberg, 1988: 145). Forced to
wear prostheses by her parents and assured by her doctors that she would
become used to them, Jill developed skill in using the prosthetic arms
and recognized that the prosthetic legs were aesthetically enhancing,
even though she moved in a wheelchair. Being continually resistant to
using the prostheses, Jill was allowed by her parents to discard the
prostheses when she turned sixteen. She

> regrets that during her first 16 years, despite her requests, no efforts were made
> to teach her to do things with the physical resources that she did possess. It was
> only 16, when she went, as she described it, "natural," that she could prevail
> upon medical staff to help her. Other people, she felt, viewed her as only part
> of a person and wanted to make her whole. But from her perspective, she was
> already whole. Having artificial limbs made her feel like an octopus. She was
> satisfied with herself, with her identity, and with her body just as it was
> (Weinberg: 1988: 146).

With the development of a disability rights movement, many disabled
people are making their disabilities integral, cherished features of their
selves (see Chapter 8).

Disabled people experience disability complexly. They learn to be
disabled through their experiences with others and themselves. They
develop orientations that may shift over time. Their experiences involve
various realms—themselves, others, and their disabilities. Though disabled people's experiences vary greatly, many do experience disability
as a personal trouble to be born, not a public issue to be addressed.

Families' Experiencing Disability

People with disabilities are family members—children, parents, spouses, relatives to others. Therefore, their families experience disability, too. Some experiences may cut across many families, such as the stigmatization of disability. However, families experience disability very differently, too. They vary because families with disabled members are families first, families with different compositions, histories, social resources, and so on. While important similarities may occur, an upper-middle class family with a disabled child will experience life differently than an impoverished minority family with a disabled child. Families' experiences of disability differ because the families differ.

Families with disabled members may experience disability differently due to the position of the disabled member(s) within the family. A family with a severely disabled child experiences disability differently than a family in which the parents are deaf (Featherstone, 1980; Walker, 1986). The challenges of being a child or a parent differ enormously whether the child or parent is disabled or not. The relations of the child to the other family members are not the same as the relations of the parents to other family members. Families do not experience disability in the abstract. They experience members who are disabled (and the challenges faced by the members and themselves). Disability is embodied in family members, whose relations to one another may vary greatly. In the following I focus on families with disabled children (though I believe much of what I discuss can be applied to families in which some other member is disabled. Much can also help us understand how people with disabilities experience the disabilities and themselves.)

Families with Disabled Children

Often unknown to them, parents and other family members bring to their disabled children great potential to raise, care for, and enjoy their children. Later that may realize that to be so. But initially they bring understandings and have experiences that make more difficult their lives and their children's lives.

Families are typically not "prepared" for disabled children. Like most people, parents and other family members typically have little intensive experience with disabled individuals. They stigmatize, stereotype, sympathize with, and/or pity disabled people. Further, they may have learned to acquiesce to doctors, teachers, and other professionals. "Professionals know best." Finally, they typically assume that nothing unusual will happen in their families (Emerson, 1970). Their children will grow up as healthy, "normal" kids. (Though they may "worry" until their children are born, they do not expect the unexpected.) Their aspirations envision a child without undue difficulties. Parents initially bring their lack of experience and knowledge, their submission to professional dominance, and their taken-for-granted belief that their children will lead untroubled lives to their becoming parents of children with disabilities (Darling, 1988).

Whether their children are born with disabilities or later acquire them, parents are initially typically bewildered. They may struggle for weeks, months, or even longer to develop tolerable understandings about what is "wrong" with their children. They likely struggle even longer in developing tolerable ways of "managing" what is "wrong." (It could be argued that tolerable understandings don't arise until tolerable strategies are developed.) The parents may encounter well-meaning professionals who do not tell them clearly and compassionately what they believe is the difficulty, who provide them misinformation, who do not know what to do, who provide conflicting advice or overwhelming suggestions about what to do, and who decide what should be done for the children and do it without fully involving them (Darling, 1979, 1988; Darling and Darling, 1982; Featherstone, 1980; Harris, 1983).

One mother of a daughter with Down syndrome recalled how their doctor told them:

> The doctor came in and said "Her cheekbones are high and her eyes . . . it could be her German ancestry." You know, he hemmed and hawed. I thought she was blind or something. He finally said it was Down's Syndrome . . . We didn't know what it was. My husband looked it up in the encyclopedia (Darling, 1979: 133).

After adopting her son who had cerebral palsy, a physical therapist, who had practiced for years, realized that she had overwhelmed parents with prescriptions for therapy:

> Before I had Peter, I gave out (physical therapy) programs that would have taken all day. I don't know when I expected mothers to change diapers, sort laundry, or buy groceries (Featherstone, 1980: 57).

Parents may struggle with a mix of emotions—fear, anger, loneliness, guilt and self-doubt (Featherstone, 1980). They worry, even fear, for themselves, their disabled children, and their children without disabilities should they have any. What will the future be like? What will their disabled children become? Will they always be responsible for caring for their disabled children? Will their nondisabled children be responsible? They may rage at the injustice of having disabled children, the insensitivity of professionals, and the overbearing sympathy of others. They may become lonely and isolated as the responsibilities of caring for their disabled children cut them off from others, as they cut themselves off from others who pity or rebuff them, as they believe they cannot share their experiences with others who have no experiences with disability, and as they try to spare their spouses their own doubts and misgivings. They may wonder what they did to bring this misfortune upon themselves, condemning themselves for "real" or imagined failings. If the daily responsibilities become overwhelming and their disabled children's development seems so meager, they may doubt their competence.

Brothers and sisters may also experience conflicting emotions. They may wonder if they can "catch" the disabilities, if they will be responsible for their siblings when they become adults, what will become of their disabled brothers and sisters, and whether or not they can genetically pass on the impairments. They, too, become angry if their disabled siblings "mess" up their possessions, but they feel guilty for feeling angry. They may resent the attention their parents and others give to their disabled siblings. If they assist to a great extent with the care of their disabled siblings, feel that they are stigmatized because of their siblings' disabilities, and keep their confusing feelings to themselves, they, too, become lonely. Like their parents, they may feel guilty because they are angry or resentful of their disabled siblings or perhaps somehow responsible for their siblings' difficulties. They may torment themselves with wondering why their siblings, not they, are impaired (Featherstone, 1980).

Out of this bewilderment, unsatisfying experiences, and mix of emotions, parents (and families) search for understanding, services, and support (Darling, 1979, 1988; Darling and Darling, 1982). Some, perhaps disadvantaged by poverty and lack of services and support, resign themselves to a hard life. Others may come in contact with fellow parents of disabled children, parents with whom they share experiences and provide support. As they live with and attend to their children with disabilities, they develop understandings of their own children and means for meeting their children's needs. They learn of services and make arrangements for their children. Many develop a satisfactory, routine way of life.

For example, parents of a daughter with Down syndrome became active members in an association for retarded citizens and friendly with another family through the association. Their daughter went to the association's nursery school and later attended a special class in a public school. The parents eventually left their pediatrician, who "kept insisting that they 'leave it up to the doctor when it comes time to put her in an institution,' " and found another one whom they liked better because he took the time to talk to them. After their daughter spent several years in a class for students designated "trainable," the parents "battled" with the school system, secured an evaluation from a private psychologist and convinced the school system to move their daughter to a class for "educable" students, where she did well. The wife's mother moved into the home, which took care of babysitting needs. The parents remained satisfied with their daughter's medical care and education. Eventually they became inactive in the association for retarded people and ceased seeing socially any families with disabled children. Their daughter played with younger, nondisabled, neighborhood children. Among their various activities, the family camped. Retardation was "not number one around" the family's house. It became "just something" that the daughter "ha(d)" (Darling, 1979: 190).

Others, creating a satisfactory life for themselves and their children, still remain active in parent-support groups and with families with disabled children. They assist other parents and families to create positive experiences for themselves. But some, not satisfied with what is available for themselves, their disabled children, and for similar families and children become crusaders who challenge the present arrangements. They lobby school boards, petition their representatives, participate in support groups, and in other ways work to improve the services and increase the opportunities for families and disabled children.

As the disabled children grow older, approaching adulthood or some other significant change in status (perhaps movement from middle school to high school), parents (and other family members) may experience again in the foreground the uncertainty and some of the mix of feelings they experienced when they first became parents of children with disabilities. Once again, they may search for information, understanding, and opportunities for their children. That searching, acceptance, or continued challenging may continue as the children become adults and move away from or remain at home (Darling, 1979; 1988; Darling and Darling, 1982).

The parents (and other family members) experience their children with disabilities within the social worlds within which the parents live. Those worlds provide obstacles and opportunities for creating more or less satisfying experiences. An active government, well-developed services, inclusive schools, parent-support groups, knowledgeable and sensitive professionals, financial assistance, and other supports enhance the capacity of parents to create satisfying experiences (see Ferguson et al., 1990). Their lack makes it more difficult. Disability may be individually experienced, but the experiences are not merely the handiwork of the experiencing individuals.

We should not think that families with disabled children experience family life primarily in terms of disability. Disabilities and the children with the disabilities are part of the mosaic of the families, being more or less prominent (and shifting so over time) in the families' lives. For that small number of children with disabilities whose parents (and even siblings) are similarly disabled, disability may only become a noticed matter when encountering the nondisabled world. Recall again Professor Sam Suppalla, whose parents and older brothers were Deaf like him.

Impersonal Others' Experiencing Disability

People unfamiliar with individuals with disabilities typically experience disability much differently than do those who are disabled. The experiences of those with disabilities varies greatly. The disabilities are only one part of the mosaic experienced by disabled people. While the disabilities may touch upon much of the individuals' lives, they are not necessarily in the foreground. They may be taken for granted, not typically remarked upon, routinely "managed" (Mest, 1988: 121).

However, to classmates, coworkers, neighbors, and others unfamiliar with disabled people, disability may be central to their experiences of disabled people. If it is, they are likely to understand disabled people as being greatly different than themselves (Fichten, 1988: 176). After all, they are *not* disabled, a typically taken-for-granted feature of themselves that becomes significant in contrast to the disabled people. If the disability is salient (and it may stand out because it is visible or contrasts greatly with expectations of "normality"), stigmatized, as it typically is, and little else is known of the disabled person, then those unfamiliar with disabled people will likely experience negatively the disabled individual. A *fundamental negative bias* is at work (Wright, 1988). The unfamiliar person has no or few other experiences of disability and disabled people to counter, to put into perspective, the salience of the stigma. Thus, those unfamiliar with disabilities typically see disabled people as more unfortunate, more troubled, and more burdened by their disabilities than do those with disabilities (or those familiar with people with disabilities) (Weinberg, 1988; Wright, 1988).

Further, being mindful of the disability, actively focusing on it, nondisabled people may notice other features of the disabled individual, such as idiosyncratic facial expressions, that are typically not noticed. These characteristics are present in nondisabled people but are noticed less because nondisabled people focus less on people they take for granted. Because nondisabled people do not notice these features as much in other nondisabled people, they take them to be unusual when they do notice them in disabled people. This becomes reason again for nondisabled people to experience disabled people as odd (Langer and Chanowitz, 1988). Those unfamiliar with disability typically attend much more to the disability than those who have lived disabled for years, they experience disabled people as greatly different from themselves, and they understand disabled people in narrow, typically negative ways.

People unfamiliar with disabled individuals may also experience existential and aesthetic anxiety (Hahn, 1988). When encountering disabled people, those unfamiliar may feel that they too could become incapable of living "normally." To combat that dreadful prospect, they separate themselves symbolically and literally from disabled people. They move away from disabled people or move disabled people away from them. By keeping their distance from disabled people, not touching them, or segregating them in facilities, nondisabled people are able to separate disabled people from themselves. They symbolically distance themselves by knowing that disabled people are not like them and depicting them so (see Chapter 3). They are different kinds of people.

Second, disabled people may arouse anxieties about one's own appearance. Some disabled people do not fit conventional standards of appearance. They look "odd." Does the appearance of nondisabled people then measure up? Once again, those not familiar with disabled people may respond to that anxiety by distancing themselves from these "less worthy" individuals. Part of that distancing, if only symbolic, is the quest for the "perfect" appearance (Glassner, 1988). The quest and better yet the achievement are shields to protect us from the possibility of our appearances no longer measuring up (Hahn, 1988).

However, disabled and nondisabled people may develop accepting relations (see Chapter 4). As they do, nondisabled people experience disabled people more complexly, less stereotypically, with less anxiety. Disability becomes part of the nondisabled people's experiential mosaic of the other who is disabled, not a single, glaring pattern poorly explored.

Conclusion

Disabilities do not determine our experiences of them. Disabled people, family members, and those less familiar with disability develop and redevelop their experiences. Disabled people learn to become who they are, though no objective lessons wait to be mastered. Family members may struggle with a mix of emotions, searching for meanings with which to manage their lives. Those unfamiliar with disability are likely to make disability the master feature of their experiences with disabled people *and* assume that it is the dominant, burdensome feature of disabled people's experiences of themselves. Disabled people, family members, and those unfamiliar with disability may experience disability in conflicting ways. That conflict itself becomes part of experiencing disability.

However, while that conflict may be recognized, the conflicting experiences may not be legitimized. We may deny the value of others', even our own, experiences. Taking their view as how the world objectively is, nondisabled people may dismiss disabled people's experiences as delusional (e.g., "Of course, disabled people would wish not to be disabled" (Weinberg, 1988).), too subjective, or irrelevant. In the face of such opposition or condescension, disabled people and their intimate others may question the validity of their own experiences. Later, if they become activists, they may similarly dismiss the experiences of nondisabled people: Those who are not disabled cannot know what it is to be disabled; therefore, nondisabled people's experiences (and concerns) are invalid.

Too rarely do we with the conflicting experiences realize that none of our experiences are (nor can be) objective reflections of how the world "really" is. Instead, all are socially produced, though individually sensed:

> The point is not to find the new, true perspective . . . The perspective of those who are labeled "different" may offer an important challenge to those who impose the label, but it is a corrective lens, another partial view, not the absolute truth. It is the complexity of our reciprocal realities and the conflict between the realities that constitute us which we need to understand (Minow, 1990: 376).

We create some of that complexity and conflict that is us through how we "service" people with disabilities. I turn now to our organizational practices and perspectives.

Endnotes

1. Approximately half of the people "with" disabilities recently interviewed in a national survey reported that they did not consider themselves to be a "disabled or handicapped person." All those interviewed had a "disability or health problem that prevented them from fully participating in work, school, or other activities;" "said (they) had a physical disability, a seeing, hearing or speech impairment, an emotional or mental disability or a learning disability;" or "considered (themselves) disabled or said that other people would consider (them disabled)" (Louis Harris and Associates, 1986: 15, iii). A large majority of those who reported that their disabilities were "slight" or "moderate" did not consider themselves to be disabled (81% and 66% respectively). Almost one-fourth of those who reported that their disabilities were "very severe" did not consider themselves to be disabled (Louis Harris and Associates, 1986: 15).

No doubt, some, perhaps most, of the people "with" disabilities who said that they did not consider themselves to be disabled or handicapped would have applied other terms to themselves that are routinely taken as associated with disability. For example, they would have applied such terms as "wheelchair mobile," "visually impaired," or "deaf." To me, such people have learned to be disabled (whatever it might mean for them), but in ways that differentiate themselves from the global, often stigmatized, identity of disabled or handicapped. The diversity of experiencing appears again. This lack of identification with a larger group of people, those with disabilities, is one of the challenges disabled people face in managing disability, in "fighting back" (see Chapter 8).

Chapter 6

SERVICING DISABILITY

Through mental health facilities, rehabilitation agencies, (special) educational programs, community care facilities, and other human service organizations, we serve people with disabilities. While no one human service organization can represent the complexity of serving disabled people and no short excerpt about a single human service organization can depict its complexity, consider the following comments about Melvin, a sixth grader attending a school in a small community of about 900 people, to which he and his adoptive mother had recently moved. Melvin had been labeled severely retarded, severely behavior disordered, hyperactive, and epileptic. At the age of five he was removed from his birth parents' home due to suspected neglect and abuse and spent several years in institutions or with foster families. At 7 Melvin knew five signs, but after moving in with his adoptive mother learned signs rapidly and then began to speak.

Not having had a student "even remotely like Melvin" before, the school was understandably anxious. The Principal expressed the concern: "We'll give it a try but I don't know how we are going to pull this off and make it work . . ." The principal also voiced the common refrain, "I will not have the other kids victimized . . ."

The first few weeks of school, Mary Lou (Melvin's mother) would get phone calls, "He's out of control. You better come up to the school . . ."

I would leave my class (in a neighboring school district) and run up there. And it would be horrendous. He would be throwing books at people and laying on the ground and I'd walk in the room and he'd jump up and sit at his desk and say, 'Hi Mary Lou,' as if to say, 'I'm alright; I'm being perfectly fine here . . .'

Within a week of having limits set, Melvin was fine . . . Within a matter of months, especially as Melvin developed friends, the other parents and principal as well as many of the teaching staff grew comfortable with Melvin . . . (However)

The principal has become a real advocate so now I have to guard against them . . . babying him. That's a major frustration too . . . If the principal is talking

to the superintendent in the hall, Mel interrupts her to stop and talk . . . in a way
that other kids would not be allowed . . .

From the start, despite the district's seeming flexibility to create a program
for Melvin at the local school, and its actual efforts to educate Mel, many
people in the district believed Mel would be better off in a neighboring district
that had a program for students with disabilities (with which Mel's mother
disagreed, especially after visiting the proposed school and observing a student without a disability calling the four students with disabilities who were
educated in a portable classroom the retard class and the principal who heard
the remark not respond) . . .

The school placed Mel in a resource room half time along with the only
other child in the school with a noticeable disability, a child with Down
syndrome . . . (eventually) the principal hired a special education teacher. This
allowed for Mel to have the community instruction (which he could have only
if certified staff took him or any student off school grounds) and to be supported
in the regular class. But it also reinforced Mel's separate status in the
school . . . The special teacher became Mel's teacher . . .

(After Mary Lou talked with the school officials about integration), the
school's response was cautious. He could be integrated some of the time, for
example in the "specials" such as music, art, and gym, and of course lunch and
recess, but he went to a special class for academics, except for (isolated)
instances . . . (Biklen, forthcoming).

Increasingly we are a service society. While we continue to manufacture great quantities of goods of all kinds (including disability), we also
provide many services (Harris, 1981; Albrecht and Levy, 1981: 24–26).
We educate, litigate, wait on, advise, clean up, assess, process, represent,
protect, invest, counsel, treat, and serve one another in many other ways.

Much of this service takes place in human service organizations such
as schools, employment offices, courts, hospitals, and social service
agencies. The primary mission of these organizations is to process people,
to change them, or to do both (Hasenfeld and English, 1974). When
processing people, human service organizations evaluate characteristics
and social situations of the people. Through interviewing, testing, and
observing among various ways, human service organizations assess people.
The organizations identify who the people are and what action to take.
When changing people, human service organizations apply "various
modification and treatment technologies" (Hasenfeld and English, 1974:
5). They counsel, instruct, medicate, rehabilitate, isolate, and in still
other ways seek to change people.

Increasingly disabled people, advocates, and human service professionals are questioning how we serve disabled people (e.g., Wolfensberger,

1972; Bogdan and Biklen, 1977; Bowe, 1978; Gliedman and Roth, 1980; DeJong, 1983; Biklen et al., 1985; Stubbins, 1988). The opening quote is itself part of a larger assessment of how we educate children and youth who are disabled. Human services may harm as well as help.

In order to understand how this could be so, I have framed this chapter with a metaphor. After briefly introducing the *metaphor* of servicing, I explore the dominant *paradigm* in serving disabled people, what I term "servicing." While servicing can assist disabled people, it diminishes them, too. It becomes *disabling service.* While I focus on how organizations service disabled people, servicing cannot be understood merely as organizational practice. Instead, like all of the means through which we make disability, we develop servicing in response to larger social concerns. Organizational servicing arises out of *societal circumstances.* In concluding the chapter, I point to alternatives to servicing.

Servicing as Metaphor

Perhaps we service disabled people as much as, if not more than, we serve them. The phrase sounds odd and its connotations are potentially uncomfortable. But the metaphor may also be meaningful.

To service an object is to fix or to maintain it. We get our television sets, refrigerators, vacuum cleaners, stereos—appliances of all kinds—serviced. We take our automobiles to mechanics for service. We call plumbers, electricians, heating and air-conditioning specialists, and telephone repairers for service. If something goes wrong, breaks, is on the blink, or in some way doesn't work quite right, we get it serviced (or perhaps discard it for a better model).

We typically get our broken or balky mechanical objects serviced by specialists. We do so, because we know relatively little about the workings of the object and, thus, take comfort in the expertise of the specialists. Often the specialists are certified or licensed, which further testifies to their expertise—and to our presumed incompetence. While we sometimes question the effort and competence of the service specialists and are often dismayed at what they charge us, we continue to frequent them. Unless the object's repair and/or maintenance is simple, friends and families often counsel us to let the specialists do it. The counsel may come after those friends and families—and we—have looked for ourselves and could not tell what was wrong or could do little about it. Our incompetence and the advice of our families and friends point us to the service specialists.

When we request service from the service specialists, we put ourselves at their mercy. They schedule us when they can fit us in—perhaps next week at the earliest. We wait for them to come, sometimes all day or more. If they don't have the right part, we're out of luck. If their mechanical ministrations fail, they still get paid. But if the circumstances seem dire, we are thankful for whatever small comfort they bring—no matter how much that relief costs.

We—and the specialists—make us compliant customers. We neither know enough nor are assertive enough (in the face of our ignorance) to question what is being done and to learn for the next time. If they suggest this, that or the other should be done, we rarely understand well enough to make an informed decision. "Do whatever is needed," comes our reply. And so they do it—whatever. When we do have hunches of what is wrong, we offer them meekly, almost self-deprecatingly, for fear of encroaching upon the specialists' playing field—and of showing how poorly we understand the game.

But the specialists are often responsible, too, for our being helpless. They neither have the time nor the inclination to explain carefully what is wrong, what they are doing, and what we can do to avoid having problems in the future. They wield their technical jargon not to enlighten us, but to put us in our place. If we complain about what they have done, they may dismiss us as ignorant or just dismiss us. They shroud their work in secrecy—behind the counter, in the back room, in the service bay, or shipped off to the service center. Even when they work in front of us, we collaborate with them to keep ourselves in the dark. We leave them to their work and don't ask them questions. We feel uneasy hanging around as they work. To do so would be an invasion of their privacy (never mind an invasion of our ignorance). When uncertain, they conspiratorily (or so it seems) consult their colleagues and then return their attention to the offending object. What they talked about with their fellow experts we have no idea. They must be satisfied with our passivity— for they are so successful in working with us to create it. The above is certainly part caricature. Yet, for us it may be a useful metaphor. Maybe we service people as well as objects.

The Servicing Paradigm

We might usefully understand much of what occurs in serving disabled people as servicing "defective" persons. Whether medicine, rehabilitation, (special) education, or some other service field is the focus, servicing dominates (See Gliedman and Roth, 1980: Chapters 3 and 8 especially; DeJong, 1983 for the basis of my discussion). However, I use servicing as a sensitizing concept, as a way of making one sense of human service agencies, not so much as a description. Servicing is not necessarily service agencies' avowed framework (though I imagine that some human service professionals would endorse much of the paradigm with the implicit criticism deleted). Many human service providers challenge the dominant paradigm in their provision of services. But to the extent that servicing makes sense of our experiences with human service agencies, then we must recognize that our services disable people, creating the difficulties that they are suppose to ameliorate.

Servicing consists of at least three important features: *individualizing disability, stratifying service,* and *surviving.* Servicing ignores the larger social arrangements (including those within their agencies) that may oppress people with disabilities to concentrate on defects assumed to be within them. They do so in order to fix disabled people. Servicing is greatly stratified. Participants and programs are unequal, often greatly so. For example, servicing takes place through a hierarchy of participants in which disabled people are at the bottom of the service agency and those with the most training and credentials are at the top. While assisting disabled people is an important goal of service agencies, surviving is perhaps the most significant one (to which assisting disabled people may contribute). Additional components make up these basic features of the servicing paradigm. While the following may seem to caricature service agencies, too many disabled people's (and their families') experiences tell us otherwise.

While I and others find great fault in servicing, I do not mean to suggest that service providers are flawed. Far from it. From my own experience and that of others, I believe that those who serve disabled people are as hard working, caring, and competent as any other group of workers. While our services may often be less successful than we had hoped, we should not believe that the problem primarily resides in the shortcomings of the providers—the teachers, counselors, psychologists, social workers, doctors, therapists, aides, attendants, and the like. While we all can improve our competence and renew our concern, our service shortcomings are due to the philosophies that underlie and the practices that make up our services. The shortcomings result from our disability policies and from the inequities within our society. Just as we should not individualize disability, nor should we individualize our service short-comings (though one of the shortcomings of servicing is its individualistic orientation) (Higgins, 1985: 13–14).

Individualizing Disability

Servicing individualizes disability (e.g., see Coles, 1987; Bines, 1988). Servicing agencies develop their philosophy and base their practices on the stance that whatever difficulties or challenges disabled people face reside within them (or within individuals close to them, typically their families). Disabled people's minds, bodies, or spirits are the problem. (Perhaps their family members' attitudes, actions and meager abilities and resources create difficulties, too.) Thus, disabled people *have* mobility, educational, adjustment, vocational, and other kinds of problems rather than wider social arrangements and others' practices being problematic for disabled people. Recall the discussion of the creation of learning disability in the Introduction and in Chapter 1.

If disabled people did not "have" deficits, then servicing agencies could not be involved (Gubrium and Buckholdt, 1982; U.S. Civil Rights Commission, 1983: 144). For example, students who are found to have a handicap that requires special education and related services must be provided a free appropriate public education according to federal regulations (Walker, 1987). Or, (until relatively recently when the mandate of state vocational rehabilitation agencies was widened) adults must have physical or mental impairments that constitute substantial handicaps to employment in order to be served by vocational rehabilitation agencies (Higgins 1985). Once the problems are identified, then service agencies strive to fix, improve, or work around the personal defects of the "clients."

Not surprisingly, an important part of servicing work is to identify those problems and characteristics that make disabled people eligible for services (Higgins, 1985). Procedures can become quite complex, taking months, even years, before eligibility is determined.

One school district ostensibly used the following procedure for identifying students as educationally handicapped: A teacher referred a student to the principal who typically referred the case to the school appraisal team, composed of the principal, the teacher of the referred student, a special education teacher, and a psychologist from the district office. If the team decided that the referral was warranted, then it recommended assessment by a school psychologist and/or other professionals (with notification and approval by parents). Once the assessment was obtained the team might take no further action, very infrequently directly place the child into some kind of educational program or refer the case to the district-wide "eligibility and placement committee." The committee, composed of the students' parents, the administrator in charge of special education, the school nurse, the psychologist who was "carrying" the case, the teacher who made the referral, and a special education teacher who would potentially work with the child, might recommend that the child remain in the regular classroom or receive some kind of special placement. In responding to various constraints in meeting governmental regulations, the school district used more complicated procedures than those described, a matter I take up later in the chapter (Mehan, Hertweck, and Meihls, 1986: Chapters 3 and 4).

The evaluation procedures further individualize disability. The procedures focus on individuals, attempt to document that the individuals *have* difficulties, and primarily explain the difficulties in term of the individuals' deficiencies. Through evaluation procedures, servicers gather information about suspected individuals (and occasionally about their families). In order to document that the suspected individuals have difficulties, they may use various approaches. They may use a "shot-gun" approach, where they probe widely, attempting to find one or more difficulties. Or they might use a "test-until-find" approach, where they evaluate until they confirm the difficulties reported by the potential client or by the referring party.

Psychologists in the school district mentioned above used this latter approach. They tested students referred to them by the school appraisal team until they found evidence to verify the reasons upon which teachers made referrals. When they did, they stopped. They did not evaluate the students further in order possibly to find other difficulties. They developed the evaluation with the referrals as a guide, choosing tests that matched the teachers' concerns. When they did not find verification, they might continue testing in order to uncover the "hidden disability." In the case of Kitty, a second grader whom her teacher referred because she was performing below grade-level in language arts and reading, the psychologist administered 19 tests without uncovering evidence of her assumed difficulty. The psychologist then recommended that Kitty remain in her regular classroom (Mehan, Hertweck and Meihls, 1986: 100–103).

When servicers evaluate potential clients, they are typically finding fault, not searching for strengths, an approach typically used by non-intimates (Goode, 1984: 232–233, 245). As difficulties are documented, then servicers typically explain them by internal defects. For example, teachers in the school district explored above overwhelmingly accounted for their referral of students for special education by pointing to students' lack of ability, behavioral difficulties, disruptive psychological states, and/or other internal limitations. Students were "two years behind in reading," had an "articulation problem," "usually out of . . . (their) seat(s)," "will argue with you," or "always in a bad mood" (Mehan, Hertweck and Meihls, 1986: 146, Chapter 5). Teachers (and even more so psychologists as they became involved in the evaluation) gave relatively little attention to the interaction between students and parents, teachers and others within diverse situations, situations not completely of the students or the other participants' own making (see also Coles, 1987).

Service providers may recognize that wider social arrangements within schools, within businesses, within the community, within government policy, even within their own organization, and elsewhere obstruct disabled people, but they do not seriously address those arrangements. That is beyond their mandate. They may also realize that they and their agencies are constrained by those arrangements, but they do not dwell on them. Schools that segregate, businesses that discriminate, governments that hesitate are by and large taken for granted (if also lamented). As one student of disability noted:

> To change the negative attitudes of the culture towards those who are judged to be disabled may require hundreds of years of systematic labor. In the meantime we are confronted with the practical problem of helping the handicapped to live with some measure of usefulness and happiness (Meyerson, 1971: 16 quoted in Gliedman and Roth, 1980: 44).

If the problem lies within disabled people, then the task is to "fix" them. If new parts won't do (though great efforts and successes are occurring in technology, but not without concern) (Tanenbaum, 1986; Cavalier, 1987; McMurray, 1987), then some kind of "retooling" may. Servicers can work with (on?) disabled people so that they can compensate, work around, adjust to, learn the limits of, modify, and in other ways address their defects. Done well, retooling enables disabled people to maneuver more successfully in the present, unchanged world. But however well it is done, "retooling" encourages us to adopt a narrow notion of what it means to be human, a narrow notion of being worthy.

Consequently, *behaving* like, if not *being* like, nondisabled people is progress within servicing agencies. When deaf children can speak and speechread even though they cannot hear well their or others' speech, progress has been made. Never mind that the cost of "progress" for a few is the needlessly diminished personal and academic growth of many (Lane, 1984 as an opponent of servicing; Lynas, 1986 as a proponent). When a person with paralysis can haltingly take a few steps or even walk laboriously, that person is to be admired even though a wheelchair may be more efficient and efforts to learn to take a few steps might be more profitably put elsewhere (Zola, 1982: Chapter 10). Years of being fitted with changing, upper extremity prostheses and learning to use them may enable a person with quadrilateral limb deficiencies to appear and seemingly to function more "normally," but the ersatz normality may come at the cost of the individual's own style of managing and sense of self, as it did for one young woman.

> It was apparent from the very beginning that no matter how competently Diane learned to use her artificial arms, she would always need to have someone place things in her reach, pre-position her terminal hooks, or prearrange objects that she needed to handle. What advantage she might gain in reach and grasp using these complex devices was canceled by the restrictions imposed by the confining equipment. Many of the tasks she learned to perform slowly and with great effort using upper prostheses—writing, reading a book, or holding a cup—were ones she could perform with her stumps (Frank, 1988: 52).

When a person known as mentally retarded can write the letters of the alphabet, without (ever?) being able to use them, that person is more "normal" when serviced. For example, at one center for mentally retarded adults, "students with no ability to recognize or make sense of characters of the alphabet could participate in an occasion of 'practice writing' by tracing through paper over large printed letters. Some students reported having practiced writing in this way for several years" (Kielhofner, 1983: 320). On one occasion at the center

> Out walked Jean with a stack of "Grade 1 workbooks" each with a very juvenile picture of alphabet blocks on it. Dorothy motioned for me to look at her workbook. On the pages were pictures of common things seen around home: a cub (sic), a bowl, a window, etc. Under the picture of the cup she had written the word, "BVOAS." This word appeared on both lines under the picture. Similarly, under the picture of a window was the word, "DROKAC," again

written twice. John was attempting to encircle the word "duck" from among a mass of letters. He had instead circled the words, "dck," "kuck," etc. The word "duck" was circled but once (Kielhofner, 1983: 320).

At times, nondisabled servicers explicitly use themselves as the standard of normality against which the disabled "clients" are judged—and assume that the disabled individuals will not measure up. Consider Sharon, a young woman recovering from a stroke, who now talks haltingly and with slurred articulation. During a therapy session to improve written communication, the speech therapist, Nancy, asks Sharon to write one-sentence descriptions that relate the various objects depicted on different cards. On the back of each card is a suggested answer.

[For a picture of houses on a mountaintop with trees below, Sharon writes: "The houses are above the treeline." The therapist is quite astounded.]

Nancy: Wow! That was a really nice way of describing it. Ver-r-r-y good! I couldn't have said it better myself. Next time, you be the teacher. [They both laugh.]

[Sharon looks at the next card, which depicts three men standing on a sidewalk with a house in the background. As Sharon thinks, the therapist puzzles over the card.]

Nancy: Gee. I don't get that one [the picture card]. I wonder what they want you to say on this one? [Turns over the card and reads the suggested sentence.] Oh, I see what they want. Let's forget this one, Sharon. It's not really clear what they want from the picture.

Sharon: Should I do it?

Nancy: No. [Pause] Now let me give you some homework. I want you to do this page of words that you have to rearrange to mean something else. Okay?

Sharon: Okay

Nancy: Let's do one first, okay, so you know what to do.

[They unscramble the first word. Sharon says that she understands. The therapist comes to the second word that Sharon is to unscramble. It is; "Change steal to something that means flavorless—_____."]

Nancy: Sharon.... Uh, you can forget about the second one. Just skip over it and just do the others for homework. Okay? Just do all of these, beginning with the third one. When I looked these over this morning, I couldn't for the life of me figure it [the second word] out myself. I asked Bea [another speech therapist] if she could figure it out at lunch and she knew what the answer was. It was "stale." So I'll forgive you if you can't come up with the right answer on that one (Gubrium and Buckholdt, 1982: 56).

Servicing takes the nondisabled world (often an idealized version of it, sometimes a very personal version of it) as the standard for evaluating the behavior of others (especially the disabled people who become its clients), developing its programs, and judging the progress of the disabled people it serves. With the nondisabled world taken for granted, servicing individualizes disability, concentrating on the "internal flaws" of its disabled clients.

Stratifying Service

Servicing is stratified, often greatly so. Inequality is pervasive. Servicing varies dramatically from the advantaged to the less advantaged, whether our concern is servicing agencies or disabled people who are served. The two typically go together. (And as I mentioned in Chapter 1, less advantaged youth are more likely to be made mentally retarded than advantaged youth.) More advantaged disabled people frequent more advantaged servicing organizations and more advantaged servicing organizations attend to more advantaged disabled people. But as important as that is, that is not my concern here. That is a concern of how we set policy and an outgrowth of social inequality (Black, 1989: 102–103).

Instead, servicing actively makes people unequal. It stratifies those involved into more or less worthy people. In doing so it creates what we often take as the consequence of being worthy but might appropriately be understood to *be* worthiness itself: being informed, influential (i.e., listened to), interdependent instead of dependent, and the like. Servicing separates disabled people (and their families) from those who service them, lowering the former, elevating the latter. Near or at the bottom of any servicing agency are the disabled people (and their families), recipients of others' assistance. Above them are the servicing staff, particularly the professionals. *Professionals dominate.* Further, servicing stratifies the services and the staff. It often does so in various ways. In particular, servicing creates a *"hierarchy of help"*. Staff arrange themselves and their work from least worthy to most worthy, from dealing directly with disabled "clients," to managing the servicing carried out by others, to setting servicing policy. Staff stratify themselves according to the tasks they perform. As the distance from the disabled people increases, so does the service worthiness of the staff. Finally (for my purposes), servicing *differentiates disabled people* into more or less worthy individuals to whom unequal amounts of service will be given. The "severity" and sincerity of the disabled people are important here. Servicing stratifies.

Professional dominance

Service staff, particularly doctors, teachers, counselors, therapists and other professionals, manage and provide servicing (Gliedman and Roth, 1980: especially Chapters 3 and 8; DeJong, 1983; Stubbins, 1988). The disabled individuals are managed. The following excerpt from a newspaper article, describing an unusual event, makes that point, perhaps even caricatures it, with great irony, an irony that seems to be lost on the professionals in the story:

MENTAL PATIENT TAKES CHARGE IN EMERGENCY

Fort Worth, Texas (AP)—It was about 10:15 p.m. when surging floodwaters from a thunderstorm knocked out power at ... Hospital and damaged the hospital's emergency generators.

In the ensuing darkness and confusion, a young mental patient stepped to the fore and "took matters into his own hands," directing the staff, giving orders, and generally coping with the emergency.

Masquerading as a medical official, the patient spent part of the holiday weekend issuing directives to employees and volunteers. With no outside power and temperatures soaring, the hospital suddenly had no lights, no air conditioning and no ventilation.

At one point, the young man dispatched his temporary charges on a midnight foray for ice.

"He did a superb job," conceded hospital administrator. ... "He was dressed in a scrubsuit, which made him look authoritative. If you had seen him standing by our interns, you would have thought he was one of them."

Security guards put an end to the pretense about 2 A.M. Sunday after an "extensive" telephone conversation between (the hospital administrator) and the patient, identified only as a man in his mid-20's (*The Columbia Record,* July 7, 1981: 4-A).

However, whether during an emergency or during the routine provision of services, professionals typically dominate, directing the disabled "clients."

The professionals' agencies' mandate to serve disabled people, their positions within the agencies, their credentials, their (seeming) expertise, and their experience, all of these are taken as pointing to the professionals as the appropriate people to be in charge. While professionals certainly talk with (though too often it seems they merely talk "to") the disabled people (and their families), they typically decide if the disabled people are eligible for services, what services are needed, if the disabled people are "making progress," if additional or different services are needed, if services should be stopped or continued, and so on.

They are the case and client managers. They declare success and reluctantly admit defeat. Through knowing their agencies' procedures, outnumbering at conferences the disabled people (and their parents/advocates), using professional jargon that may intimidate, arranging the meetings, controlling the information and the services, and in still other ways, professionals dominate. (For example, see Mehan, Hertweck and Meihls, 1986: Chapter 7 for how in one school district professionals controlled the committee which decided the eligibility and placement of students into special education programs. In part they did it through talk and the control of talk.)

Return to Diane, who was born with quadrilateral limb deficiencies. "Despite the mixed results with artificial arms, and the contrasting picture of Diane's strength and coordination in her artificial legs, a decision was made (by her specialists) when she was 12 years old to end her training with lower extremity prostheses" (Frank, 1988: 54–55). The report notes:

> This child has had a five- to six-year program during which she used experimental legs of various types. This program was not successful. It is felt that a significant part of her present enthusiasm for the use of the upper extremities is due to her release from the ordeal of struggling with lower extremity legs which gave her such limited function and satisfaction. Therefore, it is recommended that her visits to physical therapy be discontinued and her time more profitably spent in Occupational Therapy (Frank, 1988: 55).

Diane "later struggled unsuccessfully to reverse" this decision (Frank, 1988: 55).

Diane and other disabled people (and their families) are the recipients of the services bestowed upon them. What we call them tells them and us that is so. Formerly they were inmates, patients, wards of the state, but that was during less "progressive" times. Now they are residents, students, trainees, clients of all kinds. Their responsibility is to carry out dutifully the prescriptions of the professionals. They may not need to understand what they are doing or why (though understanding may also enable the disabled clients to be more dutiful). And they certainly should not question the professionals' judgment. To do so would threaten the helping relationship. Instead, they can take comfort in the professionals' expertise and good intentions. After all, according to the servicing paradigm, the professionals and their service agencies work in the best interests of the disabled people (Gliedman and Roth, 1980: Chapter 2).

Hierarchy of help

An extension of professional dominance is the stratification of staff. Service agencies, often being bureaucratic, operate through a hierarchy of staff. Directors, superintendents, administrators, assistant administrators, and the like staff the highest levels of the service agencies. Therapists, counselors, teachers, psychologists, and other professionals, who may directly service the disabled individuals, are farther down and may be stratified among themselves. For example, within one hospital that specialized in physical rehabilitation, the director of leisure services put physical therapists above occupational therapists with leisure therapists' being "OT's little cousin" (Gubrium and Buckholdt, 1982: 28). At the "bottom" are aides, attendants, instructional assistants and such. Staff with the most authority, training, credentials, prestige, and pay typically are the farthest removed from those served by the agency. Staff with the least authority, training, credentials, prestige, and pay typically interact most extensively with those served by the agency. To "advance" from directly working with those whom the agency serves to managing some portion of the agency and its staff is a goal that lower level providers may hold for themselves. The further removed from the actual provision of service, the more service worthy is the staff member.

Within a hierarchy of help, differing, often conflicting, orientations develop among the stratified staff. Those at the bottom may develop understandings that undermine the intentions of those above. Similarly, those at (or near) the top may have little understanding or appreciation for the challenges faced by those at the bottom. Stratification creates strain.

For example, consider the world of attendants in state facilities for mentally retarded individuals. Robert Bogdan and his colleagues (1974) have argued that attendants' views and subsequent behaviors may undermine the programming implemented by upper-level staff. Of particular importance are the attendants' views of their *superiors*, of their own *work*, and of the mentally retarded *residents*.

Attendants believe that their superiors do not understand "what it's really like" (Bogdan et al., 1974: 143). Not being with the mentally retarded "residents" nor on the wards very much, superiors do not have much direct experience. Consequently, the attendants question the professional jargon and procedures of their superiors. Further, attendants know that being a professional in the institution is not prestigious or well paid. Medical doctors may be foreign trained and not state certified. Communication is difficult with them. Being in much greater contact with the "residents," the attendants believe that their own experiences and understandings are better guides than are the professional pronouncements of the superiors. For example, attendants may dismiss the results of an IQ test as not reflecting the competence of the mentally retarded individual. After all, the attendant can see what the "resident" can and cannot do. (1)

While attendants may at times be gratified in working with the mentally retarded "clients," being an attendant is "just a job." Attendants emphasize the security of the job, its pay in comparison to alternatives, and other extrinsic features. (So may nursing aides, now called assistants, who work in intermediate care facilities and other "nursing homes" (Diamond, 1983).) Consequently, there is little internal reason for working at the job. Instead, attendants find ways to minimize their work—by getting more competent "residents" to do it, by "goofing off," by developing quotas as to how much they should do, and the like—while complaining about how much they must do and the trouble it is to do it. They neither have the training nor the time to work with the mentally retarded individuals. That is someone else's responsibility.

Finally, attendants view the mentally retarded "residents" in terms of their characteristics that create work for them (see also Goode, 1984). The "residents" may be known as "pukers," "headbangers," "biters," and the like. Attendants resent "residents" who are very active or who lack basic self-help skills. They hold fatalistic views of the "residents." Not much can be accomplished with them. And they may believe that too much attention may spoil the "residents"—which would create more work for them.

New attendants develop these understandings in various ways. As they first rotate from ward to ward during orientation and then later as they work with more experienced attendants, they learn from more experienced attendants these views of their superiors, their work, and the "residents." To the extent that the superiors emphasize the differentness of mentally retarded individuals in training the attendants, they help to create some of these views. To the extent that the attendants are of similar racial and socioeconomic status, perhaps relatives or friends outside of work, and segregated with one another during work, a solidarity among the attendants, a "brotherhood at the bottom," may develop in opposition to others at the institution.

The attendants' views about their superiors, their work, and the mentally retarded people may undermine programs developed by administrators. "Innovative" programming such as a "motivation program" consisting of coloring or listening to children's records on a "back ward," a behavior modification program involving a token economy on an adolescent ward, and a range of motion program on an infant/children ward to provide physical stimulation to "prevent physical regression and the development of spasticity and irreversible contractures" did not succeed well (Bogdan et al., 1974: 150). The attendants saw the programs as additional work when they were already overworked. The "patients" were too limited to improve much. At best the programs kept the mentally retarded people occupied. The attendants did not feel that they were trained to run the programs nor paid enough to do so. For example, the behavior modification program became a means for attendants to punish adolescent girls for annoying behavior rather than encourage them for appropriate behavior. However, after a while, attendants became "lax in their point recording, and many of the girls had simply forgotten about the points they had accumulated" (Bogdan et al., 1974: 149–150). The program had been subverted.

Similarly, higher-level staff's concerns may conflict with lower-level staff's everyday challenges. Being enmeshed more in the managing of the organization than in the lives of the disabled people served, upper-level staff typically have different concerns and responsibilities than do direct-care staff. Administrators must obtain funding, manage budgets, staff positions, and the like. These are not the responsibility of direct-care staff. Leaving a position unfilled in order to balance the budget may create greater work for the direct-care staff. Or, administrators and supervisors expect forms to be filled out even if service providers must do it on their "own time" or neglect disabled "clients" to do so.

Consider skilled nursing centers, intermediate care facilities and other "nursing homes" (See Diamond, 1983 for the basis of this example). Those who become nursing assistants may do so in part because they wish to care for others. However, nursing assistants may soon learn that social care-giving is not their prime responsibility. Medical and manual work is. Giving the residents their "meds" (i.e., medications), monitoring "vitals" (i.e., blood pressure, pulse, temperature, and respiration), and charting all of this are their most important responsibilities. After that comes "bed and body work" (bedmaking, cleaning, feeding the residents, and such). Talking with residents, providing emotional comfort, and other social care-giving are much less important; they're not even mentioned in the charts (nor in the training for the position). Nursing assistants may be criticized for providing such attention, as was one researcher who worked as a trained nursing assistant:

> One expressive moment of this for me was when I stopped to sit with Mary Karney, a 77-year-old resident, who was crying, on her bed. Before I could find out why she was crying, I was interrupted by my supervisor who scolded me for sitting down with Mary, reminding me that I had 16 more vitals to do before bedcheck ... This kind of incident can be recounted by nurses everywhere ... it should not be surprising that her (Mary's) blood pressure was high that day—she was upset. There was a place to record her high numbers, but not her crying (Diamond, 1983: 273–274).

However, to believe that lower-level staff or administrators and supervisors are the culprits individualizes the difficulties of servicing. While upper-level and lower-level staff are responsible for their behavior, their work is conditioned by social policies and arrangements for which all of us are responsible—either through active implementation or acquiescence. For example, large institutions cannot help but disable those they are designed to serve. Segregating mentally retarded people and persons with other disabilities in "isolated, massive facilities," providing "feeble attempts at programming," establishing a hierarchy of help that minimizes the importance of directly serving disabled people, and other practices make service agencies that are total institutions disabling (Bogdan et al., 1974: 150). Or, the "nursing homes" in which little time can be found for Mary Karney and others respond to the medical domination of care-giving within capitalism. The rational, accountable production of profit is emphasized. The government (and third party providers) pay private entrepreneurs to manage disabled people, who have now become a "commodity," a source of profits (Diamond, 1983). Our service arrangements and social policies are the culprits, not primarily the service providers.

Differentiating disabled people

When we service disabled people, we differentiate them. We divide them into categories to which we give unequal attention. Typically, we give more to those who are most advantaged and less to those who are most disadvantaged. This occurs in the unequal treatment of disabled and nondisabled people, but it takes place within servicing, too.

Many have criticized the labeling and categorization of disabled people (Gliedman and Roth, 1980; Biklen et al., 1985; Gartner and Joe, 1987).

Critics claim that such procedures separate people and often inappropriately group people for services. By categorizing some people as disabled (e.g., as learning disabled), as different than those not labeled
disabled, and then placing those with disabilities into different programs,
we make disabled and nondisabled people different. Through our procedures we created the differences (perhaps usefully so), though our common understanding is that the differences caused us to categorize and
place disabled people. Through categorization we place together disabled people who likely vary greatly, but the categorization and attendant programs and procedures channel how the people will be served.
Differences are downplayed; similarities are stressed. We both separate
people and inappropriately treat similarly those we have set apart, claim
critics.

Servicing not only separates people—disabled from nondisabled, disabled from one another—it also stratifies disabled people by worth.
Disabled people become more or less worthy of servicing attention. This
differentiation ties to service survival, as I explain later.

Severity and *sincerity* are important dimensions of stratification: typically,
the more severe, the less service; the more sincere, the greater service.

Servicing differentiates people according to the severity of their
disabilities. Severity is a shorthand (sometimes useful, often not) for
disabled people's capacity to perform according to narrow standards of
normality within narrowly constructed worlds taken for granted. Thus,
mentally retarded students may be known as EMH, TMH, and PMH—
educably mentally handicapped, trainably mentally handicapped, and
profoundly mentally handicapped. Rehabilitation clients are disabled
or severely disabled. "Nursing home" residents might be higher or lower
functioning. Typically, those with multiple disabilities or who are severely
impaired have been denied services, referred to the most segregated
servicing arrangement, shifted from one program to another as each
program claims that it cannot manage such people, left unattended when
admitted to servicing agencies, and the like (Bowe, 1978: 70; Biklen,
1985; Foster, 1987).

Nowadays professionals speak of service continuums in education,
residential arrangements, employment, and such. For example, residential arrangements for developmentally disabled individuals may run
from large-scale institutions to intermediate care facilities in the community to group homes to independent living (and still other distinctions)
(Taylor et al., 1987). Education may likewise range from segregated

insitutions serving disabled students to separate programs within a local school to being mainstreamed with nondisabled students in classes and activities. Whatever the realm, the basic assumption underlying service continuums is that the most severely impaired people should be served in the most restricted, segregated, sheltered manner. This is commensurate with their capacities. As their capacities increase, they will be served less restrictively. A service continuum provides disabled people unequal access to the larger social world. As I explain in the next chapter, this service continuum is problematic. Nevertheless, servicing differentiates disabled people according to their "severity" and typically assists less those deemed most severe (though perhaps in a more costly manner, but we should not confuse cost with quality).

Servicing also separates disabled people by their sincerity. As in human service agencies of all kind, to the most sincere goes the greatest attention (Lipsky, 1980: 152). Service providers view favorably "motivated," cooperative "clients." They appreciate disabled "clients" who (in the providers' judgments) work hard, are serious about making progress, accept the providers' statement of the problem, and actively follow the providers' prescriptions (Roth and Eddy, 1967: 199; Scott, 1969: 76–80; Gubrium and Buckholdt, 1982: 31–33; Witt et al., 1984; Higgins, 1985: 65–69, 100–102, 123). Service providers evaluate similarly family members and others who also participate in the servicing, such as parents of students receiving special education.

For example, in my field work with vocational rehabilitation counselors I learned that counselors might put "on hold" uncooperative clients. Counselors wanted to use their energies efficiently, did not believe that "clients" could be rehabilitated against their will, and enjoyed working with motivated persons. Consequently, "at times they gave less time to clients who did not follow through with planned services" (Higgins, 1985: 123). One counselor, who had "really hustled and bustled" to arrange a job interview for one of his "clients" to which the "client" was not going because of an appointment to have her hair done, kept the "client's" case opened but decided to give more attention to those more interested in "getting a job" (Higgins, 1985: 123).

Consider the staff in a midwestern physical rehabilitation hospital. To them the "ideal" disabled "patient" works hard during therapy, does therapeutic homework between sessions, doesn't criticize therapists, and (somewhat incongruously) strives to become as independent as possible while following the therapists' prescriptions. However, those who pursue their own therapeutic activties in order to become independent may be going too far. Staff may see them, as they did the following man, as "stubborn," "too independent," or "not knowing what's good" for them:

> The man was a diabetic who had had one leg amputated below the knee. Therapists and other staff members were trying to reduce the swelling in his stump and strengthen the leg so that he could begin working with a pylon (a temporary prosthesis). He was doing his exercises regularly and the leg was unusually strong, but the swelling persisted, and he would have to stay longer than expected so that the problem could be corrected. Since the patient was anxious "to go home and resume my own life," this news upset him. He was particularly angry with the staff for their failure to reduce the swelling. He claimed this was due to the fact that they did not know how to regulate his insulin intake. He had been monitoring it for thirty years by himself and knew the proper balance, but claimed that the doctor and nurses at Wilshire would not listen. As far as he was concerned, the only way he could get better was to get out of the hospital and learn to use the prosthesis on an outpatient basis. When he checked himself out of the hospital, the staff had mixed reactions. On the one hand, they were glad to be rid of a troublesome patient but, on the other, they were concerned about his condition and felt he did not know how to take care of himself properly; after all, they argued, if he had followed professional advice, he might never have lost the leg in the first place (Gubrium and Buckholdt, 1982: 32).

Servicing stratifies. Through professional dominance, a hierarchy of help, and the differentiation of disabled people, servicing makes the participants and service activities unequal, not just different. Such stratification creates shortcomings, as I explore later.

Surviving

Servicing stresses surviving. As do many organizations, servicing agencies aim to meet and manage the expectations of those upon whom they depend. Disabled people are one such group, but they are not always the most important. Funding agencies, regulatory bodies, the public, and other servicers are typically important, too. In order to survive, servicing agencies may need to demonstrate the existence of needy disabled people, their own efficiency and effectiveness, that regulations are being met, and other points. Sometimes they use great ingenuity in order to do so.

For example, recall the school district whose evaluation procedures for identifying students in "need" of special educational services I mentioned earlier. The procedures were more complicated than I previously mentioned. For example, as did all school districts, this one worked under legal requirements for evaluating students who had been referred for evaluation, developing appropriate educational programs, and implementing the programs. Given the district's resources relative to the number of children referred, the district could not meet the legal time requirements without developing some creative procedures. For example, instead of dating the referrals on the day the teachers filled them out, the district dated the referrals on the day they were presented to the School Appraisal Team. The district also made a distinction between "teacher notifications" and "official referrals." They were the "same" reports with different dates stamped on them. The notifications were the teachers' reports to the SAT about students they believed needed help. The referrals were the same reports presented to the SAT on the day that the cases were heard. The district also established a Child Guidance Team, whose composition was similar to the SAT. Referrals went first to the Child Guidance Team, which evaluated the merits of the case. The case had not yet become an official referral. If the Child Guidance Team decided that further evaluations were needed, then they were obtained without parental permission, which was necessary for official cases. After further evaluations, the Child Guidance Team might decide to refer the case to the School Appraisal Team, where it became official once presented, or recommend that nothing further be done. Through these procedures, the district was able to save time and "meet" its legal obligations (Mehan, Hertweck, and Meihls, 1986: 63–66).

Among various survival concerns, servicing agencies *create clients, address accountability,* and *pitch to the public.*

Creating clients

Without clients, servicing agencies would not survive. Without servicing agencies, clients do not exist. "Official" disabled people do not even exist without organizational certification. Without that official recognition, people known as disabled by others are not "formally" disabled. They are not recorded as disabled, and they are not served as disabled—at least not officially so (though informal arrangements may be made).

> Consider, for example, a student who is confined to a wheelchair. Certainly, one would argue, he is handicapped or has a handicap. However, such a student would not automatically be placed in a special education program for the physically handicapped. Institutional practices for identification and placement would have to be placed in motion in order for the student to achieve that designation. From this point of view, then, a physical handicap is the

product of an institutional practice. A student cannot be physically handicapped, institutionally speaking, unless there are professional practices to make that determination (Mehan, Hertweck and Meihls, 1986: 58). (2)

Servicing agencies may even be the first to transform individuals into disabled people, who then become known as disabled elsewhere, or the agencies may be the only place where the individuals are transformed into disabled people, the individuals being (known as) nondisabled outside the agencies. Servicing agencies may diagnose hearing and other impairments that were ambiguously experienced by individuals and other concerned parties (see Chapter 5). Or, only within service agencies may some individuals be known as disabled. Many children and youth who are officially classified as disabled within schools, are not understood to be disabled outside of school, either as children or later as adults. The "six-hour retarded child" refers to children known as disabled within school but who perform satisfactorily outside of school (Edgerton, 1979: 72 in Mehan et al., 1986: 161; See also Gliedman and Roth, 1980: 285 for a discussion of the vast numbers of children known as disabled who are not officially recorded as disabled as adults, though they seem to assume that the adults are indeed disabled but are simply overlooked in the counts.)

Servicing agencies certainly create their clients. They develop eligibility criteria, guidelines, and procedures or implement the criteria, guidelines, and procedures established by others. They develop sources for referrals of potential clients, screen applicants, evaluate potential clients, staff cases, develop relations with the potential clients (and possibly others related to the potential clients), make recommendations, justify their decisions, certify people as eligible, retain individuals in the status of client (instead of discharging the people), and so much more. Of course, the potential clients and many others, such as family members and professionals in the community, participate in this drama of transformation, which may make easier or more difficult the task of the service providers. Becoming a client is not inherent in the characteristics of people, just as people's makeup does not make them disabled (Prottas, 1979; Lipsky, 1980: 59–70; Gubrium and Buckholdt, 1982; Higgins, 1985; Mehan, Hertweck and Meihls, 1986; Foster, 1987; Kugelmass, 1987).

In order to survive, perhaps even to thrive (i.e., to enlarge the servicing program), servicing agencies may questionably create clients (though all creating of clients and making of disability should be questioned). Servicing agencies may "cream" applicants, accepting primarily those disabled people who seem to have good potential to benefit from the agencies' services (Scott, 1969; Safilios-Rothschild, 1970: 170). They may "bribe" disabled people (or their guardians) with the promises of benefits such as medical services or more individual attention in a special class (Higgins, 1985: 191–192; Kugelmass, 1987: 111). They may "coerce" them with the possibility that present conditions could worsen if they do not become clients. They may enlarge their criteria in order to bring more into the fold, as seems to be happening in the mushrooming of students labeled learning disabled (Coles, 1987; Walker, 1987). They may aggressively search for potential clients, painstakingly develop evidence justifying individuals' eligibility to be clients, or maintain people as clients longer in order to fill their vacancies, increase the funds other parties provide them, and/or keep a workshop productive (Buckholdt and Gubrium, 1983; Evans, 1983: Chapter 9; Mehan, Hertweck and Meihls, 1986: 62).

For example, administrators at a residential facility that treated emotionally disturbed children were concerned when the county welfare department cut funds for residential treatment at a time when several of the children in the facility were scheduled for discharge and few referrals for admission existed. Administrators urged staff to "review case files thoroughly and to document problems clearly and show progress in order to prevent further discharges" (Buckholdt and Gubrium, 1983: 253). All agencies create clients. Stress on surviving makes that creation even more problematic.

Addressing accountability

Servicing agencies are typically accountable to others who regulate them, reimburse them, fund them, or in some manner oversee them. They must document that they are properly serving the appropriate people. However, when servicing agencies address accountability, they may ironically disable people with disabilities.

When addressing accountability, servicing agencies may unintendedly make more disabled the individuals they have made clients. In order to justify their servicing of disabled people to third parties, servicing agencies may emphasize (some might argue fabricate) the limitations of the disabled people and the significant services that are needed. While concern with having sufficient clients, and thus survival, may underlie their justifications, servicers need not do this cynically. Instead, they believe that their services are useful and alternatives to their services are less desirable or are not available. For example, a family may not yet accept a disabled member or another agency is full. In the process of creating a justification for third parties, servicers may sincerely come to understand the individual in a new way—as more disabled.

For example, in the residential treatment center for emotionally disturbed children that I noted previously, a teacher, psychologist, social worker, and other caregivers "needed" to justify a continued stay of a student whom they had previously recommended be discharged. Parents, who had wanted their son to come home, changed their mind, and a suitable school had rejected the boy after he "misbehaved seriously while attending an interview with teachers and counselors" (Buckholdt and Gubrium, 1983: 260–261).

> Social Worker: We can talk all day about how things got . . . uh . . . messed up. But what are we gonna say in this report? He's got to stay here.

> Teacher: We have all the scales on him, like acting out and fantasizing. Can't we just say that he isn't as improved as we thought?

> Psychologist: I feel we may need more, . . . something harder. What I'm beginning to see is that this lad may be a sociopath. They can really fool you. He fooled us for a long time and even his parents. They seem fine one minute and then they zap you, as soon as you trust me. . . .

> Social Worker: I agree. That's a pretty strong term but I guess it's pretty close to the truth. These types (sociopaths) usually take a while to figure out. They (County Welfare) should understand why we were fooled.

> Psychologist: I really hadn't noticed but there was a hint of it in an old eval (evaluation). We should have seen it earlier but we didn't. It's that simple (Buckholdt and Gubrium, 1983: 261).

Of course, addressing accountability is not that simple. When doing so, servicers may not only come to understand people as more disabled than they had previously understood them to be, but they may also serve them in ways that lessen their lives, thereby fulfilling their lowered evaluation of them. Recall the researcher who worked as a certified nursing assistant in some "nursing homes." Instead of being encouraged or even permitted to comfort an elderly woman who was crying, his supervisor scoldingly reminded him that he had "16 more vitals to do before bedcheck" (Diamond, 1983: 273). Regulatory inspections at these "nursing homes" focused on the records, forms, and other documentation, not the interpersonal caregiving as carried out and experienced by the participants. It shouldn't surprise us that, in being accountable to regulatory overseers, these "nursing homes" made the elderly people less socially and emotionally able. Accountability can oppress people.

Pitching to the public

Servicing agencies depend on the public in order to survive. At a minimum servicing agencies depend on the community's "benign neglect" (i.e., lack of opposition). Typically they require active participation from the community. They may need clients, money, donations, cooperation, opportunities, and so on. Residential placements, job training, and jobs require community cooperation. Private programs may depend on financial support from the community. Mainstreaming students with educational handicaps requires the efforts of at least some "regular" school staff. To survive, servicing agencies must reach out to the public.

Consequently, servicers are most likely to pitch *conservatively* themselves and disabled people to the public. Confrontation and challenge are not likely. To do so jeopardizes future support. Thus, when mainstreaming students with educationally handicapping conditions, "special education" teachers may make deals with "regular education" teachers instead of insisting on more complete, integral arrangements (Biklen, 1985). As I noted in Chapter 3, fundraising activities may appeal to the sympathy of the public, thereby supporting their stereotypes. Rehabilitation counselors may literally pitch only their "best" clients to employers for fear of souring job opportunities for future prospects (Higgins, 1985: 113–114). Administrators may back off from placing "group homes" for disabled people when a community opposes the site. This can, but need not, lead to group homes primarily being placed in less advantaged neighborhoods (Rothman and Rothman, 1984: Chapter 8). Through pitching to the public, addressing accountability and creating clients among other means, agencies survive.

Disabling Service

Servicing disables people. While being serviced, disabled people develop new skills and understandings, get jobs, establish homes, and in other ways make their lives. Nevertheless, servicing is still flawed. Servicing ultimately denies the validity of being a person with varying mental, physical, and/or emotional characteristics. In making individuals disabled people, servicing makes them illegitimate. It transforms individuals with varying characteristics into *foreign* kinds of people. It makes

those foreign kinds of people *passive* participants in their lives. Consequently, servicing *preserves* our present political, economic, and other
social arrangements that may disable people. It does not challenge them.
In its failures, servicing ultimately and literally *makes death.*

Making Disabled People Foreign

Servicing produces and perpetuates narrow notions about humanity.
By taking people with varying physical, mental, and emotional characteristics and transforming them into instances of disability categories (in
part because they cannot be fit into narrow notions of normality) to be
educated, rehabilitated, housed, assisted in finding work, and in other
ways "treated" outside of the everyday routines, servicing makes people
disabled foreigners (Zola, 1989). By striving to change disabled people
into nondisabled people, or as close as as possible, servicing upholds the
primacy of being nondisabled. Anything else is alien. By unthinkingly
interpreting disabled people according to unquestioned (unrecognized?)
standards based on the routine behavior of nondisabled people, servicing reduces disabled people. It makes them less competent individuals.
The standards are taken to be objective benchmarks of humans, not the
reflections of present practices of nondisabled people, practices that can
change and that are not necessarily usefully applicable to others (Goode,
1984, 1986). Such interpretations can turn what could be understood as
the skills of disabled people into symptoms of their disability (Goode,
1986: 96).

Consider again Chris, a deaf-blind Rubella child mentioned in Chapter 4. Custodial staff, clinical staff, and teachers in the state hospital
where she lived knew her to be incompetent. They knew her primarily
as a bundle of deficits, a collection of difficulties she "posed" for them in
working with (on?) her. Her repetitive rocking, recurrent vocalizations,
masturbation, playing with her sight and sound reception (e.g., in eight
uninterrupted minutes she put a rattle to more than twenty distinct uses,
such as thumping her tongue and banging her teeth with it, rubbing it
across parts of her body, and grasping all the different surfaces), and
other behaviors were taken as symptoms of her retardation.

But what if we "freed" ourselves from an able-bodied view of reality and
from an adult view of reality, views that are understood as reality, not
"merely" ways of making reality? If we did, we could understand that
many of Chris's "seemingly pathological behaviors had a definite pur-
posiveness and rationality" (Goode, 1986: 94). Symptoms became skills,

at least to the social scientist mentioned earlier who befriended Chris. He understood the repetitive rocking as one of many activities that Chris used in occupying her time, vast amounts of time, when she was left alone. The "unusual" uses of the rattle were Chris's explorations of the object with her available senses. Her explorations were unencumbered by taken-for-granted understandings as to the appropriate way to use a rattle. "Chris was 'an alternative object reader'; that is, a person who by virtue of not knowing objects' correct uses did things with them which were completely inaccessible to most persons. Instead of equating objects with their cultural recipes Chris grasped them with an openness unavailable to the average person" (Goode, 1986: 97). But the able-bodied view of the world that underlies servicing (and that most of us unwittingly use) makes it almost impossible to see Chris's competence. Instead, Chris and others who vary physically, mentally, and emotionally are made to be alien beings.

By servicing people with disabilities in places and programs and through procedures separate from others, servicing further makes disabled people aliens. "Special" education is a prime example. It's very name tells us that the recipients are different kinds of students. Even with the legal mandate to educate together students with varying mental, physical, and emotional characteristics (i.e., handicapped and nonhandicapped students), schooling continues to separate students, putting some in separate residential schools, day schools, classrooms, and programs. While variations exist across jurisdictions and "disability categories," overall the separation of students has not changed much in America since the passage of P.L. 94-142, The Education for All Handicapped Children Act of 1975 (now termed the Individuals with Disabilities Education Act). Approximately one-third of disabled students are educated outside of general classes (Walker, 1987: 104–105; Ferguson et al., 1990). While procedures designed to ensure an appropriate, individualized education, such as the Individualized Education Program (IEP), are potentially useful (though also quite problematic), they still set disabled youth apart from nondisabled youth, who are not covered by such procedures (Gliedman and Roth, 1980: Chapters 9 and 10; Biklen, 1989). Handicap categories, legally acceptable placement options that include segregation, different funding mechanisms for "special" education and "regular" education, and other practices make youth with varying characteristics different kinds of people. Instead of creating ways to encompass more and more people of varying characteristics within the same programs, servicing makes disabled people foreign.

Making Disabled People Passive

Servicing makes disabled people (and their families) passive (Gliedman and Roth, 1980: Chapters 3 and 8; DeJong, 1983). While disabled people may exert themselve strenuously during their service, they do so in order to follow "dutifully" the prescriptions of the professionals. The professionals evaluate, plan, treat, monitor, revise, discharge, and in other ways manage disabled people. Disabled people (and their families) are expected to do what they are told. For example, while recent legislation has been intended to promote parents' involvement in their disabled children's education, typically parents remain quite passive. Special educators often write educational plans before they meet with parents, who then become passive recipients of the presented information. Yet parents may acquiesce to educators whom they view as the experts and are pleased with the educational planning. Believing they have the competence to be in charge, teachers may desire parents to acquiesce (Higgins, 1990: 67–70).

Service providers may dismiss as unreliable opinions the hard-won understanding developed by disabled people (and their families) out of their everyday experiences. Providers may downplay or disregard disabled people's desires as the unrealistic wishes of understandably unadjusted people. Service staff may dismiss as delusional parents who claim their disabled children to be more competent than the staff "know" the children to be (Goode, 1990). As a speech therapist in a rehabilitation hospital complained to a social worker about a mutual "patient":

> That guy (patient) thinks he's going to walk right out of here and go back to school and graduate next summer. No way! Yeah, he wants to get better. Sure! But he doesn't know what he's talking about. Literally! *I know* what's best for the guy and I work myself to the bone trying to get him to improve his grammar and speech. He's always saying I'm lording it over him. Boy, is he on the wrong track. Sweetheart, he just doesn't know. That's all. And I do. I wish you'd talk to him, for his own good (Gubrium and Buckholdt, 1982: 49).

Specialized professionals dominate, and we, thereby, become less competent to help ourselves (Black, 1989: 77–81). We rely on professionals, and service providers rely on more specialized providers than themselves. For example, if special education teachers are available, then regular education teachers may assume little responsibility in planning for and integrating a child with a disability (Biklen, forthcoming). Courts affirm the professionals' judgment and, thus, sustain our impotence and incompetence (Foster, 1987: 145–146; Biklen, 1988).

However, this reliance (whether willing or not) on the judgment of specialized professionals may ultimately be reliance on nothing more than a myth. This myth of professional judgment may conceal the economic, political, and other social arrangments from which our practices toward disabled people develop. Many consider the clinical judgments of professionals crucial for appropriately serving disabled people. Professionals must assess the individual needs of disabled people and then develop individualized treatment for them. This is mandated in special education and in vocational rehabilitation and is the dominant model in all kinds of services for disabled people. But is it perhaps just a myth that manages to deflect our attention from the larger economic, political and social arrangements that disable people? If so, then a reliance on professional judgment doubly handicaps disabled people. That reliance (enforced dependence?) makes them passive, and it obscures wider arrangements that must be addressed if disabled people are to become potent (Biklen, 1988).

How can we explain that states and many local jurisdictions vary widely in whether they mainstream disabled children and adults in school and in the community or segregate them in separate facilities, classes, or institutions? Nebraska segregates none of its mentally retarded students, but Maryland educates 40 percent of its mentally retarded students in schools only for disabled students. It similarly segregates more than 60 percent of its students classified as emotionally disturbed, but Wisconsin segregates none of its emotionally disturbed students. Can professional judgment vary so greatly from one state to another (Biklen, 1988)? Or might funding policies, such as 100 percent state funding for students in insititutional settings, be a reason for the wide differences in educational placement?

Residential programming for mentally retarded and other developmentally disabled people show similarly wide fluctuations from one state to another. Some states "use institutional placements at a rate seven times greater than other states." Some use Medicaid funds to "support institutions while others use them only for small community-living programs" (Biklen, 1988: 136). Differences in professional judgment cannot likely account for these great differences in placements. "Politics, state budgetary agendas, labor interests, past traditions in retardation services, court oversight, public prejudice toward people with disabilities, bureaucratic impediments, and jurisdictional disputes between human service agencies" may also be at work (Biklen, 1988: 136).

Professionals may dominate interaction with the disabled people they serve, but professionals and the agencies within which they work operate within a larger political, economic, and social context that circumscribes what they do. Professional judgment may too often be a myth that obscures those larger conditions that often oppress disabled people. A focus on clinical judgment moves again our understanding toward an individualistic view rather than a social stance.

Preserving Oppressive Arrangements

Servicing preserves our larger practices and policies that often oppress disabled people. Based on a framework that individualizes disability, servicing focuses on "defects" within disabled people. When servicing fails to "fix" the defective people, then it "blames the victim," not its practices nor the larger arrangements than oppress disabled people (Ryan, 1971). The disabled clients' severity, motivation, age, incompetence, or other shortcomings were their downfall. By making disabled people foreign, servicing upholds the primacy of the nondisabled world. In emphasizing professional judgment, servicing makes disabled people passive followers of specialists' prescriptions. Servicing discourages disabled people from questioning the larger arrangements to which they are expected to adjust, arrangements found within the servicing agencies and elsewhere. With a concern on survival, servicing agencies do not confront the community upon which they depend. They pitch conservatively themselves and their "clients" to the community.

But we should not be too surprised that servicing does not challenge the oppressive arrangements of society. Servicing is our response to the problems our oppressive arrangements and practices have created. It is not an attempt to eliminate those oppressive actions. Instead, through servicing, society "organizes the control, restriction, and maintenance of relatively powerless groups" (Lipsky, 1980: 191).

Making Death

Those most critical of our policies and practices toward people with disabilities argue that servicing not only diminishes people with disabilities but it kills many of them (Wolfensberger, 1980, 1984; Meucci, 1988). Perhaps as many as 200,000 disabled people are killed each year or their lives "seriously abbreviated" (Wolfensberger, 1984: 440). Our service agencies make death.

No doubt some of us are offended by describing the harmful practices of our service agencies as killing. The unappreciated, hard-working service providers are being unfairly, grossly indicted as killers. Not so. Such an objection again individualizes what are social practices and responsibilities. To kill is to deprive of life—and *our* service agencies (and *our* policies) deprive many disabled people of their lives, according to those most critical. To use a euphemism for our practices is to cover up those practices and, thereby, to assist in perpetuating them.

Service agencies kill disabled people in many ways. Sometimes they do so in shockingly obscene ways. Many of us are familiar with exposes of institutions that uncover grotesque practices toward mentally retarded, mentally ill, elderly, and other "residents" (e.g., Rivera, 1972; Blatt and Kaplan, 1974). The exposes momentarily shock us. For example, a nine-month investigation of the California Community Care System revealed our *inhuman* treatment of disabled people. Community care facilities for mentally retarded, developmentally disabled, or other "handicapped" persons are licensed by the state and may serve from one person to more than 100 people (Bruininks, Hauber and Kudla, 1980). They are intended to be alternatives to large total institutions. The California investigation inspected 22,000 licensed homes that housed 151,000 children and adults (Meucci, 1988). The investigation revealed

> unspeakable abuse and neglect, daily beatings, sexual abuses, people left lying in their own excrement for days, people denied medical services, cases of malnourishment, and some documented cases of murder. Many victims had contracted gangrene, resulting in the loss of limbs. Some died from the effects of bedsores; still others were cleaned up by being taken outside and hosed down (Meucci, 1988: 19).

However, we kill disabled people in much more mundane fashion than such exposes suggest. Routine, often seemingly reasonable practices of service institutions are the "weapons" in most killings. Medication, transfers from one setting to another, the withholding of basic medical care, and the like kill many more disabled people than the "unspeakable" abuses uncovered in exposes.

Servicing agencies massively drug disabled people, elderly persons, and other devalued individuals such as prisoners. Drugging is especially common in institutions. For example, according to one researcher who worked as a nursing assistant in a skilled nursing center and an intermediate care facility

> I came to realize that the director of nursing was not kidding in telling us that "the most important job you have is to get them to take their meds." According to house rules, residents must take the medications that are assigned to them. They can refuse just about everything, including eating, but they cannot refuse medications. Sedatives are prescribed as a matter of course for the diagnoses of most nursing home residents. One result was a *culture of sleep.* Residents slept so much in the homes where I worked that my conceptions of sleeping and waking were jolted. I had tended to dichotomize the two, thinking them as distinct states of consciousness. But life as a nursing home resident is, for many, somewhere between the two. It is not uncommon for a resident to fall asleep in the middle of a conversation. Some wake up only for meals and medication (Diamond, 1983: 281).

The elderly resident or disabled person who is drugged may become "too weak to resist other coercive treatment and too confused to appear believable when disclosing the truth of his or her condition to outsiders such as evaluators, inspectors, advocates, or family" (Meucci, 1988: 19). When disabled people die from cardiac arrest, pneumonia or other complications of being massively drugged, the death certificates do not show that our servicing agencies have drugged them to death. The complications are listed as the cause—the cause of 100,000 or more deaths of disabled people each year (Wolfensberger, 1980, 1984).

Other routine practices increase the death toll, too. Elderly residents of nursing homes often have too little time to eat, become emaciated, and then susceptible to death from other causes (Wolfensberger, 1984). Service institutions regularly move disabled and elderly people from "one facility to another, one wing to another, one floor to another, one room to another, or even one bed to another" (Wolfensberger, 1984: 439). The rationale is to better serve disabled people—matching services with needs. Yet, such discontinuity in disabled people's lives can "drastically contribute to disorientation, 'senility,' stress, depression, etc., and thus to death itself" (Wolfensberger, 1984: 439). Out of a mix of a fear of death without dignity (often others' deaths), a fear of being dependent on others (or on having others "burdensomely" dependent on us), a cost-benefit analysis of who deserves what kinds of medical and other services, and a disregard for those who are elderly and/or disabled, "mentally retarded people, people with other handicaps, and elderly people are commonly denied relatively elementary life supports such as antibiotics, basic resuscitation, or even the simplest medical procedures" in our hospitals (Wolfensberger, 1980: 171; Meucci, 1988). Perhaps only a "private guard" such as a family member or private duty nurse can protect moderately retarded elderly people who are admitted to many general hospitals (Wolfensberger, 1980). If we include the abortion of fetuses that are impaired and the practices of withholding routine medical assistance or sustenance from severely impaired newborns (as I explore in Chapter 7), then our service practices become disquietingly similar to the Nazi liquidation of disabled, elderly, Jewish, and other devalued people (Wolfensberger, 1980, 1981, 1984; Meucci, 1988).

Yet few of us understand servicing agencies to be killing disabled people. We may have no information, or we understand what we do have in ways different than do the critics. Euphemisms, such as calling basic resuscitation or antibiotics "heroic measures," which we then deny to disabled and other devalued people, or calling the starvation of a newborn with Down syndrome a "courageous decision" obscure what is happening (Meucci, 1988: 19; Wolfensberger, 1980). Because we still see disabled people, it becomes difficult to realize that we are killing them (in large numbers). Many of us cannot imagine that we could do this. Yet others of us may agree that such practices are appropriate, even if they make us somewhat uncomfortable. Therefore, we do not look for or think much about what is happening (Wolfensberger, 1980, 1984).

In killing disabled people, we display and produce our profound disregard for them. Because they are not equally worthy, we kill them. And because they are not equally worthy, we kill them "legitimately," routinely, typically without covering up their deaths, and with few qualms. We do not even understand that we have killed. Instead, we have enabled people to die with dignity, or we have terminated unviable fetuses. We could kill in this way only those who have little worth. Our killings proclaim so. But in killing disabled people so routinely, so easily, we also produce the disregard we hold for them. Our servicing (and our many other practices and policies) make (severely) disabled people the unworthy individuals so many of us take them to be: pitiful, maladjusted, burdensome, alien, "vegetables," and so on. The unworthiness that we have produced then becomes the justification for eliminating those who are unworthy. We have fulfilled our prophecy.

Societal Circumstances of Servicing

Servicing is not merely the practice of professionals and other staff within organizations. Recall my discussion of the myth of professional judgment. Instead, it is our organizational attempt to manage our larger societal concerns and conflicts. Often it has been a means for controlling the least advantaged in our society (Lipsky, 1980: 191). Let me illustrate with a brief discussion of special education and an even briefer one of nursing homes.

Special education developed in America primarily as a response to the challenges mainstream Americans identified in the late 1800s and early 1900s. It was a means for managing the interrelated developments of compulsory education, the wave of immigrants in the late 1800s, and the industrialization of society and its "need" for an orderly work force. Many middle class citizens believed that children of immigrants and of poor citizens were a threat to social order. The parents inadequately raised and supervised their children, who became the idle delinquents and troublemakers of growing urban areas. Compulsory education, itself a response to the industrialization of America (and to concerns about child labor, to fears of immigrants, to the social ills of a changing society) created a much greater challenge to educators. Without compulsory education, poorly performing children of immigrant and poor families did not come to school or came irregularly and eventually dropped out. An industrializing society needed trained, complacent workers to "man" the factories. Special education addressed all of these challenges.

Special education became significant in America in the late 1800s and early 1900s when schooling became mandatory. Faced with educating students with widely varying experiences, many of whom were not doing well in school, educators saw special education as the solution. Instead of building more, costly institutions, which was not practical for the great numbers of poorly performing students, educators developed segregated special education. This would provide several benefits. Poorly performing children would ceased to be hidden away and poorly cared for by parents, often foreign born, who were assumed to be undisciplined and neglectful. With appropriate training, the children could become productive citizens instead of a burden. Special education would remove handicapped children from the regular classes, where they were a detriment to the education of "normal" students and a burden to the regular teachers. By keeping handicapped children in school, the community would reduce truancy, neglect, crime, and other social ills assumed to be associated with defective youth. Special education's emphasis on individual, flexible, vocational-oriented teaching would even inform regular education. Special education developed as a humanitarian attempt to manage marginal youth.

After World War II as black children slowly left their segregated schools and entered integrated (i.e., white) schools, special education became a mechanism for resegregating schools—black and Hispanic children were disproportionately placed into special education classes. Later, the civil rights movement became a catalyst for similar concerns about equitable services within special education. America developed and modified special education (in part) as a response to broader concerns and conflicts in the country. Special education cannot be understood apart from its societal context (Sarason and Doris, 1979; Lazerson, 1983).

Recall the researcher who worked as a nursing assistant in a skilled nursing center and in an intermediate care facility. He was rebuked by his superior for sitting to comfort a distraught woman when he had "16 more vitals to do." That apparent lack of concern by the supervisor, the heavy use of medication, the inspection of documents instead of people and activities within the "nursing homes," the lack of emphasis on moving residents to a more independent living situation, and other happenings can be understood by noting the political-economic context of "nursing homes." They have become medically dominated profit makers, a capitalist growth industry, as politicians transfer the provision of social services from government to private corporations (Diamond, 1983). In a conservative, cost-conscious era, officials and others view the private sector as a means for reducing "big government." Those disabling practices are "reasonable" actions when servicing pursues the rational, accountable production of profit:

> The medical tasks are carefully monitored by the accounting systems; profit is increased if wages can be kept low and if residents' allowances can be kept to a minimum; inspection is streamlined if it is conducted totally as an analysis of quantifiable data. Permeating these dynamics is the presumption of residency based on sickness and a profitable technology based on drugs (Diamond, 1983: 283).

Much of servicing can be understood as the response of servicing agencies to the concerns encountered within the wider society.

Conclusion

Through servicing people with disabilities, we handicap them. Through servicing we individualize disability, locating the challenges disabled people experience within their "flawed" selves. Those who participate in servicing are unequal, and we provide unequal services to disabled people. Professionals dominate to the detriment of disabled people, especially to the detriment of those who challenge the professionals' dominance. With an emphasis on organizational survival, servicing agencies may serve those most easily assisted, retain others who appropriately could develop a more independent way of life, and refrain from disrupting or making uncomfortable the larger community on which the agencies depend. Consequently, servicing transforms disabled people into passive individuals who are unlike the rest of us. It preserves our social practices and arrangements that hamper disabled people.

But some are challenging our servicing of disabled people (and others, including service providers, never subscribed to the servicing paradigm). Requirements that disabled people help to develop their rehabilitation plans and that parents and their disabled children assist in developing the children's special education plans reflect the growing demand of disabled people (and their supporters) to participate actively in service decisions and delivery (Higgins, 1985, 1990). However, the "promise" of participation may often be greater than its practice. The involvement of disabled citizens as staff within, consultants to, and administrators of service organizations also speaks to the increasing claim by disabled people to control their lives. Attempts by mainstream educational programs to change the schools within which disabled children are mainstreamed, not merely change the disabled children, recognize service organizations' responsibility to work on disabling worlds, not merely "on" disabled people (Biklen et al., 1985). So, too, do the attempts of service agencies to educate and work with citizens of a neighborhood when developmentally disabled citizens come to live within them or to modify jobs in order for severely disabled people to work in private companies, not just in sheltered workshops (Taylor et al., 1987; Taylor, Biklen and Knoll, 1987). These and other changes point to a new understanding of disability. Disabled people are not flawed individuals, but citizens with varying characteristics who have the right to make their lives in a world that will include them.

However, neither the new understanding nor the new ways of serving disabled people have become widespread. Tentatively we are moving from servicing "defective" people to serving citizens—and often we are caught in the transition. For example, as I noted earlier, even with the federal requirement of P.L. 94-142 of 1975 to educate disabled children in the least restrictive environment, many disabled children are educated in segregated schools and classes (Walker, 1987). We continue to turn disabled children into educational strangers. Just as we seem to be caught in a transition in serving disabled people, so, too, are we experiencing important changes in our *disability policies,* to which I turn now.

Endnotes

1. Agency staff typically identify disabled people as less competent than do those who have developed caring relationships and who intimately interact with the disabled individuals (Goode, 1984). However, to the extent that attendants' superiors interact less with the mentally retarded "residents" than do the attendants, the attendants may develop comparatively benign views of their "charges."

2. I included this quote for several reasons. It supports the point I am making that organizations officially make people disabled. However, it also illustrates how easy it is to assume that disabilities are traits of individuals. Note that the student is said to "have a handicap." Further, the quote uses possibly disabling language: the student is "confined to a wheelchair." And some may find the masculine pronoun offensive. Yet all of this was written by extremely astute observers! The moral: Writing about disability and our lives (and, more broadly, making both of them) are difficult.

Chapter 7

POLICY(ING) DISABILITY

If we slightly alter the pronunciation of the chapter's title (so that we say "policing" disability), I believe the basis of much of our disability policy unfortunately is captured. Our policy affecting people with disabilities has primarily controlled them, has kept them in "their" place (after making a place within which to keep them). We often have not intended to do so, many times have not recognized that we were doing so, and nowadays are consciously trying to do otherwise—with some success and still many shortcomings (DeJong and Batavia, 1990; *The Disability Rag,* January/February 1991). Although our disability policy continues to be mixed, it has primarily maintained the dominant nondisabled social order. Without clearly recognizing the consequences of our policies, we have created that order.

When we think of our disability policy, we may think of worker's compensation, disability insurance, the Rehabilitation Act of 1973 (and key sections of it such as 504), The Education of All Handicapped Children Act of 1975, the Americans with Disabilities Act of 1990, and other governmental acts and programs that specifically address disability. However, until recently, most of our disability policy was developed without disabled people in mind. It was implicit. It was unrecognized. It was a disability policy without disabled people!

What we do not prohibit, we permit. What we permit often becomes legitimate—and eventually may become promoted. Without fully realizing so until recently, we have permitted or promoted the development of a society that does not "accommodate the wide variety of physical (and other) differences that exist" (McMurray, 1987: 144). Typically with no malice toward disabled people intended and little thought about them given, we have constructed a world that does not suit them (or many others) well. From housing to schooling to employment and beyond, we were building our country. Yet, in doing so, we were unthinkingly also establishing our disability policy. The

functional demands exerted on human beings by the environment are fundamentally determined by public policy. The present forms of architectural
structures and social institutions exist because statutes, ordinances, and codes
either required or permitted them to be constructed in that manner. These
public policies imply values, expectations, and assumptions about the physical
and behavioral attributes that people ought to possess in order to survive or to
participate in community life. Many everyday activities, such as the distance
people walk, the steps they climb, the materials they read, and the messages
they receive, impose stringent requirements on persons with different levels of
functional skills. These characteristics of the environment that have a discriminatory effect on disabled citizens cannot be considered simply coincidental.
Rather than reflecting immutable aspects of an environment decreed by natural law, they represent the consequences of prior policy decisions (Hahn, 1988:
40).

While those discriminatory features of our social world do reflect
policy choices, they typically do not reflect deliberate, calculated decisions to oppress citizens with disabilities. Instead, they reflect the narrow
assumptions of what is necessary to "participate in community life."
Disabled people did not fit those assumptions. Consequently, they were
omitted when such decisions were made. Much of our past, unrecognized
disability policy was intertwined with the industrialization of America.
While we have produced much progress through industrialization (and
capitalism), industrialization has also been *debilitating* for disabled people
(see also Chapter 2).

Ironically, much of our present, acknowledged "disability policy" can
be understood as responding to the obstacles we unthinkingly created
with our past, unrecognized policies. I will not explore how we developed
our policies; others have done that in great detail and with much fascina-
tion (e.g., Levine and Wexler, 1981; Scotch, 1984; Stone, 1984; Katzman,
1986; Tanenbaum, 1986; Berkowitz, 1987; Mezey, 1988; Oliver, 1988;
Percy, 1989). It has become clear, however, that our disability policy is
not a coherent, systematic approach to disability. Building upon, even
trying to undo, past policies, we have incrementally developed over
decades our present policies. We have often developed them independent of, perhaps even at odds with, other policies that may or may not be
focused on disability (Berkowitz, 1987). I will also not examine the
particulars of American disability legislation (see National Council on
the Handicapped, 1986: Appendix). Instead, I discuss basic issues of our
policy(ing) disability.

I examine the mix of *rationales* that underlie our disability policy and their shortcomings; the dominant *orientations* of our policy that until recently (but not consistently) have primarily made it difficult for people with disabilities to participate in society; and our *differentiation* of people with disabilities into categories of those more or less worthy of being assisted, even assisted to live. Given that our services to people with disabilities in part flow from our policies, my discussion in the previous chapter ties to the above concerns. Given that how we frame disability is intertwined with our policies, my discussion in Chapter 1 ties here, too. Taking off on a classic argument as to why poverty persists, I argue that disability serves many *functions*, which helps us to understand why it persists. While the oppressive making of disability ultimately harms us all, in segmental and shortsighted ways it has many positive consequences, too. I conclude the chapter with a call for policy that is inclusive, that recognizes the interdependence among us and can encompass the diversity that is us (Zola, 1989; Minow, 1990). But first, to our past, unrecognized disability policy, our debilitating industrialization.

Debilitating Industrialization

Through industrialization (based on the development of a capitalist economy), we have produced much progress: higher standards of living, more freedoms, improved health care, increased concern about health and safety, and so on. We can enable people to live who in the past would have died and improve the quality of the lives of those with serious injuries and illnesses. Industrialization, though, has produced mixed results (see Chapter 2). Through it, we have also created a disabling society. Policies that produced progress have permitted, even promoted, the debilitation of citizens with disabilities.

Life in preindustrial societies was difficult and often short. Harsh conditions prevailed for most citizens. No doubt, citizens with disabilities often lived particularly hard, short lives in an inhospitable environment. At times, their communities even killed them. However, disabled people did not live uniformly dreary lives. Instead, preindustrial societies also provided opportunities for disabled people to participate in the lives of their families and communities.

Prior to industrialization, "most persons with disabilities were integrated into community roles, protected by ties of kinship and participation in wider social networks" (Scheer and Groce, 1988: 32). We mistakenly think that the abandonment, neglect, or killing of disabled people was and is routine in preindustrial societies. Not so (Scheer and Groce, 1988). While some societies killed disabled infants, they also practiced infanticide on nondisabled infants (Harris, 1989: 210–214). Others killed neither their disabled nor nondisabled infants. Rarely were disabled infants who survived past the neonatal period killed, though disabled children were likely neglected more so than nondisabled children. The killing of elderly, disabled members was/is also rare. Instead, preindustrial families and communities often felt obligated to take care of their members (Rothman, 1971: Chapter 1, Scheer and Groce, 1988).

In turn, disabled citizens participated in their families' and communities' affairs and contributed to the welfare of both. For example, until recent modernization altered life in a peasant community in the highlands of Mexico, blind male elders wove nets, sorted produce, tended gardens, and socialized the young by interpreting their dreams (Scheer and Groce, 1988: 29–30). Deaf citizens on Martha's Vineyard from the late 17th to early 20th century constituted an unusually large percent of the island's population (due to the inheritance of a recessive gene). Consequently, many hearing islanders were related to or knew deaf islanders and, therefore, learned to sign. In a society without telephones, television, and other communication devices that emphasize the ability to hear, being deaf was less of an obstacle to participating in community affairs. Thus, the deaf islanders participated in the life of the community—working, marrying, holding public office, and such (Groce, 1985; but see Crouch, 1986).

In small-scale societies nondisabled citizens knew disabled citizens (Scheer and Groce, 1988). People who many of us take to be "bizarre or disturbed" in today's urban areas often would have become familiar, accepted (if not well understood) neighbors to members of rural communities (Hahn, 1987: 558). Even in the more impersonal cities of preindustrial societies, disabled people were highly visible. The "*maimed,* the *lame,* the *feeble-minded,* the *blind,* the *scarred,* and the *diseased* were . . . present to a degree incomprehensible to a modern Westerner" (Lofland, 1973: 42). Through war, disease, accident, poor health and poor health care, unsanitary living conditions, and mutilation as punishment for many infractions, disability was widespread (Lofland, 1973: 42). It was a routine part of everyday life.

While disabled people lived widely varying lives in preindustrial societies, lives that were often short and difficult, they also participated in their families and communities in ways that might surprise many of us today. Further, in preindustrial societies, where a

> rigid separation had not yet been made between home and work and where travel was difficult for anyone, citizens with disabilities may not have been exposed to some of the egregious inequities that have subsequently become apparent in highly impersonal and autonomous cultures (Hahn, 1987: 557).

Industrialization (through the development of capitalism) changed greatly the lives of disabled and nondisabled citizens. While those intertwined developments eventually "led" to significant advances in disabled people's lives, they have also set in concrete, literally and metaphorically, many oppressive arrangements and attitudes with which disabled people and our disability policy presently struggle.

Industrialization and capitalism dramatically altered community life. Modernization encouraged, even forced, people to leave their small, traditional communities in search of paid labor and tore people from their communities due to dramatic shifts in employment opportunities. It threw together great numbers of people who did not know one another well. It segregated work from home, which cheapened those left at home and made worthy primarily those who contributed through their paid labor to the further building of the country. Capitalism tilted social life toward the satisfaction of individual desires and away from meeting communal responsibilities. The goal became to enhance oneself (Shorter, 1975). Order and stability seemed threatened.

Consequently, community and family obligations to its needy members decreased in favor of more impersonal means of assistance. With that impersonal help came the rise of massive institutions for society's dangerous, deprived, and disabled citizens. While those large total institutions were erected in a spirit of optimism that society could restore order to the lives of those disordered (and perhaps thereby illustrate to all the necessity of order and stability), they eventually became warehouses for those who were taken to be a threat to conventional society (Rothman, 1971, Wolfensberger, 1975).

Industrialization also rebuilt our environment. In place of small villages, great cities with their massive buildings rose. Trains, streetcars, subways, and motor vehicles became the means for getting around these cities and from one to another. Time and space were being conquered, but not for all citizens. While industrialization enabled, even forced, citizens to assemble in order to work, play, worship, and so on, it isolated many disabled people. What brought together nondisabled people kept out disabled people. Life became less accessible to many citizens with disabilities.

Industrialization emphasized standardization. In preindustrial societies, clothes, tools, household goods, and the other necessities of everyday life were tailored to the individuals who used them and often made by those who used them (Harris, 1981: Chapter 2, Hahn, 1987: 556). But industrialization proceeded through standardizing both what was produced as well as how it was produced. Standardization left out those who did not fit the narrow notions of normality that we were developing (Hahn, 1987).

The same happened within schools, which became the educational factories producing capable and compliant workers for the industrial factories (Sarason and Doris, 1979, Lazerson, 1983). School standardization (in the face of what seemed to be a rising threat from lower class, often immigrant children) led to special education or pepetuated no education for disabled youth (see Chapter 6). In the hopes of helping those who did not do well in these standardized schools, we even created learning disabilities to which our special education was a response (see Chapter 1).

With the rise of mass production came the necessity for and the development of mass consumption. In promoting consumption, businesses advertised an idealized image of people to which most might aspire. The message was clear: Appearance was worth—as an individual, as a colleague, as a potential employee, as a citizen. An unacceptable appearance was a sign of lower moral worth. (To avoid that taint one needed, of course, to purchase and use the appropriate products.) This idealized image excluded minorities of all kind, including those with disabilities (Hahn, 1987). While eventually our industrialization and capitalism gave rise to the recognition of many that we must respond more equitably to our disabled citizens and also "provided" resources and technology to do so, our modernization initially made them marginal, even invisible citizens (Hahn, 1987: 562). Our policies that promoted development became unrecognized, but disastrous disability policies. In many ways, our present policies are responses to our past, unrecognized policies.

Rationalizing Policy

Our policies toward citizens with disabilities have been based on various rationales. *Charity* and *utility* have been the most prominent. In the past several decades *rights* have become increasingly important. Nowadays all three exist in shifting combinations. These rationales view disabled people in different ways. They (and the policies based on them) empower disabled people or diminish them. They enable them to challenge their oppression, their enforced dependence, or they require them to be grateful for what is given to them. These rationales conserve present arrangements that oppress disabled people, or they challenge those practices. Used with the best of intentions, these rationales have very different consequences. All have shortcomings.

Charity

Charity provides a handout to "handicapped" people. Those of us who are more fortunate appropriately assist those less fortunate than us. In return, we expect them to be grateful for what we generously provide. Provisions are a gift, not a right (Bogdan and Biklen, 1977: 18). Charity draws upon and creates sympathy and pity for individuals with disabilities. With often the best of intentions, charity diminishes those of us with disabilities. Instead of recognizing and emphasizing the complexity of people with disabilities and the essential similarity between those with and without disabilities, charity turns people with disabilities into heartbreaking and heartwarming cases. Charitable fund-raising campaigns ask us to help organizations "make . . . the life that's saved worth living," to "help paint a rainbow of hope against a dark sky especially for children with epilepsy," or to realize that we "are the foundation on which the handicapped build their entire lives" (*The Disability Rag,* Winter 1990: 23, 25, 28). These campaigns are a major means through which we display disability (see Chapter 3).

Charity diminishes the significance of disability. When the good will of givers is piqued, when funds dry up, or when some other concern takes center stage, charity will be withdrawn. We provide it if we like and when we can. Under charity, disability and the lives of those with disabilities are not a fundamental concern of society.

Thus, charity also makes disabled people less powerful. Recipients of charity have relatively little say in how that charity is handled. They can either accept it on the terms given, or they can do without. "Poor souls cannot be choosy."

Charity is fundamentally a conservative rationale. It typically locates the problem of disability within the individual. It focuses on individual traits that must be fixed or worked around. Charity does not draw our attention to our practices and policies that may be oppressing disabled people. It does not encourage us to challenge those present, handicapping arrangements. Thus, it conserves them.

Charity continues to be a major rationale of our disability policy, even though nowadays we have developed numerous governmental programs. Our governmental policies would be even more inadequate without charitable activities. But our governmental policies themselves are often based on charitable or "humanitarian" concerns (Higgins, 1985: 29–30). "Support of specific programs invariably include . . . humanitarian pleas about the essential worth of the individual and the need for compassion for the less fortunate" (Newman, 1987: 32).

For example, "blindness became the only disability to be included within the protections of the Social Security Act," the landmark social welfare legislation of 1935 (Scotch and Berkowitz, 1990: 9). During the debate about its inclusion, members of Congress emphasized pity and charity.

> Using . . . what was the norm in discussions of public charity at the time, an influential Ohio Republican led the fight in the House on behalf of the blind. "Who is it," asked the Congressman, "that elicits your sympathies more than the poor blind beggar? I am sure that you will agree with me that there is no affliction worse than blindness when accompanied by poverty . . . With the rich man flying by in his limousine, with the athlete skipping by in the full flower of health, with the grand lady in her rustling silks passed by with her vain superiority complex, with the happy carefree children . . . there sits the poor blind with his little tin cup extended. Are you going to leave him on the street or will you assist me to put him upon his feet?" (Scotch and Berkowitz, 1990: 10).

However, to the extent that governmental policies provide benefits, not protect rights, then government can more easily take away what it gives. Compassion, after all, might become too costly.

> In periods of limited resources, which is to say virtually always, it is politically acceptable to limit benevolent acts of charity because of budgetary constraints, traditional practice, or administrative difficulty. Reducing benefits may be legitimate, while violating rights is not (Scotch, 1984: 42).

Utility

Utility underlies much of our disability policy. Are the practices toward disabled people beneficial to society? Are they cost effective? Utility comes in many, related forms.

We often develop and justify disability policies because they improve the economy, or we oppose them because they may harm the economy. Disability policies may improve the economy by increasing the productivity of disabled people, turning them into tax payers instead of allowing them to remain tax users. Justification for special education has often taken that position, as it did in England in the late 1800s. A royal commission report in 1889 noted:

> The blind, deaf, dumb and the educable class of imbecile . . . if left uneducated become not only a burden to themselves but a weighty burden to the state. It is in the interests of the state to educate them, so as to dry up, as far as possible, the minor streams which must ultimately swell to a great torrent of paupersim (Tomlinson, 1982: 38).

Even eliminating discrimination against disabled people may be justified not because discrimination is fundamentally "wrong" and violates the rights of disabled individuals, but because to do so improves the economy. "The benefits of eliminating discrimination in the labor market can be summarized as more efficient use of labor, improved efficiency in the human capital market, and increased incentives for labor force participation by impaired workers" (Johnson, 1986: 254). However, others may oppose disability policies because they believe the policies will harm society. For example, many "fear that income-support programs will substantially discourage work and retard economic growth" (Burkhauser and Hirvonen, 1989: 167; Yelin, 1989).

In an economy where work is the central mechanism for distributing what is desirable, where people are expected to work, but not all may be able to do so, do disability policies undermine or support that work-based distributive system (Stone, 1984)? Overly generous disability payments may draw potential workers from the labor market, thereby undermining the economy. After all, why work if it is so easy to qualify for disability payments? (However, disability payments do not seem to lure many out of the labor force (Yelin, 1989).) But if all are expected to work, but many are not needed, then the work ethic of the country is undermined. However, flexible disability programs can expand their definitions of who is disabled and thereby "soak up" some of the unemployment (Stone, 1984: 168).

Utility focuses on the costs and benefits of disability policy. Most crudely, does the policy make sense—dollars and cents? The "bottom line" is the "return on the dollar"—the return on the dollars spent on the particular program for disabled individuals. Consequently, proponents and opponents may argue about whether more money will be saved (e.g., through reduced future dependency on governmental assistance) than spent within a particular disability program. Supporters may tout how for every dollar invested in a particular disability program a much larger number of dollars is saved. State vocational rehabilitation agencies have often done so (Berkowitz, 1987: Chapter 5). Still others may sound the alarm when a program appears to become too costly, as disability insurance became to some officials in the late 1970s and early 1980s in America (Berkowitz, 1987: Chapter 4; Mezey, 1988; Yelin, 1989). (However, some countries such as Sweden and Germany seem to emphasize less the economic cost-benefit analysis than does the United States (Burkhauser and Hirvonen, 1989: 188).)

Utility pervades our present disability policies. Even as we move toward rights as a rationale, we hold to cost-benefit considerations. The legal standard of "reasonable accommodation" has been used in deciding the extent to which work, education, and other realms of society will be accessible to those with disabilities. While the standard has developed differently in various societal areas, cost has been held to be a legitimate ground upon which accommodations do not need to be made or in deciding which ones may be used. For example, The Supreme Court ruled in 1979 in *Southeastern Community College v. Davis* that accommodations that would result in "undue financial and administrative burdens" were not required under Section 504 of the Rehabilitation Act of 1973 (U.S. Commission on Civil Rights, 1983: 113). The recently passed Americans with Disabilities Act allows "undue hardship" and "readily achievable" considerations to be used in deciding whether or not accommodations must be made or barriers removed (*The Disability Rag,* January/February 1991: 12–13).

Costs have been central to the continuing controversy over transportation accessibility. Will equal access to transportation be provided to all citizens no matter what the cost or will less costly transportation that provides so-called "effective mobility," if also segregated mobility, become the standard?

One view maintains that each individual has a right to be fully integrated into society and thus public transportation—buses and subways—must be made accessible to everyone. Barrier-free transit is a right, impervious to considerations of cost. Another perspective regards the question of providing transportation not as one of rights, but as one of cost effectiveness—securing the most out of a given input. In principle, such separate, specialized services as taxis and minivans would be acceptable. In one respect, then the fundamental debate is about values—the trade-offs between equity and efficiency (Katzmann, 1986: 2).

Disability-rights groups and their supporters have pushed a rights-oriented approach of equal access, while local government officials who would implement the transportation policy have favored what they see to be a less costly effective-mobility approach. While the Americans with Disabilities Act of 1990 moves more toward a rights-oriented approach of equal access than has previous legislation (e.g., New public buses ordered on or after August 26, 1990 must be accessible to people with disabilities.), it provides up to 30 years to make various components of our transportation system accessible. Moreover, given that disability activists and the transportation industry have skirmished for more than ten years over implementing previous legislation, it is much too soon to tell how accessible our public transportation system will become (*The Disability Rag*, January/February 1991).

If utility is the logic underlying our disability policy, then disabled people may become too costly. "In the extreme there are instances where taking cost-benefit criteria to their logical conclusion could entail withholding essential life-support systems" (DeJong and Lifchez, 1983: 49). Hasn't this already happened? "Economists have begun to apply cost-benefit analysis to the decision-making process and have identified the birthweight below which intensive care yields a net economic loss in terms of the 'quality-adjusted-life-years gained' " (Noble, 1987: 67–68).

Costs are a central concern in what have come to be known as "Baby Doe" cases. As two advocates for those with disabilities put it, one of the questions in such cases is, "Do you really want to spend a million dollars and end up with so little? Is society ready to pay to care for the most severely disabled people?" (Biklen and Ferguson, 1984: 7). The answer often seems to be no, as evidenced by the University of Oklahoma Health Sciences Center's project that used a quality of life formula to decide for which newborns with spina bifida aggressive treatment would be recommended and for which newborns only supportive care (i.e., death) would be recommended.

Utility, even more so than charity, cheapens people with disabilities. Charity exceeds utility in its concern for those with disabilities, no matter how pitying that concern may be. Utility merely "uses" disabled people. If they (and policy addressed toward them) cannot produce a "profit" (i.e., if benefits do not exceed cost), then they have little or no value.

Rights

With recent political struggles, court cases, and federal (and other governmental) legislation, rights have become an important feature of disability policy. Rights proclaim that those with disabilities are entitled to the fundamental protection and opportunities enjoyed by any citizen. As Section 504 of the Rehabilitation Act of 1973 states: "No otherwise qualified handicapped individual in the United States, as defined in Section 7(6), shall, solely by reason of his handicap, be excluded from the participation in, be denied the benefits of, or be subjected to discrimination under any program or activity receiving federal financial assistance" (Scotch, 1984: 52). While Section 504 is considered by many to be the landmark civil rights provision for disabled people, dozens of federal laws and many more state and local laws prohibit discrimination against people with disabilities (U.S. Commission on Civil Rights, 1983: 1). The Americans with Disabilities Act of 1990 extends to "disabled Americans civil rights protections that are analogous to those accorded to racial minorities in the Civil Rights Act of 1964, as amended" (DeJong and Batavia, 1990: 66). It goes beyond previous policy, such as Title V of the Rehabilitation Act of 1973, which proscribed discrimination in the public sector (i.e., government or government supported) to reach "deep into the private sector" to protect the civil rights of Americans with disabilities (Bowe, 1990: 90).

Rights are a much more powerful approach than charity or utility. If donations dry up or costs exceed benefits, then people with disabilities may be left out. But rights are more resistant to costs and other conflicting concerns (Scotch, 1984). Rather than (primarily) looking to individual characteristics to understand the difficulties experienced by people with disabilities, rights encourage us, even require us, to evaluate our practices that may limit people with disabilities. Rights empower people with disabilities. With rights, people with disabilities may legitimately contest what they perceive to be illegitimate treatment of them. (However inadequately understood and achieved at present), rights most importantly proclaim that people with disabilities are equal to those without disabilities. People with disabilities are to enjoy no less the opportunities and safeguards of their society than those without disabilities, because they are no less than their fellow citizens without disabilities.

Consequently, disability rights are controversial. To provide rights to disabled people in education, work, public accommodations, transportation, and elsewhere is to alter the relation between those with and without disabilities. With rights, those with disabilities increase their standing relative to those without disabilities. No longer must they endure arrangements that disadvantage them to the advantage of nondisabled citizens. Hence, nondisabled citizens may feel threatened. Further, it may be costly to ensure rights, especially when what is now understood to be the denial of the rights of disabled citizens has become so deeply built into our society. As I noted earlier, nondisabled citizens may object to what they take to be the high cost of rights, especially when they believe that the resources spent to ensure the rights of disabled citizens could be spent more usefully elsewhere (i.e., on those without disabilities). Utility becomes promoted at the expense of rights.

Thus, the controversy about disability rights policy continues to be strong. Writing the regulations to implement legislation has in some cases taken years and even nationwide demonstrations (Scotch, 1984; Bowe, 1986; Katzmann, 1986). Backlash against disability rights legislation appeared even before the regulations were written and continue today (*The Disability Rag*, January/February 1991).

For example, the chairman of the Metropolitan Transit Authority of New York claimed that it would cost $100 million to make the subways accessible to riders with mobility impairments. However, to do so would benefit few because few "handicapped" people would use the subways. According to the chairman, less than three dozen "handicapped" riders used the Washington, D.C., subway with their expensive elevators (Berkowitz, 1987: 219). Reasonable accommodation, a touchstone of much of the rights legislation, seemed to lead to costly, even absurd requirements, claimed critics. One widely reported story concerned the

small town of Rudd, Iowa. This farming community of less than five hundred people had no one in a wheelchair, but it did have a public library. A regional office of HEW's Office of Civil Rights informed the town of Rudd that the library had to be made accessible. The townspeople claimed it would cost $6,500 to build a ramp for no one but the bureaucrats (Berkowitz, 1987: 222).

In another widely publicized instance, a national magazine reported that a California business spent $40,000 to make its drinking fountains accessible to those in wheelchairs. The firm did so by lowering all of its drinking fountains (U.S. Commission on Civil Rights, 1983: 2).

We should wonder, however, whether those concerned about disability rights are primarily worried about cost. To make and keep people with disabilities dependent is very costly (Bowe, 1978, 1980; Chirikos, 1989). Further, except perhaps for the expense of making transportation accessible (and not necessarily even then), reasonable accommodation is often not costly (U.S. Commission on Civil Rights, 1983: 106–108; Collignon, 1986). The business that spent $40,000 to lower all of its water fountains did so foolishly. Paper cup dispensers work very well. To equip buses with ramps costs half as much as to air-condition them (Berkowitz, 1987: 220). However, citizens have not cried out about air-conditioning buses. Actually, separate transportation systems for disabled citizens may often be more costly than making existing ones accessible (Bowe, 1980: 75). Making new and existing buildings accessible to all is not particularly expensive either.

> A National League of Cities study found that it costs less than one-half of one percent of the total cost of constructing a new building to make it it completely accessible to and usable by disabled people. Mainstream, Inc., a Washington, D.C., consulting firm, estimates that it costs about 1c per square foot per month to make most existing facilities accessible, compared to a monthly cost of 12–13c per square foot just to polish floors and clean carpets (Bowe, 1980: 84).

Modifying existing arrangements, structures and transportation systems are more costly, but existing legislation provides the opportunity to do so over several, sometimes many, years, where "readily achievable," and not at the expense of "undue hardship" (which, of course, some disability activists criticize as a retreat from securing the rights of disabled citizens).

Criticisms of the cost of implementing rights legislation obscures a much more fundamental concern of the critics and others: People with disabilities are not like those without disabilities. They are not equal. They are not as worthy. Therefore, those without disabilities need not, even should not, provide disabled people what they provide themselves. To do so seemingly lessens who nondisabled people are. To do so takes away from what they, the nondisabled, *deserve.* Of course, charity shows the moral superiority of the nondisabled and utility is practical. But rights speak to people's most fundamental worth. For that reason rights will remain controversial in policy debates.

In the provision of "rights," in the day-to-day lives of those with disabilities, rights are even more precarious. Legislation goes underfunded and (more to the point about rights) unimplemented through delayed regulations (Ferguson et al., 1990; *The Disability Rag,* January/February 1991). Legislation, even with regulations, does not guarantee changed practices. For example, even though the Education of All Handicapped Children Act of 1975 emphasized educating students with disabilities in the least restrictive environment, the educational segregation of today's disabled youth is about as extensive as it was when the legislation was enacted (Walker, 1987; Ferguson, et al., 1990). Anyone who has participated in service agencies, such as schools, in which some of those rights are to be implemented, knows how easily the grand rhetoric of rights legislation can be so easily overlooked in everyday life (see Chapter 6).

Perhaps because of the precarious state of rights for people with disabilities, some champions of disabled people have questioned the wisdom of pushing the rights rationale. For example, the disability rights movement has increased its

> political sophistication by learning how to temper and tailor its rhetoric. In the past, leaders had spoken of entitlements and inherent rights. Now, with the arrival of Reagan and George Bush, who led an important Task Force for Regulatory Relief, the leaders stressed independence (Berkowitz, 1987: 222).

Independence seems to speak first to utility, to the cherished (if also somewhat mythical) American value of self-reliance, and perhaps only afterwards to rights.

Others wonder how effective a rights approach will be in achieving autonomy for disabled people. While an adversarial approach has enabled disabled people to obtain the "legal recognition of their independent rights—to life, to work, to treatment or habilitation," that approach may not be very effective in implementing those rights day by day, which requires cooperation, not competition (Weinberg, 1988: 290). But doesn't cooperation depend on equality, otherwise it becomes coercion, no matter how subtle?

In a complementary fashion, some disability activists wonder whether rights are becoming the rationale for "integration on the cheap" (Barton and Tomlinson, 1984: 71; Minow, 1990: 138). Moving people with disabilities out of institutions without providing community services or physically mainstreaming students with disabilities without providing appropriate education may be an unintended consequence of a rights rationale. The rationale of rights has led to great progress for citizens with disabilities (and ultimately for all citizens), but it continues to be precarious and controversial.

As I noted in Chapter 1, I believe that we must move beyond a minority-group approach. It does not push us far enough to examine how we make our lives as disabled and nondisabled people. Much of my concern in Chapter 1 is equally applicable to a rights rationale, which is so intertwined with a minority-group perspective. I will not repeat that discussion, though it may be useful to return to it.

A rights rationale is, ironically, still very much an individualistic approach from a taken-for-granted center of a "normal" person. Instead of being automatically cast into the devalued status of abnormal person, people with disabilities might be able to enjoy the rights of any citizen. They will as long as they are essentially "normal." (Recall the phrase, "otherwise qualified.") Some people with disabilities, however, are "really different." Their essential differences (differences from the nondisabled center that are taken to be the natural standard), not merely unacceptable prejudice, have denied them full participation in society. For them, "special" accommodations may be appropriate. Thus, the rights perspective

> retains a general presumption that differences reside in the different person rather than in relation to norms embedded in prevailing institutions . . . (It) also presumes that the status quo is natural and good, except where it has mistakenly treated people who are really the same as though they were different . . . (It) takes as given and as a measure for the future the pattern of rights that developed for those historically included. New rights, responsive to the needs of the historically excluded, both lack foundation and strengthen the divide between those who fit and those who do not fit the norm (Minow, 1990: 108, 109).

A rights rationale says to people with disabilities: If you measure up, then you have rights—the rights that those of us who are nondisabled have enjoyed and that have suited us. We may extend some special treatment, but that is what it is—special—because (some of) you do not "really" measure up, you are not "really" the same. I do not mean to be harsh, but I urge us not to rest on our laurels—on our rights!

Consider the Americans with Disabilities Act of 1990. Employers are exempted from meeting the requirements of the Act when to meet the requirements would create an "undue hardship" or when they have fewer than 15 employees. Physical barriers to public facilities do not need to be removed when to do so is not "readily achievable." Transportation officials have up to 30 years to make parts of their transportation systems accessible. We can understand these and other exemptions and lag times as practical adjustments to a rights approach. We can also understand those "loopholes" as indications of fundamental shortcomings in our present rights approach, shortcomings I have mentioned above.

In the conclusion of this chapter, I return to my concern with the rights rationale and other rationales and (American) disability policy. Neither the rationales nor the policies, including a rights rationale, satisfactorily emphasize the interconnectedness of human life, the partiality of our experiences, the commonality/communality that can bind us, and therefore, the importance of developing universal policies that encompass us all (Zola, 1989; Ferguson et al., 1990; Minow, 1990).

Orienting Policy

We might assume that our disability policy is oriented toward enabling citizens with disabilities to participate as fully as possible within their communities. However, given our still dominant individualistic view of disability as an individual defect and all that has accompanied that view (recall the previous chapters) and given our mixed rationales and conflicts that underlie our policies, we should not be surprised if the orientations are otherwise.

Our disability policy might be better understood as primarily, certainly not completely, "designed" to make it difficult for citizens with disabilities to participate in their communities. Often with the best of intentions, we have *individualistically* managed the challenge of disability through *segregating* citizens with disabilities into *exceptional* programs that made them *dependent*. Even with the increasing recognition of the rights of disabled citizens, we have had difficulty in moving away from these orientations (Bowe, 1978, 1980; Erlanger and Roth, 1985; National Council on the Handicapped, 1986: vi; Berkowitz, 1987; Biklen, 1988; Ferguson et al., 1990).

Individualizing

Our disability policies have primarily focused on the individual flaws of citizens with disabilities to the exclusion of the social barriers they encounter. Our policies have been built upon and, in turn, support our individualistic conceptions of disability (see Chapter 1). They have informed our service practices (see Chapter 6). The flaws of disabled individuals prevented them from learning or earning, from participating satisfactorily in social life. Or, their defects threatened the rest of us. Whether with sympathy or fear, we killed, sterilized, institutionalized, medicated, serviced, compensated, tried to fix, or neglected them because the "problem" of disability was inside them. Though we often did not call it what it was or admit to it, at times we killed them, because they were a burden, they or their parents had offended the (supernatural) order of the world, or their lives were not worthy enough to maintain at such expense and sorrow (see Chapter 6; Scheer and Groce, 1988).

Out of hope, pity, or fear we have institutionalized disabled citizens. "For their own good" or for ours, we separated them from us. As for citizens known as mentally retarded, we first institutionalized them in the middle 1800s because we believed that within separate schools they could develop adaptive, compensatory skills and return to the community. When our results fell short of our expectations, we continued to institutionalize mentally retarded citizens out of pity for them. We protected these "unfortunate" people by separating them from an inhospitable world into asylums. But pity turned to resentment, and paternalistic charity to brutalization. In the latter 1800s, urban problems seemed to be increasing—crime, drinking, ungoverned children, sexual deviance, and so on—problems often attributed to the large waves of immigrants, many of whom were not from Great Britain or Northern and Western Europe as many early Americans had been. Social Darwinism became fashionable. It emphasized that people with fewer natural endowments would naturally fall to the bottom of society. (It provided justification for some of the profound changes that an industrializing, capitalistic society was producing, changes I briefly mentioned earlier.) However, such people could be a menace if they reproduced themselves. Concern about "defective" people swept the country in the late 1800s and early 1900s (Rothman, 1971: especially Chapters 10 and 11; Wolfensberger, 1975; Lane, 1984: 358–361). Mentally retarded citizens were a prime target of this fear. Out of fear we continued to institutionalize some of them. And hoping to prevent their reproduction, we prohibited the procreation of retarded (and other "defective") citizens and their marriages, sterilized them, and, when those measures failed, tried to strictly separate them from nondisabled citizens and from the opposite sex, a "sexual quarantine" (Wolfensberger, 1975: Chapter 2). Compulsory sterilization continued in some locales until the 1960s (Minow, 1990: 134).

More recently we "service" those with disabilities (see Chapter 6). We treat, counsel, medicate, rehabilitate, and educate. With "space-age" technology we can improve greatly the capacity of disabled people to participate in social life. For example, a

> communication device called the Eyetyper is currently available for use by nonspeaking persons with severe physical limitations. The system consists of an upright display module divided into nine cells on which are displayed pictures or words. A sensor uses an infrared video camera to sense which of the nine display areas a person is looking at, and an output module translates the selection into a voice appropriate to the age and sex of the user. With this system, a person can "speak" to another person with no greater effort than subtle eye movements (Cavalier, 1987: 131).

We also compensate disabled people for their loss of earnings and provide for those who cannot support themselves through workers' compensation, disability insurance, and supplemental income (Erlanger and Roth, 1985). From destruction to compassion, we respond to the challenges of disability by focusing on the disabled individual. Sometimes we succeed; other times not.

Segregating

When responding to the challenges of disability, we have often segregated disabled people from nondisabled people. Destruction was permanent separation and institutionalization sometimes equally so.

Consider the education of children with disabilities. While separate educational institutions were created for deaf and for blind children in the 1800s, with the emphasis on mandatory education came separate education for disabled youth (Sarason and Doris, 1979: Chapter 13; Lazerson, 1983; see Chapter 6). While educators today point to clinical judgment as the basis for educational decisions concerning disabled youth, the variation in segregated placement of disabled students is so large that clinical judgment cannot account for it. Instead, as I noted in Chapter 6, funding policies that favor segregated placements are important. If a "state provides 100% of the funding for institutional placements, local school districts will find this an attractive option for eligible students" (Biklen, 1988: 134). As I noted earlier, even with the enactment of PL 94-142, The Education for All Handicapped Children Act of 1975, which emphasized that students with educational handicaps should be educated in the least restrictive environment, the "percentage of disabled students served in the general school environment has remained constant" (Walker, 1987: 104; see also Ferguson et al. 1990).

> Furthermore, there have been disturbing trends within other categories (categories other than learning disabled): placement in separate classes and separate schools has increased for orthopedically impaired students and for mentally retarded youngsters, numbers which can only be partially explained by the decrease in enrollment in separate nonschool environment. The fact that school officials explain the increase in separate, more restrictive placements for orthopedically disabled students with the rationale that it is more effective and economical to centralize these services raises serious questions ... These data, combined with reports from advocacy organizations about struggles over placement because of a lack of commitment to general classroom placements, reports from evaluation studies about the slowdown of development of multiple options for placement for children by category, the fact that placement of students after evaluation often is determined by available space and (dis)-incentives within funding categories, and research on referral practices indicates (sic) that placement and integration of disabled students in the school environment leaves much yet to be achieved (Walker, 1987: 105).

Even when we educate students with disabilities in the same schools and even in the same classes as nondisabled children, we may have only achieved physical integration, not social integration (Higgins, 1990: especially Chapter 4). Placing a disabled child in a regular class but not including that child in the life of the class and of the school is perhaps a more cruel segregation than educating that child in a separate institution. We provide the illusion of integration while producing isolation.

So, too, does the deinstitutionalization of mentally retarded individuals and others with disabilities leave much left to be achieved. While many mentally retarded individuals left large total institutions in the 1970s, the decrease in the number of mentally retarded citizens in large institutions has slowed dramatically (Biklen, 1988). Our "irrational" funding policies are partly at fault. For example, approximately "75 percent of the federal reimbursement to states for intermediate care facility/mental retardation (ICF/MR) programs currently goes to support 3 percent of mentally retarded people still living in large institutional settings" (Ferguson et al., 1990: 12). Because of that "irrational" policy, government poorly provides attendant services that could enable citizens with disabilities to live and work in the community (DeJong and Batavia, 1990; *The Disability Rag,* January/February 1991).

Nowadays, a continuum of service—residential, vocational, and educational—is becoming an important component of disability policy. Services may be provided from the most segregative setting to the least (Taylor et al., 1987). For example, governments may provide residential services for developmentally disabled individuals that range from large total institutions to intermediate care facilities in the community to smaller group homes to foster care to supported independent living (Taylor et al., 1987). The rationale is that more severely disabled citizens will be served in more restrictive environments. As their skills develop, then they will be moved to less restrictive settings. Policies that promote a continuum of services legitimate segregation under the rationale that providers and participants are always working toward integration. A continuum of services encourages officials to evaluate some disabled citizens as so impaired that more restrictive services are appropriate. Otherwise, why have a continuum? If less restrictive services are not presently successful, the alternative of more segregative services is always available.

A fundamental flaw in this policy is the confusion of restrictiveness with intensity. Severely disabled citizens may need intensive services, but they do not need to receive them in restrictive settings. A growing number of programs in Michigan, Nebraska and elsewhere are showing that severely disabled citizens can live successfully within the community (Taylor et al., 1987). However, other states are much more likely to segregate their severely disabled citizens in large-scale institutions (Biklen, 1988).

We also segregate disabled citizens in workshops, in separate transportation systems, in service agencies geared only toward them, and through a housing policy that has attempted to build accessible housing but has not yet succeeded (*The Disability Rag,* May/June 1990, March/April 1991, May/June 1991). Our policies often encourage, even require, segregation. But why shouldn't they, if we "know" people with disabilities to be fundamentally different than those without.

Making Exceptional

Correspondingly, our disability policy has emphasized exceptional approaches to "handling" disability. This exceptional orientation proclaims that disabled citizens are not ordinary people. If we segregate disabled people from nondisabled people and justify that isolation by appealing to the individual "defects" of disabled citizens that make them different, then our programs must be different, too. Instead of enlargening our arrangements and practices, making them flexible/adaptable, so that we can deal with our collective diversity within the same programs, we develop special, exceptional arrangements, procedures and programs for disabled citizens (Zola, 1989). The continuing debate over equally accessible transportation or transportation that is separate but provides "effective mobility" illustrates this issue.

Policy that makes disability exceptional also separates disabled people from nondisabled people. It does so not only physically, but more important, socially. It indicates that disabled people are different kinds of people instead of proclaiming disabled people are ordinary people with varying attributes. Policies that enable us to respond to the diversity of our citizens within a common framework proclaim that we are all fundamentally similar. Such policies are much different than those that establish separate programs for separate categories of people. The latter is "exceptionalistic" (see Chapter 6).

Special education is a prime example. When we have responded to the varying needs of students with educationally significant disabilities, we have done so through exceptional means. We have established separate schools and classes, even separate intermediate districts. We have established separate, specialized training for teachers who educate disabled students. They speak a jargon of EMH, IEP, and LEA. We have separate administration and funding mechanisms. For example, subsidies may be provided for specific services such as transportation, funds provided for personnel such as an itinerant teacher, or money allocated per disabled student served. "Each mechanism, whether for specific services, personnel, or students, differentiates education funding for students labelled disabled from that of their nondisabled peers" (Biklen, 1989: 7). "Irregular" practices abound.

In attempting to ensure that youth with disabilities received a free, appropriate education, The Education for All Handicapped Children Act of 1975 (and subsequent legislation) have perpetuated policies that are exceptional. Among many consequences, the law proclaimed that in contrast to nondisabled youth, youth with disabilities are different kinds of youth, with different needs that must be addressed through different procedures. (Ironically, observers have questioned what is special about

much of special education (Algozzine, Morsink and Algozzine, 1986).)
These exceptional procedures include evaluations by multidisciplinary
teams, a continuum of educational placements (that legitimates segregation), the Individual Educational Program (the IEP), and due process
provisions that enable parents to challenge educational decisions. While
the intent of these and other provisions is to serve better those youth
with educationally significant disabilities, they also set disabled youth
apart. Nondisabled youth are not responded to in this manner. These
procedures make it difficult for school participants to see disabled youth
as ordinary people, who, whether disabled or not, are tremendously
diverse. Unusual, irregular, special procedures make youth with disabilities exceptional children, not regular kids (Biklen, 1989).

Producing Dependence

Finally, our disability policy has primarily promoted the dependence
of disabled people. Typically believing people with disabilities to be
incapable of contributing (much) to society, we spend most of our disability funds on programs that require disabled people to be and remain
dependent (DeJong and Batavia, 1990). "Simply put, this nation spends
most of the money allocated to disability on programs that provide the
handicapped with tickets out of the labor force" (Berkowitz, 1987: 4).

For example, workers' compensation, Social Security Disability Insurance and Supplemental Security Income are income maintenance programs that dominate our disability policy (Berkowitz, 1987: Part 1). They
provide income and other benefits to disabled people who are "needy"—
who cannot work due to an occupational injury or disease, have reduced
earning capacity, or are unable to engage in "substantial gainful activity."
Through these programs we presumably ameliorate the consequences of
disability. However, with average SSDI benefits to disabled workers of
less than $500 per month in 1985, we cannot be ameliorating the conse-
quences very successfully (Yelin, 1989). To receive the benefits, disabled
recipients (particularly recipients of SSDI and SSI) must be dependent,
must remain dependent, and must prove that they are dependent (Bowe,
1980: 4, Berkowitz, 1987). The process of obtaining those benefits is not
conducive to thinking of oneself as independent (DeJong and Batavia,
1990). If workers' compensation recipients undertake rehabilitation, they
may fear that their settlements will be reduced (Berkowitz, 1987: 158).
SSDI and SSI recipients may hesitate to "risk losing their program
eligibility through employment, even if they are assured that they will

probably be able to regain eligibility in the future if necessary (DeJong and Batavia, 1990: 69). (In contrast, several European countries provide assistance to disabled people irrespective of their being employed (DeJong and Batavia, 1990).)

Until recently, strong disincentives in the disability insurance program have existed that discourage disabled people from working or trying to work. The earnings ceiling above which recipients are denied benefits has been low, $713 for SSI recipients in 1984 (National Council on the Handicapped, 1986: 29). Thus a disabled recipient could work for modest wages and have benefits terminated. However, even with good wages, to work may require the assistance of attendants, a specially equipped van, and other expenses that nondisabled people do not incur. Hence, the "real" take-home pay may be much smaller than the paycheck. Further, in being terminated, recipients have also lost other support services such as medical assistance. It would be a significant, added burden to pay for medical care, which is typically much greater for disabled citizens (Bowe, 1980: Chapter 5). Many may not be able to get private health insurance (National Council on the Handicapped, 1986: 28). Recent changes have removed some of those disincentives, but they still exist (National Council on the Handicapped, 1986: 27–29; Berkowitz, 1987: 107; DeJong and Batavia, 1990).

Even our state-federal vocational rehabilitation system, America's major (or largest-budgeted) program to enable disabled citizens to become independent (Berkowitz, 1987: 154) has not promoted independence as well as we might have expected or hoped. Minimal funding in comparison to income supplement programs such as SSDI and SSI make it impossible for the vocational rehabilitation program to serve more than a small percentage (perhaps less than 10%) of potentially eligible citizens (Bowe, 1980: 100). While the federal government spends more than $1 billion on vocational rehabilitation, the "Social Security Disability Insurance program costs at least 17 times more" (Berkowitz, 1987: 154). With modest funding and with the concern among officials that they must show that the funds bring results, vocational rehabilitation agencies have often focused on less severely disabled individuals who were more likely to return to work (or remain working). The more severely disabled individuals, who needed greater assistance and who may not become employed, were often denied services. This procedure of "creaming," which I mentioned in the previous chapter, enabled vocational rehabilitation agencies to show through a simple cost-benefit analysis that they "paid" their way by saving many tax dollars for every tax dollar spent (Berkowitz, 1987: Chapter 5). Our funding of vocational rehabilitation and the agencies' approach to rehabilitation perpetuated a great deal of dependency. Recent federal legislation has mandated that vocational rehabilitation address the needs of severely disabled individuals who may become more independent through employment or through developing independent living skills even if they do not hold a job (Bowe, 1980: Chapter 4; Berkowitz, 1987: Chapter 5). The disability movement, however, continues to criticize our approach to rehabilitation (DeJong, 1983; see Chapter 6).

However, even when we enable severely disabled citizens to develop their abilities to work, if we do not enable them to get out of their home and go to work and then ensure that jobs are arranged so that they can work successfully, we still will have perpetuated dependence. "Rehabilitating" disabled individuals succeeds best when we also rehabilitate the world in which they—we—live (Bowe, 1980; Erlanger and Roth, 1985: 338–339).

Our traditional disability policy gives much less attention to enabling disabled people to develop the skills to become self-controlling, to creating opportunities for disabled people to use their hard-earned skills in work, to reducing the barriers to being independent (Bowe, 1980; Erlanger and Roth, 1985; Berkowitz, 1987). The increasing emphasis on rights has begun to challenge our traditional disability policy, but as I noted earlier, a rights rationale is still precarious and controversial. With often good intentions and some success, our disability policy has also disabled those it was intended to assist.

Differentiating Disabled People

Policies cannot be neutral. They promote courses of action and often categories of people. Typically some individuals benefit, while others do not. Thus, policies usually treat people unequally. Our policies (and practices) have typically made people known as disabled less worthy individuals, lessening their opportunities to participate fully in their society's affairs (Hahn, 1983; Minow, 1990). That is a crucial point of this entire book. However, we also respond more generously to some with disabilities than to others. These unequal responses are tied to our policy rationales, particularly to the rationale of utility.

While we typically understand disability as a stigma, ironically, our policies also cast disability as a "political privilege" (Stone, 1984: 28). It is a

> political privilege because, as an administrative category, it carries with it permission to enter the need-based system and to be exempt from the work-based system. It can also provide exemption from other things people normally consider worth avoiding: military service, debt, and criminal liability. Disability programs are political precisely because they allocate these privileges (Stone, 1984: 28).

Disability programs allocate other desirables as well, primarily services and monetary benefits. However, to some we allocate more than to others.

Typically, our disability policy has promoted disabled individuals who are "most valuable to national and industrial interests" (Albrecht and Levy, 1984: 72). Defense and work are the key. Disabled veterans, disabled workers, and disabled youth who we believe will eventually work have benefitted most from our disability policy.

We assist most generously those who become disabled in defense of the country, disabled veterans. With the enactment of the first national pension law in 1776 to compensate men with service-related disabilities, the nation began its special commitment to assist disabled veterans (Obermann, 1965: Chapter 8). We assist disabled veterans in order to meet our self-proclaimed obligations to those who sacrificed themselves in defense of the country. Therefore, as a former Rehabilitation Services Administration commissioner concluded, "the veterans system is a benefits, not a rehabilitation, system because the disabled veterans are not required to work" (Tanenbaum, 1986: 64). Disabled veterans have strongest claim on our disability dollars. Thus, veterans are typically "entitled to more generous benefits and their programs are older and better established than civilian programs" (Berkowitz, 1987: 169). For example, in a recent year the Veterans Administration spent an average of $5,000 on the vocational rehabilitation of veterans, but the state vocational rehabilitation agencies spent just $800 (Tanenbaum, 1986: 62; but see Yelin, 1989: 149–150). Those who become disabled in defense of the country are most worthy within our disability policy.

We also assist most those who best embody the work ethic/ideology of our society. We do so when dispensing services as well as monetary (and other) benefits. To those disabled individuals who we believe can work or can return to work, we provide vocational rehabilitation, which may include an array of medical, educational, counseling, and other services.

To the others, vocational rehabilitation agencies typically have provided regrets (until the recent focus on serving those with severe disabilities and on providing independent living services for more severely disabled individuals who may not work) (Berkowitz, 1987: Chapter 5). To those individuals who become disabled "on the job," we provide worker's compensation (Berkowitz, 1987: Chapter 1). For those who work steadily, we have created insurance benefits should they become disabled, Social Security Disability Insurance. Their work history (and Social Security taxes) entitle them to the disability insurance. However, to those who have not worked sufficiently but become disabled, we provide less generous welfare, Supplemental Security Income, in order to insure a minimum income (Erlanger and Roth, 1985; Yelin, 1989). With our disability policies focused on those who have worked or can work, we have in various shifting ways slighted women, elderly people, and those most severely disabled (Mudrick, 1988).

Our educational policies also stratified youth with disabilities according to how likely they might become productive citizens. As I have already noted, special education (in part) developed out of the concern to make disabled youth employable. It was "economic good sense to make as many citizens, even the handicapped, productive as possible" (Tomlinson, 1982: 36). And those disabled youth viewed as most likely to become productive have been provided the most attention. The most severely disabled youth were typically excluded from school or placed in segregated institutions. Within the past several decades a continuum of services from the most restrictive to the least restrictive became a guide in serving disabled youth and adults. The assumption is that "people with the most severe disabilities will be served at the most restrictive end of the continuum and those with the mildest disabilities will be at the least restrictive end" (Taylor et al., 1987: 7). The recent emphasis on mainstreaming has not fundamentally changed that assumption. Instead, it has modestly shifted the continuum toward less restrictive educational placements primarily by diminishing the role of large total institutions. But the more severely disabled youth are still likely to be educated in more segregated settings (Walker, 1987; Ferguson et al., 1990; Higgins, 1990).

In still other ways we differentiate people with disabilities. The social status of disabled people matters just as it does for nondisabled people. To those with higher status comes more. For example, higher status workers who become disabled may be treated more generously than lower status workers who become disabled. Both worker's compensation and Social Security Disability Insurance in the U.S. provide greater benefits for recipients who are financially more well off, through either (very roughly) compensation for lost wages or the equivalent of social security retirement benefits (which may be offset by benefits from other programs) (Erlanger and Roth, 1985; Berkowitz, 1987: 26–30). As I previously noted, SSDI for those who have worked is more generous than SSI for those who have not worked (much, if at all).

America is not alone in providing preferences to higher status workers who become disabled. Class distinctions have been important in German social insurance policy. Early in this century separate schemes for white- and blue-collar workers were established. To become eligible white-collar workers needed to show only a 50 percent loss in earning capacity compared to a comparable, healthy worker, but blue-collar workers needed to show a loss of two-thirds. Further, when deciding if other employment was feasible, the range of potential employment was drawn more narrowly for the white-collar workers who became disabled than the blue-collar, disabled workers. Changes in the past several decades have not fundamentally altered the preference shown German white-collar workers (Stone, 1984: 56–68).

And still other people with disabilities are favored. Visually impaired people "enjoy special privileges" in American disability policy (Berkowitz, 1987: 168). For example, at Congressional hearings on rehabilitation, representatives of visually impaired people often testify first. Vocational rehabilitation regulations permit states to maintain separate rehabilitation systems for visually impaired people—and 32 states do so. The Social Security Act singled out only visually impaired people among those with disabilities to qualify for welfare. Visually impaired people may run newsstands or snack bars in federal buildings. It is not clear why we provide special privileges to visually impaired people.

> Possibly it is because the unimpaired can easily imagine and sympathize with their plight; unlike mental illness, for example, the state of blindness involves little stigma. Possibly it is because blindness has existed since the beginning of history, so that the blind have had more time to secure a place for themselves as legitimate objects of aid from the state. The very fact that their impairment is less disabling than others gives the blind advantages in political organization (Berkowitz, 1987: 168).

Our (and other societies') disability policies make unequal those whom we have already made less worthy. As we do throughout society, we differentiate disabled people. We typically provide more to those who already have the most or seemingly have the most to offer in the future.

I wonder if we are not creating (at least) two tiers of disabled citizens, much as we seem to have among black Americans. We enable some disabled citizens and black citizens to participate in the mainstream. But many others are left increasingly farther behind (Wilson, 1987). For disabled citizens whom we now see as essentially "normal," we provide them rights and opportunities. We enroll them in regular classes, even academically advanced classes. We "ensure" that colleges are accessible and accommodating. We modify the work environment where needed so that they can be productive, and we guard against discriminatory pay and promotions. We remove physical barriers so that they can get around. But for those who are older (perhaps elderly), poor, more severely impaired, our policies and our emphasis on rights do not touch them as much. They still do not fit our slightly expanded notion of worth. They are not seen as valuable citizens.

These two tiers among disabled citizens appear in the significant differences between disabled citizens who work and those who do not (Bowe, 1985; Louis Harris and Associates, 1986: Chapter 5). Disabled citizens who work are better educated, have higher incomes, and feel more satisfied with life than those who do not work (though variation within each group and overlap between the two groups exist) (Louis Harris and Associates, 1986: Chapter 5). We continue to make some disabled people more valuable than others. We even make some inhuman.

Dehumanizing Disability

Many have recently become concerned with our treatment of severely disabled infants born with a correctible but life-threatening health condition, "Baby Doe's" as they are impersonally referred to in the media (and in the courts). Government response to this concern was perhaps largely symbolic: vaguely worded legislation with few sanctions and little meaningful oversight that did not address the lack of serious support for parents and their severely disabled infants, which may make the future (seem) "bleak" to the parents and observers (Moss, 1987).

That concern, treatment, and government response explicitly point to how our policies may figuratively and literally dehumanize people with disabilities (Biklen and Ferguson, 1984; Hentoff, 1987; see also Chapter 6). We may first figuratively dehumanize infants by claiming that should they survive the medical procedure they will be "vegetables," their lives will be "meaningless," they will not achieve "humanhood," or in other ways they will not be persons (Hentoff, 1987). We may then fulfill our prophecy by not providing the medically indicated care to enable the disabled infants to live. However, should these infants live, we may serve them and their families in ways that make it difficult, if not impossible, to become human. Having done so, we may then knowingly, but also sympathetically, assert that we told you so. We have, indeed, dehumanized the infants.

The debate about what constitutes being human is ancient. It has assumed especially poignant significance with our increasing capacity to sustain the lives of infants and others with severe disabilities (Duncan and Woods, 1989). In the context of assisting severely disabled people to live, the discussion may be quite vague. If a person does not have the "ability to form relationships," then perhaps the life is not worth living. Or might those with Down syndrome face a future too bleak to be assisted? Others would point to the so-called "really" severely disabled, such as "Baby Jane Doe" born with spina bifida, as someone whose life is not worth preserving (Biklen and Ferguson, 1984). Some develop more specific indicators of who is human or a person (the latter in some way being more of a being than the former). Some use IQ scores. One medical ethicist suggests that anyone with an IQ below 40 is "questionably a person; below the mark of 20, not a person" (Fletcher, 1979: Chapter 1). Others develop a "scientific" formula to decide who is worth treating and who isn't, in effect, who is human enough to live and who is not.

Doctors and other health care professionals at the University of Oklahoma Health Sciences Center conducted a five-year project to evaluate an early selection and treatment procedure of infants born with spina bifida. Other doctors had previously conducted similar projects. However, due to the commentary of disability rights activists and columnists, this experiment received widespread attention, well beyond the circle of health care professionals who read the medical journal in which the report of the project appeared. Based on the evaluation of the infants, the management team recommended to the parents either vigorous treatment or supportive care. Vigorous treatment seems to have been successful. The infants lived. However, supportive treatment was successful, too. The babies died, which, of course, was the goal of that "treatment."

However, not all parents agreed with the recommendation. Five families did not, and with early, vigorous treatment, three of the babies survived. Three other babies who were not sloted for vigorous treatment did not have the good grace to die and eventually received treatment. As the management team noted of one of these children:

> At age 6 months, one baby was noted to be robust and thriving and a decision for vigorous treatment was made by the family at that time. The child is now 3 years old and lives at home with his family (Gross et al., 1983: 453).

(This child who had not been initially recommended for treatment does not seem to have become the "hopeless case" with a "meaningless" life, the foundation upon which such infanticide is presently practiced.)

The treatment management team was influenced by a quality of life formula developed by a respected pediatric surgeon and clinical professor of surgery (Gross et al., 1983; Hentoff, 1987). The formula, $QL = NE \times (H + S)$, predicts the quality of life the child will likely have if the child lives. The quality of life (QL) is a result of the child's natural endowment (NE) as influenced by the child's contribution from home and family (H) and society (S).

Besides formalizing and publicizing a practice that has been occurring informally and without much discussion for many years, the management team expressed and operated on (no pun intended) common, disabling assumptions and practices. As they recognized, using the quality of life formula more likely leads to recommendations of vigorous treatment for infants who are advantaged by "accident of birth," by having the good fortune to have wealthier parents. Their practices continued the unequal consequences of our disability policies. More broadly, they recognized that the practices of others are of enormous consequences for the lives of those with disabilities. However, instead of challenging the resulting inequities (not to mention oppression), their practices took for granted the present arrangements. Their practices also fulfilled their prophecies. Infants judged to have a poor quality of life, indeed, did. They died! Though not all did (once treatment was started sometimes months later). People have an annoying knack of confounding experts. Those who do, though, are the exception. They must have been because the management team said so little about them. The team's practices also supported professional dominance, even though the survival of babies sloted to die disconfirmed the expertise of the professionals.

The management team did not recognize, as most of our policy and thinking about disability do not recognize, that their view as nondisabled professionals is just one view among great diversity. Instead, they took their nondisabled view to be the bedrock standard, the "natural" center, from which to evaluate the lives of others. That fundamental error is the most disabling of all.

The management team (and many of their colleagues) have merely made "professional" what all societies do and must do—ration fundamental resources among people, even to the extent of allocating life and death. Here is not the place to examine that overwhelmingly complex and controversial issue (see Duncan and Woods, 1989 for a start). However, we must clearly recognize that when our rationing routinely puts those with disabilities at the end of line, we make clear their worth as people.

The Functions of Disability

Disability persists. It even expands. We turn ever more human characteristics into differences and then into disabilities. We manufacture those human conditions that we know as disabilities. We continue to create a world based on narrow notions of who we are. Consequently, many people with and without disabilities encounter great difficulty in their lives. Our specific responses to disability (from "benign" neglect to gross negligence, from public inaccessibility to educational segregation) often have the (unintended?) consequence of handicapping those who are disabled.

Ironically, our disability policy (and much of how we make disability) might be partly understood as a means for maintaining disability.

> Suppose there were more seriousness about the perpetuation of the category of "handicap" than about the employment of handicapped people: the current mix of policies would then be entirely rational (Roth, 1981: 209).

Perhaps disability serves useful purposes that (often unrecognized by us) undermine the impetus to reduce or prevent disability and dependence (Albrecht, 1976; Zola, 1979; see Gans, 1971 for the positive functions of poverty, the "model" for my discussion). However, to suggest that disability serves positive functions does not mean that we willfully disable one another in order to benefit from those positive outcomes, though at times that has happened. (For example, people have purposefully disabled themselves or often others, particularly children, in order to beg more successfully.) It does not mean that beneficiaries of disability are ignoble. Just the opposite; many have the best of intentions. Nor does it mean that disability serves positive purposes for all segments of society. Some benefit more than others, and varying functions may benefit differing people. More important, basic societal arrangements may be supported by disability. (Ultimately, our disabling practices harm us all, but shortsigthedly we resist changes that we recognize may immediately, directly disadvantage us.) Nevertheless, to the extent that disability functions positively in important ways, then we will less likely address effectively disability. Among the positive functions of disability are the following:

1. Disability is big business. Medical professionals, counselors, special educators, and other human service professionals earn their living by serving disabled people. So do aides, secretaries, clerks, and other workers who support the efforts of the professionals. Attorneys who litigate disability claims likewise profit from the existence of disability. Hospitals, rehabilitation agencies, manufacturers of all kinds of "disability items," and other organizations exist because of disability. Academics do, too. Rehabilitation agencies have "hung on" to clients in order to keep their rolls full or their workshops productive (Scott, 1969; Buckholdt and Gubrium, 1983; Evans, 1983: Chapter 9). Consequently, we should not be surprised when such organizations and professionals expand disability to encompass more conditions and more people or perpetuate people's status as disabled (with the well meaning intention of serving the individuals). Many organizations and professionals "live off of" disability (Lane, 1988; Albrecht, forthcoming).

2. Disability enables others to ennoble themselves. Through charitable work or contributions, those without disabilities demonstrate, even elevate, their moral worth. Those paid to work with disabled people may also receive praise. Special education teachers, therapists, counselors, and other human service professionals who work with disabled people are lauded for their patience, concern, and kindness (though occasionally condemned if the service seems unsatisfactory). Disability enables us to "do—and be—good."

3. Disability also enables nondisabled people to define and elevate their existential status. Being able-bodied after all only has meaning in contrast to those known as disabled (Higgins, 1980: 175–179). Being sighted makes sense in contrast to those who are not sighted; being hearing in contrast to those not hearing; and so on. In contrast to those who are disabled, nondisabled people are *not* that. They are *other* than that. They are *better* than that. By portraying disabled people as "different, odd, or not quite normal and by routinely putting them in an inferior position, the nondisabled assert their moral superiority" (Higgins, 1980:

178). While nondisabled people may experience existential anxiety because they, too, could become disabled (Hahn, 1988), they seemingly comfort themselves in knowing that they can do what disabled people presumably cannot do and they are what disabled people presumably cannot be. Disability becomes a "foil" through which nondisabled people identify themselves as morally worthy.

4. Disability absorbs the costs of societal change. As we knowingly and unknowingly create a hazardous world, those who become disabled are the unfortunate, but to-be-expected, "victims" of progress. They bear the costs of our accidents, unsafe work places, toxic environments, and the like. Thus, (in New Zealand) becoming disabled through accidents is the result of the "normal operation of the society: the production, distribution, and consumption of goods and services ... a chance and undesired byproduct of these activities" (Kronick, Vosburgh, and Vosburgh, 1981: 191).

5. Disability protects our political economy. As I noted earlier, a significant cornerstone of that economy is a work ideology. We believe that through work people obtain what is desirable, and everyone should work (or take care of the children). However, not everyone can work. More important, not everyone is needed to work. We have more workers than jobs. Disability, a flexible category, can be used to "absorb" some of the surplus workers, thereby reducing unemployment and its pressures on society. When

> ideology mandates that everyone should work but society cannot provide employment for large segments of its population, the dilemma can be reconciled by *defining* a higher proportion of the population as disabled ... An expansion of the definition of disability can reduce the pressures of unemployed workers on the work-based distributive system and at the same time preserve the legitimacy of the work ideology (Stone, 1984: 168).

Disability is a societal safety valve.

6. Disability provides an escape from onerous obligations. Individuals who encounter difficulty meeting the demands of work, family, school and other responsibilities can bow out, if not gracefully, then at least somewhat more legitimately through disability (Cole and Lejeune, 1972). Thus, disability can be a personal escape hatch from the rigors of burdensome responsibilities. Not coincidentally, these responsibilities may become most burdensome for those with fewest resources.

7. Disability can be used to control people and protect social arrangements. In the Soviet Union, those who threaten the legitimacy of the state have been routinely institutionalized as mentally ill. However, we do not need to go abroad to recognize that disability can be used to control. Through special education we have segregated lower and working class children, immigrant youth, and black, Hispanic and other minorities from the middle class white majority. We managed those who did not conform to white, middle class standards by relegating them to the rolls of "the disabled," particularly "the retarded" (Sarason and Doris, 1979: Chapter 16; Lazerson, 1983). Or, troubles that women experience that could be seen as arising out of gender and family inequities may be handle as an individual, personal problem of mental illness (Warren, 1987). If such troubles become individualized, then gender and family arrangements that disadvantage women are protected. Disability can be used to protect social arrangements (Coleman, 1986: 228) just as it can be used to protect our political economy (the two being interrelated).

   8. Disability subsidizes many of us. While we spend billions of dollars in responding ineffectively to disability (Bowe, 1978; Berkowitz, 1987) we also indirectly benefit from disability. To the extent that disabled workers have fewer alternatives, then they are less likely to leave undesirable employment. Their lack of alternatives provides less impetus for employers to improve the pay, promotion opportunities, and other conditions of work (Johnson and Lambrinos, 1983). Employers' profits are improved. Nondisabled workers are subsidized, too. When disabled people are excluded from employment or have fewer alternatives to pursue, non-disabled people have fewer competitors for jobs. Having fewer competitors, they may be more successful in obtaining employment and in "demanding" better wages.

   9. Disabled people may be convenient scapegoats for societal problems (Albrecht, 1976). They may be exterminated to improve the genetic stock of the people. They are feared as the perpetrators of crime and other danger (witness the stereotype of the disabled criminal, particularly the deranged criminal). Biological inferiority becomes an acceptable explanation for the great disparities in the social conditions of minorities and majorities. Disablitiy becomes a convenient excuse for inhumanely treating "expendable" people, such as the elderly in nursing homes (see Chapter 6). Scapegoating disabled people or disability encourages us to overlook the deep-seated social bases for our difficulties, as it did in our creation of learning disabilities (see Chapter 1).

   10. Disability provides us amusement and entertainment. From the court jesters of the middle ages (and before) to the freak shows of the mid-1800s to the mid-1900s to the movie and television portrayals of disabled characters, we have been repulsed and fascinated by disability (Bogdan, 1988; Hahn, 1988; See Chapter 3). Some of our most powerful literary and cinematic characters are disabled.

11. Disability is a basic means for structuring social life. We must categorize our world. Otherwise, it would not exist. By categorizing people we produce but also reduce the (potentially) great variation among ourselves. By interacting with one another and arranging our various organizations and practices on the basis of those categories, we simplify social life. We identify our interactional partners or place our associational participants in terms of categories such as "able-bodiedness," sex, race, age, and many others. We create routines, rules, laws, and other guides for acting toward those whom we have categorized. This simplifies and orders social life. For example, we can patronize a mentally retarded person (which requires much less interactional and existential effort than to interact with the person on more profound levels); a school can entrust students with educational handicaps to its special education component, which momentarily takes care of the matter; and, until recently, a business did not have to bother with a disabled applicant seeking work. Through disability we order social life—making it more routine, manageable, predictable.

Disability "serves" all of these functions and more. Being so important in our lives, it is no wonder that our policies (and our other ways of making disability) may help to produce and sustain it. However, they do so in ways that ultimately harm us all.

Conclusion

Our disability policy has primarily controlled people with disabilities. With good intentions and at times with no intentions at all, recognized or not, we have developed a disability policy that has often created a subservient place for people with disabilities and kept them in it. Industrialization (based on capitalism) produced great progress but also fundamentally altered our society in ways that debilitated people with disabilities. We have rationalized our disability policy in changing, conflicting ways—charity, utility, rights—that have primarily made people with disabilities marginal members of their society. We have pursued policies that individualize disability through segregated, exceptional responses that make people with disabilities dependent, even unworthy to live. We have also tried to do otherwise, but have yet to succeed.

We have not succeeded because our disability policies (and almost all of our making of disability) are fundamentally flawed. Our policies and our making do not adequately emphasize the interconnectedness of our lives, the partiality of our experiences, the potential for a commonality/communality that can bind us, and, therefore, the importance for developing universal policies that encompass us all without sacrificing the rich diversity that can be us (Zola, 1989; Ferguson et al., 1990; Minow, 1990). Even a rights rationale, as I noted earlier, which has enabled us to make such great progress, falls short.

Consider the progress we have made within the past twenty years. That progress is both inspiring and vastly disappointing. Instead of systematically excluding students with disabilities from school, we are now opening the schoolhouse door for them. However, as I noted earlier, the "mainstreaming" of students with disabilities has not changed nearly as much as some imagine; neither has the quality of their schooling (Ferguson et al., 1990). Work sites are becoming accessible, but a smaller proportion of citizens with disabilities are working or looking for work now than twenty years ago (Bowe, 1990). Although many citizens who are developmentally disabled have "moved" out of large public, residential institutions since the late 1960s, more than 135,000 such citizens still live in large institutions (Ferguson et al., 1990). Housing and transportation remain inaccessible for many citizens with disabilities, and without attendant services, others unnecessarily remain in institutions. We can understand this slow, mixed progress as the result of the difficulty in remaking an oppressive world. No doubt, that is so. But we can also see in these disappointing results the shortcomings of our policies, including a rights approach.

We must build on rights to encourage relations, the complex, diverse relations among our citizens. Consider a child with a disability, perhaps a severe disability. The child has parents. Those parents are employees (perhaps employers). They are neighbors, and they participate in community organizations as does/should the child. Thus, the family, the work organization, the neighborhood, and the community (and its organizations) are implicated in the life of the child with the disability. A policy that does not enable people to maintain those relations and draw upon those relations will not succeed. For example, a policy that does not enable the parents to meet their responsibilities as employees (perhaps in flexible, shifting ways) while also being parents to their disabled child and their other children cannot succeed. Our policy will fail if it does not enable the parents to be husband and wife to one another (e.g., through respite services or a neighbor's help that permit the parents to have time to themselves). A policy that does not help the child with the disability to develop friendships with neighborhood children and take those friendships into the community's school and back out again will not work well. A policy that does not use the community in which the child lives to prepare the child for living in the community is surely one that alienates the child from the community. A policy that does not engender a desire in neighbors, local employers, and other community citizens to make a valued place for the disabled child and the child's family will not be satisfactory. And so on.

Supported Community Life approaches used with developmentally disabled citizens are promising attempts to enable citizens with disabilities to be members of their communities, not merely exist within their communities. These approaches complement formal support in the community with informal support. For example, a nondisabled colleague's showing a disabled colleague how to perform a work task is just as good as, if not better than, using a "job coach." Or, when we educate children with disabilities in their local schools, adults with disabilities can participate as guest speakers, workshop leaders and in other ways in addition to being paid staff. They can also participate in situations that do not directly involve mainstreaming such as volunteering in the school office. Likewise, the larger community and its nondisabled members can participate in mainstreaming programs (Higgins, 1990). Participants use (and alter) existing community facilities and opportunities; relying less on special, segregated services (e.g., vocational training in a community business, not in a workshop). Assistance is tailored to the local nature of the community; standardized goals or approaches are inappropriate (e.g., learning to travel by subway in New York, but perhaps learning to snowmobile in Anchorage). Disabled citizens and/or their families decide what suits them best. By using the community and informal assistance, these approaches expand the community's capacity to assist all (Ferguson et al., 1990).

Supported Community Life approaches call upon the community to assist citizens with disabilities and aim to enable citizens with disabilities to live and participate within the community. While such approaches have potential risks such as unintentionally emphasizing a charity-response to disabled citizens, they are promising, too (Ferguson et al., 1990). These approaches speak to the interconnectedness of our lives, to the rebuilding of community that includes us all.

Universal policies that encompass the diversity of our citizens and that recognize that many, if not all, of us will experience some of the consequences of disability or chronic illness (especially as we age) will serve us best (Zola, 1989). For example, making new housing that is flexible and adaptable to those with disabilities will enable many elderly citizens to remain in the community, not just younger citizens with disabilities. It will enhance the lives of those temporarily impaired through accidents and illnesses. Transportation that is accessible to people who move in wheelchairs also helps those pushing carriages or who have difficulty walking. Redesigning work tasks, relations, machines, and layouts may not only enable people with disabilities to work productively, but those changes may increase the productivity of other workers, too. For example, when one company "altered an assembly line supervisor's task to aid a man with mental retardation, all 12 workers output rose and errors fell" (Zola, 1989: 420). (I imagine similar results can occur in school.) Flexible work schedules and arrangements, part-time work, and work at home speak not only to the needs of some people with disabilities but to many others as well, such as parents with young children or those who might wish to avoid long commutes and horrendous traffic. It also speaks to the "shrinking" of work in our lives (Zola, 1989: 416). Inclusive, flexible approaches, not special, exceptional ones are most promising.

This shift in policy—away from charity, with less emphasis on the narrowest notions of utility, building on but recognizing the shortcomings of rights—will not come easily. A policy that emphasizes our interconnectedness, our commonality/communality, while also respecting our diversity, entails a fundamentally different way of making our world. No longer can being nondisabled be the unrecognized center. Instead, we enlarge the center, making it more varied to include us all.

People with disabilities are managing, even challenging, our present world. In *managing* the disability that we make, they are creating new possibilities. To their efforts, I turn.

Chapter 8

MANAGING DISABILITY

W e make disability. Typically, we have made disability a defect to be endured by individuals. We have made less worthy those we made disabled. We have portrayed them as dangerous, evil, pitiful, or maladjusted. Interactions between disabled and nondisabled people have often been awkward, the identities of disabled people spoiled, and the experiences of disability too often dissatisfying. We directed disabled people to put themselves in the hands of professionals, who so often worked on a "broken" person instead of serving a fellow citizen. Our policies have intentionally, at times unwittingly, and at other times in spite of good intentions typically oppressed disabled people. With all of this making, disabled people have contended.

Disabled people manage what others have made of them. They live in a world primarily built *by* those without disabilities *for* those without disabilities. From acquiescing to "fighting back," disabled people contend with that world. From individual responses to collective action, disabled people manage the making of disability.

People with disabilities may try to *live with* the making of disability with as few difficulties as possible. Whether they acquiesce to that making or try to lessen the impact of that making upon them, disabled people try to create satisfactory lives without directly countering the oppressive actions of others. However, disabled people may also *challenge* the making of disability. They may reject the stigma of disability and try to create new understandings and opportunities for themselves and other disabled people. They seek to gain control over their lives. When successful, they have remade disability.

People with disabilities manage disability in various ways. When encountering others in public, some disabled citizens may put up with rude remarks and stares, whereas others may rebuke those who act offensively. Disabled people may (gently) reeducate neighbors and colleagues, but others may ignore them. Relatively few work with others who are disabled to change policies, such as the national efforts to implement the Rehabilitation Act of 1973 and the Americans With Disabilities Act of 1990. Most disabled people, like nondisabled people, are not involved in organized efforts to address their concerns. Disabled people may manage disabilities in different ways as they encounter differing others and as their experiences of disability change (e.g., see Schneider and Conrad, 1980).

Disabled people's specific responses to the making of disability may primarily enable them to live with that making, challenge it, or do both. For example, concealing one's disability in order to avoid the negative reactions of others primarily enables disabled people to live with the disability (see Chapter 4). Challenging the insensitive remarks of others momentarily challenges the oppression of disabled people. However, through participating in a community of disabled people, members may not only live more successfully with the disability but also develop understandings that counter the prevailing negative images of them. Becoming politically active through participating in an organization of disabled people directly, overtly challenges the oppression of disabled people, but that political activism may also enable disabled people to develop more satisfying relations among one another, to live more successfully with the disability.

Disabled people are *more likely to live with their disability than to challenge its oppressive making* (see Scotch, 1989). I believe this is so for many reasons. Where disability is not readily evident, living with disability through concealing it becomes possible. People with epilepsy or mental health difficulties can do so. For those who develop a sense of belonging and create a comfortable existence among similarly disabled people, as deaf people may, living with disability again becomes a satisfying strategy. Perhaps more important are the obstacles to challenging disability.

Challenging disability is difficult. When challenging the oppressive actions of individuals, disabled people do not know what the individuals' reactions will be. To the extent that disabled people have been made dependent on others—on parents, spouses, service providers, employers, and such—challenging those others' behaviors means risking the loss of needed support, no matter how belittling it may be. Some disabled people know no others who are similarly disabled. Thus, support for challenging others may not be available (Schneider and Conrad, 1980; Scotch, 1988).

Collective challenging is even more difficult. Disabled people who know no others similarly disabled not only lack support in challenging specific individuals, but they also lack the social ties that can provide a path to collective resistance. Being poorer and less educated than nondisabled individuals, disabled people may find it even more difficult to mount collective, political challenges to their oppression. While disproportionately poor and less educated, disabled people are nevertheless heterogeneous. They differ by race, ethnicity, sex, age, social class, disability experience, and so on. Those differences, which point to differing experiences, responsibilities, and concerns, can work against collective challenges. For example, people with a particular disability and their advocates may believe that working with other disability groups will "dilute" their own claims (Bowe, Jacobi and Wiseman, 1978; Minow, 1990: 37). Disabled people experience barriers to assembling to overcome those barriers, such as the lack of accessible public transportation for mobility impaired citizens (Anspach, 1979). Until recently, severely disabled people were often so confined in institutions that political confrontation was almost unimaginable. To organize politically necessitates stepping into a devalued status, even if one doesn't believe the devaluation fits (Scotch, 1988). Therefore, some disabled people may distance themselves from others who are disabled. That lack of self-identification precludes joining with others to challenge present arrangements (Scotch, 1988).

> Persons with disabilities often are understandably reluctant to focus on that aspect of their identity that is most negatively stigmatized by the rest of society and to mobilize politically around it. Yet this hesitancy can only contribute to their oppression (Hahn, 1985: 310).

Many disabled people already use great ingenuity and effort to manage their everyday lives—to attend to their daily needs, to move about their communities, to work, and so on. Less energy, time, and will are left for collectively challenging societal oppression (Roth, 1983).

The individualism of America and our pervasive individualizing of disability also work against collective challenges. "In a society that celebrates the individual . . . it is all too natural to seek solutions to our problems as individuals rather than as members of an excluded class" (Scotch, 1988: 162). We are expected to handle what troubles us as personal problems rather than encouraged to transform those difficulties into public issues (Mills, 1959). Thus, deaf people typically called on family members, friends, and colleagues to make telephone calls for them. Only recently have they pushed for telephone relay systems as a matter of right (now federally mandated in the Americans with Disabilities Act of 1990).

Correspondingly, an individualistic, professional paradigm has dominated our modern making of disability. Disability has been an individual defect that disabled people are to bear or adjust to as best as possible under the management of professionals—doctors, special education teachers, rehabilitation professionals, and the like. Alternatives to be contemplated, tried, and worked out have not been readily available until recently, or they have been resisted by those professionals who have been in charge. Collective challenges have had to overcome these and other obstacles (Anspach, 1979; Hahn, 1983; Zola, 1983; Scotch, 1988, 1989). However, disabled people have overcome those obstacles to create a disability rights movement, which I explore later in the chapter.

We must be cautious in how we evaluate the responses of disabled people. It may be too easy to regard living with the disability as less worthy than challenging the oppressive making of disability. Evaluations, of course, are important in the creation of disability. Through evaluations we separate people into categories, making them different kinds of people, perhaps rendering them more manageable. We have separated disabled from nondisabled people and then separated disabled people from one another (e.g., through "disability-specific" programs and organizations and through severity classifications). Our evaluations of how disabled people manage disability may only have the similar (though unintended) divisive effect.

While I primarily focus on how disabled people manage disability, family members, advocates, and others also live with and/or challenge disability. They, too, confront disability. As I explored in Chapter 5, parents of disabled children search for understanding, services, and support. Some fail and resign themselves to a hard life. Others succeed. Some succeed but continue their involvement with families with disabled children, altruistically helping others develop satisfactory experiences. Others, dissatisfied with what is available, challenge present arrangements by lobbying school boards, petitioning representatives, organizing and participating in support groups, demonstrating, and the like. Family members deal with disability, too. Others, such as professionals and advocates, may work alongside of (and at times out in front of) disabled people in challenging present arrangements (Scotch, 1984, 1989). However, I primarily focus on the actions of disabled people.

Living with Disability

Disabled people may live with their disability individually and collectively. Through *normalizing*, they attempt to become as much like nondisabled people as possible—in their behaviors, beliefs, and even their being. Through passing and covering (which I explored in Chapter 4), disabled people lessen their spoiled identities by concealing their disabilities or making them less obtrusive. Through self-help groups, voluntary associations, and communities of disabled people, those with disabilities *collectively* live with their disability. They assist one another in managing the constraints of disabilities. They also provide social support in living with the oppression created by others. Within the camaraderie of often similarly disabled people who share a wealth of experiences, that oppression becomes less burdensome. Collectively living with a disability even provides the opportunities for disabled people to challenge their oppression.

Normalizing

Those who live with a disability may embrace the world of nondisabled people. Some who do may attempt to participate within it as much as possible on its terms. They strive to "normalize" their behavior, beliefs, even their being (Anspach, 1979: 769; Phillips, 1985: 50). They accept the assumptions of nondisabled people about what it means to be normal—how one should behave, think, feel, communicate, and so on. While they may believe that they do not measure up, they make a "concerted effort to minimize, rationalize, explain away, and downplay" any differences between themselves and those not disabled (Anspach, 1979: 769). Where possible, they compensate for their impairments by developing alternative means for performing conventionally. Deaf people who normalize may work arduously to develop speechreading and speaking skills. Even though they may not understand aurally what others say, they can understand visually and respond orally. By doing so, they perform more conventionally than deaf people who depend on writing or gestures when communicating with hearing people. Some disabled people become "super crips" (a disparaging term among disabled people), defying our expectations as to what those with that disability can do. They are the ones often depicted in the media as a model for what others with disabilities might aspire to become and as a caution to nondisabled people that people with disabilities must be given a chance *because* not all become the helpless, dependent, pitiful people that nondisabled people assume them to be. Some, like Franklin D. Roosevelt, normalize so "well" that others may not realize that they are disabled or never think of them as disabled (Zola, 1982: Chapter 10; Gallagher, 1985).

Others, less successful, more clearly struggle to act "conventionally." For example, one young woman, with cerebral palsy, has chosen not to use any devices to aid her communication with others, such as a communication board. Instead, she attempts to

> speak normally. In spite of her efforts, those who know Rebecca well still have some difficulty understanding her particular style of speech. Others, however, find her way of speaking extremely difficult to comprehend, straining to listen to each syllable and then piecing together words they do understand with phrases that they do not. Because Rebecca has some control over her speech, she attempts to potentiate whatever ability she has. On the other hand, in her struggle for what appears to be normalization, an independence from nonconventional methods and devices, she restricts the number of those with whom she can interact (Phillips, 1985: 52).

However, we need to be careful not to "blame the victim" (Ryan, 1971). If we attribute Rebecca's communication difficulties to her cerebral palsy and her apparent commitment to nondisabled people's standards of communication, then we overlook others' actions that help produce the communication difficulties. At a minimum we overlook the inability of nondisabled people to attend carefully to her speech. More fundamentally, we overlook the pervasive individualizing of disability as a defect, which may underlie that (unsuccessful?) commitment to the standards of nondisabled people.

Rebecca's approach to communication differs from another young person, David, also with cerebral palsy but with less speech ability than Rebecca. David uses a communication board to communicate with others. While this nonconventional device has limitations, it enables David to communicate with a wider audience:

> although communicating with the board takes time for David and the reader, the reader's patience is not overly taxed . . . (more important, David) is assertive and in control of the communication process. First, he has immediate access to interaction with strangers. It is true that many may react negatively to his disability and his physique. Yet, because of the communication board, he is approachable to the extent that his "speech" is universalized, and can be understood even by strangers. Second, he adapts these aids not only to his own physiological limitations, but also to others' limitations (tolerance and time). Perhaps his is not a radical approach, but he achieves success by accomplishing

social interaction otherwise unavailable to him, as well as easing some of the personal isolation resulting from his physiological limitations (Phillips, 1985: 52–53).

Again we need to be careful not to attribute so easily David's personal isolation to his physiological limitations.

David, perhaps because he has less "choice" than Rebecca, does not normalize his communication to the extent that Rebecca does. Relying on artificial devices to communicate is unconventional. However, we must be careful that we do not quickly conclude that David is being more "authentic" than is Rebecca, more "true" to who he is than is Rebecca to who she is. We make and manage disability in diverse ways.

Ironically, deaf people who do not speak to hearing people even though their speech is intelligible may be normalizing. While using pencil and paper may be a repudiation of the hearing world's emphasis on speaking and hearing, it may also be an acquiescence to that emphasis. Some deaf people do not like their voices (from partially hearing their voices or by being told by others). Their silence "respects" the demands of the hearing world.

When disabled people normalize, they acquiesce to the making of disability. They accept the legitimacy of the world made by nondisabled people (or resign themselves to it) and attempt to fit themselves within it as best as possible.

Others may not accept the legitimacy of the nondisabled world, but they may not challenge it either. Instead, through passing and covering they attempt to minimize their own stigmatization. As I noted in Chapter 4, some disabled people whose disabilities are not readily apparent may present themselves as nondisabled. However, they often encounter various difficulties when they do so. Others whose disabilities are apparent or known about may try to lessen the disabilities' obtrusiveness. Through various strategies, they reduce the attention others give their disabilities. (Return to Chapter 4 for a fuller discussion of these management strategies.) When people with disabilities normalize, pass, and/or cover, they individually attempt to live with the disability.

Collectively Living with the Disability

Normalizing, passing, and covering are primarily individualistic approaches to living with a disability. Individual disabled people embrace the standards of the nondisabled world, conceal the disability, or try to make the disability less obtrusive, even if they may be assisted at times by others. Participating in self-help groups, voluntary associations, and even communities of disabled people can be a collective approach to living with disability. (Of course, these approaches can also become means for challenging the making of disability, which I take up later.)

Disability groups may provide information, support, training, and other help that enable their members to meet better the challenges created by their physical, mental, and emotional characteristics within the constraints of the conventional world. For example, within Little People of America, people of short statue, midgets and dwarfs, may learn more about medical and health issues affecting them, where to buy appropriate clothing or how to tailor clothing to suit their bodies, the availability of devices that enable them to participate in a world built for much larger people, employment and educational opportunities, and similar matters (Weinberg, 1968; Ablon, 1984: Chapters 8 and 9, 1988: Chapter 8). Or, through self-help groups, those with diabetes, epilepsy and other conditions may learn better how to manage them through medication, diet, life style and the like (Maines, 1984).

Perhaps even more important, disability groups also assist their participants to live with their disability, with the oppression made by others. Participants provide the opportunity for similarly (though not by any means identically) oppressed people to develop ties among one another, casually communicate, develop and share a wealth of experiences, engage in pleasurable activities, and so on. Within such groups disabled people may be able to turn their backs on the oppression created by others and develop feelings of belonging among one another (Higgins, 1980; Higgins and Butler, 1982: 210–216; Ablon, 1984, 1988: Chapter 8; Padden and Humphries, 1988). Their disabilities do not disable them among one another. Instead, the disabilities may become an unremarkable feature of one another and their collective activity. Such groups also may provide the opportunity for people with disabilities to identify themselves as a person with a disability, to make the disability a significant feature of themselves (as I noted in Chapter 5).

For example, one member of Little People of America explained that becoming a member:

> did everything. It saved my life. You wouldn't know it, but I was the most depressed college freshman, introverted, shy, miserable. When I found LPA, it was everything. And it only took me one month till I had totally reversed my life. Until I was about 20, I really thought I was the only dwarf in the world. I knew that somewhere there were other dwarfs, but I didn't see them and what

I got out of it, the most important thing, was just knowing there were other people. There were other dwarfs. I think if these kids could just come to this and know that there are other dwarfs, then go back and really do well—whatever it is they're doing (Ablon, 1984: 168).

Disabled people make friends, acquaintances, colleagues, and more intimate partners within disability groups. Social life and personal existence may become richer than what is possible within the nondisabled world. And in becoming so, the nondisabled world becomes perhaps less burdensome because it is no longer the only world within which one must live.

When living with disability, disabled people attempt to minimize the difficulties they experience. Through embracing the nondisabled world, concealing or covering their disabilities, or associating with others made disabled, disabled people may successfully live with disability. However, the oppression made by others goes unchallenged. Thus, when living with disability, disabled people help to maintain the oppression with which they live.

Challenging Disability

Disabled people do not only live with disability. Some *individually and/or collectively* challenge the oppressive making of disability. Challenging another's inappropriate comment, breaking through to a more satisfying relation with a colleague, or talking to a group of nondisabled people about disability are individualistic ways of challenging disability. Individual disabled citizens challenge their stigmatization by particular nondisabled people. The oppressive behavior and beliefs of individual people, even aggregates of individual people, are countered.

Individualistic approaches are important and necessary. However, by themselves they are limited. Individualistic approaches generally leave untouched wider social arrangements, practices, and policies that make people disabled. Segregated schooling, poorly accessible public transportation, unaccommodating employers, inadequate attendant services, and other practices persist in the face of individualistic approaches. Individualistic approaches may also maintain the isolation of people with disabilities from one another. In countering the stigmatization by others, disabled people may develop more satisfying relations, but they do not develop common bonds with others similarly disabled, common bonds that may be helpful in further challenging disability.

Collective strategies enable disabled people to challenge more profoundly the oppressive making of disability. Self-help groups, voluntary associations, and communities of disabled people may initially enable their members to live with the disability. In doing so, participants are likely to develop understandings that counter the dominant disabling belief that they are defective. Out of the interaction within disability groups and the redefinition of themselves to themselves, some disabled people (and allies) may directly challenge others' oppressive disabling of them. They may lobby, protest, or in other ways push for practices and policies that liberate instead of debilitate.

Individual Challenging

Through momentary responses and more extended disavowals, disabled people may challenge the belittling behaviors of others. Instead of letting the offensive remarks or actions pass, disabled people may criticize, educate, or otherwise counter the offender. Others may work to break through their stigmatization. Gradually nondisabled people realize that the disability may be something other than they had taken it to be, that it is not all of the disabled person, that it does not lessen the disabled person's worth.

For example, in schools that educate disabled and nondisabled students, disabled students and the staff may momentarily respond to others' offenses (Higgins, 1990: 134–135). A teacher's aide who is disabled and works in a mainstream program counters barriers to the integration of the disabled youth. "When he sees a student showing negative attitudes toward somebody because of their disability, he is not afraid to speak up":

> If it's on a one-to-one situation and a kid does something, then I have the opportunity. I'll call him over and sit down with him and talk to him a little bit. And nine times out of ten, he won't do that again. I just say, "Hey, look, I'm different from you, but you have two feet and I've got four wheels." And that's about it (Biklen, 1985: 17).

Perhaps less successfully, deaf children mainstreamed in an elementary school may respond equally rudely to hearing students who make fun of their signing (Higgins, 1990: 135). Other disabled people momentarily challenge the disability by "fend(ing) off the 'patronizing' gestures" of others who try to take care of them (Fisher and Galler, 1988: 178).

A handful of people identified as mentally retarded or psychiatrically impaired who were friends and colleagues in a rehabilitation center typically responded to cruel remarks in public by ignoring the remarks. They avoided the offender or paid little attention, " 'walk(ing) to the other side of the street' " or letting the remark " 'go in one ear and out the other' " (Mest, 1988: 122). However, they occasionally chastised the offender. As one of the colleagues/friends remarked:

> I talk back to them and tell them what I think, you know. I say, "This is not right for you to stand there and make fun of somebody. You're just making fun of your own self" (Mest, 1988: 122).

Through momentarily challenging offensive others, disabled people assert themselves. Disabled people may "rightly feel proud of standing up to a put down" (Higgins, 1990: 135). However, by themselves, momentary challenges are not likely to be very effective. They may escalate unpleasant reactions. They don't systematically or extensively counter the offensive attitudes of others. They may not produce positive perceptions. More sustained, individual challenges would be useful.

Through disavowal, disabled people deny being spoiled. As I explored more fully in Chapter 4, they attempt to break through others' stigmatization. Through building upon the civil, superficial acceptance that nondisabled people often give them, disabled people may be able to develop fuller, more satisfying relations in which they become complex individuals, not stereotyped objects.

Through disavowal and momentary responses, disabled people individually challenge disability. They challenge the offensive behaviors and attitudes of specific disabled people. To do so likely requires that disabled people have already developed understandings that counter the dominant oppressive beliefs. Disabled people may develop those beliefs through participating with others who are also disabled. That participation may be a basis for collectively challenging disability.

Collective Countering

Disabled people may also collectively counter their oppression. Through participation in groups, associations, and communities of disabled people and in organized efforts to develop new policies, practices, and opportunities, disabled people collectively counter their oppression. Through collectives they counter their oppression, and the target of their countering are larger social arrangements. Such countering is doubly collective.

Collective countering may be directed toward one another (and implicitly toward the oppression) or more pointedly toward those people, policies, and practices that burden them. Developing an in-group ideology that enables them to cast off the belittling beliefs of their oppressors is first used among one another. The ideology *provides another way of being.* The "alternative" beliefs may be a basis for more overtly challenging the arrangements and attitudes that oppress them, perhaps through political action designed to rewrite governmental regulation. Through directly challenging oppression, disabled people further develop alternative understandings.

The minority-group perspective that has been developing for the past two decades provides an important alternative to the individualistic, defective view that has dominated our understanding of disability. While I believe that we must eventually move beyond a minority-group perspective, it encourages us to legitimate human diversity and to challenge arrangements and attitudes that deny dignity and opportunity to all (see Chapter 1).

For example, visually impaired members of an advocacy organization for/of blind people on the East Coast challenged the dominant view of blind people. They denied the legitimacy of "experts" to set policy. Instead, visually impaired "consumers," like themselves, were better qualified. They rejected the view that blindness produced incapacitation. Instead, blindness was an "inconvenience"; the attitudes and actions of the sighted world were incapacitating. Disabling language such as "client" was replaced with assertive terminology such as "worker" or "employee" (in workshops). They decried the exploitation of workshops and other "blindness institutions" through a mocking song, "Bringing in the Thieves," which began: "Working in the broom shop, it's a full-of-gloom shop." Out of this alternative view, members unsuccessfully attempted to unionize blind employees of a "sheltered" workshop and were involved in other collective challenges. Through the union and other advocacy activities, the members further developed their alternative understandings (Goldin, 1984).

Deaf community

Perhaps more so than any other group of people regarded as disabled, deaf people have developed fundamental ways of living/being that counter the oppression of others. Communities of Deaf people in which signed languages are embraced and are the fundamental means of communication provide an "alternative" to the dominant hearing world (Jacobs, 1980, Gannon, 1981; Lane, 1984; Padden and Humphries, 1988).

Today, more so than ever, Deaf people have self-consciously developed and embraced that alternative way of being, though Deaf people have been creating that alternative way of being for hundreds of years, if not longer.

Deaf people have developed a rich culture and complex communities. Possessing the innate capacity to learn language but experiencing the difficulty/inability to do so auditorily, deaf people have created over generations signed languages (though the "solutions" vary from one society of deaf people to another, say the Italian deaf in contrast to deaf Americans). They also make their way in a world dominated by hearing people and hearing people's assumptions and practices as to what is necessary to live satisfactorily, even to be human. Out of this, Deaf people have created their own communities and culture (Padden and Humphries, 1988). Through marriages, friendships, clubs, networks of acquaintances, organizations, churches, publications, and other means, members give body to their community. Through their signed languages, cultural beliefs, and symbolic representations of their being (e.g., stories), they provide their soul (Higgins, 1980; Padden and Humphries, 1988).

Certainly part of that richness and complexity builds upon and manages the tension of being Deaf in a hearing world that does not recognize the validity of being Deaf. The hearing world continues to demand (if more subtly nowadays) that Deaf people be as much like hearing people as possible (see Chapter 1). That demand was crudely made in the past when signed languages were forbidden in schools that educated deaf students and oral approaches were emphasized. That demand is made more subtly when total communication replaces oralism, but artificial sign systems that manually represent English are stressed to the neglect of signed languages. Deaf people feel the burden of that demand when mainstreaming is emphasized both to the neglect of meaningful interaction and inclusion and to the perceived peril of residential schools, the heart of being Deaf and of Deaf communities for so long (Lane, 1987; Padden and Humphries, 1988).

But that richness and complexity also comes from Deafness being at the *center* of being Deaf (Padden and Humphries, 1988). Recall Professor Sam Suppalla (Chapter 5). As a Deaf child in a Deaf family, being both deaf and Deaf was a "natural," unremarkable feature of his life. If Deafness is at the center, then the practices of the hearing world become unconventional, even strange. If Deafness is at the center, then signed languages are not unusual, "adaptive," or "artful" means of communication, but legitimate, effective, and richly expressive linguistic ways of communicating to others (Padden and Humphries, 1988: Chapter 4 and throughout). If Deafness is at the center, then "a-little hard-of-hearing" means that an individual can hear only a little, is only a little like hard of hearing people, the opposite of what it means for hearing people (Padden and Humphries, 1988: 39). If Deafness is at the center, then Deaf communities, signed languages, and Deaf culture are not "alternatives" to the larger hearing world. They are valid ways of living and being in their own right.

Members of the Deaf community create tales, jokes, plays, poems, and other cultural stories that affirm basic beliefs about themselves, give expression to the tension of living among hearing people who deny the validity of being Deaf, tell one another how they should live, and further enrich their lives (Padden and Humphries, 1988: 33). For example, one story, which developed out of a family anecdote and exists in various versions, emphasizes that sign language is necessary for the well being of Deaf people; gestures and speech will not enable them to survive (Padden and Humphries, 1988: 32–33):

> Eighteen-year-old Joshua Davis was squirrel hunting one day on his parents' southern plantation . . . during the Civil War. Suddenly he found himself surrounded by Union Soldiers. Davis was deaf but he could tell that they were shouting at him . . . Davis pointed to his ears and gestured that he was deaf but the soldiers did not believe him. They suspected that he was a spy and was trying to fool them by pretending to be deaf. They shoved and pushed the youth to a nearby house where a couple standing in front of it informed them that the youth was their son and that he was, indeed, deaf. The captors did not believe them either and they were looking for a rope to hang young Davis as a spy when a mounted officer rode up. The officer was informed that they had caught a spy who was "playing deaf." The officer (as it was later learned had a deaf brother) rode over to the youth and fingerspelled to him: "Are you deaf?" The youth responded in signs, "Yes." "Where were you educated?" the officer asked next to which the young man told him at the school for the deaf . . . With that information the officer ordered the youth's release and the family's house spared (Gannon, 1981: 9).

Deaf people's typical inability to understand sounds well and to learn spoken languages auditorily is a fundamental feature of their lives. However, they know that sounds are a crucial component of control. Hearing people demand that they see sounds through lipreading, produce sounds through speech training, and if they cannot make conventional sounds, then to be quiet. Deaf people may be concerned about bodily sounds they make and whether it is permissible to make such sounds. But, through a classic joke within the Deaf community, Deaf citizens turn the table on hearing people and their (now seen from a center of deafness) obsession with sounds:

> A Deaf couple check into a motel. They retire early. In the middle of the night, the wife wakes her husband complaining of a headache and asks him to go to the car and get some aspirin from the glove compartment. Groggy with sleep, he struggles to get up, puts on his robe, and goes out of the room to his car. He finds the aspirin, and with the bottle iń hand he turns toward the motel. But he cannot remember which room is his. After thinking a moment, he returns to the car, places his hand on the horn, holds it down, and waits. Very quickly the motel rooms light up, all but one. It's his wife's room, of course. He locks up his car and heads toward the room without a light (Padden and Humphries, 1988: 103).

As two Deaf scholars note about this joke:

> The joke is not on the Deaf man who has inconveniently forgotten which room is his, but on hearing people, who conveniently help him to find his room. The joke's hero knows he can count on hearing people to be extraordinarily attentive to sound — to his gain and their detriment. Their predictable behavior, to respond to sound even in the middle of the night, is what makes the joke wickedly funny. The audacity of the hero, having the nerve to prey upon the automatic instincts of hearing people, is for a moment, thrilling (Padden and Humphries, 1988: 103–104).

Deaf poets express both the tension of deaf people's being outsiders in a hearing world and the integrity of sign language in and of itself. "You Have to be Deaf to Understand," translated into seven languages, expresses the difficulties of living in a hearing world in contrast to the "serenity" of signing (Gannon, 1981: 380). It is a poem written in English by a deaf poet. But more recently, Deaf poets are creating signed poems, some of which can be put into English. These poems are built upon a "detailed awareness of how signs are assembled and the relationship of structure to meaning" (Padden and Humphries, 1988: 84). Deaf poetry is increasingly putting Deafness at the center (Padden and Humphries, 1988: Chapter 5).

In increasingly, self-consciously putting Deafness at the center of their rich culture and satisfying communities, some Deaf people experience difficulty identifying with people who have other disabilities (Padden and Humphries, 1988: 43–44). Disabled people are those with visual or physical impairments. Deaf people are a distinct language and cultural group, which has been oppressed. Disabled people do not have that rich heritage, claim Deaf people. However, recognizing that the "public understands" the modern concerns and language of "access" and "civil rights" and "knowing well the special benefits, economic and otherwise, of calling themselves disabled, Deaf people have a history, albeit an uneasy one, of alignment with other disabled groups" (Padden and Humphries, 1988: 44). Thus, some Deaf people may take advantage of a "handicapped" discount when using public transportation but feel uneasy with the implied identification that they are disabled (Padden and Humphries, 1988: 43–44).

In (at times so fundamentally) transcending hearing people's individualistic, defective conceptualizations of deafness, some Deaf people may have ironically and unintentionally disabled others with disabilities. Have they set themselves apart from, even "above," disabled people without similarly rich cultures and satisfying communities? Has Deaf people's success in countering the oppressive making of disability produced another instance of a persistent problem people with disabilities encounter in collectively challenging disability: How can people made disabled in differing ways create and unite for their common good?

Disability Rights Movement

Since the 1960s people with disabilities (and allies such as parents) have more visibly, assertively collectively challenged their oppression. Whether through confrontation or cooperation to acquire rights and opportunities long believed denied or through providing services (or developing new means of providing services) to disabled people (which are often run by disabled people), those with disabilities are countering their oppression.

For example, associations of disabled people, some of which, such as the National Association of the Deaf, have existed more than 100 years, have become more overtly political in their activities: lobbying government, challenging discrimination through court action, demonstrating, organizing at the local level, and the like. Court suits challenging the custodial care (or is it neglect) of mentally retarded citizens or the inadequate education of youth with disabilities indicate that some parents no longer acquiesce to professionals. The rise of the independent living movement in the past several decades shows that people with disabilities, including severe disabilities, can take control of their lives. The massive, national demonstrations organized by the American Coalition of Citizens with Disabilities, ACCD, in spring 1977 to demand the issuance of regulations implementing Section 504 of the Rehabilitation Act of 1973 in which, among other tactics, protesters occupied regional offices of the then Department of Health, Education, and Welfare and the national office in Washington, D.C. pointed to the commitment and skills of the protesters (Bowe, 1986: Chapter 13). The protest of deaf students and others at Gallaudet University in March 1988, which led to the naming of the first hearing impaired president of the university, told the nondisabled world that disabled people would not be denied their opportunities for full participation (Gannon, 1989). In Spring 1990, citizens with disabilities demonstrated again in Washington, D.C., this time in support of the Americans with Disabilities Act, which became law that summer (Johnson, 1990). The development of an international organization of disabled people, Disabled People's International, attests to the ability of citizens with disabilities to transcend the obstacles of nationality and language in pushing for greater opportunities and fuller civil rights (Driedger, 1989). The less widely publicized but more widespread work of local associations and groups of disabled citizens provides commitment upon which the more publicized, often national, efforts build. Through these and other means, people with disabilities have challenged their oppression.

In the past twenty years, people with disabilities have created a disability rights movement. This "loosely coupled network of organizations whose goals and objectives are focused on empowerment and collective rights—human, civil, and legal—for disabled people" is an important component of the wider, varied movement of disabled people to challenge how disability is made (Scotch, 1989: 383). At times, the rights movement has been less a loosely coupled network of organizations than a striking instance of collective opposition, such as the protest at Gallaudet University.

Developing a rights movement

Disadvantaged status does not produce a rights movement; people do (Scotch, 1989). Disabled people developed their rights movement within a larger *social landscape*. Through *mobilizing* themselves they turned personal troubles into public issues (Mills, 1959: 8–11). They managed the difficulties of collectively opposing oppression that I mentioned earlier: heterogeneity, reluctance to emphasize a status that others devalue, dispersion, society's individualism, and so on.

Disabled Americans developed a rights movement out of a changing social landscape with many important features. With the end of World War II, America turned its attention toward some of the challenges at home, such as unequal opportunities for black citizens and poverty. World War II and subsequent wars such as the one in Southeast Asia (i.e., Vietnam War) disabled many men who formerly had taken for granted their participation in society. So did polio and automobile accidents. With improved medical and rehabilitative technology, many more disabled people survived life-threatening conditions and were more active than in the past. The middle class members of the "baby-boom generation" were reared with high aspirations and a self-confident view of personal achievement" (Scotch, 1989: 386). Some of these "boomers" who became disabled expected to return to the mainstream. As one activist member of this generation has written:

> Many activists, then, are not people who were kept out of the mainstream as children; they had been in the mainstream and never questioned their right to be there. So, when others questioned it, they were ready with armor and anger to fight to preserve their sense of themselves that the adult world was trying to shatter (Asch, 1984: 551).

The social conflict of the 1960s and beyond provided examples of how disabled people might respond to and understand their own oppression. The civil rights movement, antiwar and student movements, and a revitalized feminist movement dramatically provided different possibilities for how disabled people might respond to their troubles. Some disabled people gained experience and developed more liberating understandings through participating in those other social movements. Less confrontational, the "consumers movement," which emphasized a distrust of the service or product provider and the need for consumers to make informed choices, supported a basic concern of other movements that people control their lives. That concern to take charge of one's life also found expression in the rise of self-help groups and the attempts to limit or develop alternatives to the medical monopoly of health care. Political activism, including public protest, became more widespread and legitimate. That activism broadened the public debate by focusing "not only along lines of established economic conflicts but also around issues of identity and social roles" (Scotch, 1989: 386; see also DeJong, 1983; Zola, 1983; Scotch, 1988).

Within that changing social landscape, some disabled people mobilized themselves. Out of the tens of millions of disabled Americans, perhaps less than 100,000 belong to organizations that work for the rights of disabled people; perhaps only a few thousand "actively participate in movement activities on an ongoing basis" (Scotch, 1989: 382). However, not all those who are similarly disadvantaged need to mobilize themselves in order to succeed.

Disabled people mobilized themselves by transforming their personal troubles into public issues. They developed/used a rights perspective, which countered the prevailing individualistic, defective view. Through newsletters, magazines, and other media they ran (such as *The Disability Rag* and "single-disability-specific" material) and through the wider mass media, they educated other disabled (and nondisabled) people who had yet to become active. Through building organizations of disabled citizens and coalitions of organizations—recruiting and maintaining members, securing funds, planning activities, developing and sustaining consensus, managing conflict among the members, developing contacts with officials, and much more—the disability movement became more cohesive. Without cohesion, disability activists would have been ineffectual, isolated protesters to whom policy makers would have been unlikely to listen (Bowe, Jacobi and Wiseman, 1978). Perhaps ironically, the policies and actions of government assisted disabled people in mobilizing themselves to challenge government.

Government policies and actions provided opportunities and resources for disabled people to mobilize themselves to challenge government and the private sector. Segregating disabled people in educational and other facilities brought together people who were otherwise dispersed. The President's Committee on the Employment of the Handicapped, established after World War II to promote employment opportunities of disabled veterans, did too, a point to which I return. The Rehabilitation Act of 1973, whose Title V "prohibited discrimination on the basis of handicap by recipients of federal grants and contracts and in federally-operated programs" and which used civil rights language, was passed with little involvement from the disability rights movement (Scotch, 1989: 390; 1984). However, it and other legislation in the 1970s such as the Education for All Handicapped Children Act of 1975 (now officially named the Individuals with Disabilities Education Act) legitimated a minority group/rights perspective of disability. Disability activists used that perspective to develop further a collective conscience among disabled citizens. That perspective enabled disabled activists to enter the larger network of civil rights activists. Pursuant to this legislation, the federal government contracted with organizations of disabled citizens to "provide technical assistance and organize public education campaigns" (Scotch, 1989: 391). Conferences, independent living centers, demonstration projects, and other activities that brought disabled people together were sponsored by the government. The "federal government provided a massive infusion of resources, including legitimacy, for the movement" (Scotch, 1989: 392).

The government even provided the focus for the first, major, nationwide protest of the nascent disability movement: the nationwide demonstrations demanding the issuance of regulations implementing Section 504 of the Rehabilitation Act of 1973. A very brief discussion of the development of that nationwide protest illustrates how disabled citizens have organized themselves to challenge collectively their oppression.

The President's Committee on the Employment of the Handicapped sponsored annual meetings that brought together disabled citizens from throughout the country. While dominated by service providers and an incremental approach to change, it enabled disabled people who were less complacent to communicate with one another. Some remained in contact between the annual meetings. Out of those meetings disabled activists began to develop a network throughout the country and organized demonstrations against President Nixon's vetoes in 1972 and 1973 of The Rehabilitation Act. Ties were strengthened. In 1974 at the annual PCEH meeting, disabled participants held alternative sessions. Out of this meeting of approximately 150 people, activists with disabilities developed the American Coalition of Citizens with Disabilities. The ACCD tied local and single-disability organizations into a coalition that could more cohesively address disability concerns. With a grant from the Rehabilitation Services Administration, staff were hired in 1976. By using the perception that it represented many disabled people, the ACCD placed four people with disabilities on the Carter-Mondale transition team in 1976. It also helped to make President Carter's inauguration accessible to people with disabilities. Through news conferences such as one protesting the inaccessibility of the subway being developed in Washington, D.C., the ACCD was beginning to be perceived as what it was trying to becoming, a powerful coalition of disability organizations.

The ACCD and its first director focused on Section 504 of The Rehabilitation Act of 1973. That civil rights section prohibited discrimination on the basis of handicap by any program or activity receiving federal financial assistance. Three years after the passage of The Rehabilitation Act, regulations had not been implemented. Through a letter to the

secretary of HEW and then continuing contacts with the General Counsel-
designate of HEW and members of his staff, the ACCD was able to voice
the concerns of disabled citizens to high-level officials working on the
regulations. Becoming dissatisfied with the delay in issuing regulations,
the ACCD organized massive, nationwide demonstrations in April 1977.
For example, protesters sat in the regional office of HEW in San Francisco
for a record 25 days and nights. On May 4 the regulations were issued.
The ACCD's rights activities and demonstrations, their mobilization of
diverse organizations and people, made visible the developing disability
rights movement and provided further support to its development (Bowe,
Jacobi and Wiseman, 1978; Bowe, 1986: Chapter 13; Scotch, 1984, 1989).

However, the disability rights movement "faces an uncertain future" of
(possible) successes and certain struggles (Scotch, 1989: 380). With the
national government's support of rights issues becoming mixed and with
economic concerns growing, some disability organizations have closed
or reduced their activities (Scotch, 1984: 151). Primarily due to lack of
funds, the ACCD disbanded in 1986 (Bowe, 1986). Opposition to the
implementation of rights for disabled citizens, which critics charge is
costly, continues. Relations between movement leaders and a more conservative executive branch have become more "distant" (Scotch, 1989:
394).

Yet, the disability rights movement has not disappeared. Some members have "moved inside," becoming part of the government and private
sector that they had challenged. Being inside, they hope to be able to
influence policy more directly and provide services more effectively.
Most, remaining on the "outside," continue to push for the rights of
disabled citizens as witnessed by activists' demonstration in Washington,
D.C. in March 1990 to urge passage of the Americans with Disabilities
Act, which was signed by the President in July.

Disability activists with the support of the government have established more than 300 independent living centers since the 1970s. These
community centers may provide various services: housing, attendant
care, interpreting, transportation, equipment repair, transitional services,
counseling, advocacy, and so on. Typically run by disabled people, the
independent living centers demonstrate that disabled citizens can control their lives in the community. The centers, like the disability movement,
challenge the individualistic view of disability as a personal defect. *The
Disability Rag*, which began as a newsletter at an independent living
center in Louisville, Kentucky, has become a national voice in challeng-

ing that burdensome view (but a national voice with financial concerns). The centers have been a reflection of, a resource for, and a success of the disability rights movement. Through empowering disabled citizens and enabling them to more fully participate in their communities, independent living centers will continue to be an important feature of the disability rights movement (Kleinfield, 1979; Crewe and Zola, 1983; Scotch, 1989).

Disability rights groups have broadened their ties in an effort to promote their concerns. They have joined with civil rights groups and "ad hoc coalitions concerned with social policy" to fight "budget cuts and conservative civil rights policies" of recent years (Scotch, 1989: 395). They helped to secure passage of civil rights legislation in 1988 that restored coverage of federal antidiscrimination statutes that had been narrowed through a 1984 Supreme Court decision. When cases concerning the life-saving medical treatment of disabled newborns became visible in the early 1980s, segments of the disability rights movement warily joined forces with right-to-life advocates. The two very different movements "jointly issued statements, lobbied government officials, and filed court briefs in support of policies of government intervention on behalf of disabled newborns" (Scotch, 1989: 396). This alliance has not lead to the disability rights movement's sustained collaboration with conservative political movements. However, disability groups have formed coalitions with senior citizens concerning the provision of human services. While senior citizens may resist identification with disabled people, the two groups often experience common concerns. Conversely, while "people with HIV infection and related diseases are covered by laws protecting disabled people from discrimination," the disability rights movement is wary of allying with a group that many Americans morally reject (Scotch, 1989: 397).

However, I wonder if the future, "long-term" success of the disability rights movement will depend on forming coalitions with other groups that transcend disability. Through such coalitions, citizens with disabilities and others who have been disadvantaged become partners rather than competitors for seemingly scarce opportunities (Scotch, 1989: 390). It will not be easy. By working with other groups on common concerns, disability activists empower themselves. By increasing their numbers, they are harder to dismiss. More important, by working with other groups, disability activists demonstrate that their concerns are many people's concerns. Disability becomes an integral issue for us all, not a separate, "private" problem for some. Such coalitions could promote inclusive policies, discussed in the previous chapter.

By forming coalitions that transcend disability, disability activists and their partners may educate us about the making of disability. They may teach us what I consider to be a fundamental lesson. Though we presently believe otherwise, when we make disability, we make all of us.

Conclusion

People with disabilities live in a world largely made by others without disabilities. Those without disabilities have primarily made disability an individual, burdensome defect. However, how those with disabilities manage others' making becomes part of the world within which they—and those without disabilities—live. Responsibility is mutual even if resources and capacities differ.

Disabled citizens may manage disability in various ways. Some try to live with their disabilities with as few difficulties as possible. While perhaps individually satisfying, this approach leaves in place the disabling practices and policies that burden them. Instead, disabled citizens are increasingly confronting their oppression. Whether individually or collectively, they are challenging how we make disability. They are "standing up" to the belittling actions of others, developing "alternative" ways of being, and working to revise the disabling practices and policies of their society. When citizens with disabilities (and others) succeed, they have remade disability. With a discussion of basic considerations, not specific strategies, I turn to the challenge of *remaking disability* in concluding this book.

Conclusion

REMAKING DISABILITY

We make disability—and we can remake it. We can remake disability better than we have presently made it if we understand that:

Disability is not an inherent, essential feature of people. We differentiate ourselves according to our ability to sense, symbolize and exert force. Through interpersonal, organizational, and societal practices, we transform that variation into disability (and nondisability). With good intentions and sometimes with no intentions at all, we create disability. While we cannot make disability successfully in any imaginable way, we can make disability in more ways than we presently do or than we presently imagine. Some of those ways yet tried will be more successful than our present accomplishments.

Through framing disability, we tell ourselves what disability is and who is to manage it. By primarily individualizing it, by acting toward disability as an internal defect of flawed people, whether a moral, medical or economic flaw, we make people with disabilities separate, less worthy "kinds" of people. But through framing disabled people as a minority group, we may challenge the practices that oppress us. Yet we should not be satisfied with our present minority-group framework. It does not push us enough to realize how completely we make disability; it does not encourage us enough to recognize how nondisability remains the unstated center of our world.

Through injuring, warring, working, poverty, and self-disabling practices among other means, we literally manufacture the characteristics that we turn into disabilities. Even as we have produced great progress through our industrializing society, we have continued to manufacture great quantities of disability. Yet, our modernization has also provided us the way to do otherwise, to reduce the manufacturing of disability. Do we have the will?

As we manufacture disability, we depict it. Through how we name disability, portray disabled people in the media, and other displays, we present disability as an individual defect that separates people with dis-

250

abilities from those not disabled. Disabled people are the negation of "normal" people (e.g., abnormal). They are "afflicted," monstrous, demonic, objects of charity, "vegetables," or maladjusted. But as we begin to remake disability, as people with disabilities (and supporters) participate more forcefully in displaying disability, we are slowly presenting disabled people as welcomed members in the diversity of humanity.

Through interaction, disabled and nondisabled people create one another's identities, and based on those identities manage their interactions. Nondisabled people have typically spoiled the identities of disabled people, and together disabled and nondisabled people have often created awkward, unsatisfying interactions. However, disabled and nondisabled people can break through the stigmatization to create accepting relations. While the interplay between interactions and identities is interpersonal, disabled and nondisabled people produce that interplay out of the larger social worlds they create and encounter. For example, in creating the large schools, housing developments, businesses, and other organizations of our modern world, we make it difficult for all of us to develop ties that bind.

Through our interactions with one another and ourselves, we experience disability. Disabilities do not determine our experiences. We create them as we encounter the opportunities and obstacles of our larger world. People with disabilities make much more complex, varied, and changing experiences of disability than imagined by nondisabled people. Some may make it the cherished, "natural," (almost) taken-for-granted center of their lives, which bewilders most people without disabilities. However we experience disability, each of our experiences is a partial experience, not the one, "true" experience.

Through working on people with (assumed) flawed minds and/or bodies in order to "fix" them, we service disabled people. By serving disabled people in separate programs and facilities dominated by professionals in which disability is individualized, we make disabled people passive strangers, people unlike those without disabilities and with little control of their lives. However, to the extent that we enable people with disabilities to become informed, confident, powerful consumers who determine their goals and courses of action, then our society serves well its citizens.

As we industrialized, creating great progress and profound changes (through capitalism), we created a world in which people with disabilities were the odd ones out. Often with good intentions, we have kept them in that marginal position. Through charitable policies we turned disabled people into poor souls, and through an emphasis on utility we cheapened them even more (when it was uneconomical to do otherwise). Even as we "haltingly" move toward a rights rationale, we have continued to pursue policies that individualize disability through segregated, exceptional responses that make (many) people with disabilities dependent. Policies that stress and support the interconnectedness of our lives and encompass us all, disabled or not, will serve us best.

People with disabilities live in a world largely made by others. However, how they manage the making of disability becomes part of the world within which they and those without disabilities live. While many people with disabilities try to live with disability with as few difficulties as possible, others challenge the making of disability. They question a world centered on one narrow notion of humanity, a notion that constrains us all.

We can challenge our present making of disability and remake it more successfully if we understand that:

Disability does not determine what we do. Our bodies do provide us capacities to sense, symbolize and exert force. But our bodies do not dictate how we live and act together (Stewart, forthcoming). To claim that disability requires us to manage ourselves in one way or another may comfort us as it enables us to turn away from the awesome responsibility of making our lives. But if we do so, we dangerously deceive ourselves even as we imprison ourselves by our unexamined, unrecognized handiwork (Stewart and Reynolds, 1985).

We cannot make disability, we cannot make ourselves, anything we might wish. Breta and Chris, of whom I have spoken several times, will never be able to read these words. But whatever we make disability, whatever Breta and Chris become, will be our and their doing. If we lose the ability to "wish," to see our lives as *our* responsibility and to wonder what we could do, then we will have truly disabled us all.

We can remake disability more successfully if we understand that:

Disability is an integral feature of our lives, of our world. To think that disability is somehow "over there," that "thank goodness" it touches only "those" people's lives, serves us poorly. Many of us are disabled or know well someone who is disabled. Almost all of us will personally experience disability (when we age). *We* are "the disabled" (Zola, 1983; 1989). We are increasingly recognizing the pervasiveness and significance of disability (though we have a long way to go on both accounts).

We are increasingly using disability as a means for creating our worlds—witness the explosion of disability laws in the past two decades. We are becoming a *"disabled society."* To most that is frightening. We would be wise to *embrace* it. But how we embrace it is the challenge.

Many of us think that to assist disabled people takes away from nondisabled people. That "zero-sum" mentality is pervasive. It appears in the charges that "accommodating" people with disabilities is too expensive. Our "zero-sum" thinking shows so little understanding, so little imagination. If we realize that in reducing the obstacles for those with disabilities, we are ultimately reducing the barriers that we all (will) face (though not at the same time and in the same way), then we will be more successful in reducing those barriers. If we realize that by enlargening our world to include those with disabilities, we can make it easier for all of us to live, then we may challenge ourselves to do so. However, if the interests of those presently with and without disabilities are pitted against one another, then we are the ones who have put them at odds. It need not be.

We can remake disability more successfully if we realize that:

To remake disability, we must remake our world, which burdens us all. Focusing solely on those with disabilities will not succeed. Instead, we must examine our narrow, rigid notions of normality upon which we have made our world. We take our arrangements as necessary, even as natural, rather than recognizing that we made them in ways that suit (at best) a fraction of our citizens.

For example, many of us find it difficult to move from one destination to another, not just citizens who move in wheelchairs. We fume behind the wheel as we breathe in the fumes of our congested highways. We wait away our lives at bus stops, airline terminals, and in snarled traffic. We try to find a place to sit on the subway at rush hour. Yet, we champion our "right" to drive individually. Few people are in the position (of power and privilege) to escape all of the above and more. An accessible transportation system would be one that is friendly to us all.

Consider schools. We have typically educated well only a small fraction of our population. Until recently, most children were not welcomed at school, or once they came they eventually dropped out—often with our blessing and relief (Sarason and Doris, 1979; Coles, 1987). How many people do you know who enjoyed school, were enthralled by it, could not be kept away from it? We cannot merely aim to bring children with disabilities into the educational mainstream. We must develop an educational stream through which all children can navigate successfully.

Or consider our cherished notion that we govern ourselves by the rule of law, not by the "might of men." We apply the laws to all in order to ensure everyone's rights. For women, people of color, those without property (literally and figuratively), gays and lesbians, immigrants ("illegal" and otherwise), people with disabilities, those of various nationalities (e.g., Japanese Americans), and many others, rights have not always, not fully, been part of their realities. The independent, white, propertied male was the person for whom rights were developed and upon whom they were most fully bestowed through law. That was the unstated, even unacknowledged norm. Even as we extended rights to others, we still retained that unexamined starting point (Minow, 1990).

For example, as we have grappled with issues about health benefits, unemployment benefits, job discrimination and other work-related matters experienced by women who worked outside of the home for pay, we have typically taken the male worker as the standard in making our decisions or challenging the decisions that have been made. If we made "accommodations" to women and their potential for becoming pregnant (e.g., perhaps by a state providing a "limited right to resume a prior job following an unpaid pregnancy disability leave"), then our generosity implicitly recognized the unstated norm (Minow, 1990: 58). (Notice how pregnancy, a natural potential of women, becomes marginalized as disability, itself marginalized from the variation of humanity.) However, no narrow set of experiences can be the blueprint for us all.

We will need to remake all realms of our world in order to "accommodate" us all, not just those of us with disabilities (Zola, 1989). Flexible, diverse work arrangements (and complementary support systems) are needed to meet the challenges of our varied population. We even need to rethink our work ideology. Our housing policy fails not only those with disabilities, but also millions of our citizens who do not live in decent, affordable housing. Many people with disabilities are burdened by the cost, uncertainty, or unavailability of medical care, but few citizens are satisfied with their coverage and cost. Our large schools, businesses, housing developments, and other organizations that we have developed as we modernized make it difficult for all of us to develop supportive, caring relations (Harris, 1981). The stratification of our society separates us into clashing classes and categories of people. To remake disability, we will need to refashion our world to include us all.

To remake disability successfully is to remake ourselves, our worlds. It cannot be easy. It cannot be done at once. But if we do not realize that such is our challenge, then we cannot succeed.

I do not know what disability will become if we take up that challenge. Will we transcend the idea of disability so that it no longer is a major means for ordering our world? Will we turn disability into a valued feature of the diversity of humanity? Will we make it many different things? How will our makings and remakings vary? I know they will never cease.

Whatever disability becomes, we will have made it. Our humanity does not determine what we will do, what we will make disabled and nondisabled people, what we will make ourselves. It does not guarantee that we will live and act together successfully. But our humanity provides us the capacity to make our selves, to try to live and act together well. In taking up the challenge, we can embrace our humanity.

REFERENCES

Ablon, Joan. 1984. *Little People in America: The Social Dimensions of Dwarfism.* New York: Praeger.

Ablon, Joan. 1988. *Living with Difference: Families with Dwarf Children.* New York: Praeger.

Ainlay, Stephen C. 1988. "Aging and New Vision Loss: Disruptions of the Here and Now." *Journal of Social Issues* 44 (1):79–94.

Ainlay, Stephen C., Gaylene Becker, and Lerita M. Coleman (eds.). 1986. *The Dilemma of Difference: A Multidisciplinary View of Stigma.* New York: Plenum.

Albrecht, Gary L. 1976. "Social Policy and the Management of Human Resources." Pp. 257–85 in *The Sociology of Physical Disability and Rehabilitation,* edited by G. Albrecht. Pittsburgh, PA: University of Pittsburgh Press.

Albrecht, Gary L. 1981. "Cross-National Rehabilitation Policies: A Critical Assessment." Pp. 269–77 in *Cross National Rehabilitation Policies: A Sociological Perspective,* edited by G. Albrecht. Beverly Hills, CA: Sage.

Albrecht, Gary L. forthcoming. *The Disability Business.* Newbury Park, CA: Sage.

Albrecht, Gary L. and Judith A. Levy. 1981. "Constructing Disabilities as Social Problems." Pp. 11–32 in *Cross National Rehabilitation Policies: A Sociological Perspective,* edited by G. Albrecht. Beverly Hills, CA: Sage.

Albrecht, Gary L. and Judith A. Levy. 1984. "A Sociological Perspective of Physical Disability." Pp. 45–106 in *Advances in Medical Social Sciences,* vol. 2, edited by J. Ruffini. New York: Gordon and Breach.

Algozzine, Kate M., Catherine V. Morsink, and Bob Algozzine. 1986. "Classroom Ecology in Categorical Special Education Classrooms: And so, They Counted the Teeth in the Horse!" *The Journal of Special Education* 20 (Summer):209–17.

Altman, Barbara M. 1981. "Studies of Attitudes Toward the Handicapped: The Need for a New Direction." *Social Problems* 28 (February):321–37.

American Psychiatric Association. 1980. *Diagnostic and Statistical Manual of Mental Disorders.* 3rd ed. Washington, D.C.: APA.

Anspach, Renee R. 1979. "From Stigma to Identity Politics: Political Activism Among the Physically Disabled and Former Mental Patients." *Social Science and Medicine* 13A (November):765–73.

Asch, Adrienne. 1984. "Personal Reflections." *American Psychologist* 39 (May):551–52.

Asch, Adrienne and Michelle Fine. 1988. "Introduction: Beyond Pedestals." Pp. 1–37 in *Women with Disabilities: Essays in Psychology, Culture, and Politics,* edited by M. Fine and A. Asch. Philadelphia: Temple University Press.

Asch, Adrienne and Michelle Fine. 1988. "Shared Dreams: A Left Perspective on

Disability Rights and Reproductive Rights." Pp. 297–305 in *Women with Disabilities: Essays in Psychology, Culture, and Politics*, edited by M. Fine and A. Asch. Philadelphia: Temple University Press.

Baker, Charlotte and Robbin Battison. 1980. "Editors' Note." P. xi in *Sign Language and The Deaf Community: Essays in Honor of William C. Stokoe*, edited by C. Baker and R. Battison. Silver Spring, MD: National Association of the Deaf.

Baker, Susan P., Brian O'Neill, and Ronald S. Karpf. 1984. *The Injury Fact Book*. Lexington, MA: D.C. Heath.

Barnartt, Sharon N. and Katherine Seelman. 1988. "A Comparison of Federal Laws Toward Disabled and Racial/Ethnic Groups in the USA." *Disability, Handicap and Society* 3 (1):37–48.

Barol, Bill. 1987. "I Stayed Up with Jerry." *Newsweek* (September 21):66–68.

Barton, Len (ed.). 1988. *The Politics of Special Educational Needs*. London: Falmer.

Barton, Len. 1988. "Research and Practice: The Need for Alternative Perspectives." Pp. 79–95 in *The Politics of Special Educational Needs*, edited by L. Barton. London: Falmer.

Barton, Len and Sally Tomlinson. 1984. "The Politics of Integration in England." Pp. 65–80 in *Special Education and Social Interest*, edited by L. Barton and S. Tomlinson. London: Croom Helm.

Becker, Gaylene. 1980. *Growing Old in Silence: Deaf People in Old Age*. Berkeley: University of California Press.

Bell, Alexander Graham. 1883. "Upon the Formation of a Deaf Variety of the Human Race." Presented to the National Academy of Sciences.

Berk, Marc L. 1985. "Medical Manpower and the Labeling of Blindness. *Deviant Behavior* 6 (3):253–65.

Berkowitz, Edward D. 1987. *Disabled Policy: America's Programs for the Handicapped*. Cambridge: Cambridge University Press.

Best, Joel. 1989. "Dark Figures and Child Victims: Statistical Claims about Missing Children." Pp. 21–37 in *Images of Issues: Typifying Contemporary Social Problems*, edited by J. Best. New York: Aldine De Gruyter.

Biklen, Douglas. 1985. "Getting Started." Pp. 1–29 in *Achieving the Complete School: Strategies for Effective Mainstreaming*, D. Biklen with R. Bogdan, D. Ferguson, S. Searl, Jr., and S. Taylor. New York: Teachers College Press.

Biklen, Douglas. 1986. "Framed: Journalism's Treatment of Disability." *Social Policy* 16 (Winter):45–51.

Biklen, Douglas. 1987. "The Culture of Policy: Disability Images and Their Analogues in Public Policy." *Policy Studies Journal* 15 (March):515–35.

Biklen, Douglas. 1988. "The Myth of Clinical Judgment." *Journal of Social Issues* 44 (1):127–40.

Biklen, Douglas P. 1989. "Redefining Schools." Pp. 1–24 in *Schooling and Disability*, edited by D. Biklen, D. Ferguson, and A. Ford. Chicago: National Society for the Study of Education.

Biklen, Douglas. Forthcoming. *Schooling Without Labels*. Philadelphia: Temple University Press.

Biklen, Douglas with Robert Bogdan, Dianne L. Ferguson, Stanford J. Searl, Jr., and

Steven J. Taylor. 1985. *Achieving the Complete School: Strategies for Effective Mainstreaming.* New York: Teachers College Press.

Biklen, Douglas P. and Philip M. Ferguson. 1984. "In the Matter of Baby Jane Doe: Does Reagan Really Agree with Us?" *Social Policy* 15 (Summer):5–8.

Bines, Hazel. 1988. "Equality, Community and Individualism: The Development and Implementation of the 'Whole School Approach' to Special Educational Needs." Pp. 145–60 in *The Politics of Special Educational Needs,* edited by L. Barton. London: Falmer.

Black, Donald. 1989. *Sociological Justice.* New York: Oxford University Press.

Blatt, Burton and Fred Kaplan. 1974. *Christmas in Purgatory: A Photographic Essay on Mental Retardation.* Syracuse, NY: Human Policy Press.

Blythman, Marion. 1988. "From the Other Side of the Wall." Pp. 32–57 in *The Politics of Special Educational Needs,* edited by L. Barton. London: Falmer Press.

Bogdan, Robert. 1988. *Freak Show: Presenting Human Oddities for Amusement and Profit.* Chicago: University of Chicago Press.

Bogdan, Robert and Douglas Biklen. 1977. "Handicapism." *Social Policy* 7 (March/ April):14–19.

Bogdan, Robert and Douglas Biklen. 1985. "The Principal's Role in Mainstreaming." Pp. 30–51 in *Achieving the Complete School: Strategies for Effective Mainstreaming.* D. Biklen with R. Bogdan, D. Ferguson, S. Searl, Jr., and S. Taylor. New York: Teachers College Press.

Bogdan, Robert, Douglas Biklen, Arthur Shapiro, and David Spelkoman. 1982. "The Disabled: Media's Monster." *Social Policy* 13 (Fall):32–35.

Bogdan, Robert and Steven Taylor. 1976. "The Judged, Not the Judges: An Insider's View of Mental Retardation." *American Psychologist* 31 (January):47–52.

Bogdan, Robert and Steven J. Taylor. 1982. *Inside Out: The Social Meaning of Mental Retardation.* Toronto: University of Toronto Press.

Bogdan, Robert and Steven Taylor. 1987. "Toward a Sociology of Acceptance: The Other Side of the Study of Deviance." *Social Policy* 18 (Fall):34–39.

Bogdan, Robert and Steven J. Taylor. 1989. "Relationships with Severely Disabled People: The Social Construction of Humanness.(April):135–48.

Bogdan, Robert, Steven Taylor, Bernard deGrandpre, and Sondra Haynes. 1974. "Let Them Eat Programs: Attendants' Perspectives and Programming on Wards in State Schools." *Journal of Health and Social Behavior* 15 (June):142–51.

Booth, Tony. 1988. "Challenging Conceptions of Integration." Pp. 97–122 in *The Politics of Special Educational Needs,* edited by L. Barton. London: Falmer Press.

Bowe, Frank. 1978. *Handicapping America: Barriers To Disabled People.* New York: Harper and Row.

Bowe, Frank. 1980. *Rehabilitating America: Toward Independence For Disabled and Elderly People.* New York: Harper and Row.

Bowe, Frank. 1985. *Black Adults With Disabilities: A Statistical Report Drawn From Census Bureau Data.* Washington, D.C.: U.S. Government Printing Office.

Bowe, Frank. 1985. *Disabled Adults in America: A Statistical Report Drawn From Census Bureau Data.* Washington, D.C.: U.S. Government Printing Office.

Bowe, Frank. 1986. *Changing the Rules.* Silver Spring, MD: T.J. Publishers.

Bowe, Frank. 1990. "Employment and People With Disabilities: Challenges for the Nineties." *OSERS News in Print* 3 (Winter):2–6.

Bowe, Frank G. 1990. "Into the Private Sector: Rights and People with Disabilities." *Journal of Disability Policy Studies* 1 (Spring):89–101.

Bowe, Frank, Jan E. Jacobi, and Laurence D. Wiseman. 1978. *Coalition Building: A Report on a Feasibility Study to Develop a National Model for Cross-Disability Communication and Cooperation.* Washington, D.C.: American Coalition of Citizens with Disabilities, Inc.

Brodsky, Carroll M. 1976. *The Harassed Worker.* Lexington, MA: D.C. Heath.

Bruininks, Robert H., Florence A. Hauber, and Mary J. Kudla. "National Survey of Community Residential Facilities: A Profile of Facilities and Residents in 1977." *American Journal of Mental Deficiency* 84 (5):470–78.

Bruner, Jerome. 1986. *Actual Minds, Possible Worlds.* Cambridge, MA: Harvard University Press.

Buckholdt, David R. and Jaber F. Gubrium. 1983. "Practicing Accountability in Human Service Institutions." *Urban Life* 12 (October):249–68.

Budnick, Lawrence D. 1987. "Injuries." Pp. 165–77 in *Preventive Medicine and Public Health,* edited by B. Cassens. New York: Wiley.

Burkhauser, Richard V. and Petri Hirvonen. 1989. "United States Disability Policy in a Time of Economic Crisis: A Comparison with Sweden and the Federal Republic of Germany." *The Milbank Quarterly* 67 (Supplement 2, Part 1):166–94.

Byrne, John and Cecilia Martinez. 1989. "Ghastly Science." *Society* 27 (November/December):22–24.

Cartwright, Frederick F. *A Social History of Medicine.* London: Longman.

Cavalier, Al. 1987. "The Application of Technology in the Classroom and Workplace: Unvoiced Premises and Ethical Issues." Pp. 129–41 in *Images of the Disabled, Disabling Images,* edited by A. Gartner and T. Joe. New York: Praeger.

Chambliss, William J. 1974. "The State, the Law, and the Definition of Behavior as Criminal or Delinquent." Pp. 7–43 in *Handbook of Criminology,* edited by D. Glaser. Chicago: Rand McNally.

Chirikos, Thomas N. 1989. "Aggregate Economic Losses from Disability in the United States: A Preliminary Assay." *The Milbank Quarterly* 67 (Supplement 2, Part 1):59–91.

Cockerham, William C. 1981. *Sociology of Mental Disorder.* Englewood Cliffs, NJ: Prentice-Hall.

Cole, Stephen and Robert Lejeune. 1972. "Illness and the Legitimation of Failure." *American Sociological Review* 37 (June):347–56.

Coleman, Lerita M. 1986. "Stigma: An Enigma Demystified." Pp. 211–32 in *The Dilemma of Difference: A Multidisciplinary View of Stigma,* edited by S. Ainlay, G. Becker, and L. Coleman. New York: Plenum.

Coles, Gerald. 1987. *The Learning Mystique: A Critical Look at "Learning Disabilities".* New York: Pantheon.

Collignon, Frederick C. 1986. "The Role of Reasonable Accommodation in Employing Disabled Persons in Private Industry." Pp. 196–241 in *Disability and the Labor*

Market: Economic Problems, Policies, and Programs, edited by M. Berkowitz and M. Hill. Ithaca, NY: ILR Press.

The Columbia Record. 1981. "Mental patient takes charge in emergency." July 7: 4–A.

The Columbia Record. 1982. "Ex-mental patient held in Starlet's stabbing carried 'Death Petition'." March 17: 6–A.

The Commission on Education of the Deaf. 1988. *Toward Equality: Education of the Deaf.* A Report to the President and the Congress of the United States. Washington, D.C.: U.S. Government Printing Office.

Conrad, Peter and Joseph W. Schneider. 1980. *Deviance and Medicalization: From Badness to Sickness.* St. Louis: C.V. Mosby.

Crewe, Nancy M., Irving Kenneth Zola, and Associates. 1983. *Independent Living for Physically Disabled People.* San Francisco: Jossey-Bass.

Crouch, Barry A. 1986. "Martha's Vineyard, 1700–1900: A Deaf Utopia?" *Sign Language Studies* 53 (Winter):381–87.

Darling, Rosalyn Benjamin. 1979. *Families Against Society: A Study of Reactions to Children with Birth Defects.* Beverly Hills, CA: Sage.

Darling, Rosalyn Benjamin. 1988. "Parental Entrepreneurship: A Consumerist Response to Professional Dominance." *Journal of Social Issues* 44 (1):141–58.

Darling, Rosalyn Benjamin and Jon Darling. 1982. *Children Who Are Different: Meeting the Challenges of Birth Defects in Society.* St. Louis: C.V. Mosby.

Davis, Fred. 1961. "Deviance Disavowal: The Management of Strained Interaction by the Visibly Handicapped." *Social Problems* 9 (Fall):120–32.

Davis, Townsend. 1988. "Hearing Aid." *The New Republic* 199 (September 12 and 19):20, 22.

DeJong, Gerben. 1983. "Defining and Implementing the Independent Living Concept." Pp. 4–27 in *Independent Living for Physically Disabled People: Developing, Implementing, and Evaluating Self-Help Rehabilitation Programs,* N. Crewe, I. Zola, and Associates. San Francisco: Jossey-Bass.

DeJong, Gerben and Andrew L. Batavia. 1990. "The Americans with Disabilities Act and the Current State of U.S. Disability Policy." *Journal of Disability Policy Studies* 1 (Fall):65–75.

DeJong, Gerben and Raymond Lifchez. 1983. "Physical Disability and Public Policy." *Scientific American* 248 (June):40–49.

Deshen, Shlomo. 1991. "Mutual Rejection and Association among the Discredited: The Case of Blind People in Israel." *Human Organization* 50 (Spring):89–96.

Diamond, Timothy. 1983. "Nursing Homes as Trouble." *Urban Life* 12 (October):269–86.

The Disability Rag. 1990. "Are These 'Our' Films?" 11 (May/June):32–34.

The Disability Rag. 1990. 11 (May/June):passim.

The Disability Rag. 1990. 11 (Winter):passim.

The Disability Rag. 1991. 12 (January/February):passim.

The Disability Rag. 1991. "The Americans with Disabilities Act: Where We Are Now." 12 (January/February):11–12, 14–15, 18–19.

The Disability Rag. 1991. "Highlights from the ADA." 12 (January/February):12–13.

The Disability Rag. 1991. "Why the Nation Doesn't Have Attendant Services." 12 (January/February):1, 4–5, 8, 10.

The Disability Rag. 1991. 12 (March/April):passim.

The Disability Rag. 1991. 11 (May/June):8.

The Disability Rag. 1991. "Fields of Dreams?" 12 (May/June):10.

Driedger, Diane. 1989. *The Last Civil Rights Movement: Disabled People's International.* London: Hurst.

Duncan, Barbara and Diane E. Woods (eds.). 1989. *Ethical Issues in Disability and Rehabilitation: Report of a 1989 International Conference.* New York: World Rehabilitation Fund, Rehabilitation International, and World Institute on Disability.

Edgerton, Robert B. 1979. *Mental Retardation.* Cambridge, MA: Harvard University Press.

Ehrlich, Paul R. and Anne H. Ehrlich. 1989. "Intelligent Planning for Safety." *Society* 27 (November/December):15–16.

Elliott, Gregory C., Herbert L. Ziegler, Barbara M. Altman, and Deborah R. Scott. 1982. "Understanding Stigma: Dimensions of Deviance and Coping." *Deviant Behavior* 3 (April–June):275–300.

Emerson, Joan P. 1970. "Nothing Unusual is Happening." Pp. 208–22 in *Human Nature and Collective Behavior* edited by T. Shibutani. Englewood Cliffs, NJ: Prentice-Hall.

Erlanger, Howard S. and William Roth. 1985. "Disability Policy: The Parts and the Whole." *American Behavioral Scientist* 28 (January/February):319–45.

Evans. A. Donald and William W. Falk. 1986. *Learning to be Deaf.* Berlin: Mouton de Gruyter.

Fagerhaugh, Shizuko. 1975. "Getting Around with Emphysema." Pp. 99–107 in *Chronic Illness and the Quality of Life,* A. Strauss and B. Glaser. Saint Louis: C.V. Mosby.

Farer, Laurence S. and Carl W. Schieffelbein. 1987. "Respiratory Diseases." Pp. 115–24 in *Closing the Gap: The Burden of Unnecessary Illness,* edited by R. Amler and H. Dull. New York: Oxford University Press.

Featherstone, Helen. 1980. *A Difference in the Family: Life with a Disabled Child.* New York: Basic Books.

Ferguson, Philip M. 1987. "The Social Construction of Mental Retardation." *Social Policy* 18 (Summer):51–52.

Ferguson, Philip M., Michael Hibbard, James Leinen, and Sandra Schaff. 1990. "Supported Community Life: Disability Policy and the Renewal of Mediating Structures." *Journal of Disability Policy Studies* 1 (Spring):9–35.

Fichten, Catherine S. 1988. "Students with Physical Disabilities in Higher Education: Attitudes and Beliefs That Affect Integration." Pp. 171–86 in *Attitudes Toward Persons with Disabilities,* edited by H. Yuker. New York: Springer.

Fine, Michelle and Adrienne Asch. 1988. "Disability Beyond Stigma: Social Interaction, Discrimination, and Activism." *Journal of Social Issues* 44 (1):3–21.

Fine, Michelle and Adrienne Asch (eds.). 1988. *Women with Disabilities: Essays in Psychology, Culture, and Politics.* Philadelphia: Temple University Press.

Fisher, Bernice and Roberta Galler. 1988. "Friendship and Fairness: How Disability Affects Friendship Between Women." Pp. 172–194 in *Women with Disabilities: Essays in Psychology, Culture, and Politics,* edited by M. Fine and A. Asch. Philadelphia: Temple University Press.

Fletcher, Joseph. 1979. *Humanhood: Essays in Biomedical Ethics.* Buffalo, NY: Prometheus Books.

Foster, Glen G., James E. Ysseldyke, and James H. Reese. 1975. " 'I Wouldn't Have Seen It If I Hadn't Believed It'." *Exceptional Children* 41 (April):469–73.

Foster, Susan Bannerman. 1987. *The Politics of Caring.* London: Falmer.

Frank, Gelya. 1988. "On Embodiment: A Case Study of Congenital Limb Deficiency in American Culture." Pp. 41–71 in *Women with Disabilities: Essays in Psychology, Culture, and Politics,* edited by M. Fine and A. Asch. Philadelphia: Temple University Press.

Freidson, Eliot. 1966. "Disability as Social Deviance." Pp. 71–99 in *Sociology and Rehabilitation,* edited by M. Sussman. Washington, D.C.: American Sociological Association.

Furth, Hans G. 1966. *Thinking Without Language.* New York: Free Press.

Gallagher, Hugh Gregory. 1985. *FDR's Splendid Deception.* New York: Dodd, Mead.

Gannon, Jack R. 1981. *Deaf Heritage: A Narrative History of Deaf America.* Silver Spring, MD: National Association of the Deaf.

Gannon, Jack R. 1989. *The Week the World Heard Gallaudet.* Washington, D.C.: Gallaudet University Press.

Gans, Herbert J. 1971. "The Uses of Poverty: The Poor Pay All." *Social Policy* 2 (July/August):20–24.

Gartner, Alan and Tom Joe. 1987. "Conclusions." Pp. 205–8 in *Images of the Disabled, Disabling Images,* edited by A. Gartner and T. Joe. New York: Praeger.

Gartner, Alan and Tom Joe (eds.). 1987. *Images of the Disabled, Disabling Images.* New York: Praeger.

Glassner, Barry. 1988. *Bodies.* New York: G.P. Putnam.

Gliedman, John and William Roth. 1980. *The Unexpected Minority: Handicapped Children in America.* New York: Harcourt.

Gluckman, Max (ed.). 1962. *Essays on the Ritual of Social Relations.* Manchester, England: Manchester University Press.

Goddard, Henry H. 1912. *The Kallikak Family.* New York: Macmillan.

Goddard, Henry H. 1915. "The Possibilities of Research as Applied to the Prevention of Feeble-Mindedness." Pp. 307–312 in the *Proceedings of the National Conference of Charities and Correction.*

Goffman, Erving. 1963. *Stigma: Notes on the Management of Spoiled Identity.* Englewood Cliffs, NJ: Prentice-Hall.

Goffman, Erving. 1974. *Frame Analysis.* Cambridge, MA: Harvard University Press.

Goldin, Carol S. 1984. "The Community of the Blind: Social Organization, Advocacy and Cultural Redefinition." *Human Organization* 43 (Summer):121–31.

Goldstein, Paul J., Dana Hunt, Don C. Des Jarlais, and Sherry Deren. 1987. "Drug Dependence and Abuse." Pp. 89–101 in *Closing the Gap: The Burden of Unnecessary Illness,* edited by R. Amler and H. Dull, New York: Oxford University Press.

Goode, David A. 1984. "Socially Produced Identities, Intimacy and the Problem of Competence Among the Retarded." Pp. 228–48 in *Special Education and Social Interests,* edited by L. Barton and S. Tomlinson. London: Croom Helm.

Goode, David A. 1986. "Kids, Culture and Innocents." *Human Studies* 9 (1):83–106.

Goode, David A. 1990. "On Understanding Without Words: Communication Between a Deaf-Blind Child and Her Parents." *Human Studies* 13 (January):1–37.

Groce, Nora Ellen. 1985. *Everyone Here Spoke Sign Language: Hereditary Deafness on Martha's Vineyard.* Cambridge, MA: Harvard University Press.

Groce, Nora Ellen. 1990. "Cross-Cultural Research: From Here to the 21st Century." *Disability Studies Quarterly* 10 (Spring):1–3.

Gross, Richard H., Alan Cox, Ruth Tatyrek, Michael Pollay, and William Barnes. 1983. "Early Management and Decision Making for the Treatment of Myelo-meningocele." *Pediatrics* 72 (October):450–58.

Gubrium, Jaber F. and David R. Buckholdt. 1982. *Describing Care: Image and Practice in Rehabilitation.* Cambridge, MA: Oelgeschlager, Gunn and Hain.

Hahn, Harlan. 1983. "Paternalism and Public Policy." *Society* 20 (March/April):36–46.

Hahn, Harlan. 1985. "Introduction: Disability Policy and the Problem of Discrimination." *American Behavioral Scientist* 28 (January/February):293–318.

Hahn, Harlan. 1985. "Toward a Politics of Disability Definitions, Disciplines, and Policies." *The Social Science Journal* 22 (October):87–105.

Hahn, Harlan. 1987. "Advertising the Acceptably Employable Image: Disability and Capitalism." *Policy Studies Journal* 15 (March):551–70.

Hahn, Harlan. 1987. "Civil Rights for Disabled Americans: The Foundation of a Political Agenda." Pp. 181–203 in *Images of the Disabled, Disabling Images*, edited by A. Gartner and T. Joe. New York: Praeger.

Hahn, Harlan. 1988. "Can Disability Be Beautiful?" *Social Policy* 18 (Winter):26–32.

Hahn, Harlan. 1988. "The Politics of Physical Differences: Disability and Discrimination." *Journal of Social Issues* 44 (1):39–47.

Hanks, Michael and Dennis E. Poplin. 1981. "The Sociology of Physical Disability: A Review of Literature and Some Conceptual Perspectives." *Deviant Behavior* 2 (July–September):309–28.

Harris, George A. 1983. *Broken Ears, Wounded Hearts.* Washington, D.C.: Gallaudet College Press.

Harris, Marvin. 1981. *America Now: The Anthropology of a Changing Culture.* New York: Simon and Schuster.

Harris, Marvin. 1989. *Our Kind: Who We Are, Where We Came From, Where We Are Going.* New York: Harper and Row.

Hasenfeld, Yeheskel and Richard A. English. 1974. "Human Service Organizations: A Conceptual Overview." Pp. 1–32 in *Human Service Organizations: A Book of Readings*, edited by Y. Hasenfeld and R. English. Ann Arbor, MI: University of Michigan Press.

Henderson, George and Willie V. Bryan. 1984. *Psychosocial Aspects of Disability.* Springfield, IL: Charles C Thomas.

Hentoff, Nat. 1987. "The Awful Privacy of Baby Doe." Pp. 161–79 in *Images of the Disabled, Disabling Images*, edited by A. Gartner and T. Joe. New York: Praeger.

Herring, Christina L. 1987. "Substance Abuse." Pp. 201–09 in *Preventive Medicine and Public Health*, edited by B. Cassens. New York: Wiley.

Higgins, Paul C. 1980. *Outsiders in a Hearing World: A Sociology of Deafness.* Beverly Hills, CA: Sage.

Higgins, Paul C. 1985. *The Rehabilitation Detectives: Doing Human Service Work.* Beverly Hills, CA: Sage.

Higgins, Paul C. 1987. "Introduction." Pp. vii–xvii in *Understanding Deafness Socially,* edited by P. Higgins and J. Nash. Springfield, IL: Charles C Thomas

Higgins, Paul C. 1990. *The Challenge of Educating Together Deaf and Hearing Youth: Making Mainstreaming Work.* Springfield, IL: Charles C Thomas.

Higgins, Paul C. and Richard R. Butler. 1982. *Understanding Deviance.* New York: McGraw-Hill.

Hollinger, Chloe S. and Reginald L. Jones. 1970. "Community Attitudes Toward Slow Learners and Mental Retardates: What's in a Name?" *Mental Retardation* 8 (February):19–23.

Horne, Marcia D. 1988. "Modifying Peer Attitudes Toward the Handicapped: Procedures and Research Issues." Pp. 203–22 in *Attitudes Toward Persons with Disabilities,* edited by H. Yuker. New York: Springer.

Hughes, Dana, Kay Johnson, Sara Rosenbaum, Elizabeth Butler, and Janet Simons. 1988. *The Health of America's Children: Maternal and Child Health Data Book.* Washington, D.C.: Children's Defense Fund.

Jacobs, Leo M. 1980. *A Deaf Adult Speaks Out.* 2nd ed. Washington, D.C.: Gallaudet College Press.

Johnson, Mary. 1990. "'Wheels of Justice' Week." *The Disability Rag* 11 (May/June): 19–25.

Johnson, William G. 1986. "The Rehabilitation Act and Discrimination Against Handicapped Workers: Does the Cure Fit the Disease?" Pp. 242–61 in *Disability and the Labor Market: Economic Problems, Policies, and Programs,* edited by M. Berkowitz and M. Hall. Ithaca, NY: ILR Press.

Johnson, William G. and James Lambrinos. 1983. "Employment Discrimination." *Society* 20 (March/April):47–50.

Jones, Edward E., Amerigo Farina, Albert H. Hastorf, Hazel Markus, Dale T. Miller, Robert A. Scott with Rita de S. French. 1984. *Social Stigma: The Psychology of Marked Relationships.* New York: W. H. Freeman.

Jones, Lesley, Jim Kyle, and Peter Wood. 1987. *Words Apart: Losing your hearing as an adult.* London: Tavistock.

Kaiser, Susan B., Carla M. Freeman, and Stacy B. Wingate. 1985. "Stigmata and Negotiated Outcomes: Management of Appearance by Persons with Physical Disabilities." *Deviant Behavior* 6 (2):205–24.

Kaplan, George A., Mary N. Haan, S. Leonard Syme, Meredith Minkler, and Marilyn Winkleby. 1987. "Socioeconomic Status and Health." Pp. 125–29 in *Closing the Gap: The Burden of Unnecessary Illness,* edited by R. Amler and H. Dull. New York: Oxford University Press.

Katzman, Robert A. 1986. *Institutional Disability: The Saga of Transportation Policy for the Disabled.* Washington, D.C.: The Brookings Institution.

Kent, Deborah. 1987. "Disabled Women: Portraits in Fiction and Drama." Pp. 47–63 in *Images of the Disabled, Disabling Images,* edited by A. Gartner and T. Joe. New York: Praeger.

Kielhofner, Gary. 1983. "'Teaching' Retarded Adults: Paradoxical Effects of a Pedagogical Enterprise." *Urban Life* 12 (October):307–26.

Kiser, Bill. 1974. *New Light of Hope.* New Canaan, CT: Keats.

Kleinfield, Sonny. 1979. "Declaring Independence in Berkeley." *Psychology Today* 13 (August):67–78.

Krause, Elliott A. 1976. "The Political Sociology of Rehabilitation." Pp. 201–221 in *The Sociology Of Physical Disability and Rehabilitation,* edited by G. Albrecht. Pittsburgh, PA: University of Pittsburgh Press.

Kriegel, Leonard. 1982. "The Wolf in the Pit in the Zoo." *Social Policy* 13 (Fall):16–23.

Kriegel, Leonard. 1987. "The Crippled in Literature." Pp. 31–46 in *Images of the Disabled, Disabling Images,* edited by A. Gartner and T. Joe. New York: Praeger.

Kronick, Jane C., Miriam G. Vosburgh, and William W. Vosburgh. 1981. "Changing Principles for Disability in New Zealand: The Accident Compensation Act." Pp. 185–204 in *Cross National Rehabilitation Policies: A Sociological Perspective,* edited by G. Albrecht. Beverly Hills, CA: Sage.

Kugelmass, Judy W. 1987. *Behavior, Bias, and Handicaps: Labeling the Emotionally Disturbed Child.* New Brunswick, NJ: Transaction Books.

Lane, Harlan. 1984. *When the Mind Hears: A History of the Deaf.* New York: Random House.

Lane, Harlan. 1987. "Mainstreaming of Deaf Children — From Bad to Worse." *The Deaf American* 38 (Spring):15.

Lane, Harlan. 1988. "Is There a 'Psychology of the Deaf?'" *Exceptional Children* 55 (September):7–19.

Langer, Ellen J. and Benzion Chanowitz. 1988. "Mindfulness/Mindlessness: A New Perspective for the Study of Disability." Pp. 68–81 in *Attitudes Toward Persons with Disabilities,* edited by H. Yuker. New York: Springer.

LaPlante, Mitchell P. 1990. "Who Counts as Having a Disability? Musings on the Meaning and Prevalence of Disability." *Disability Studies Quarterly* 10 (Summer): 15–17.

Lazerson, Marvin. 1983. "The Origins of Special Education." Pp. 15–47 in *Special Education Policies: Their History, Implementation, and Finance,* edited by J. Chambers and W. Hartman. Philadelphia: Temple University Press.

Lehrer, Steven. 1979. *Explorers of the Body.* Garden City, NY: Doubleday.

Lenihan, John. 1976/1977. "Disabled Americans: A History" *Performance* 27 (November–December, January):1–72.

Lennon, Mary Clare, Bruce G. Link, Joseph J. Marbach, and Bruce P. Dohrenwend. 1989. "The Stigma of Chronic Facial Pain and Its Impact on Social Relationships." *Social Problems* 36 (April):117–34.

Levine, Erwin L. and Elizabeth M. Wexler. 1981. *PL 94-142: An Act of Congress.* New York: Macmillan.

Lindesmith, Alfred R., Anselm L. Strauss, and Norman K. Denzin. 1975. *Social Psychology.* Hinsdale, IL: Dryden.

Link, Bruce G. and Francis T. Cullen. 1986. "Contact with the Mentally Ill and Perceptions of How Dangerous They Are." *Journal of Health and Social Behavior* 27 (December):289–302.

Link, Bruce G., Francis T. Cullen, Elmer Struening, Patrick E. Shrout, and Bruce P.

Dohrenwend. 1989. "A Modified Labeling Theory Approach to Mental Disorders: An Empirical Assessment." *American Sociological Review* 54 (June):400–23.

Lipsky, Michael. 1980. *Street-Level Bureaucracy: Dilemmas of the Individual in Public Services.* New York: Russell Sage.

Locker, David. 1983. *Disability and Disadvantage: The Consequences of Chronic Illness.* London: Tavistock.

Lofland, Lyn H. 1973. *A World of Strangers: Order and Action in Urban Public Space.* New York: Basic Books.

Longmore, Paul K. 1985. "A Note on Language and the Social Identity of Disabled People." *American Behavioral Scientist* 28 (January/February):419–23.

Longmore, Paul K. 1985. "'Mask': A Revealing Portrayal of Disabled." *The Los Angeles Times Sunday Calendar* (May 5):22–23.

Longmore, Paul K. 1985. "Screening Stereotypes." *Social Policy* 16 (Summer):31–37.

Louis Harris and Associates, Inc. 1986. *The ICD Survey of Disabled Americans: Bringing Disabled Americans into the Mainstream.* New York: ICD–International Center for the Disabled.

Lynas, Wendy. 1986. *Integrating the Handicapped into Ordinary Schools: A Study of Hearing-Impaired Pupils.* London: Croom Helm.

MacMillan, Donald L. 1977. *Mental Retardation in School and Society.* Boston: Little, Brown.

Maines, David. 1984. "The Social Arrangements of Diabetic Self-Help Groups." Pp. 111–26 in *Chronic Illness and the Quality of Life,* 2nd ed., A. Strauss and J. Corbin, S. Fagerhaugh, B. Glaser, D. Maines, B. Suczek, and C. Wiener. St. Louis: C.V. Mosby.

Mairs, Nancy. 1986. *Plain Text.* Tucson: University of Arizona Press.

Makas, Elaine. 1988. "Positive Attitudes Toward Disabled People: Disabled and Nondisabled Persons' Perspectives." *Journal of Social Issues* 44 (1):49–61.

McCaffrey, David P. 1982. *OSHA and the Politics of Health Regulation.* New York: Plenum.

McMurray, Georgia L. 1987. "Easing Everyday Living: Technology for the Physically Disabled." Pp. 143–60 in *Images of the Disabled, Disabling Images,* edited by A. Gartner and T. Joe. New York: Praeger.

Mehan, Hugh, Alma Hertweck, and J. Lee Meihls. 1986. *Handicapping the Handicapped: Decision Making in Students' Educational Careers.* Stanford, CA: Stanford University Press.

Mercer, Jane R. 1973. *Labeling the Mentally Retarded: Clinical and Social System Perspectives on Mental Retardation.* Berkeley, CA: University of California Press.

Merton, Robert K. 1957. *Social Theory and Social Structure.* Rev. ed. Glencoe, IL: Free Press.

Mest, Grace M. 1988. "With a Little Help from Their Friends: Use of Social Support Systems by Persons with Retardation." *Journal of Social Issues* 44 (1):117–25.

Meucci, Sandra. 1988. "Death-Making in the Human Services." *Social Policy* 18 (Winter):17–20.

Meyerson, Lee. 1971. "Somatopsychology of Physical Disability." Pp. 1–74 in *Psychology of Exceptional Children and Youth*, 3rd ed., edited by W. Cruickshank. Englewood Cliffs, NJ: Prentice-Hall.

Meyerson, Lee. 1988. "The Social Psychology of Physical Disability: 1948 and 1988." *Journal of Social Issues* 44 (1):173–88.

Mezey, Susan Gluck. 1988. *No Longer Disabled: The Federal Courts and the Politics of Social Security Disability.* New York: Greenwood Press.

Mills, C. Wright. 1959. *The Sociological Imagination.* London: Oxford University Press.

Minow, Martha. 1990. *Making All the Difference: Inclusion, Exclusion, And American Law.* Ithaca, NY: Cornell University Press.

Moss, Kathryn. 1987. "The 'Baby Doe' Legislation: Its Rise and Fall." *Policy Studies Journal* 15 (June):629–51.

Mudrick, Nancy R. 1988. "Disabled Women and Public Policies for Income Support." Pp. 245–68 in *Women with Disabilities: Essays in Psychology, Culture, and Politics*, edited by M. Fine and A. Asch. Philadelphia: Temple University Press.

National Council on the Handicapped. 1986. *Toward Independence: An Assessment of Federal Laws and Programs Affecting Persons With Disabilities — With Legislative Recommendations.* Washington, D.C.: U.S. Government Printing Office.

National Council on the Handicaped. 1986. *Toward Independence: An Assessment of Federal Laws and Programs Affecting Persons With Disabilities — With Legislative Recommendations*, Appendix. Washington, D.C.: U.S. Government Printing Office.

National Council on the Handicapped. 1988. *On the Threshold of Independence: Progress on Legislative Recommendations From 'Toward Independence'*, A Report to the President and to the Congress of the United States. Washington, D.C.

National Research Council. 1985. *Injury in America: A Continuing Public Health Problem.* Washington, D.C.: National Academy Press.

Newman, Joseph. 1987. "Background Forces in Policies for Care and Treatment of Disability." Pp. 25–44 in *Childhood Disability and Family Systems*, edited by M. Ferrari and M. Sussman. New York: Haworth Press.

Newsweek, 1989. "Pregnancy + Alcohol = Problems." July 31:57.

Noble, John H. Jr. 1987. "Ethical Considerations Facing Society in Rehabilitating Severely Disabled Persons." Pp. 65–82 in *Childhood Disability and Family Systems*, edited by M. Ferrari and M. Sussman. New York: Haworth Press.

Obermann, C. Esco. 1965. *A History of Vocational Rehabilitation in America.* Minneapolis, MN: T. S. Denison.

Oliver, Mike. 1988. "The Social and Political Context of Educational Policy: The Case of Special Needs." Pp. 13–31 in *The Politics of Special Educational Needs*, edited by L. Barton. London: Falmer Press.

Oliver, Michael. 1990. *The Politics of Disablement: A Sociological Perspective.* New York: St. Martin's Press.

Padden, Carol. 1980. "The Deaf Community and the Culture of Deaf People." Pp. 89–103 in *Sign Language and The Deaf Community: Essays in Honor of William C. Stokoe*, edited by C. Baker and R. Battison. Silver Spring, MD: National Association of the Deaf.

Padden, Carol and Tom Humphries. 1988. *Deaf in America: Voices from a Culture.* Cambridge, MA: Harvard University Press.

Percy, Stephen L. *Disability, Civil Rights, and Public Policy.* 1989. Tuscaloosa, AL: The University of Alabama Press.

Petrunik, Michael and Clifford D. Shearing. 1983. "Fragile Facades: Stuttering and the Strategic Manipulation of Awareness." *Social Problems* 31 (December):125–38.

Pfeiffer, David. 1989. "Just How Many Disabled Persons Are There in the United States?" *AADC News* (Winter):1, 6.

Phillips, Marilyn J. 1985. " 'Try Harder': The Experience of Disability and the Dilemma of Normalization." *The Social Science Journal* 22 (October): 45–57.

Phillips, Marilyn J. 1986. "What We Call Ourselves: Self-Referential Naming Among the Disabled." Presented at the Seventh Annual Ethnography in Research Forum, University of Pennsylvania, Philadelphia, April 4–6.

Phillips, Marilyn J. 1988. "Disability and Ethnicity in Conflict: A Study in Transformation." Pp. 195–214 in *Women with Disabilities: Essays in Psychology, Culture, and Politics,* edited by M. Fine and A. Asch. Philadelphia: Temple University Press.

Ponse, Barbara. 1977. "Secrecy in the Lesbian World." Pp. 53–78 in *Sexuality: Encounters, Identities, and Relationships,* edited by C. Warren. Beverly Hills, CA: Sage.

Prottas, Jeffrey Manditch. 1979. *People-Processing: The Street-Level Bureaucrat in Public Service Bureaucracies.* Lexington, MA: D.C. Heath.

Quart, Leonard and Albert Auster. 1982. "The Wounded Vet in Postwar Film." *Social Policy* 13 (February):24–31.

Rains, Prudence M., John I. Kitsuse, Troy Duster, and Eliot Freidson. 1975. "The Labeling Approach to Deviance." Pp. 88–100 in *Issues in the Classification of Children.* vol. 1, edited by N. Hobbs. San Francisco: Jossey-Bass.

Raspberry, William. 1989. "African American Usage Examined." *The State* (January 6):15-A.

Raspberry, William. 1989. "Former HUD chief not only 'silent,' but also 'blind'." *The State* (July 6): 11-A.

Reiman, Jeffrey. 1984. *The Rich Get Richer and the Poor Get Prison: Ideology, Class, and Criminal Justice.* 2nd ed. New York: Wiley.

Reiman, Jeffrey. 1991. *The Rich Get Richer and the Poor Get Prison: Ideology, Class, and Criminal Justice.* 3rd ed. New York: Macmillan.

Rivera, Geraldo. 1972. *Willowbrook: A Report on How it is and Why it Doesn't Have to Be That Way.* New York: Random House.

Robertson, Leon S. 1983. *Injuries: Causes, Control Strategies, and Public Policy.* Lexington, MA: D.C. Heath.

Robinson, James C. and Glenn M. Shor. 1989. "Business-cycle Influences on Work-related Disability in Construction and Manufacturing." *The Milbank Quarterly* 67 (Supplement 2, Part 1):92–113.

Rosen, Ephraim and Ian Gregory. 1965. *Abnormal Psychology.* Philadelphia: W.B. Saunders.

Rosenberg, Charles E. 1989. "Disease in History: Frames and Framers." *The Milbank Quarterly* 67 (Supplement 1):1–15.

Rosenberg, Charles and Janet Golden (eds.). 1989. "Framing Disease: The Creation and Negotiation of Explanatory Schemes." *The Milbank Quarterly* 67 (Supplement 1): Issue.

Roth, Julius A. and Elizabeth M. Eddy. 1967. *Rehabilitation for the Unwanted.* New York: Atherton.

Roth, William. 1981. *The Handicapped Speak.* Jefferson, NC: McFarland.

Roth, William. 1983. "Handicap as a Social Construct." *Society* 20 (March/April):56–61.

Rothman, David J. 1971. *The Discovery of the Asylum: Social Order and Disorder in the New Republic.* Boston: Little, Brown.

Rothman, David J. and Sheila M. Rothman. 1984. *The Willowbrook Wars.* New York: Harper and Row.

Ruffner, Robert H. 1987. "504 and the Media: Legitimatizing Disability." *American Rehabilitation* 13 (April–May–June):4–7, 25.

Ryan, William. 1971. *Blaming the Victim.* New York: Pantheon.

Rynders, John E. 1987. "History of Down Syndrome." Pp. 1–17 in *New Perspectives on Down Syndrome,* edited by S. Pueschel, C. Tingey, J. Rynders, A. Crocker, and D. Crutcher. Baltimore, MD: Paul H. Brookes.

Rynders, John E. 1987. "Introduction." Pp. 147–48 in *New Perspectives on Down Syndrome,* edited by S. Pueschel, C. Tingey, J. Rynders, A. Crocker, and D. Crutcher. Baltimore, MD: Paul H. Brookes.

Safilios-Rothschild, Constantina. 1970. *The Sociology and Social Psychology of Disability and Rehabilitation.* New York: Random House.

Safilios-Rothschild, Constantina. 1981. "Disability and Rehabilitation: Research and Social Policy in Developing Nations." Pp. 111–22 in *Cross National Rehabilitation Policies: A Sociological Perspective,* edited by G. Albrecht. Beverly Hills, CA: Sage.

Sagatun, Inger J. 1985. "The Effects of Acknowledging a Disability and Initiating Contact on Interaction Between Disabled and Non-Disabled Persons." *The Social Science Journal* 22 (October):33–43.

Sarason, Seymour B. and John Doris. 1979. *Educational Handicap, Public Policy, and Social History: A Broadened Perspective on Mental Retardation.* New York: Free Press.

Scheer, Jessica and Nora Groce. 1988. "Impairment as a Human Constant: Cross-Cultural and Historical Perspectives on Variation." *Journal of Social Issues.* 44 (1):23–37.

Scheerenberger, R. C. 1983. *A History of Mental Retardation.* Baltimore, MD: Paul H. Brookes.

Schein, Jerome D. 1968. *The Deaf Community: Studies in the Social Psychology of Deafness.* Washington, D.C.: Gallaudet College Press.

Schneider, Joseph W. 1988. "Disability as Moral Experience: Epilepsy and Self in Routine Relationships." *Journal of Social Issues* 44 (1):63–78.

Schneider, Joseph W. and Peter Conrad. 1980. "In the Closet with Illness: Epilepsy, Stigma Potential and Information Control." *Social Problems* 28 (October):32–44.

Schneider, Joseph W. and Peter Conrad. 1983. *Having Epilepsy: The Experience and Control of Illness.* Philadelphia: Temple University Press.

Scotch, Richard K. 1984. *From Good Will to Civil Rights: Transforming Federal Disability Policy.* Philadelphia: Temple University Press.

Scotch, Richard K. 1988. "Disability as the Basis for a Social Movement: Advocacy and the Politics of Definition." *Journal of Social Issues* 44 (1):159–72.

Scotch, Richard K. 1989. "Politics and Policy in the History of the Disability Rights Movement." *The Milbank Quarterly* 67 (Supplement 2, Part 2):380–400.

Scotch, Richard K. and Edward D. Berkowitz. 1990. "One Comprehensive System? A Historical Perspective on Federal Disability Policy." *Journal of Disability Policy Studies* 1 (Fall):1–19.

Scott, Robert A. 1969. *The Making of Blind Men: A Study of Adult Socialization.* New York: Russell Sage.

Shapiro, Michael J. 1981. "Disability and the Politics of Constitutive Rules." Pp. 83–96 in *Cross National Rehabilitation Policies: A Sociological Perspective,* edited by G. Albrecht. Beverly Hills, CA: Sage.

Shorter, Edward. 1975. *The Making of the Modern Family.* New York: Basic Books.

Sivard, Ruth Leger. 1989. *World Military and Social Expenditures.* 13th ed. Washington, D.C.: World Priorities.

Skrabanek, Petr and James McCormick. 1990. *Follies and Fallacies in Medicine.* Buffalo, NY: Prometheus Books.

Smith, David J. 1985. *Minds Made Feeble: The Myth and Legacy of the Kallikaks.* Rockville, MD: Aspen Systems Corp.

Smith, Gordon S. and Henry Falk. 1987. "Unintentional Injuries." Pp. 143–63 in *Closing the Gap: The Burden of Unnecessary Illness,* edited by R. Amler and H. Dull. New York: Oxford University Press.

Sowell, Thomas. 1987. *A Conflict of Visions.* New York: Morrow.

Stark, Rodney. 1989. *Sociology.* 3rd ed. Belmont, CA: Wadsworth.

Stewart, Robert L. Forthcoming. *Living and Acting Together.*

Stewart, Robert L. and Larry T. Reynolds. 1985. "The Biologizing of the Individual and the Naturalization of the Social." *Humanity and Society* 9 (May):159–67.

Stone, Deborah A. 1981. "The Definition and Determination of Disability in Public Programs." Pp. 49–64 in *Cross National Rehabilitation Policies: A Sociological Perspective,* edited by G. Albrecht. Beverly Hills, CA: Sage.

Stone, Deborah A. 1984. *The Disabled State.* Philadelphia: Temple University Press.

Strauss, Anselm L. and Barney G. Glaser. 1975. *Chronic Illness and the Quality of Life.* Saint Louis: C.V. Mosby.

Stubbins, Joseph. 1988. "The Politics of Disability." Pp. 22–32 in *Attitudes Toward Persons with Disabilities,* edited by H. Yuker. New York: Springer.

Sweidel, Gabriele. 1989. "Stop, Look and Listen! When Vocal and Nonvocal Adults Communicate." *Disability, Handicap and Society* 4 (2):165–75.

Tanenbaum, Sandra J. 1986. *Engineering Disability: Public Policy and Compensatory Technology.* Philadelphia: Temple University Press.

Taylor, Steven J., Douglas Biklen and James Knoll (eds.). 1987. *Community Integration for People with Severe Disabilities.* New York: Teachers College Press.

Taylor, Steven J. and Robert Bogdan. 1989. "On Accepting Relationships between

People with Mental Retardation and Non-disabled People: Towards an Understanding of Acceptance." *Disability, Handicap and Society* 4 (1):21–35.

Taylor, Steven J., Julie A. Racino, James A. Knoll, and Zana Lutfiyya. 1987. *The Nonrestrictive Environment: On Community Integration for People with the Most Severe Disabilities.* Syracuse, NY: Human Policy Press.

Temkin, Oswei. 1971. *The Falling Sickness.* 2nd ed. Baltimore, MD: Johns Hopkins Press.

Thomas, Elizabeth. 1958. *The Harmless People.* New York: Knopf.

Tomlinson, Sally. 1982. *A Sociology of Special Education.* London: Routledge and Kegan Paul.

U.S. Bureau of the Census. 1990. *Statistical Abstract of the United States: 1990* (110th edition) Washington, D.C.

U.S. Department of Education. 1990. *"To Assure the Free Appropriate Public Education of All Handicapped Children": Twelfth Annual Report to Congress on the Implementation of The Education of the Handicapped Act.* Washington, D.C.: Government Printing Office.

U.S. Department of Health and Human Services. 1986. *The 1990 Health Objectives for the Nation: A Midcourse Review.* Washington, D.C.: Office of Disease Prevention and Health Promotion, Public Health Service.

U.S. Department of Health and Human Services. 1986. *Types of Injuries and Impairments Due to Injuries: United States.* Hyattsville, MD: Public Health Service, National Center for Health Statistics, (PHS) 87–1587.

U.S. Department of Health and Human Services. 1988. *Disease Prevention/Health Promotion: The Facts.* Palo Alto, CA: Bull Publishing.

U.S. Department of Health and Human Services. 1988. *The Health Consequences of Smoking: Nicotine Addiction. A Report of the Surgeon General.* Rockville, MD: Public Health Service, Centers for Disease Control, Center for Health Promotion and Education, Office on Smoking and Health.

U.S. Department of Health and Human Services. 1988. *The Nature and Extent of Lead Poisoning in Children in the United States: A Report to Congress.* Washington, D.C.: Public Health Service, Agency for Toxic Substances and Disease Registry.

U.S. Department of Health and Human Services. 1989. *Reducing the Health Consequences of Smoking: 25 Years of Progress. A Report of the Surgeon General.* Rockville, MD: Public Health Service, Centers for Disease Control, Center for Chronic Disease Prevention and Health Promotion, Office on Smoking and Health. DHHS Publication No. (CDC) 89-8411, Prepublication version, January 11, 1989.

U.S. Department of Labor. 1988. "Replacement Issued for Release on Occupational Injuries and Illnesses in 1987." Washington, D.C.: Bureau of Labor Statistics.

U.S. Department of Transportation. 1988 (August). "Drunk Driving Facts." Washington, D.C.: National Highway Traffic Safety Administration.

U.S. Department of Transportation. 1988. *National Accident Sampling System 1986: A Report on Traffic Crashes and Injuries in the United States.* Washington, D.C.: National Highway Traffic Safety Administration.

U.S. Department of Transportation. 1989 (June). "Occupant Protection Facts." Washington, D.C.: National Highway Traffic Safety Administration.

United States Commission on Civil Rights. 1983. *Accommodating the Spectrum of Individual Abilities.* Washington, D.C.: U.S. Government Printing Office.

Van Riper, Charles. 1971. *The Nature of Stuttering.* Englewood Cliffs, NJ: Prentice-Hall.

Viscusi, W. Kip. 1989. "Safety through Markets." *Society* 27 (November/December): 9–10.

Walker, Lisa J. 1987. "Procedural Rights in the Wrong System: Special Education is Not Enough." Pp. 97–115 in *Images of The Disabled, Disabling Images,* edited by A. Gartner and T. Joe. New York: Praeger.

Walker, Lou Ann. 1986. *A Loss for Words: The Story of Deafness in a Family.* New York: Harper and Row.

Warren, Carol A. B. 1987. *Madwives: Schizophrenic Women in the 1950s.* New Brunswick, NJ: Rutgers University Press.

Weinberg, Joanna K. 1988. "Autonomy as a Different Voice: Women, Disabilities, and Decisions." Pp. 269–96 in *Women with Disabilities: Essays in Psychology, Culture, and Politics,* edited by M. Fine and A. Asch. Philadelphia: Temple University Press.

Weinberg, Martin S. 1968. "The Problems of Midgets and Dwarfs and Organizational Remedies: A Study of the Little People of America" *Journal of Health and Social Behavior* 9 (March):65–71.

Weinberg, Nancy. 1988. "Another Perspective: Attitudes of Persons with Disabilities." Pp. 141–53 in *Attitudes Toward Persons with Disabilities,* edited by H. Yuker. New York: Springer.

Werner, David. 1990. "Visit to Angola, Where Civilians are Disabled as a Strategy of Low Intensity Conflict (LIC)." *Disability Studies Quarterly* 10 (Spring):36–39.

Wilcox, Sherman. 1984. " 'Stuck' in School: A Study of Semantics and Culture in a Deaf Education Class." *Sign Language Studies* 43 (Summer):141–64.

Wildavsky, Aaron. 1989. "The Secret of Safety Lies in Danger." *Society* 27 (November/December):4–5.

Will, George F. 1986. "Immersed in a Sea of Silence." *Newsweek* (October 27):112.

Wilson, Graham K. 1985. *The Politics of Safety and Health: Occupational Safety and Health in the United States and Britain.* Oxford: Clarendon.

Wilson, William J. 1987. *The Truly Disadvantaged: The Inner City, the Underclass, and Public Policy.* Chicago: University of Chicago Press.

Withers, Rob and John Lee. 1988. "Power in Disguise." Pp. 175–89 in *The Politics of Special Educational Needs,* edited by L. Barton. London: Falmer Press.

Witt, Joseph C., C. Dean Miller, Robert M. McIntyre, and Dave Smith. 1984. "Effects of Variables on Parental Perceptions of Staffings." *Exceptional Children* 51 (September):27–32.

Wolfensberger, Wolf. 1972. *The Principle of Normalization in Human Services.* Toronto: National Institute on Mental Retardation.

Wolfensberger, Wolf. 1975. *The Origin and Nature of our Institutional Models.* Syracuse, NY: Human Policy Press.

Wolfensberger, Wolf. 1980. "A Call to Wake Up to the Beginning of a New Wave of 'Euthanasia' of Severely Impaired People." *Education and Training of the Mentally Retarded* 15 (October):171–73.

Wolfensberger, Wolf. 1981. "The Extermination of Handicapped People in World War II Germany." *Mental Retardation* 19 (February):1–7.

Wolfensberger, Wolf. 1984. "Holocaust II?" *Journal of Learning Disabilities* 17 (August/September):439–40.

Wood, Philip H.N. 1980. "The Language of Disablement: A Glossary Relating to Disease and Its Consequences." *International Journal of Rehabilitation Medicine* 2 (2):86–92.

Worrall, John D. and Richard J. Butler. 1986. "Some Lessons from the Workers' Compensation Program." Pp. 95–123 in *Disability and the Labor Market: Economic Problems, Policies, and Programs,* edited by M. Berkowitz and M. Hill. Ithaca, NY: ILR Press.

Wright, Beatrice A. 1960. *Physical Disability — A Psychological Approach.* New York: Harper and Row.

Wright, Beatrice A. 1988. "Attitudes and the Fundamental Negative Bias: Conditions and Corrections." Pp. 3–21 in *Attitudes Toward Persons with Disabilities,* edited by H. Yuker. New York: Springer.

Yelin, Edward. 1989. "Disabled Concern: The Social Context of the Work-disability Problem." *The Milbank Quarterly* 67 (Supplement 2, Part 1):114–65.

Ysseldyke, James E. and Bob Algozinne. 1990. *Introduction to Special Education.* 2nd ed. Boston: Houghton Mifflin.

Yuker, Harold, E. 1988. "The Effects of Contact on Attitudes Toward Disabled Persons: Some Empirical Generalizations." Pp. 262–74 in *Attitudes Toward Persons with Disabilities,* edited by H. Yuker. New York: Springer.

Zola, Irving Kenneth. 1979. "Helping One Another: A Speculative History of the Self-Help Movement." *Archives of Physical Medicine and Rehabilitation* 60 (October):452–56.

Zola, Irving Kenneth. 1982. *Missing Pieces: A Chronicle of Living with a Disability.* Philadelphia: Temple University Press.

Zola, Irving Kenneth, 1983. "Developing New Self-Images and Interdependence." Pp. 49–59 in *Independent Living for Physically Disabled People: Developing, Implementing, and Evaluating Self-Help Rehabilitation Programs,* N. Crewe, I. Zola and Associates. San Francisco: Jossey-Bass.

Zola, Irving Kenneth. 1985. "Depictions of Disability — Metaphor, Message, and Medium in the Media: A Research and Political Agenda." *The Social Science Journal* 22 (October):5–17.

Zola, Irving Kenneth. 1987. "The Portrayal of Disability in the Crime Mystery Genre." *Social Policy* 17 (Spring):34–39.

Zola, Irving Kenneth. 1989. "Toward the Necessary Universalizing of a Disability Policy." *The Milbank Quarterly* 67 (Supplement 2, Part 2):401–28.

Zola, Irving Kenneth. forthcoming. "The Naming Question: Reflections on the

Language of Disability." In *Report of the American Association for the Advancement of Science Workshop on the Demography of Scientists and Engineers with Disabilities*. Washington, D.C.: American Association for the Advancement of Science.

Zola, Irving Kenneth and Corrine Kirchner (eds.). 1990. "Disability Demographics," Issue theme. *Disability Studies Quarterly* 10 (Summer).

AUTHOR INDEX

A

Ablon, Joan, 234, 235, 257
Ainlay, Stephen C., 36, 136, 137, 138, 257, 260
Albrecht, Gary L., 6, 21, 28, 37, 132, 152, 213, 219, 222, 257, 266, 270, 271
Algozzine, Bob, 28, 50, 52, 210, 257, 274
Algozzine, Kate M., 210, 257
Altman, Barbara M., 82, 106, 109, 110, 257, 262
Amler, R., 262, 263, 265, 271
Anspach, Renee R., 229, 230, 231, 257
Asch, Adrienne, 7, 15, 18, 60, 63, 125, 141, 244, 257, 258, 262, 263, 268, 269, 273
Auster, Albert, 87, 269

B

Baker, Charlotte, 85, 258, 268
Baker, S., 68, 69, 70, 76, 258
Barnartt, Sharon N., 35, 43, 258
Barnes, William, 218, 264
Barol, Bill, 94, 258
Barton, Len, 12, 95, 96, 202, 258, 259, 263, 273
Batavia, Andrew L., 188, 199, 208, 210, 211, 261
Battison, Robbin, 85, 258, 268
Becker, Gaylene, 36, 135, 257, 258, 260
Bell, Alexander Graham, 33, 34, 135, 258
Berk, Marc L., 57, 258
Berkowitz, Edward O., 12, 39, 40, 41, 189, 195, 197, 200, 201, 202, 204, 210, 211, 212, 213, 214, 215, 222, 258, 271
Berkowitz, M., 261, 265, 274
Best, Joel, 68, 258
Biklen, Douglas, 6, 48, 80, 83, 84, 87, 88, 91, 94, 111, 112, 134, 152, 153, 167, 168, 175, 177, 179, 180, 186, 194, 198, 204, 207, 208, 209, 210, 214, 216, 217, 236, 258, 259, 271
Bines, Hazel, 156, 259

Black, Donald, 161, 178, 259
Blatt, Burton, 181, 259
Blythman, Marion, 32, 259
Bogdan, Robert, 6, 37, 52, 80, 83, 84, 87, 88, 93, 94, 111, 112, 113, 114, 134, 153, 164, 166, 167, 186, 194, 223, 258, 259, 271
Booth, Tony, 35, 259
Bowe, Frank G., 11, 26, 32, 55, 57, 60, 61, 62, 75, 153, 168, 199, 200, 201, 204, 211, 212, 222, 224, 229, 243, 245, 247, 259, 260
Brodsky, Carroll M., 73, 74, 260
Bruininks, Robert H., 181, 260
Bruner, Jerome, 23, 260
Bryan, Willie V., 83, 264
Buckholdt, David R., 133, 156, 160, 164, 169, 170, 173, 174, 178, 220, 260, 264
Budnick, Lawrence D., 68, 77, 260
Burkhauser, Richard V., 196, 197, 260
Butler, Elizabeth, 76, 265
Butler, Richard R., ii, 57, 72, 234, 265, 274
Byrne, John, 66, 260

C

Cartwright, Frederick F., 7, 8, 260
Cassens, B., 260
Cavalier, Al, 158, 206, 260
Chambers, J., 266
Chambliss, William J., 27, 260
Chanowitz, Benzion, 110, 148, 266
Chirikos, Thomas N., 11, 201, 260
Clerc, Laurent, 33
Cockerham, William C., 50, 260
Cole, Stephen, 221, 260
Coleman, Lerita M., 36, 222, 257, 260
Coles, Gerald, 9, 12, 25, 32, 51, 53, 54, 55, 156, 158, 173, 253, 260
Collignon, Frederick C., 201, 260

Conrad, Peter, 7, 22, 26, 27, 49, 50, 51, 52, 106, 107, 108, 127, 129, 228, 261, 270
Corbin, J., 267
Cox, Alan, 218, 264
Crewe, Nancy M., 248, 261, 274
Crouch, Barry A., 191, 261
Crocker, A., 270
Crutcher, D., 270
Cullen, Francis T., 108, 130, 266

D

Darling, Jon, 144, 145, 146, 261
Darling Rosalyn Benjamin, 144, 145, 146, 261
Davis, Fred, 109, 112, 113, 261
Davis, Townsend, 43, 46, 261
deGrandpre, Bernard, 164, 166, 167, 259
De Jong, Gerben, 29, 39, 153, 155, 162, 178, 188, 198, 199, 208, 210, 211, 212, 244, 261
Denzin, Norman K., 36, 266
Deshen, Shlomo, 136, 261
Des Jarlais, Don C., 77, 263
Diamond, Timothy, 165, 166, 167, 174, 182, 185, 261
Dohrenwend, Bruce P., 130, 136, 266, 267
Doris, John, 8, 44, 185, 193, 206, 222, 253, 270
Driedger, Diane, 243, 262
Dull, H., 262, 263, 265, 271
Duncan, Barbara, 217, 219, 262
Duster, Troy, 36, 269

E

Eddy, Elizabeth M., 169, 270
Edgerton, Robert B., 58, 172, 262
Ehrlich, Anne H., 71, 262
Ehrlich, Paul R., 71, 262
Elliott, Gregory C., 106, 109, 110, 262
Emerson, Joan P., 118, 144, 262
English, Richard A., 152, 264
Erlanger, Howard S., 204, 206, 212, 214, 215, 262
Evans, A. Donald, 128, 134, 173, 220, 262

F

Fagerhaugh, Shizuko, 138, 262, 267
Flak, William W., 70, 134, 262, 271
Farer, Laurence S., 73, 77, 262

Farina, Amerigo, 36, 106, 265
Featherstone, Helen, 143, 144, 145, 262
Ferguson, Dianne L., 6, 134, 153, 167, 186, 198, 217, 258, 259
Ferguson, Philip M., 41, 42, 147, 177, 202, 204, 207, 214, 216, 224, 225, 226, 259, 262
Ferrari, M., 268
Fichten, Catherine S., 105, 147, 262
Fine, Michelle, 7, 15, 18, 60, 63, 125, 141, 257, 268, 269, 273
Fisher, Bernice, 113, 236, 262
Fletcher, Joseph, 217, 263
Ford, A., 258
Foster, Glen G., 82, 263
Foster, Susan Bannerman, 168, 172, 179, 263
Frank, Gelya, 137, 159, 163, 263
Freeman, Carla M., 106, 108, 265
Freidman, Eliot, 36, 263, 269
French, Rita, 36, 106, 265
Freud, 51
Furth, Hans G., 32, 263

G

Gallagher, Hugh Gregory, 232, 263
Galler, Roberta, 113, 236, 262
Gannon, Jack R., 238, 240, 241, 243, 263
Gans, Herbert J., 219, 263
Gartner, Alan, 80, 167, 260, 263, 264, 265, 266, 273
Glaser, Barney G., 262, 271
Glaser, D., 139, 260
Glaser, P., 267
Glassner, Barry, 148, 263
Gliedman, John, 13, 30, 31, 39, 40, 41, 42, 56, 57, 58, 153, 155, 162, 167, 172, 177, 178, 263
Gluckman, Max, 10, 263
Goddard, Henry, H., 96, 263
Goffman, Erving, 36, 105, 106, 107, 117, 263
Golden, Janet, 8, 270
Goldin, Carol S., 136, 238, 263
Goldstein, Paul J., 77, 263
Goode, David A., 16, 31, 99, 100, 103, 104, 108, 114, 115, 121, 125, 158, 165, 176, 177, 178, 187, 263, 264
Graham, K., 273
Gregory, Ian, 49, 269

Groce, Nora Ellen, 10, 17, 26, 66, 75, 122, 190, 191, 205, 264, 270
Gross, Richard H., 218, 264
Gubrium, Jaber F., 133, 156, 160, 164, 169, 170, 173, 174, 178, 220, 260, 264

H

Haan, Mary N., 75, 265
Hahn, Harlan, 29, 30, 35, 37, 38, 39, 42, 43, 57, 58, 84, 148, 189, 191, 192, 193, 212, 221, 223, 229, 230, 264
Hall, M., 265
Hanks, Michael, 37, 264
Harris, George A., 144, 264
Harris, Louis, 39, 59, 60, 61, 139, 140, 150, 216, 267
Harris, Marvin, 43, 66, 122, 152, 191, 193, 254, 264
Hartman, W., 266
Hasenfeld, Yeheskel, 152, 264
Hastorf, Albert H., 36, 106, 265
Hauber, Florence A., 181, 260
Haynes, Sondra, 164, 166, 167, 259
Henderson, George, 83, 264
Hentoff, Nat, 216, 217, 218, 264
Herring, Christina L., 77, 264
Hertweck, Alma, 58, 157, 158, 163, 171, 172, 173, 267
Hibbard, Michael, 147, 177, 202, 204, 207, 214, 224, 225, 226, 262
Higgins, Paul C., ii, iii, iv, 11, 13, 32, 33, 34, 36, 56, 116, 117, 118, 119, 121, 127, 134, 135, 136, 141, 156, 169, 173, 175, 178, 186, 195, 207, 214, 220, 225, 234, 236, 237, 239, 264, 265
Hill, M., 261, 274
Hirvonen, Petri, 196, 197, 260
Hobbs, N., 269
Hollinger, Chloe S., 82, 265
Horne, Marcia D., 91, 265
Hughes, Dana, 76, 265
Humphries, Tom, 124, 127, 132, 135, 136, 234, 238, 239, 240, 241, 242, 269
Hunt, Dana, 77, 263

J

Jacobi, Jan E., 229, 245, 247, 260
Jacobs, Leo M., 238, 265
Joe, Tom, 80, 167, 260, 263, 264, 265, 266, 267, 273
Johnson, John M., ii
Johnson, Kay, 76, 265
Johnson, Mary, 265, 243
Johnson, William JG., 196, 222, 265
Jones, Edward E., 36, 106, 265
Jones, Lesley, 128, 132, 265
Jones, Reginald L., 9, 82, 265

K

Kaiser, Susan B., 106, 108, 265
Kaplan, Fred, 181, 259
Kaplan, George A., 75, 265
Karpf, Ronald S., 68, 69, 70, 76, 258
Katzman, Robert A., 189, 265
Katzmann, 198, 200
Kent, Deborah, 80, 87, 265
Kielhofner, Gary, 159, 160, 266
Kirchner, Corrine, 55, 56, 57, 275
Kiser, Bill, 141, 266
Kitsuse, John I., 36, 269
Kleinfield, Sonny, 248, 266
Knoll, James, 168, 186, 208, 214, 271, 272
Krause, Elliott A., 72, 75, 266
Kriegel, Leonard, 87, 88, 89, 266
Kronick, Jane C., 12, 67, 221, 266
Kudla, Mary J., 181, 260
Kugelmass, Judy W., 23, 172, 173, 266
Kyle, Jim, 9, 128, 132, 265

L

Lambrinos, James, 222, 265
Lane, Harlan, 33, 34, 51, 52, 53, 96, 135, 159, 205, 220, 238, 239, 266
Langer, Ellen J., 110, 148, 266
La Plante, Mitchell P., 29, 266
Lazerson, Marvin, 12, 185, 193, 206, 222, 266
Lee, John, 11, 273
Lehrer, Steven, 8, 266
Leinen, James, 147, 177, 202, 204, 207, 214, 224, 225, 226, 262
Lejeune, Robert, 221, 260

Lenihan, John, 95, 266
Lennon, Mary Clare, 136, 266
Levine, Erwin L., 189, 266
Levy, Judith A., 21, 28, 37, 152, 213, 257
Lifchez, Raymond, 198, 261
Lindesmith, Alfred R., 36, 266
Link, Bruce G., 108, 130, 136, 266
Lipsky, Michael, 169, 172, 180, 184, 267
Locker, David, 29, 136, 137, 138, 267
Lofland, Lyn H., 191, 267
Longmore, Paul K., 30, 82, 83, 84, 85, 987, 88, 89, 90, 91, 92, 267
Lutfiyya, Zana, 272
Luther, 26
Lynas, Wendy, 34, 119, 159, 267

M

MacMillan, Donald L., 27, 51, 267
Maines, David, 234, 267
Mairs, Nancy, 84, 267
Makas, Elaine, 105, 267
Marbach, Joseph J., 136, 266
Markus, Hazel, 36, 106, 265
Martinez, Cecilia, 66, 260
McCaffrey, David P., 66, 74, 267
McCormick, James, 7, 271
McIntyre, Robert M., 169, 273
McMurray, Georgia L., 12, 158, 188, 267
Mehan, Hugh, 58, 157, 158, 163, 171, 172, 173, 267
Meihls, Lee, 58, 157, 158, 163, 171, 172, 173, 267
Mercer, Jane R., 37, 58, 59, 267
Merton, Robert K., 105, 267
Mest, JGrae M., 134, 147, 237, 267
Meucci, Sandra, 96, 180, 181, 182, 183, 267
Meyerson, Lee, 12, 158, 267, 268
Mezey, Susan Gluck, 12, 189, 197, 268
Miller, C. Dean, 169, 273
Miller, Dale T., 36, 106, 265
Mills, C. Wright, 229, 243, 268
Minkler, Meredith, 75, 265
Minow, Martha, 8, 13, 30, 32, 41, 42, 45, 103, 142, 149, 190, 202, 203, 204, 206, 212, 224, 229, 254, 268
Morsink, Catherine V., 210, 257
Moss, Kathryn, 91, 216, 268
Mudrick, Nancy R., 214, 268

N

Nash, Jeffrey, ii, 265
Neisser, 32
Newman, Joseph, 195, 268
Noble, John H., Jr., 198, 268

O

Obermann, C., 26, 72, 213, 268
Oliver, Michael, 20, 21, 25, 37, 86, 189, 268
O'Neill, Brian, 68, 69, 70, 76, 258

P

Padden, Carol, 32, 124, 127, 132, 135, 136, 234, 238, 239, 240, 241, 242, 268, 269
Percy, Stephen L., 189, 269
Petrunik, Michael, 106, 107, 116, 117, 118, 137, 269
Pfeiffer, David, 55, 269
Phillips, Marily J., 27, 85, 120, 231, 232, 233, 269
Pollay, Michael, 218, 264
Ponse, Barbara, 106, 269
Poplin, Dennis E., 37, 264
Prottas, Jeffrey Manditch, 172, 269
Pueschel, S., 270

Q

Quart, Leonard, 87, 269

R

Racino, Julie A., 272
Rains, Prudence M., 36, 269
Raspberry, William, 83, 92, 269
Reese, James H., 82, 263
Reiman, Jeffrey, 70, 71, 72, 73, 74, 76, 269
Reynolds, Larry T., 10, 32, 252, 271
Rivera, Geraldo, 181, 269
Robertson, Leon S., 69, 70, 269
Robinson, James C., 74, 269
Rosen, Ephraim, 49, 269
Rosenbaum, Sara, 76, 265
Rosenberg, Charles E., 7, 8, 269, 270
Roth, Julium A., 169, 270
Roth, William, 13, 30, 31, 39, 40, 41, 42, 56,

57, 58, 82, 129, 130, 131, 153, 155, 158,
162, 163, 167, 172, 177, 178, 204, 206, 212,
214, 215, 219, 229, 262, 263, 270
Rothman, David J., 91, 96, 175, 191, 192, 205,
270
Rothman, Sheila M., 91, 175, 270
Ruffini, J., 257
Ruffner, Robert H., 89, 92, 270
Ryan, William, 14, 31, 180, 232, 270
Rynders, John E., 47, 270

S

Safilios-Rothschild, Constantina, 38, 56, 60,
62, 66, 75, 173, 270
Sagatun, Inger J., 105, 270
Sarason, Seymour B., 8, 44, 185, 193, 206, 222,
253, 270
Schaff, Sandra, 147, 177, 202, 204, 207, 214, 224,
225, 226, 262
Scheer, Jessica, 10, 26, 122, 190, 191, 205, 270
Scheerenberger, R.C., 27, 49, 50, 270
Schein, Jerome D., 32, 270
Schieffelbein, Carl W., 73, 77, 262
Schneider, Joseph W., 7, 8, 22, 26, 27, 49, 50,
51, 52, 106, 108, 127, 129, 131, 132, 228,
261, 270
Scotch, Richard K., 38, 40, 77, 84, 189, 195, 199,
200, 228, 229, 230, 243, 244, 245, 246, 247,
248, 271
Scott, Deborah R., 106, 109, 110, 262
Scott, Robert A., 13, 36, 95, 106, 127, 130, 132,
133, 169, 173, 220, 265, 271
Searl, Stanford J., Jr., 134, 153, 167, 186, 258,
259
Seelman, Katherine, 35, 43, 258
Shapiro, Arthur, 87, 88, 259
Shapiro, Michael J., 271
Shearing, Clifford D., 106, 107, 116, 117, 118,
137, 269
Shibutani, T., 262
Shor, Glenn M., 74, 269
Shorter, Edward, 192, 271
Shrout, Patrick E., 130, 266
Simons, Janet, 76, 265
Sivard, Ruth Leger, 71, 72, 75, 271
Skrabanek, Petr, 7, 271
Smith, Gordon S., 70, 271
Smith, Dave, 169, 273

Smith, JDavid, 96, 271
Sowell, Thomas, 10, 271
Spelkoman, David, 87, 88, 259
Stark, Rodney, 66, 271
Stewart, Robert L., vii, 7, 10, 32, 101, 252, 271
Stokoe, William C., 258
Stone, Deborah A., 12, 21, 30, 189, 196, 197,
213, 215, 221, 271
Strauss, Anselm L., 36, 139, 262, 266, 268, 271
Struening, Elmer, 130, 266
Stubbins, Joseph, 153, 162, 271
Suczek, B., 267
Sussman, M., 263, 268
Sweidel, Gabriele, 117, 120, 271
Syme, S. Leonard, 75, 265

T

Tanenbaum, Sandra, 158, 189, 213, 271
Tatyrek, Ruth, 218, 264
Taylor, Steven J., 37, 52, 111, 113, 114, 134, 153,
164, 166, 167, 168, 186, 208, 214, 258, 259,
271, 272
Temkin, Oswei, 26, 272
Thomas, Elizabeth, 10, 272
Tingey, C., 270
Tomlinson, Sally, 196, 202, 214, 258, 263, 272

V

Van Riper, Charles, 273
Viscusi, W. Kip, 66, 68, 79, 273
Vosburgh, Miriam G., 12, 67, 221, 266
Vosburgh, William W., 12, 67, 221, 266

W

Walker, Lisa J., 51, 55, 62, 156, 173, 177, 187,
202, 207, 214, 273
Walker, Lou Ann, 143, 273
Warren, Carol A.B., 222, 269, 273
Weinberg, Joanna K., 202, 273
Weinberg, Martin S., 234, 273
Weinberg, Nancy, 140, 141, 142, 148, 149, 273
Werner, David, 66, 71, 273
Wexler, Elizabeth M., 189, 266
Wiener, C., 267
Wilcox, Sherman, 135, 273
Wildavsky, Aaron, 66, 273

Will, George F., 78, 273
William, J., 273
Wilson, 67, 74, 216
Wingate, Stacy B., 106, 108, 265
Winkleby, Marilyn, 75, 265
Wiseman, Laurence D., 229, 245, 247, 260
Withers, Rob, 11, 273
Witt, Joseph C., 169, 273
Wolfensberger, Wolf, 26, 80, 96, 152, 180, 181,
    182, 183, 192, 205, 206, 273, 274
Wood, Peter, 128, 132, 265
Wood, Philip H.N., 21, 274
Woods, Diane E., 9, 217, 219, 262
Worrall, John D., 72, 274
Wright, Beatrice A., 38, 130, 147, 148, 274

Y

Yelin, Edward, 196, 197, 210, 213, 214, 274
Yesseldyke, James E., 28, 50, 52, 82, 263,
    274
Yuker, Harold E., 121, 262, 265, 266, 271, 273,
    274

Z

Ziegler, Herbert L., 106, 109, 110, 262
Zola, Irving Kenneth, 11, 20, 46, 48, 55, 56,
    57, 59, 60, 62, 82, 83, 85, 86, 87, 90, 159,
    176, 190, 204, 209, 217, 219, 224, 226, 230,
    232, 244, 248, 252, 254, 261, 274, 275

SUBJECT INDEX

A

Americans with Disabilities Act of 1990, 188
   civil rights protections in, 199
   exemptions in, 203–204
   use of reasonable accommodations
      standard, 197
Alcohol
   disability due excessive use of, 77–78
   number alcoholics in America, 77
   responses to alcoholism, 22
American Coalition of Citizens with
     Disabilities
   development of, 246
   disbanding of, 247
   protests organized by, 246–247
   work of, 246–247
American Sign Language
   problems use in classrooms, 135
   use of, 135
Americans with Disabilities Act, demonstra-
     tion for, 243, 247
Asbestos fibers, lung disease disability due
     to, 73

C

Categorizing disability, 49–55
   differentiation of human variation, 49–52
      development of, 49–50
      of hearing impairment, 51
      of mental retardation, 49, 50, 51
      of psychiatry, 50, 51
   discovery characteristics of, 51–52
   learning disability (see Learning
      disability)
   paternalism of nondisabled, 52
   terms describing youth, 51–52
Challenging disability, 235–249

collective countering, 237–242
   deaf community, 238–242 (see also
      Deaf people)
   development in-group ideology, 238
   development minority group
      perspective, 238
   methods of, 237–238
   visually impaired, example, 238
   disability rights movement (see Disability
      rights movement)
   individual challenging, 235, 236–237
      of negative attitudes, 236
      of offensive behaviors, 236, 237
Charity rationale, 194–195
   effects of on disabled people, 194–195
   government programs and, 195
Communicative disabilities/conversational
     disruptions, 117–120
   basis of conversation, 117
   by persons who stutter, 117
   navigating encounters, 116
   transactional disruptions, 119–120
   with deaf persons, 118–119
Conceptualizing disability, 18, 25–35
   economic/work-limitation, 25, 29–30
   individualizing disability, 25–26
      economic/work-limitation, 25, 29–30
      medical-clinical conception, 25, 27–29
      traditional, 25–26, 26–27
   medical-clinical, 25, 27–29 (see also
      Medical-clinical conception)
   traditional conceptions, 25, 26–27
Counting disability, 55–63
   consequences of, 56
   dependence of definition of disability,
      56–57
   effects of, 62
   future of, 62
   health-conditions approach to, 57, 59

Counting disability (*continued*)
  ICD survey of disabled Americans (*see*
    International Center for the
    Disabled survey)
  in less developed countries, 56, 66
  making disability by (*see* Making
    disability)
  variations in, 55–56
  work-disability approach to, 57
    criticisms of, 57–58, 58–59
Deaf people (*see also* Hearing impairment)
  alternative way of being, 237–238
  as a deficit, 32
    example, 32–35
  as newscasters, 46
  attempts to "fix" deaf people, 33
  attempts to normalize, 231
  burden of mainstreaming on, 239
  collective challenging by, 238–242
  deaf community, 238–242
  deaf poetry, 241
  deafness at the center, 239–240
  development signed language, 239
  education of, 34–35
  individualizing deafness
    of Bell, 33–34
    of Clerc, 33
    of today, 34
  obsession with sounds, 240–241
    case illustration, 241
  problems identifying with other
    disabilities, 241–242
  signing as necessary for well being, 240
    case illustration, 240
  student protest at Gallaudet University,
    243
  tension between students and education
    of officials, 135
  terms describing characteristics of, 52
  traditional attitude toward, 32
  use of terms "deaf and dumb," 32
  use of term Deaf, 122
Depicting disability, 80–98
  conclusions, 97
  displaying disability (*see* Displaying
    disability)
  endnotes, 97–98
  methods of, 19, 80–81
  naming disability (*see* Naming disability)

Diagnosis, definition, 28
Disability rights movement, 242–249
  American Coalition of Citizens with
    Disabilities, 246–247
  association with civil rights groups, 248
  association with coalitions with senior
    citizens, 248
  description of, 243
  development of, 243–249
  drug in social conflict of 1960's, 244–245
  for the Americans with Disabilities Act,
    243
  future of, 247, 248–249
  government policies and actions, 245–246
  independent living centers established
    by, 247–248
  making public issues of personal troubles,
    245
  organizations involved, 242–243
  President's Committee on the Employment
    of the Handicapped, 245, 246
  protest at Gallaudet University, 243
  Rehabilitation Act of 1973, 245, 246
Disabled people
  care in small-scale societies, 191
  concept of, 47
  demographics of, 62–63
  handling of in preindustrial societies,
    190–191
  role of in premodern society, 191
  similarities disabled and nondisabled,
    63
  use of term, 20–21
Disabled People's International, development
  of, 243–244
Disabled veterans
  first national pension law for, 213
  most worthy for disability dollars, 213
Disability
  absorbs costs of societal change, 221
  as a basic means for structuring social
    life, 223
  as a social phenomenon, 25
  as big business, 220
  as socially constructed, 8
  can be used to control people and protect
    social arrangements, 221–222
  categorizing (*see* Categorizing disability)
  conception of, 18

Disability (*continued*)
  conceptualizing (*see* Conceptualizing disability)
  consequences of individualizing, 30–35
    blaming the victims, 31
    conserving present arrangements, 31–32
    example, 32–35
    lessening those disabled, 31
    placing burden on the disabled, 30
    segregation disabled people, 30–31
  consequence of normal functioning of society, 12
  definition, 15, 28
  demography of, 60–63
  depicting, 19 (*see also* Depicting disability)
  early beliefs regarding, 26–27
  enabling nondisabled people to define and elevate existential status, 220
  enabling others to ennoble themselves, 220
  experiencing of (*see* Experiencing disability)
  framing of (*see* Framing disability)
  hearing impairments, 9
  individualizing, 25–26
  interacting and identifying (*see* Interacting and identifying disability)
  learning (*see* Learning disability)
  making (*see* Making disability)
  managing of (*see* Managing disability)
  manufacture of (*see* Manufacturing disability)
  may be convenient scapegoats for societal problems, 222
  paternalistic characterizations of, 52–53
  percent of in developing world, 17
  policing of (*see* Policy(ing) disability)
  protects our political economy, 221
  provides amusement and entertainment, 222–223
  provides an escape from onerous obligations, 221
  remaking (*see* Remaking disability)
  servicing of (*see* Servicing disability)
  social deviance of, 36–38
  subsidizes many people, 222
  use of term, 29
  variation as creation of, 8

Disabled worker, use of term, 30
Disabling service, 175–183
  flaws in service, 175–176
  making death by, 180–183
    definition of, 181
    use of drugs, 181–182
    ways of, 181, 182–183
  making disabled people foreign, 176–178
    case illustration, 176–177
    methods of, 176
    "special" education illustration, 177–178
  making disabled people passive, 178–180
    domination of specialized professionals, 178–179
    role of professionals, 178
  preserving oppressive arrangements, 180
Disease, as socially constructed, 8
Displaying disability, 93–97
  freak shows, 93–94
  fundraising, 94
  methods of, 93
  scholarly works, 95–96
  summary, 96–97
  telethons, 94
  tours of facilities, 95
Down syndrome, attitudes of the past, 47
Drug addiction, disabilities due to, 77, 78

E

Economic/work-limitations, view of disability, 29–30
Education of All Handicapped Children Act of 1975 (*see also* Individuals with Disabilities Education Act)
  exceptional policies of, 209–210
  segregation of disabled students, 206–207
  unimplemented legislation, 202
Education of disabled persons (*see* Special education)
Emotionally disabled, due problems at work, 73–74
Epilepsy
  as socially constructed, 8
  disabling lessons by parents, 131–132
Experiencing disability, 123–150
  by people with or without disability, 124
  case illustration, 123–124

Experiencing disability (*continued*)
 conclusion, 149–150
 disability as an individual phenomenon,
   139–140
  employment difficulties, 140
  factors in difficulties of, 139
  solving barriers faced, 139–140
 disabled people's experiencing disability,
   126–142
  development experiential orientations,
    126–127
  experiential orientations, 140–142
  learning to be disabled, 127–136
  realms of disability experience, 136–140
  effective communication, case
    illustration, 16–17, 125
 endnotes, 150
 experiential orientations, 140–142
  complexity of, examples, 140
  disability complexly of disabled
    persons, 142
  experiencing disabilities and
    themselves, 140–142
 families' experiencing disability, 143–147
 families with disabled children, 143–147
  changes in parents, 145–146
  effect on siblings, 145
  effect position in family, 143
  emotions parents face, 144–145
  lack preparation for disabled children,
    143–144
  parents creation of satisfying
    experiences, 147
  variations of, 143
 first lesson in, 127–130
 impersonal others' experiencing disability,
   147–149
  anxieties of, 148
  fundamental negative bias and,
    147–148
  reactions to unfamiliarity with
    disabilities, 147–148
 learning to be disabled, 127–136
  application stereotypes about disability,
    127
  dealing disabled with organization
    designed to serve, 127
  encounters people with disabilities
    have with nondisabled, 127

  first lesson in, 127–130
  interaction with similarly disabled,
    127
  teaching disability lessons, 130–136
 making of, 19
 primary lesson, 129–130
 realization of disability, 128–129
 realms of disability experience, 136–140
  disability is the person, 137
  disruption of everyday order, 136–137
  focus on features of their disabilities,
    136
  managing the disability, 137–139
  redesigning lifestyles to manage.
    138–139
  uncertainly as central feature, 137
 simplification of, 125–126
 teaching disability lessons, 130–136
  disabled people differentiating
    themselves from other disabled
    people, 134–135
  encounters with nondisabled people
    as instructive, 132
  initial negative evaluation due
    sterotypes, 130
  interacts disabled people with one
    another, 135–136
  learning from disabled people, 134
  learning through encounters with
    service agencies, 132–133
  mainstreaming in schools, 133–134
  parents as teachers, 131
  visually impaired people, 133
 use of term Deaf, 123–124 (*see also* Deaf
    people)
 variation of, 125, 127–128
Eyetyper, use of, 206

F

Feebles (*see also* Weaklings)
 attitudes society toward, 3–4
 definition, 3
 past attitudes society toward, 3
 use of term, 3
Framing disability, 18, 22–64
 as means for managing ourselves. 24
 as practical, 23–24
  examples, 22–23, 23–24

Framing disability (*continued*)
   categorizing disability, 24–25, 49–55
   conceptualizing disability (*see*
      Conceptualizing disability)
   conclusions, 63–64
   counting disability, 25, 55–63
   creation disability, 63
   examples of, 22–23
   of human variation, 23
      examples, 22–23
   problem drinking, 22
Functional limitations, use of term, 28, 29

H

Handicap
   definition, 28
   use of term, 21, 29
Hearing impairment (*see also* Deaf
      people)
   changes in person with, 9
   due on the job noises, 73
   due use of Walkman radios, 78
   due work problems, 73
   encounters with deaf people, 118–119
   obsession with noises, 13
   special services open to, 51
Hyperkinesis, learning disabilities and, 51

I

Identifying disability (*see* Interacting and
      identifying disability)
Illness, as socially constructed, 8
Impaired vision, preparation for seeing less
      well, 138
Impairment
   definition, 28
   use of term, 21
Individualizing disability, 155, 156–161, 204,
      205–206, 223–224
   compensation given, 206
   difficulties of, 156
   "fixing" problems within disabled people,
      158–159
   focus on flaws of person, 205–206
   identifying problems of disabled people,
      156–158

evaluation procedures, 157–158
   procedures for educationally
      handicapped, 156–157
   recognition wider social arrangements
      for, 158
   servicing agencies definition of success,
      159
      case illustration, 159
   servicing those with disabilities, 206
   standard used by some nondisabled
      servicers, 160–161
Individuals with Disabilities Education Act,
      47–48, 177, 188
Industrialization and disabled persons,
      189–190, 190–193
   care of disabled in preindustrial societies,
      190–192
   effects industrialization on disabled
      people, 192–193
   handling of disabled people in
      preindustrial societies, 190–191
   progress made through industrialization,
      190–191
Injuries and disability, 68–71
   due to vehicle crashes, 69–70
   incidence rate of, 68
   methods of preventing, 70
   permanent impairment statistics, 68
   reduction of possible, 69
   work related injuries, 70–71
Interacting and identifying disability (*see*
      Interacting and identifying disability)
   conclusion, 120–122
   creating identities for one another,
      103–105
      case illustration, 103–104
   interactional identities, 101–105
      case illustration, 99–100, 102, 103
   navigating encounters, 116–120 (*see also*
      Navigating encounters)
   of disabled and nondisabled people, 19
   spoiled identities, 105–116 (*see also*
      Spoiled identities)
International Center for the Disabled survey
      (ICD)
   definition disabled used, 59–60
   demography of disability from, 60–63
   future of, 62
   purpose of, 59

L

Learning disability
  beginning use of term, 9
  categorization helpful or harmful, 55
  categorizing, an example, 53–55
  changes since World War II, 54
  creation of, 54
  definition, 53
  hyperkinesis and, 51
  minimal neurological dysfunction and,
    53–54, 54–55
  number children identified as, 9, 55
Lung disease causing work disability, 73

M

Making disability, 3–21
  and understanding ourselves, 11–12, 13
  as more or less useful to us, 10–11
  challenge of, 14–17
    example, 16–17
    limitations created and limitations
      imposed, 15–16
    obstacles due barriers imposed
      externally, 15
  effect on our lives, 11
  endnotes, 21
  examples of, 9
  importance of bodies, 7–8
    variation in, 8
  in mosaic of humanity, 13–14, 18
  remaking (*see* Remaking disability)
  terms used, 20–21
  understanding of, 6
  ways of, 6–7
Managing disability, 20, 227–249
  challenging disability, 228, 235–249
  collective challenging, 228–229 (*see also*
    Challenging disability)
  collectively living with the disability,
    233–235
  conclusion, 249
  disabled people and challenges to
    making of, 228
  evaluations and creation of disability,
    230
  family and advocates confront disability,
    230

  living collectively with their disability, 231
  living with disability, 231–235
  normalizing, 231–233
  reactions of disabled people to making of
    disability, 227
  responses to making of disability, 228
  use of disability groups
    disability rights movement, 242–243
    example, 234–235
  ways of, 20, 227–228
Manufacturing disability, 67–79
  accidents which may disable, 67
  conclusion, 79
  methods of, 65
  prevention of, 79
  production characteristics of disability,
    18–19
  role of "manufacturing" in, 66–67
  sources of creating disability, 67–79
    injuries, 67, 68–71
    poverty, 67, 75–76
    self-disabling practices, 67, 76–79
    war, 67, 71–72
    work, 67, 72–74
  sources where disability is created, 67
  use of term, 66, 67
Medical-clinical conception
  attitudes toward, 27
  definitions concepts, 28
    different uses of terms, 29
  mental retardation, 27–28
Mental retardation
  as a physiological deficiency, 36–37
  as a social invention, 43–44
  categories of in 1887, 49–50
  classifications of, 50–51
  concept of, 27–28
  concerns about in 1800s, 205–206
  definition, 28
  deinstitutionalization to intermediate
    care, 207–208
  displaying disability of, 96
  early definition of retardation, 50–51
  "six-hour" disability defined, 58
Minority group concept of disabled people,
  38–48
  civil rights legislation and, 40–43, 44
  contrasts with individualistic conceptions,
    39

Minority group concept of disabled
people (*continued*)
    lack common characteristics, 40, 44
    legislation contributing to, 38–39
    problem of accommodating "normal" and
        average citizens, 44–46
    problems with, 38, 43
    Public Law 94-142 intentions, 47–48
    questioning of, 39–43
    severely disabled as "naturally" limited,
        46–47

N

Naming disability, 80, 81–86
    by nondisabled people, 81–82
    dehumanized names, 83
    guidelines for referring to those with
        disabilities, 83
    medicalized names, 82–83
    new terms used, 83–84, 84–86
    use of names, 81
National Association of the Deaf, work of,
    242–243 (*see also* Deaf people)
Navigating encounters people with and
    without disabilities, 116–120
    communicative disabilities (*see*
        Communicative disabilities)
    conversational disruptions (*see*
        Communicative disabilities)
    identification as disabled by guide dogs,
        canes, etc., 116

P

Pathology, definition, 28
Policy(ing) disability, 188–226
    as response to obstacles created, 189
    charity, 194–195
    conclusions, 223–226
    consequences of, 188–189
    control of disabled people by, 188, 223
    debilitating industrialization, 189–190,
        190–193 (*see also* Industralization
        and disabled persons)
    dehumanizing disability, 216–219
        defining the term human, 217
        study infants born with spinal bifida,
            217–218

        treatment of severely disabled infants,
            216–217
    differentiating disabled people,
        212–219
        by social status, 214–215
        by the visually impaired people, 215
        by vocational rehabilitation agencies,
            213–214
        dehumanizing disability, 216–219
        for who can work, 213–214, 224
        use special education, 214
        veterans system as benefits, 213
    disability as a political privilege,
        212–213
    disability policy, 188
    discriminatory feature of social world,
        188–189
    exceptional approach to, 204, 208–210
    functions of disability, 219–223
    impossibility of being neutral, 212
    individualizing, 204, 205–206 (*see also*
        Individualizing concepts of
        disability)
    need for flexible/adaptable programs, 209
        example, 209
    orienting policy, 204–212
        exceptional approach to, 204, 208–210
        individualizing, 204, 205–206
        producing dependence, 204, 210–202
        segregating, 204, 206–208 (*see also*
        Segregating disabled persons)
    producing dependence, 210–212
        by programs offered, 210
    rationales underlying, 189–190, 223
    rationalizing policy, 194–204, 223
        charity, 194–195
        rights, 199–204, 224 (*see also* Rights of
        disabled citizens)
        utility, 196–199
    study infants born with spina bifida,
        217–218
        quality of life formula, 218
        results of study, 218
    tiers of disabled citizens, 216
    types of, 188
    utility, 196–199
        costs and benefits of disability policy,
        197
        disability policy in 1800s England, 196

Policy(ing) disability (*continued*)
    effects of disability payments, 196–197
    eliminating discrimination's effect on
        economy, 196
    equal access approach, 198
    opposition to disability policies, 196
    quality of life and economic costs,
        198–199
    transportation accessibility and costs,
        197–198
    use of reasonable accommodation
        standard, 197
    ways of, 19–20
Portraying disability, 80, 86–93
    as dependent persons, 88
    by media, 86–87, 88–89
    changing media, 91–93
    disabling images, 87–89
    future of, 92–93
Poverty and disability
    conditions producing disability, 75
    incidence of malnutrition, 75
    ways disabilities occur, 75–76
President's Committee on the Employment
    of the Handicapped, 245, 246
Public Law 94-142, 47–48, 177 (*see also*
    Individuals with Disabilities Education
    Act)

R

Rehabilitation Act of 1973, 188, 243, 246–247
Remaking disability, 250–255
    accessible transportation, 253–254
    challenge of, 20
    conditions for, 250
    creation identities of disabled persons, 251
    depicting disability, 250–251
    effect industrialization on disabled,
        251–252
    framing disability, 250
    future of disability, 255
    individualizing disability, 250
    making of (*see* Making of disability)
    managing disability, 252–253
    manufacture of characteristics that
        become disability, 250
    negative terms used for disabled persons,
        251

    rights of disabled persons, 252,
        253–254
    serving disabled people, 251
    stratification of our society, 254
    work-related concerns of the disabled, 254
Rights of disabled citizens, 199–204
    as defined in Rehabilitation Act of 1973,
        199
    controversies over disability rights, 200
    criticisms of cost of implements,
        201–202
    definition in Rehabilitation Act of 1973,
        199
    power of, 199–200
    rationale of and measuring up, 203–204
    rights-oriented approaches to equal
        access, 198
      to a quality life, 198
      to public transportation, 198
    unimplemented legislation, 201–202
    use of reasonable accommodation,
        200–201
      examples, 200–201

S

Segregating disabled persons, 204, 206–208
    by educators, 206–207
    continuum of service as, 208
    deinstitutionalization mental retardated
        and funding, 207–208
    methods of, 208
    of severely disabled citizens, 208
"Self"-disablement, 76–79
    complications of smoking, 76–77
    drug use, 77, 78
    excessive drinking, 77–78
    inadequate diet, 78
    inadequate exercise, 78
    methods of, 76
    number adults who smoke, 76
Servicing disability, 151–187
    complexity of, 151
      case illustration, 151–152
    conclusion, 186–187
    disabling service, 175–183 (*see also*
        Disabling service)
    endnotes, 187
    evaluation procedures, 157

Servicing disability (*continued*)
    human service organizations role in, 152
    servicing as a metaphor, 153–154
        definition of service, 153
        use of specialists expertise, 153–154
    servicing paradigm, 155–175 (*see also*
        Servicing paradigm)
    societal circumstances of servicing, 184–185
    types organizations, 151
    variations in of states, 179–180
    ways of, 19
Servicing paradigm, 155–175
    features of, 155
    individualizing disability, 155, 156–161
    providers of, 155–156
    servicing "defective" persons, 155
    stratifying service, 155, 161–175 (*see also*
        Stratifying service)
    surviving, 155
Smoking and disability
    complications from smoking, 76–77
    COPD due to, 77
    number adults who smoke, 76
Social deviance of disability, 36–38
    definition, 36
    mental retardates as, 36–37
    minority groups, 37
    reactions to, 36, 37
    responsibility for disability on us, 48
Social Security Disability Insurance (SSDI)
    description of program, 210, 214
    disincentives of, 210–211
Socializing disability, 35–48
    as a social phenomenon, 35
    deviance (*see* Social deviance of
        disability)
    disabled people as a minority group,
        38–48 (*see also* Minority group
        concept)
    embodied in our actions, 35–36
Southeastern Community College v. Davis
    decision, 197
Special education
    development of, 184–185
    Individuals with Disabilities Education
        Act, 47–48, 177
    mainstreaming disabled children, 179
    mainstreaming physically, but not socially,
        207

    making program exceptional, 209
    mandated individual treatment plan, 179
    procedures for, 210
    purpose of, 184, 214
    role of parents, 178–179
    societal context of, 184–185
Spoiled identities, 105–116
    developing accepting relations, 111–115
        basis for, 111–112
        examples, 112–113, 113–114, 115
        stages of, 112
        with severely disabled people, 113,
            114–115
    disabled people's managing stigma,
        106–109
        covering, 108
        disavowal, 108–109
        passing, 106–108
    interrelations of, 115–116
    nondisabled people's managing stigma,
        109–111
        ignore disability, 110
        lowered expectations, 110–111
        minimize contacts, 109–110
    public encounters of disabled &
        nondisabled, 105–106
Stratifying service, 155, 161–175
    addressing accountability, 173–175
        padding reports, 173–174
    creating clients, 171–173
        making disabled, 172
        official disabled, 171–172
        questionable clients, 172–173
    differentiating disabled people, 167–170
        according to severity of disabilities,
            168
        by sincerity, 169
        criticisms of, 167–168
        ideal rehabilitation patient charac-
            teristics, 169–170
        service continuums, 168–169
    dimensions of, 169
    domination of professionals, 161, 172–163
        case example, 163
        role of, 162–163
    hierarchy of help, 161, 164–167
        importance of profit, 167
        orientations developed among staff,
            164

Stratifying service (*continued*)
role of nursing assistants, 166–167
undermining programs, 166
views of attendant's of superiors,
164–165
work as a job only to attendants, 165
pitching to the public, 175
separation disabled people from servicing
persons, 161
servicing differentiates disabled people, 161
surviving, 170–171
variation servicing from advantage to
disadvantage, 161
Strength
definition, 3
feebles (*see* Feebles)
use in living, 3
use of term, 3
weaklings (*see* Weaklings)
Stuttering, conversational disruption,
117–118
Supplemental Security Income (SSI)
disincentives of, 211
eligibility requirements for, 210, 214
Supported Community Life
approaches of, 225–226
use of, 225

V

Visual impairment
collective challenging by, 237–238

experiencing disability, 133
special privileges for, 215
Vocational rehabilitation program
clients of, 213–214
effectiveness of, 211–212
funding of, 211
purpose of, 211

W

War disabilities
direct injuries, 71–72
indirect injuries, 71–72
number injuries annually due to, 71
Weaklings
attitudes society toward, 4
benefits paid to, 5
causes of, 4
concerns needs of, 5
confrontation society by, 5–6
educational practices for, 4–5
problems due to attitudes nonweaklings,
5
use of term, 4
Word blindness (*see* Learning disability)
Workplace injuries, 72–74
due to stress, 73–74
exposure to chemicals, 73
hearing impairment, 73
number of annually, 72
occupational lung diseases, 73
permanent disabilities from, 72